When Paris Sizzled

When Paris Sizzled

*The 1920s Paris of Hemingway, Chanel, Cocteau,
Cole Porter, Josephine Baker, and Their Friends*

Mary McAuliffe

ROWMAN & LITTLEFIELD
Lanham • Boulder • New York • London

Published by Rowman & Littlefield
A wholly owned subsidary of The Rowman & Littlefield Publishing Group, Inc.
4501 Forbes Boulevard, Suite 200, Lanham, Maryland 20706
www.rowman.com

6 Tinworth Street, London SE11 5AL, United Kingdom

Distributed by NATIONAL BOOK NETWORK

British Library Cataloguing in Publication Information Available

Library of Congress Cataloging-in-Publication Data

Names: McAuliffe, Mary Sperling, 1943– author.
Title: When Paris sizzled : the 1920s Paris of Hemingway, Chanel, Cocteau, Cole
Porter, Josephine Baker, and their friends / Mary McAuliffe.
Description: Lanham : Rowman & Littlefield, [2016] | Includes bibliographical
references and index.
Identifiers: LCCN 2016017189 (print) | LCCN 2016019010 (ebook) | ISBN
9781442253322 (cloth : alkaline paper) | ISBN 9781538121801 (pbk. : alk. paper) |
ISBN 9781442253339 (electronic)
Subjects: LCSH: Paris (France)—Intellectual life—20th century. | Intellectuals—
France—Paris—History—20th century. | Artists—France—Paris—History—20th
century. | Authors—France—Paris—History—20th century. | Arts—France—Paris—
History—20th century. | Social change—France—Paris—History—20th century. |
World War, 1914–1918—Influence. | Paris (France)—Social life and customs—20th
century. | Paris (France)—Biography.
Classification: LCC DC737 .M35 2016 (print) | LCC DC737 (ebook) | DDC
944/.3610815—dc23
LC record available at https://lccn.loc.gov/2016017189

♾™ The paper used in this publication meets the minimum requirements of
American National Standard for Information Sciences—Permanence of Paper
for Printed Library Materials, ANSI/NISO Z39.48-1992.

Printed in the United States of America

In memory of

Saville and Anita

dear friends and mentors

~

Contents

Chapter 13   Cocktails, Darling? (1928)   237

Chapter 14   The Bubble Bursts (1929)   253

              Notes   273

              Bibliography   305

              Index   315

              About the Author   329

Illustrations

~

Acknowledgments

As I reflect on the years I have spent writing about Paris, especially about the Belle Epoque and now *les Années folles*, I am more than ever grateful for those friends and mentors who, over the years, have shared with me their knowledge and love of history, art, architecture, and music. High on this list are Saville and Anita Davis, to whom this book is dedicated. By their enthusiasm and example, they encouraged me to follow, at least in part, along some of the same paths that so enriched their lives and the lives of those around them.

Many of these friends, sadly, are now deceased, and I miss them greatly, but I hope that by exploring Paris during the culturally rich years of the Third Republic, including the Belle Epoque and the period between the two world wars, that I have in some measure expressed my thanks for their encouragement and guidance.

In addition, I would like to thank the New York Public Library for providing me a place in its Wertheim Study Room, a sanctuary for scholars within its vast research facilities. I am also indebted to those research librarians in the NYPL's Art and Architecture division as well as in its Library for the Performing Arts for their ever-ready assistance.

During the past several years, I have been blessed by the guidance of my editor at Rowman & Littlefield, Susan McEachern, who has shepherded four books, including this one, into publication. Her knowledge, judgment, and taste have made a difficult task easier and far more rewarding. I have also been fortunate in once again having Jehanne Schweitzer as my expert production editor, smoothing out the variety of bumps that can crop up along the way to publication. My thanks as well to assistant editor Audra Figgins for her assistance in leading me through the complex publication process.

As always, my deepest thanks to my ever-supportive family, especially to my husband, whose beautiful photos enhance these pages, and without whose enthusiastic support this book would not be possible.

~

Introduction

The Twenties, or the Roaring Twenties, as they are known in America, had a distinctive name in Paris—*les Années folles*, or, roughly translated, the Crazy Years. This era began after the war's end, in late 1918, and continued through the decade, until brought to a halt by the Wall Street crash of 1929 and subsequent worldwide depression.

These years, stretching scarcely over a decade, saw great change on almost every front, from art and architecture to music, literature, fashion, entertainment, transportation, and, perhaps most notably, behavior. Most of what appeared at the time to be revolutionary had roots that went back to the war or even the prewar years, but these trends fully flowered—and drew the most notice—during the postwar decade.

Readers of my previous books on Paris—*Dawn of the Belle Epoque* and *Twilight of the Belle Epoque*—will recognize many of the cast of characters, including Gertrude Stein, Marie Curie, Jean Cocteau, Picasso, Stravinsky, Diaghilev, and Proust, as well as Clemenceau, Sarah Bernhardt, and Claude Monet. But others now make their appearance, most notably Ernest Hemingway, Coco Chanel, Cole Porter, Josephine Baker, and Le Corbusier, in addition to Jean Renoir, Man Ray, Sylvia Beach, James Joyce, and Kiki, the famed Queen of Montparnasse.

Photography and cinema were the new vehicles for artistic expression during these vibrant years, but the era's innovative spirit also fostered the more traditional art forms as well as high-decibel factories run by entrepreneurs such as André Citroën, Louis Renault, and the Michelin brothers. The hard metallic clang of the assembly line and the roar of automobile traffic were reflected in the clean-edged and streamlined forms of Art Deco, while architects such as Le Corbusier found inspiration in the new gods of machinery, industrialization, and technology.

The epicenter of all this creativity, as well as of the era's good times, was that unsightly quarter known as Montparnasse. There, impoverished artists and writers found colleagues and cafés, while tourists discovered, at least for a night or two, the wild escapades of their dreams. A swelling population of expats, dubbed the "Lost Generation," either found themselves or became permanently mired in a haze of fantasy and booze. Escapism and creativity mingled for a decade in this fizzy atmosphere, until the tourists vastly outnumbered the locals and the party came to an end.

Throughout the decade, the sheer hedonism of those with money and leisure contrasted starkly with the many who, in the war's aftermath, struggled to rebuild their lives. And, in an ominous counterpoint to the new in all its forms, including hairstyles, hemlines, and women in the workplace, gangs and armies of the extreme right emerged, seething with righteous indignation.

Rather than a decade of unmitigated bliss, *les Années folles* thus encompassed a striking degree of tension, a combustible mixture that produced not only a remarkable surge of creativity but also a ruthless attempt to annihilate whatever threatened tradition and order—a battle that would only escalate in the decade that followed.

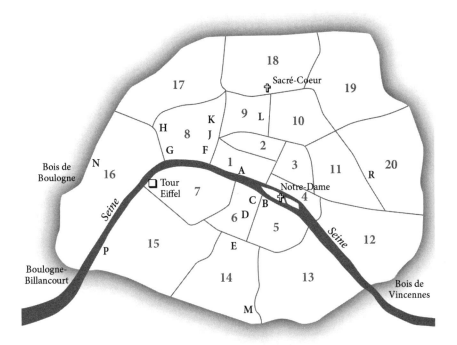

PARIS, 1918–1929
Key

A. Musée du Louvre
B. Sorbonne and Latin Quarter
C. 12 Rue de l'Odéon (Shakespeare and Company)
D. 27 Rue de Fleurus (Gertrude Stein)
E. Café du Dôme, Café de la Rotonde, and La Coupole (Montparnasse)
F. Place de la Concorde
G. Théâtre des Champs-Elysées
H. Arc de Triomphe and Place de l'Etoile
J. 28 Rue Boissy d'Anglas (original site, Boeuf sur le Toit)
K. 102 Boulevard Haussmann (Proust)
L. Folies Bergère (32 Rue Richer)
M. Parc Montsouris
N. Villa La Roche (now Fondation Le Corbusier, 10 Square du Docteur-Blanche)
P. Citroën factory, Quai de Javel (now Parc André-Citroën, Quai André-Citroën)
R. Père-Lachaise Cemetery

Paris's twenty arrondissements are indicated by number.

Mapping Specialists

Crowds in the streets of Paris on Armistice, November 11, 1918. Photo © Tallandier / Bridgeman Images

CHAPTER ONE

~

Out of Darkness
(1918)

At 11 a.m. on November 11, 1918, Marie Curie was in her lab, working as usual, when guns sounded over Paris. Not German guns, but French guns. Guns that for the first time in four years were firing without hostile intent. It was an extraordinary moment, signaling that Armistice had come and that the war, that never-ending nightmare of carnage and atrocity, was truly over.

Helen Pearl Adam, the British journalist who had remained in Paris for the war's duration and faithfully recorded her impressions, wrote that "it would have been a strange thing if Paris had kept her head when the Armistice was signed, and accordingly she did not." For three days Paris and all of France celebrated, as people surged into the streets, popped arcs of champagne into the air, and enthusiastically embraced one another. But it was a relatively orderly celebration. Adam noted that "about the most desperate crime committed by the Paris populace in those three days was the theft of flags." Indeed, shops quickly sold out of Allied flags, and soon those fortunate enough to own their own found they had to look sharp to keep them.[1]

Wanting to join in the celebration, but discovering that no flags were to be had, Madame Curie promptly bought blue, white, and red fabric and, with the help of her cleaning lady, sewed flags to drape from the Radium Institute windows. Then, accompanied by a building attendant, she and a friend took to the streets in Curie's old radiology car, the one she had driven so many times to the front to care for the wounded. But now, instead of cratered roads and desperate measures to x-ray and save shattered soldiers, she found herself part of a massive celebration. She and her colleague got only as far as the Place de la Concorde when the crowd surged around them, climbing onto the old Renault's roof and fenders and bringing it to a halt. It was a glorious moment.

On the Left Bank, the gentle Abbé Mugnier heard the bells for Armistice ring from Saint-Germain-des-Prés and then was swept into a crowd of boisterous students parading along the Boulevard Saint-Germain. The mist lifted a little, and he was moved to see flags flying everywhere, especially Allied flags. Somewhere along the way he encountered an American who told him that the Armistice had been signed and, in one of those little gestures that seemed so very American, gave him a chocolate bar.

Later that day, and on a more reflective note, Marcel Proust—holed up as usual in his cork-lined bedroom on Boulevard Haussmann—wrote his dear friend Madame Geneviève Straus: "We have thought too much about the war not to say a tender word on this evening of victory, joyous on account of victory, melancholy on account of all those we loved who will not see it." He added, "One weeps so much for the dead that a certain form of gaiety is not the form of celebration that one would prefer."[2]

Almost one and one half million French died in the war, with three million more wounded—many so severely that they would not be able to work or function normally again. This, out of a prewar population of forty million. The numbers were shattering; the reality was even worse. Much of the northern third of France had been laid waste, and the nation's treasury had reached rock bottom, with staggering war debts as well. As if this were not enough, the worldwide influenza epidemic, which had already killed millions, was now sweeping through Paris. One of its victims was the poet Apollinaire, weakened from a head wound he had received at the front, who died on November 9. News of the Armistice broke as his friends gathered around his body, laid out in his Boulevard Saint-Germain apartment.[3] Seeing all the flags flying along the boulevard, Jean Cocteau later wrote that Apollinaire's friends "were able to believe, in the confusion of kinds of heroism, that Paris was bedecked in his honor."[4]

～

The young Swiss architect Charles-Edouard Jeanneret, who would soon change his name to Le Corbusier, viewed the scene from beneath the seventeenth-century mansard roof of his Left Bank apartment on Rue Jacob.[5] He had arrived in Paris early in 1917, during some of the most difficult months of the war, and found this tiny apartment in what had been the building's servants' quarters. Charmed by the location as well as by the building's provenance—it had once belonged to a celebrated eighteenth-century actress, whose romance with a dashing nobleman led to her poisoning by a rival—Jeanneret transformed his garret into a cozy den filled with cushions, pillows, and a huge divan. Unlike the streamlined Le Corbusier interiors to come, with their bare floors and white walls, Jeanneret decorated this modest flat with black wallpaper accented with medallions of fruit, and with rugs of black, white, and red stripes. Perhaps to divert himself from the bitter cold and the coal shortages of wartime Paris, he also painted one wall of his diminutive apartment with a landscape of sun-washed tropical palms.

Freezing in the winter and often hungry, Jeanneret nonetheless committed himself to Paris and to the new spirit that already was emerging in the war-torn city. During his first spring there, he attended the avant-garde production of *Parade*, the iconoclastic joint creation of Jean Cocteau (scenario), Erik Satie (music), Pablo Picasso (sets and costumes), and Léonide Massine (choreography). Jeanneret loved it. Everything about it was new, brazen, and bold, and he eagerly embraced its spirit.

What this actually meant in his own life, though, was less clear. Struggling to establish himself professionally while riding the emotional roller coaster of his own mood swings, the end of the war—"this horrible and empty war"—left him with one question: "What will tomorrow bring?"[6]

The day after Armistice, Claude Monet wrote his good friend Georges Clemenceau to offer two of what he called his "decorative panels" to the state. "It's little enough," he said, "but it's the only way I have of taking part in the victory."[7]

The panels were a portion of Monet's huge project that he called his *Grandes Décorations* (later known simply as his *Water Lilies*), on which he had been laboring for years. It was, as their mutual friend and art critic Gustave Geffroy commented, as if Monet had offered "a bouquet of flowers to honour victory in war and the conquest of peace."[8] By this time Clemenceau was prime minister of France and, having won the war for his nation, was now launched in the equally fraught process of winning the peace. But six days after receiving Monet's offer, Clemenceau dropped everything and went with Geffroy to Giverny to make his choice.

There is some disagreement over what exactly Monet proposed to give the state in this initial offer. By the time of their visit, Geffroy was already referring to the proffered gift as "several" rather than "two." If so, Clemenceau had been working successfully to increase the number of canvases. But, however pleased Monet was by Clemenceau's visit, he quickly retracted his offer. By the month's end, he was flatly refusing to donate or sell any of the enormous canvases, even though he acknowledged that they were "cluttering up" his studio. "Impossible," he told his art dealer, Gaston Bernheim-Jeune. "I need each of them to work on the others." "I am not very fond of public displays," he added in a subsequent letter and backed off.[9]

Thus began a tortuous affair, in which Georges Clemenceau heroically worked to obtain Monet's water-lily panels for the nation and, at the same time, valiantly sought to convince his longtime friend to undergo a much-needed operation to save his eyesight before it was too late.

⌒

"Peace," the painter Fernand Léger exultantly wrote his good friend, the painter André Mare. Léger had been severely gassed while serving at Verdun, and Mare was badly wounded on the Picardy front while camouflaging artillery with Cubist designs. "Finally," Léger went on, "after four long years, exasperated, keyed-up, depersonalized man opens his eyes, takes a look, relaxes and rediscovers life, gripped by a wild desire to dance, let off steam, scream, at long last stand upright, shout, scream and squander." Keenly attuned to the moment, he added, "A hurricane of life forces fills the world."[10]

Death and destruction had at long last given way to life. Hope had triumphed. This was, after all, the war to end all wars. H. G. Wells had coined that famous phrase, or at least a close approximation of it, in a series of articles that appeared in 1914 as *The War That Will End War*.[11] Woodrow Wilson readily adopted it, along with the renowned promise that this war would make the world "safe for democracy." The war-weary and battered denizens of the Western world had found in these words the hope and will to struggle on.

French author Joseph Kessel later wrote that "we'd won the war, the war to end all wars; life lay open before us and we were convinced everything would be fine."[12] But others were not so sure. The British prime minister, David Lloyd George, is said to have cynically remarked, "This war, like the next war, is a war to end war."[13] And a growing number, like the British poet Siegfried Sassoon—a decorated war hero—came to believe that "the war was a dirty trick which had been played on me and my generation."[14]

Still, as Jean Cocteau's young lover and protégée, Raymond Radiguet, wrote in his 1924 novel, *Le Bal du Comte d'Orgel*, it was a mistake to view frivolity as unpardonable at such a moment in Europe's history. "It is at these troubled periods," Radiguet explained, "that frivolity, even license, are most easily understood." Why? Because "one enjoys with gusto what tomorrow may belong to somebody else."[15] Certainly, in the aftermath of Armistice, Paris partied, and Paris partied hard. In the words of the gifted and proudly debauched young writer Maurice Sachs, "At the close of the war . . . Paris was the indispensable place, the ample city into which the world poured its treasures."[16] The *couturier* Paul Poiret celebrated Armistice with an enormous victory party, despite having lost two of his children, the eldest (Rosine) and the youngest (Gaspard), to the influenza epidemic. Jean Cocteau left the deathbed of Apollinaire to attend and was enchanted. Poiret had been in the business of enchantment for years, with over-the-top parties attracting the *crème de la crème* of Paris's social set, most notably with his glittering 1911 Thousand and Second Night extravaganza and his follow-up 1912 *Les Festes de Bacchus*, a champagne-fueled affair held in the forest of Versailles. According to Cocteau, the war had not diminished Poiret's touch. Later, Cocteau rapturously recalled that "when daybreak came we thought it was still only eleven, like the travelers in the German ballad held spellbound by the nightingale."[17]

Despite this success, Poiret—who had spent the war years designing uniforms for French soldiers, to the detriment of his *couturier* business—was about to experience the difficulties of reestablishing himself in Paris, both on the social and the fashion front. Until the war, he had been the self-proclaimed king of fashion. Ready to defend his title as the war ended, he nonetheless was well aware of the threat that others, especially the gamine-like newcomer, Coco Chanel, posed to his supremacy.

Unlike Poiret, who was a Parisian by birth, Gabrielle Chanel—whose early biography is murky—was not. A mother who died, a father who disappeared, long years in a Catholic orphanage, and even longer years of deprivation in the ungentle regions of the Auvergne, where she was born and raised—these, along with the taint of illegitimacy, emerge as fleeting images in a web of changing stories and outright fabrications. Late in life, when a young woman suggested that she see a psychiatrist, Chanel promptly retorted, "I, who never told the truth to my priest?"[18]

She seems to have tried her hand at a variety of menial jobs, as well as a brief turn as a music-hall singer, where her rendition of "Qui qu'a vu Coco?" (Who Has Seen My Dog, Coco?) may have inspired the audience to call her "Coco." She later denied this story, conveying—in long interviews with her trusted friend, the writer, socialite, and diplomat Paul Morand—that she had received the nickname "Little Coco" in early childhood. But whatever the actual details, somewhere along the line she acquired the name, and it stuck.

In addition to her nickname, Chanel also acquired a lover, a wealthy young cavalry officer, Etienne Balsan, with whom she spent several years at his estate, the Château de Royallieu, where he bred horses, played polo, and raced. It was through Balsan that she met Arthur ("Boy") Capel, the scion of a prosperous English family, who became the great love of her life. Balsan seemed ready enough to share her, and so, moving to Balsan's apartment in Paris, she turned her hand to making hats, whose sleek and elegant lines brought attention and customers. In 1910, Boy Capel financed her first independent millinery shop, Chanel Modes, on fashionable Rue Cambon. Soon after, with Capel's funding and encouragement, she opened a boutique in the seaside resort of Deauville. It was then that she ventured into clothing, designing corset-free sailor blouses and sweaters to be worn over soft skirts, which were as comfortable and attractive as they were revolutionary. Deauville's society women flocked to the new styles, which quickly earned the stamp of *le vrai chic*, in contrast to the uncomfortable, constricting, and overornamented styles of the past.

The war imposed its own constraints on Chanel, much as it did on Poiret and other Paris *couturiers*, most of whom virtually or completely closed down for the duration. Chanel remained for a time in Deauville, where she worked with jersey, a readily available fabric more commonly used in underwear. Using this, she continued to create clean-lined and comfortable clothing, much of it inspired by menswear. The summer residents of Deauville, cut off from Paris by the German advance, were delighted to supplement their wardrobes with Chanel fashions, which were as practical as they were attractive. Soon Chanel—who by this time was earning enough to operate without Boy Capel's or anyone's financial support—moved to Biarritz, where she opened her first *maison de couture* and took up residence in a villa that she bought, for cash, at the war's end.

Abandoning the waistline, as she did, and shortening skirts to allow more freedom of movement (as well as a shocking glimpse of ankle), her clothing freed women at a time when increasing social emancipation as well as the demands of war called for exactly what she was providing. "One world was ending," she later told Paul Morand; "another was about to be born. I was in the right place; an opportunity beckoned, I took it."[19]

She also took the shears to her long hair, freeing women from yet one more burdensome style. It was a bold move, and one that other women quickly imitated. As Paul Poiret later remarked, "We ought to have been on guard against that boyish head. It was going to give us every kind of shock, and produce, out of its little conjuror's hat, gowns and coiffures and jewels and boutiques."[20]

Gabrielle "Coco" Chanel, 1929. Private Collection / Alinari / Bridgeman Images

～

Her real name was Alice Prin, but she became known simply as Kiki. Born in 1901 into abject poverty in the Côte d'Or region of eastern France, she joined cousins in her grandmother's household after her mother "traipsed off to Paris," as Kiki later put it. "We were six little love-babies," she added, "our fathers having overlooked the little matter of acknowledging us," and like Coco Chanel, she quickly learned to make her way in a tough world.[21]

At the age of twelve she joined her mother in Paris, where she went to work in a series of menial jobs, including a bakery as well as a wartime factory, where she repaired soldiers' shoes. Meals, when available, consisted largely of beans, and so when she met up with some painters who asked her to pose in the nude for them, she readily accepted. Money, however little, was money. And as she put it, "the truth is, if you want to know, I had a figure that you'd have a hard time passing up anywhere."[22]

Her mother's apartment was located near the Gare Montparnasse, a quarter that had rapidly become a center for artists and bohemians. Kiki soon made the acquaintance of Chaim Soutine, who occupied a studio in a cluster of ramshackle buildings called the Cité Falguière, just to the west of the train station. Amedeo Modigliani, another artist well acquainted with poverty, had moved there first, and others followed. These flimsy shacks were hot in the summer and freezing in the winter—so cold that, as Kiki remembered, Soutine "spent the night burning up everything in his place to keep us warm."[23]

After losing her wartime factory job (women with children to support or a husband at the front received priority), Kiki worked in earnest to find modeling jobs, regularly cruising the famed Montparnasse cafés, the Dôme and the Rotonde, to see if she could spot any artists. It took nerve, she confessed, especially as the Rotonde's owner, Victor Libion, didn't like her because she didn't wear a hat—the sure sign of a streetwalker. Her first jobs were with painters as poor as she was, but in time she did more and more posing. Blessed with a cheerful personality and a rare talent for singing ribald songs, as well as a striking figure, she slowly became a fixture in the Montparnasse scene.

By 1918, at the age of seventeen, she could report that she was keeping house with a painter. "It's not exactly what you would call high life," she added, "but anyway, we eat!"[24] The painter was Maurice Mendjizky, with whom Kiki lived for almost four years. At this point, no one, least of all Kiki, could have predicted her future reign as Queen of Montparnasse.

⌒

Montparnasse—a name that summoned up images of bohemianism, shabby-chic stylishness, and adventure—had for almost a decade replaced Montmartre as the place where artists wanted to live and work. Picasso's move from Montmartre to Montparnasse in 1912 had confirmed Montparnasse's newly acquired reputation, but even before that it had been attracting impoverished painters and sculptors, who gravitated to the insalubrious La Ruche at the quarter's southwestern tip, as well as to a variety of hovels and shacks throughout the quarter.

Picasso had by this time become a name to reckon with in the art world, with a steadily growing income to match, and his sequence of Montparnasse apartments—although located in unpicturesque spots along the cemetery—were in buildings of comfort if not of style. Having left behind his longtime mistress Fernande Olivier in Montmartre, Picasso settled, first in a ground-floor apartment at 242 Boulevard Raspail, then in a larger apartment at 5 bis Rue Schoelcher, with his new love, Eve Gouel. It was easy enough to conclude that Picasso found Montparnasse attractive because of its distance from Montmartre and Fernande, who did not take well to being dumped. But even before this breakup, Picasso had been drawing closer to Montparnasse and its cafés. It was only following Eve's death and his subsequent (July 1918) marriage to the Russian ballerina Olga Khokhlova that Picasso took yet another step toward respectability and relocated to a large Right Bank apartment on Rue La Boétie, next door to the opulent gallery and residence of his art dealer, Paul Rosenberg. The proximity was no coincidence: it allowed Rosenberg (who made the arrangements) to keep an eye on his valuable artist, and the Picassos did not object. Olga yearned for the kind of life that she felt her husband deserved, and Picasso—now thirty-seven—felt that he had done quite enough suffering in the cause of art and was ready for more of the perks of fame.

The Picassos moved into their new quarters shortly after Armistice. It was a gracious and spacious apartment, with a butler, cook, and maid to maintain the premises and decorum. Soon the Picassos were attending dinners and suppers at all the right places and giving sparkling little parties of their own.

Other artists who had scrabbled out of poverty into success soon abandoned Montparnasse and even Paris. As Gertrude Stein later put it, "the old crowd had disappeared."[25] Henri Matisse, long a fixture in the Latin Quarter, was now living in Nice, and Chaim Soutine, although still broke, was about to spend most of the next three years in the south of France, preferring to settle near beautiful Parc Montsouris when he found fame. The sculptor Ossip Zadkine remained on the edge of Montparnasse but retreated to a location deep in a garden on Rue d'Assas. Marc Chagall, when he returned from Russia, lived the bourgeois married life in comfortable surroundings, first on what now is Avenue du Général-Leclerc (14th), then in Boulogne-sur-Seine and, by the 1930s, in fashionable Passy (16th). Fernand Léger kept his studio on Rue Notre-Dame-des-Champs and participated in Montparnasse's artistic life, but not in its nightlife. André Derain—when not partying—also lived in bourgeois respectability, joining Georges Braque near Parc Montsouris. This meant that as prewar Montparnasse disappeared into the realm of legend, only Moïse Kisling remained of the old guard to revel in the quarter's nonstop round of festivities.

For a few, the war had offered opportunity on a grand scale. Among these, some of the most prominent were the automaker Louis Renault and his soon-to-be rival, the industrialist André Citroën. Renault had spent the prewar years building his auto business on an ever-larger scale, expanding his product line into trucks, taxis, and buses for the international market, as well as airplane engines for the French military at home. The war brought him impressive government contracts, as he shifted to produce war materiel and developed the first truly functional armored tank—a late addition to the war effort that contributed significantly to Allied victory. Citroën, whose initial foray into the world of manufacturing had been his invention and production of the double-helical gearwheel, had, like Renault, already made his fortune when the advent of war launched him into the mass production of artillery shells. Both men emerged from the war as industrial titans, even wealthier and more successful than before.

But there the similarity ended. In background, personality, and approach to their work, they could hardly have been more different. Renault, the youngest surviving son of a Parisian drapery dealer and button manufacturer, had been a backyard mechanic who designed his own automobiles— light, fast, quiet, and inexpensive to purchase and maintain. Bringing them to the public's attention through the turn of the century's brutal road races, in which he and his brother actively took part (until his brother's tragic death at the wheel), Renault steadily and ruthlessly expanded his Billancourt factory and his product line to meet the growing demand. He was a notoriously hard worker and a difficult man to work for, as demanding of others as he was of himself. Taciturn, even grim, he had no use for socializing or for what he termed "coddling" his workers. "Working for him," one of his employees later commented, "was like being with a volcano." Outside the factory, he was boorish. According to one acquaintance, he was "the rudest man I've ever known."[26]

Citroën, on the other hand, was an attractive and sociable fellow, who enjoyed Paris nightlife and took an interest in his workers' welfare. The youngest child of a prosperous Jewish diamond merchant who had originally hailed from Amsterdam, Citroën, like Renault, had been raised in middle-class Parisian comfort. But unlike Renault, who was a mechanic turned businessman, Citroën—although a product of the Ecole Polytechnique—was a businessman with an understanding of mechanics. He also had an understanding of human nature. Citroën was charming and knew how to use his charm. He mingled easily with his colleagues and his workers and, unlike Renault, had no qualms about borrowing for his escalating projects. He also understood the value of publicity, of which Renault was contemptuous but at which Citroën would prove extraordinarily adept.

Although both men had made a point of separately visiting Henry Ford before the war, to witness firsthand the miracles that Ford was working using the Frederick Winslow Taylor method of scientific management and mass production, it was Citroën who first took full advantage of the Taylor method in his wartime munitions factory on Paris's Quai de Javel (now Quai André-Citroën). Renault later claimed that he paid little attention to Citroën at the time, except to note that Citroën had obtained a substantial government contract and produced shells in exceptionally large quantities using the Taylor method. Whether or not this was the case, Renault would soon find it difficult to avoid Citroën; as the war ended, the former gear manufacturer was about to embark on a new enterprise of automobile manufacture, in direct competition with Renault and Renault's established automobile works.

Maurice Ravel spent Armistice Day in the hospital. He was a small man and had always been frail; yet when war came, he did his utmost to enlist—startlingly enough, as a bombardier. The romance of flight captivated him, but this did not persuade army medics that it was his calling. Finally, after repeated applications, Ravel managed to win an assignment as an army truck driver, and he spent long, grueling months hauling supplies in the Verdun sector—"exhausting, insane, and perilous service," as he wrote a friend.[27] He never was injured, but he became ill. Adding to his woes, during the height of this turmoil, his beloved mother died.

Ravel was not in good health when he received a temporary discharge from military service that became permanent. Although he made arrangements with his friends the Godebskis for lunch on the Sunday following his Armistice operation, he was unable to keep the appointment. Instead, he went for a rest cure in the Haute-Savoie, where he found "charming" people but felt isolated and bored.[28] Although he had completed his lovely *Le Tombeau de Couperin* during a previous recuperation, dedicating each of its six movements to a fallen friend or friends, he would compose nothing new for three years.

Twenty-eight-year-old Captain Charles de Gaulle had spent most of the war years as prisoner in a series of high-security German camps, from which he regularly attempted to escape. He had begun the war at the head of a platoon of frontline troops before being severely wounded. After recovery, he returned to the front, only to be captured at Verdun. For the remainder of the war, he did his utmost, along with equally determined colleagues, to throw a monkey wrench into whatever prisoner-of-war camps they were in, creating havoc (setting fire to straw mattresses, throwing water bombs, or performing "concerts" on food tins at all hours of the night) and concocting ever-more-daring means of escape.

His escape attempts were dramatic and, against all odds, successful—at least for remarkably long periods of time before exhaustion, illness, or just plain bad luck caught up with him. But on September 1, as it became clear that the end of the war was coming, he wrote to his mother, "If I cannot get into the fighting again between now and the end of the war, shall I stay in the army? And what commonplace kind of a future would I have there?" Having missed almost three years of the fighting, he despaired of his future career as an army officer. "I am buried alive," he added despondently.[29]

And yet he *was* alive, and so far as his parents were concerned, that was miracle enough. Three weeks after the Armistice, de Gaulle crossed the Swiss frontier to arrive, via Geneva and Paris, at his Parisian family's country home in the Dordogne in early December. There, he joined his three brothers, who had also survived the fighting.

It was a thankful family gathering. Still, as Captain de Gaulle contemplated the war's end, he was troubled—not only for his own career, but for the future of France. In his opinion, armistice did not mean peace, and France now had two enemies instead of one: Germany and Bolshevik Russia.

Moreover, as he trenchantly put it to his fellow prisoners near the war's end, "The nations of old Europe will end by signing a peace that their statesmen will call a peace of mutual understanding and which in fact will be a peace of exhaustion." Such a peace could not be a real peace. It was only "a shabby cloak thrown over unsatisfied ambitions, hatred more inveterate than ever and unextinguished national anger."[30]

France and its allies had emerged from the darkness of war. On November 11, there was joy everywhere as the war-weary celebrated. But at least a few were already wondering what lay ahead.

Jean Cocteau, circa 1917. Photo © Tallandier / Bridgeman Images

CHAPTER TWO

~

Going Forward
(1918–1919)

"J'ai tué" (I have killed), wrote the poet Blaise Cendrars, at the war's end, of his blistering experience as a soldier. Cendrars, a Swiss national who joined the French Foreign Legion, had lost his right hand in combat in 1915. Now, in November 1918, he wrote, "I have defied the shelling and the bombardment, the mines, fire, gas and artillery: all the anonymous, demonic and blind machinery of war. . . . I acted and I killed. Like a man who wants to live."[1]

Not long after, his friend Fernand Léger told an audience that the experience of war (at Argonne and Verdun) had heightened his sense of life, "accelerated, deep and tragic. There men and things are seen in their fullest intensity, their values are in full focus, stretched to [the] breaking point." Léger had emerged from the shelling and the gassing as a different man, one who viewed life even after Armistice as "a state of war," an existence that was "hard and shrill," turbulent and fast paced, but conducive to creativity.[2]

The mauve-colored romanticism of prewar days had disappeared in the shock of aerial bombardment and mustard gas. Necessity and opportunity had combined to free women from claustrophobic styles and ankle-length hair, even while their husbands, sons, and lovers returned from the war wounded, bitter, and dazed to take up lives that no longer looked or felt the same. Machinery clanged, automobiles roared, music pounded to a turbulent beat, and everything was moving faster than ever before. Some found the newness liberating and exciting, while others felt pummeled by it. For more than four terrible years, Parisians had yearned for peace, and now peace had come. But after the celebrations came difficult adjustments—or failures to adjust—as life went on.

Léger himself, a gentle giant of a man and a trained architect, had moved from Normandy to Paris at the turn of the century, where for several years he eked out an existence as an architectural draughtsman while painting off hours in the Impressionist style. And then, late in the decade, he discovered the work of Cézanne and Braque and made his break with the past. Having discovered the importance of geometric shapes, he struggled with the concept of volume ("I wanted to push volume as far as possible") and strove to "dislocate the human body,"[3] creating a startling style of cylindrical forms that soon earned the name "Tubism," indicating its close relationship with Cubism.[4] Moving in the same Montparnasse artistic circles as Archipenko, Soutine, Lipchitz, and Chagall, Léger was included in the mind-boggling 1913 New York Armory Show, where he impressed Picasso's art dealer, Daniel-Henry Kahnweiler, who offered him the financial security of an exclusive contract.

After his traumatic war experience, Léger embraced the new with fervor, painting people as well as industrial and mechanical objects in pared-down, streamlined shapes. It would not be long before his path would cross that of others adopting the same clean-lined Purist aesthetic—especially the young architect Le Corbusier.

⌒

Charles Jeanneret, who was about to become Le Corbusier, was in a funk. Armistice was all right, of course—who didn't want this ghastly war to end? But Armistice had landed on an inconvenient date. Jeanneret, along with his friend, adviser, and collaborator Amédée Ozenfant, had been working almost nonstop on paintings for a small exhibition that was scheduled to open on November 11.[5] The exhibition was postponed, much to Jeanneret's annoyance. "The armistice has disorganized a lot of things," he wrote a friend on November 20. "People have been celebrating for the last eight days. Not me, of course."[6]

Jeanneret may have been working as an architect, but what he really wanted to be was a painter. He had met Ozenfant near the end of the war (he later recalled the date as 1918, while Ozenfant remembered it as May 1917).[7] Whatever the exact timing, the occasion was momentous. Le Corbusier later underscored Ozenfant's "clear understanding" and reminisced that they shared the perception that "an age of steel was beginning." A new era was coming following the war's turmoil, upheaval, and destruction.[8]

What this new era would be was a question that preoccupied Jeanneret and Ozenfant alike, and along with preparations for their art exhibition, they had also been hard at work in producing a small book, *After Cubism*, which appeared shortly after Armistice. Cubism, in their eyes, had once possessed merit, even though it was the "troubled art of a troubled era."[9] But Cubism had become merely decorative and therefore inadequate for the postwar world. Even *Parade*, the ballet that only shortly before had delighted Jeanneret with its boldness and newness, now served the authors as an example of facile and decorative diversion. Hailing the new gods of machinery, industrialization, and technology, Jeanneret and Ozenfant proclaimed that both art and architecture should reflect these modern deities. "The great Competition," as they called the war, "has gotten rid of aging methods and imposed in their place others that the struggle has proven their betters. . . . Not since Pericles has thought been so lucid."[10]

The term they used to describe their new movement was Purism, and it became their rallying cry. Out with Cubism! Down with Dada and Expressionism! Instead, with their joint vision regarding change and progress, they reduced a disorderly world to an orderly one, a realm with the clean undecorated lines and balanced forms of Classical Greece. For two young men, one of whom (Jeanneret) had accomplished little in Paris to date except to open a small factory manufacturing reinforced-concrete bricks, while the other, the slightly older Ozenfant, ran a couture salon owned by Paul Poiret's sister, it was quite a bold undertaking. Even though both were painters and Ozenfant had once founded an avant-garde literary review (*L'Elan*), they still were far from being recognized authorities on the question of art and architecture—or on anything else, for that matter.

But this was about to change.

The Americans were coming! They had come, famously, to the Allies' rescue in 1917 and 1918, and their sheer numbers had helped bring the interminable conflict to a close. Now American soldiers were demobilizing, and many made a point of seeing Paris en route home. Hearing tales of Paris's bright lights, their sisters, cousins, and aunts soon followed.

Relatively few Americans had visited France before the war. One account has a total of only about fifteen thousand Americans visiting annually in the prewar years. Compared with the four hundred thousand about to descend annually by 1925, this was peanuts. The falling franc made Paris an affordable as well as glamorous destination, beckoning those with lighter pocketbooks as well as the well-to-do. Many chose to stay, creating a growing expat community that swelled from eight thousand in 1920 to thirty-two thousand by 1923,[11] drawn by the low cost of living and the sheer fun the city provided. America was entering the era of Prohibition, and Paris's flowing booze as well as its nonchalance about anything sexual provided special appeal. Naughty revues and casual café culture enticed, and even those like Ernest Hemingway who found themselves in fourth-floor walk-ups with insalubrious toilet facilities were enchanted with the place. Those with more money could of course afford even more enchantment.

One of these was young Cole Porter, grandson of J. O. Cole, a self-made man who had shrewdly established a dry-goods store in California during the gold rush, profitably selling basic necessities to miners instead of panning for gold. After marrying a local girl from his hometown in Peru, Indiana, J. O. soon moved permanently back home, where he invested in Indiana farmland as well as West Virginia forests. Beneath all that West Virginia timber lay vast deposits of coal and oil, making J. O. the richest man for miles around.

J. O.'s son died, leaving as his only heir a beloved daughter, a plain but determined young woman named Kate, who despite her father's opposition married a local druggist, the handsome and musically inclined Samuel Porter. Porter was not nearly grand enough for J. O., but Kate insisted, and Kate usually got her way. She married Sam in 1884, and their only surviving child, Cole, was born seven years later.

Sam was gentle and Kate was not, but this made little difference to young Cole, whom Kate spoiled as freely as she had been indulged by her own father (who contributed significantly to the family's financial well-being). Given piano and violin lessons by his mother, Cole hated the violin but took to the piano, especially when he was accompanying his own witty lyrics—an ability that he honed at prep school (Worcester Academy in Massachusetts) and Yale. A clotheshorse and a dandy from childhood (one acquaintance recalled that his mother dressed him like Little Lord Fauntleroy), young Cole brought paintings and an upright piano with him to school, as well as trunks filled with dapper clothes. But the boy from Peru, Indiana, chiefly shone as a whiz at entertaining. He easily became the center of parties and quickly went on to create entire evenings of entertainment, honing his charm and social graces along the way.

At Yale he became an almost immediate social success, writing football songs ("Bull Dog") and college shows, establishing lifelong friendships with elite Yalies, and spending more money (courtesy of his grandfather) than almost anyone else. In return, J. O. demanded that Cole do something sensible, like study law. This meant Harvard Law School, where Cole stuck it out for only a brief time before boredom prevailed and he transferred to Harvard's School of Music. Grandpa was not pleased, but Kate ran interference for her beloved son, and Cole continued to live exactly the life he wanted.

New York City followed, where for the first time Cole Porter experienced failure. In 1916, his musical *See America First* bombed on Broadway. But by this time the Great War was practically on America's doorstep, and soon after U.S. entry in April 1917, Cole embarked for France, drawn as much by the excitement of what was going on as by patriotism. What he did there, exactly, has been difficult to pin down. Initially he worked for a relief organization, and then he may have entered the Foreign Legion. Or else he served in a Franco-American ambulance unit. In any case, wherever he served, his music came with him: accompanying him across the Atlantic was a piano keyboard with collapsible legs.

By early 1918, Porter seems to have managed to land in Paris, possibly in a division of the American Expeditionary Forces headquartered on Avenue Montaigne. At that time a coterie of well-off young British and American officers frequently met at his apartment on stylish Place Vendôme, lent him by a French friend. There, elegance, rapier wit, and cosmopolitanism reigned. By the war's end, Cole Porter had become the toast of the town among Paris's international set.

In this, Porter was aided by professional hostess Elsa Maxwell, whom he had met two years earlier at a party in Greenwich Village, where he overheard her arguing with a friend about the merits of *See America First.* "Pardon me for eavesdropping, but are you paging me?" he asked, smoothly insinuating himself into her group. He was so slickly dressed that Maxwell immediately assumed he was a gigolo, but Porter shrugged and told her it was "all on tick," adding that it was "Grandpa's tick."[12] And then he sat down at the piano and began to sing, holding Maxwell and the crowd in delighted rapture. It was then that he won Maxwell's lasting friendship, including her invaluable social connections.

"I wish I could say that I fell for him in the first ten seconds," Maxwell later wrote, but "on the contrary, I felt antagonistic toward him. I thought he was trying to be excessively cute, and I've always been allergic to that approach."[13] Maxwell, a short, dumpy dynamo with a penchant for gaiety and a talent for fun, had grown up in modest circumstances in San Francisco. Her father, an indifferent insurance salesman with little interest in money, was far more interested in his less-than-lucrative career as a music and drama critic for the *New York Dramatic Mirror.* His connections to a variety of celebrities as well as Maxwell's own talents as a play-by-ear pianist gave her a lifelong interest in the music and theater world. Starting as a pianist

Cole Porter, circa 1930s. Culver Pictures / The Art Archive at Art Resource, NY

for silent films, she went on to music halls and a career as an accompanist before finding her true calling as "the hostess with the mostest," as she would in time be dubbed.

Early in 1918 Porter also met a Southern beauty, Linda Lee Thomas, a wealthy divorcée who had shed an abusive husband and fled to wartime Paris, where she did relief work for soldiers' families and moved in an international set. She and Porter struck up a close friendship, and soon after Armistice they announced their engagement, prompting Porter to travel back to America to ask his grandfather to increase his allowance—with the aim of matching his future wife's substantial funds. J. O. objected strenuously, feeling that he had already wasted enough money on a young man who persisted in "musical nonsense." But Kate liked the idea of a socially connected daughter-in-law and arranged to increase Porter's income behind J. O.'s back. In addition to this good news, Porter received a job offer: on the boat to New York he had entertained fellow passengers with lounge shows and, as a consequence, met a theatrical producer who asked him to write the score for a new Broadway show, *Hitchy-Koo of 1919*. The show opened in New York in October 1919 and played only fifty-six performances, but it provided Porter with welcome encouragement as well as royalties.

This, in addition to the largess his mother wangled, gave Porter the financial backing he felt he needed to marry Linda in December 1919 in the *mairie* (town hall) of Paris's eighteenth arrondissement. Linda and Cole seemed delighted with one another, but Linda's friends were not so pleased. The art historian Bernard Berenson, who described Linda as a "lovey, lovely creature," was taken aback by her decision to marry "a little musical man from the Middle West fifteen years younger than herself." In actuality, their difference in age was eight years rather than fifteen, but nonetheless, this age difference as well as the dissimilarity of their backgrounds did not seem auspicious. But it was the unmentionable, Porter's homosexuality, that clearly posed the most difficulties. Writing the Boston art collector Isabella Stewart Gardner, Berenson concluded that he had met the pair on honeymoon in Italy and "saw their future in the blackest terms."[14]

∿

Another unlikely union took place shortly before Armistice, this one between Louis Renault and Christiane Boullaire, the daughter of a Parisian notary. She was only twenty-one, while her husband was forty. Moreover, he was notoriously hard driving, brusque, and a force to be reckoned with. But he was rich, with a town house on Avenue Foch and a country estate on the Seine, and Christiane decided to take her chances and see what could be done with him. For his part, Renault wasn't getting any younger, and he wanted an heir. It may not have been a perfect match, but it had possibilities.

By this time Renault had amassed a fortune and was ready to spend some of it—an inclination much to Christiane's liking. He had already built a luxurious mansion at Herqueville—a verdant four-thousand-acre property on the Seine, within easy reach of Paris—where he could go and, if not relax, at least tinker in his private workshop. It was at Herqueville that he and Christiane exchanged their vows on September 26, 1918, prompting a complete upheaval in Renault's world.

Christiane had a taste for the best, whether in jewelry, flowers, antiques, paintings, yachts, or any of the other paraphernalia of the very rich, in which Renault could and did easily indulge her. But she was also intelligent, ambitious, and determined to win her way, with her husband's money, into the realms of high society. At the same time, she was equally determined to upend bourgeois conventions whenever it suited her. She considered herself avant-garde and enjoyed attention-getting amusements such as keeping snakes that crawled about the house or entwined themselves around her arms and neck. They were not poisonous, but they scared the daylights out of some of her guests, whom she took great glee in shocking. These absurd pets normally resided in a bathtub, but on one occasion they somehow escaped and slithered throughout the house, sending the servants fleeing for shelter elsewhere.

In the turbulent social atmosphere of postwar France, money now counted for far more than did titles or family lineage, and Christiane made the most of this new world, giving herself a short course on the latest topics in art and politics and introducing her boorish husband to good music and the requisite social graces. She also worked to attract the best names to Herqueville and the Renaults' Avenue Foch townhouse, where she entertained an increasingly impressive list of celebrities and dignitaries. Château de Herqueville, with one of the best "shoots" in France, offered a special appeal to her guests, and Christiane herself was an excellent shot, in addition to being an accomplished rider, swimmer, and skier. Apparently an avid markswoman, she famously attended a shooting party immediately following her wedding ceremony.

Louis Renault never did quite adjust to the social whirl, although to his credit, he tried. He loved Christiane and wanted to please her—especially after the prompt birth of a son and heir, Jean-Louis, in January 1920. But Louis remained ill at ease in social situations and vastly preferred the factory floor or his own private workshop to any of the events his wife cooked up. Given the challenges he was about to face, it was probably a good thing that he did not retire to a life of leisure but kept an active hand in his business.

Helena Rubinstein was another who saw little point—or enjoyment—in leisure. Following the Armistice, this Polish powerhouse returned to Europe from America, where she had occupied herself during the war by brilliantly choreographing a huge expansion of her cosmetics empire. Reestablished in London and Paris, she continued her drive toward new pinnacles of success, finding ever-more-innovative and irresistible ways to sell magic in a jar to women eager to believe in miracles.

Rubinstein needed more than a miracle, though, to save her marriage. Her journalist husband, Edward Titus, whom she had left in charge of their two children in New York, was growing restless and bored with his parental duties. At length, after Madame's departure, he placed the children in the hands of a nanny and headed for Paris. There he renewed his Left Bank contacts and reestablished his ties to Parisian expats that he had made in New York during the war. Soon he found his niche in Montparnasse, establishing a bookshop for rare books along with what would become a revered Left Bank publishing house, the Black Manikin Press. Here he would publish limited editions of authors such as D. H. Lawrence that more mainstream publishers would not touch.

Rubinstein footed the bill for her husband's Montparnasse venture, and it was an arrangement that worked for the moment. By this time she was beginning to use her wealth to collect paintings, jewelry, and sculpture—although her taste ran more to quantity than quality. An avant-garde publishing house was not especially showy, but it loosely fit into her scheme of artistic acquisition.

Still, the dissimilar trajectories of the Rubinstein and Titus careers, as well as Titus's numerous affairs with other women, meant trouble ahead.

L'Oréal's founder, Eugène Schueller, was another who was bored by leisure. A brilliant chemist as well as businessman, Schueller had worked his way out of poverty by the time the war began, having successfully parlayed his discovery of a safe and natural-looking hair dye into a moneymaking venture. On the strength of his early success he married, and when war came, he enlisted, leaving his business in the capable hands of his wife. Upon returning safely from the war, where he acquitted himself with honors,[15] he was pleased to find his business flourishing. But rather than take it easy, he then began to branch into other areas that interested him, including celluloid combs, cellulose acetate, artificial silk, Bakelite, cellulose paints, and cinema and photographic film. In this last venture, his company, Plavic Film, took control of the film-manufacturing company run by the legendary Lumière brothers, who had invented motion pictures.

In the meantime, L'Oréal continued its rapid growth, aided by the new hairstyle, the bob—the short, cropped hair for women that had begun to appear during the war and that Coco Chanel as well as movie stars such as Clara Bow and Louise Brooks made popular. Instead of leading to a drop in demand for hair dye, as Schueller initially feared, the new style increased demand, as it required frequent cutting and dying. Seeing another new niche, Schueller now produced a bleach, L'Oréal Blanc, that created the rage for blonde and platinum hair that continued for decades.

Soon Schueller, like Renault, would have his own luxurious country estate—his in Brittany, overlooking the sea—as well as his own yacht. Yet unlimited wealth wasn't enough for him. Like Renault, he was chafing under governmental constraints. But unlike Renault, Schueller would turn his dissatisfaction with the current state of the economy into carefully calibrated theories on a new-model economy to replace it.

In December 1918, Charles Jeanneret and Amédée Ozenfant finally had the exhibition of their paintings that they longed for, but to their great disappointment it was not well reviewed. The art critic Louis Vauxcelles wrote that the two young painters were "like clergymen putting on blinders when they walk down the grand boulevards, in order to keep from being tempted by the pretty girls."[16] His point was the paintings' lack of spontaneity, but he certainly spotted a fundamental tension within Jeanneret, who had been brought up in the strict Calvinist environment of La Chaux-de-Fonds, a somber watchmaking town in the Swiss Jura. Now and in the future, Jeanneret would venture into wild and usually (but not always) imaginary sexual fantasies, which he seemed to find necessary to relate in detail to his parents via long letters.

Ironically, it was at this exhibition that Jeanneret met the pretty young saleswoman and model Yvonne Gallis, who would eventually become his wife. But at the moment, things looked bleak for him, especially in comparison with others' success. At almost the same time as his and Ozenfant's failed exhibition, the Japanese artist Tsuguharu Foujita had his first solo exhibition at Galerie Devambez (at 49 Boulevard Malesherbes), where he rocketed to fame using French techniques in Japanese-style paintings. Earlier that year Foujita had painted in the south of France with Modigliani and Soutine, and now he became one of the few among his Montparnasse buddies to be making money. To celebrate his newfound wealth, he installed a bathtub with hot running water in his studio, making him the envy of his crowd.

Much to Marcel Proust's relief, both his brother, Dr. Robert Proust, and Proust's former lover, Reynaldo Hahn, returned from the war unharmed—perhaps a miracle, given Dr. Proust's continuous exposure to danger throughout the war. Marcel Proust's own doctor reassured him that he was not suffering from any grave illness, but Proust still clung to the deep fear that he would die before completing his multivolume *oeuvre*. Despite this constant apprehension, his epic work, *In Search of Lost Time*, continued to go forward, with the printer finishing *Within a Budding Grove* as well as the proofs for *The Guermantes Way* (parts 1 and 2) on November 30. Proust was disappointed that only the second volume of his work was coming out, unaccompanied by volumes 3, 4, 5, and 6. His publisher had finally hired two printers in an attempt to step up the process, and a huge proofing job was landing on Proust all at once—a dismal job, he told his publisher, "so wearying in my current state."[17]

Just as worrying, if not more so, was the news that Proust was going to have to move. He had lived at 102 Boulevard Haussmann since 1906, where in 1910 he famously lined his bedroom with cork to deaden the boulevard's noise. Soon after the New Year, he learned that his landlady (his aunt by marriage) had just sold the building to a banker, who was prepared to turn it into a bank and offices. Proust was thunderstruck. His aunt had given him no hint that this was about to happen, and since he had only a verbal agreement rather than a formal lease, he feared that the new owner would evict him while at the same time requiring immediate payment of the large sum that Proust owed in back rent—"a double nightmare for me," as he put it.[18]

Reaching out as usual to friends for help, he enlisted the aid of Walter Berry, president of the American Chamber of Commerce in Paris, to sort out his financial and legal difficulties as well as to find him buyers for two large tapestries and other pieces of furniture that Proust trusted would bring him the cash he so badly needed. Complicating matters were the constant demands of Proust's health and his nocturnal habits, which required absolute silence during the day while he slept or rested. Proust, as always, was fortunate in his friends: Berry replied that he would be "enchanted" to receive Proust's furnishings on his premises and show them to his friends without revealing the owner's name.[19]

After years of resounding financial success, even during the war years, François Coty—that perfumer *extraordinaire*—was facing a new challenge. He had taken care well before the war to found subsidiaries in other countries and to fabricate most of his products outside of France. This strategy served him well, for in 1918 he sold almost thirty thousand compacts of perfumed face powder alone, much of it made and sold in the United States. He also shipped all the parts of his perfumes separately to avoid import taxes. He maintained twenty-one different luxury perfume lines during the war, with their corresponding beauty products, and in drawing up his ledgers he found that, financially speaking, he had not suffered from the war—with the exception of his business in Russia, where the Bolshevik Revolution led to a huge financial loss. The damage he suffered there contributed significantly in coming years to his deep and abiding hatred of the Bolsheviks.

Yet all seemed well with Coty's empire, except that in the war's aftermath, the public no longer was satisfied with a rehash of prewar perfumes. It was a new world, and the public wanted something new to go with it. This represented a major challenge, for it was one thing to create something novel, but quite another to blot out the ghastly memories of trench warfare and mass death. Dreaming of the wild maquis of his Corsican youth and of the forest groves on the Loire, where he had bought a château, Coty set to work to create a perfume evoking the amber-scented mosses that fragranced these forests at certain hours. The outcome was a triumph. Paris enthusiastically took to Coty's new perfume, Chypre, the first of his perfumes to reach the greater public. Coty had unquestionably joined the club of great perfumers.

Still, his life had somehow become emptier as his fortune burgeoned. His children, a son born in 1902 and a daughter in 1904, were growing up, while his wife, Yvonne, who had so significantly helped him during the early days of their marriage, had become distant. Whether their marriage's deterioration or Coty's philandering came first, by the war's end Coty was filling his private life with mistresses, on whom he lavished expensive gifts. His expenditures were endless: in addition to properties in Corsica and Nice, he bought and extensively remodeled that château on the Loire, domiciled his mistresses and his illegitimate children in pricey residences, and housed his own family in an exclusive property near the Bois de Boulogne. Despite his expenditures, his wealth continued to grow. At the beginning of the 1920s, his fortune was estimated at one hundred million francs.

Yet as Coty's business continued to prosper, he would find life a little less enjoyable than he had perhaps expected. He would also discover, as had Napoleon Bonaparte, that it was easier to conquer an empire than to keep it.

∽

The young composer Darius Milhaud returned "to a Paris jubilant with victory celebrations." After the gloom of war, he felt that "now at last the victory that had been paid for so dearly was felt to be something tangible, visible, making our hearts swell with boundless hope."[20]

Milhaud had spent the latter part of the war years in Brazil, where he served as secretary to the French ambassador Paul Claudel, a highly regarded poet and dramatist as well as diplomat. Less well known was the fact that Claudel was also the brother of Camille Claudel, that remarkable sculptor who had been the great love of Rodin's life. Since then, she had sunk intermittently into paranoia, leading Paul and their mother to commit her to an asylum. There—despite her doctors' reluctance, but in accord with her mother and brother's insistence—Camille would remain for the rest of her long life.

This part of Paul Claudel's life was little known, and he evidently preferred it that way. Camille's bohemianism had been an embarrassment, and as a devout Catholic he perhaps had been appalled by her relationship with Rodin, even before her mental instability became obvious. (His own subsequent relationship with a married woman, who bore his child, left its own psychic scars.) Paul Claudel and his mother were adamantly opposed to having Camille's work shown, even (and perhaps especially) in the new Musée Rodin that opened in 1919 in the Hôtel Biron, the beautiful mansion where Rodin had worked and welcomed friends. Long after Camille's death, Claudel would change his mind and donate several of his sister's sculptures to the museum. But that time was still a long way off.

A devout Catholic and mystic who was deeply conservative and even reactionary in his politics, Claudel was, like so many other conservative Catholics, anti-Semitic. But he nonetheless befriended Darius Milhaud, a Jew from Aix-en-Province, who for many years would collaborate with Claudel in setting Claudel's work to music. Although Jewish, Milhaud early on had learned to love the music of the Roman Catholic Church. From his grandfather's country estate, he could "hear the Angelus from the Convent of St. Thomas chiming out in triple time a major sixth that hung in the air nearly as long as the note whose harmonic it was. Far off, like an echo, the bells of the Cathedral Church of St. Saviour and of St. Mary Magdalen faintly answered." In addition, one of his best friends was a devout Catholic who "worshipped music and admired my early efforts [at composition] with passionate conviction."[21]

Milhaud was the pampered and musically inclined only child of a well-to-do family of almond exporters. Taking to the violin as a youngster, he soon found that "music was becoming a more and more imperious necessity for me."[22] But since his health was delicate, his parents put off sending him to the Paris Conservatoire until he was older. In the meantime, they took him to concerts in Marseilles, where he heard Sarasate, Eugène Ysaÿe, and the Cortot-Thibaud-Casals Trio. His parents also brought him to Paris on short holidays, where he took lessons with a teacher at the Conservatoire. At last in 1909, at the age of seventeen, he enrolled in the Conservatoire and moved permanently to Paris. There he became an avid concertgoer, gallery attender, and enthusiast of the Ballets Russes, especially when the scores were by Stravinsky. But his classes in chamber music and orchestral playing bored him. What he now wanted was to become a composer.

It was at this point in his development that Milhaud's Catholic friend from Aix enthused over a play by Francis Jammes, whose writing reflected a return to the Catholic faith under the influence of none other than Paul Claudel. Milhaud requested Jammes's permission to turn the play, *La Brebis égarée* (*The Lost Sheep*), into an opera—a request that Jammes granted. Then, learning of Jammes's high opinion of Claudel, Milhaud began to read Claudel's poetry. Soon Milhaud was part of a group of young Catholic writers gravitating around Jammes, Claudel, and André Gide. "Between Claudel and me," he later wrote, "understanding was immediate, mutual confidence absolute. . . . It marked the first step not only in a faithful collaboration, but in a precious friendship."[23] Along with Maurice Barrès, whom Milhaud also admired, his new companions were intensely conservative, devoutly Catholic, and stridently nationalist.

At the same time, other connections were drawing Milhaud more deeply into Paris's music world. Maurice Ravel made it possible for one of Milhaud's early works to be performed at the Société Musicale Indépendante (SMI), which Ravel and others had recently formed, under the presidency of Gabriel Fauré, in protest against the ultraconservative policies of the Société Nationale de Musique, bastion of composers such as Camille Saint-Saëns and Vincent d'Indy. Ravel also connected him with the salon of Cipa Godebski, brother of arts patron Misia Natanson Edwards, where Milhaud met Erik Satie and the pianist Ricardo Viñes. Another important salon opened its doors to Milhaud through the society portrait painter Jacques-Emile Blanche, who brought him to perform at one of Princesse Edmond de Polignac's musical evenings, where he became a regular. In addition, his Conservatoire friends and acquaintances included important future connections, such as Georges Auric and Arthur Honegger, who would become his companions in the Groupe des Six following the war.

Rejected for military service on medical grounds, Milhaud assisted in refugee work before Paul Claudel requested that he be sent to Brazil as his secretary. Milhaud arrived in 1917, during Carnival, and was "fascinated by the rhythms of this popular music." Rio "had a potent charm,"[24] he added, and after his return to Paris, it would continue to exert its considerable attraction.

Once back in Paris, Milhaud linked up with old friends from prewar days, including Arthur Honegger and Georges Auric. During his time away, these young composers and their friends had performed their works at small venues such as the Salle Huyghens in Montparnasse—a painter's studio where bohemians and the most avant-garde of Paris's upper crust mingled in democratic discomfort. Erik Satie was the leader of these young composers—"our mascot," as Milhaud called him. "The purity of his art, his horror of all concessions, his contempt for money, and his ruthless attitude toward the critics were a marvelous example for us all."[25]

Satie dubbed four of these young composers—Auric, Honegger, Louis Durey, and Germaine Tailleferre—Les Nouveaux Jeunes. Soon Francis Poulenc and Milhaud joined the group, and a critic named them Les Six, or the Groupe des Six, a name that stuck. Although each of the six had a decidedly individualistic approach to composition, they shared in the birth of a new kind of French music, which as Milhaud later put it, was "fresh, jazzy, unpretentious, [and] ideally suited to the 'modern-dress' ballets that stemmed from *Parade* and [Debussy's] *Jeux*."[26] They and their friends, who included poets, painters, writers, actors, and singers as well as composers and musicians, began to meet regularly on Saturday evenings at Milhaud's apartment at 5 Rue Gaillard (now Rue Paul-Escudier) at the foot of Montmartre. Delighting in one another's company, they took equal delight in setting the conventional world on its ear.

After cocktails and hijinks, including occasional bicycle races around the dining-room table, they typically moved on to dinner at a small restaurant followed by the Montmartre fair or the circus Médrano. After that, they returned to Milhaud's place, where they sang, played, and read poetry. This was a group that was more than willing to combine high art with low, appreciating American ragtime and jazz as well as the music halls of Maurice Chevalier and Mistinguett. Instead of endless discussions of music and theory, they clearly preferred fun.

By this time Jean Cocteau had established himself as the Groupe des Six's spokesman.[27] After all, his *Le Coq et l'Arlequin* (*The Cock and the Harlequin*), published in early 1918, had served as a kind of manifesto for the new music that the group embraced, despite differences in the individual members' characters, temperaments, and compositional styles. In it, Cocteau pleaded for a purely French music that "shuns the colossal" (meaning German music), and he proclaimed Satie as the leader of this musical breakthrough. Although the Gallic rooster became Cocteau's symbol for such purely French music, which included provincial French folk tunes, he envisioned the new music as also welcoming American jazz. "The music-hall, the circus, American Negro bands—all this," he wrote, "is as fertilizing to an artist as life itself."[28]

One of Cocteau's earlier books of poetry (1911) was titled *Le Prince frivole* (*The Frivolous Prince*), a designation that still seemed a fitting description of its author, for even at the age of thirty, Jean Cocteau remained the *enfant terrible* of Paris's foremost artistic circles. Born and raised in an artistically inclined and well-traveled Parisian family, he had left home at the age of fifteen for a life of adventure in Marseilles—an adventure that abruptly ended when his exasperated uncle sent the police to bring him home. Handsome, temperamental, and thoroughly pampered by his widowed mother, Cocteau quickly learned that indulgence came as a reward for being charming. He also learned that audacity won attention, which was just as good a way as any for achieving fame.

Although he would in time make his mark as a novelist, playwright, artist, and filmmaker, Cocteau preferred to be known as a poet, which was how he first came to the attention of the elite in prewar artistic Paris—especially Countess Anna de Noailles, author of several acclaimed books of poetry and the undisputed queen of the prewar literary salons. Cocteau quickly became Countess de Noailles' devoted attendant and companion, mirroring her to an extraordinary degree—especially in his endless conversation and monologues, which echoed the brilliant torrent of words that were her trademark.

Cocteau also attached himself to Sergei Diaghilev and Diaghilev's retinue during the brilliant prewar years of Diaghilev's Ballets Russes, where he endeavored to make himself indispensable. He fumbled badly on his first major outing, the libretto for a 1912 ballet, *Le Dieu bleu*, which fell flat and quickly disappeared from the Ballets Russes repertory. It was around this time that Diaghilev famously told Cocteau, "Astound me! I'll wait for you to astound me!"[29] It took Cocteau five years, but he succeeded with *Parade*, the 1917 Ballets Russes production with music by Erik Satie, sets and costumes by Pablo Picasso, and choreography by Léonide Massine. Cocteau prided himself in having provided the scenario for *Parade* and in having pulled together the principals—especially since this turned into an event of considerable notoriety. *Parade* may not have caused quite as much stir as Cocteau later claimed, but even though not of the decibel level or caliber of *Rite of Spring*, it created a satisfying amount of consternation among the traditionalists and, better yet, got Diaghilev's attention.

Quite a few people did not like Jean Cocteau. Picasso, who found that a little of Cocteau went a long way, once acidly remarked that Cocteau was "becoming terribly famous: you will find his works at every hairdresser's." (Taking a sideswipe at Cocteau's unabashed homosexuality, Picasso was also heard to remark that Cocteau was "born with a pleat in his trousers.")[30] Diaghilev, who put up with years of Cocteau's attempts to crash the inner Ballets Russes circle, found him exasperating. (Cocteau in turn called Diaghilev "that ogre, that sacred monster," and described Diaghilev's laugh as that of "a very young crocodile.")[31] Erik Satie was heard to make gibes about Cocteau, and André

Gide was especially contemptuous, on the grounds that he found Cocteau superficial—although it certainly did not help matters when, one evening in late 1917, Cocteau made off with Gide's current love interest.

Perhaps most painful of all was Apollinaire's snub of Cocteau in the program notes for *Parade*. *Parade* had accomplished all that Cocteau hoped for, yet there was one sour note, and that was Apollinaire's failure to mention Cocteau at all. After Apollinaire's death, Cocteau envisioned himself as the Polish poet's successor, the one person who could pull together all the disparate factions of the postwar modern movement, or *l'esprit nouveau*. Cocteau also positioned himself—and possibly even came to view himself— as Apollinaire's close friend. This was far from the truth, and several among Apollinaire's followers, founders of literary magazines who battled constantly among one another, were united in their poor opinion of Cocteau. These included André Breton, Louis Aragon, and Philippe Soupault, as well as the editors of the influential *Nouvelle Revue Française* (*NRF*)—Jean Schlumberger, Jacques Copeau, and especially the future Nobel Prize winner for literature André Gide. Despite Cocteau's frantic attempts to win Gide's approval (and a favorable review in the *NRF*), Gide from the outset had regarded Cocteau as little more than a frivolous addition to the Paris literary scene. Nothing in the years to come did much to change his mind.

Yet Cocteau always had alternatives. Writing soon after Armistice to Count Etienne de Beaumont, Cocteau told him that "peace touches me like grace, and I wear its dove on my shoulder amidst the monkeys and the wolves."[32] Whomever Cocteau had in mind in the monkeys and wolves category—and it well could have been Breton or any of his associates—it was not difficult for him to escape to a far more refined society. On Christmas Eve following Armistice, he dined at the Ritz (along with Marcel Proust and others) as the guest of the Princesse Lucien Murat. Following this, the young man-about-town entertained the group with songs of the Belle Epoque at the apartment of one of the members of the Italian armistice delegation.

Years later, the talented but trouble-prone writer Maurice Sachs recalled that Cocteau was what he termed an "animator"—a remarkable individual who, together with Diaghilev, "was the most enchanting magician of our time."[33] That post-Armistice Christmas of 1918, Cocteau had no way of predicting his future, but he keenly felt that he was ready to soar. In a Christmas poem for his mother, he wrote that the year's end was bringing to a close the war "with its cruel discords." And then, referring to his brother, who had fought in the air corps and survived, he added, "One of your sons closes his wings." As for himself, he concluded, "And the other feels his [wings] grow again."[34]

The year was closing on a note of relief, hope, and joy.

Delegates witnessing the signing of the Treaty of Versailles, Hall of Mirrors, Palace of Versailles, June 28, 1919. Photo © Tallandier / Bridgeman Images

CHAPTER THREE

~

Versailles and Victory

(1919)

The Versailles Peace Conference did not officially open until January 18, 1919, two long months after Armistice was declared, and further delays plagued it until March. Upheaval and revolution in Germany as well as in Russia were partly to blame, but the Allied leaders did not seem in a hurry to begin negotiations. Britain's prime minister, David Lloyd George, first wanted to hold British elections, and U.S. president Woodrow Wilson set off for London and Italy soon after arriving in Paris. In February, Wilson returned to America to deal with growing opposition in Washington to the League of Nations, while Lloyd George again returned to London to address domestic issues. As Harold Nicolson (then a junior member of the British delegation) later noted, the central element of the Versailles Peace Conference was "the element of confusion."[1]

In the meantime, Helen Pearl Adam reported "enormous crowds of secretaries and under-secretaries and private secretaries" who crowded into the city, cramming the hotels to capacity and (to the infinite dismay of Parisians) raising the cost of living. The secretaries and undersecretaries ended up in bathrooms and on sofas, and "it is said that three lieutenant-generals slept together in a servant's attic of one of the big hotels."[2]

Paris celebrated Christmas, that first Christmas of the peace, with excitement, joy, and high prices. Holly was scarce, while butter was maddeningly absent. Coal and milk were also in short supply, but game, poultry, meat, vegetables, fish, and fruit were available, although at a price. On Christmas Eve, Charles-Edouard Jeanneret attended what he called "an extremely select *soirée*" at the house of Paul Poiret's sister, Germaine Bongard, owner of the exclusive dress shop where Jeanneret's partner, Amédée Ozenfant, worked and where Jeanneret and Ozenfant had held their exhibit (rumor had it that Bongard was Ozenfant's lover). Helen Pearl Adam ate at a famous restaurant (charitably left nameless) that charged exorbitant prices for a meal that marched from oysters and oxtail soup through lobster, venison, chicken, and a long succession of other dishes, ending with cream cake and ices. "I believe there was a salad," she reported, "and there may have been other things too, but one could only regard with dazed wonder the spectacle of so much to eat and so much to pay."[3]

Reviving prewar dress codes, evening dress at such an affair was the rule. This meant boiled shirts (stiff dress shirts) and white ties for the men and low-cut gowns for the ladies. At Adam's dinner, the ladies received great bouquets of flowers as a famous singer sang the Marseillaise to the accompaniment of an orchestra of three performers—"the first heard in a Paris restaurant for four years."[4]

Amid the celebrations of this first postwar holiday season, Marcel Proust extricated himself from his bedclothes to attend a grand New Year's Eve dinner given by Count Etienne de Beaumont in honor of the British ambassador Lord Derby. Count Beaumont, whose lifestyle served as a model for his young friend Jean Cocteau, would soon be leading the way as master of the postwar revels—those elaborately staged and glittering Beaumont parties and costume balls that would so memorably define the decade. This dinner was merely a prelude to far greater things to come.

Yet beneath the expressions of relief and joy lay nagging concerns about the future. Winning the peace might well be even more difficult than winning the war, as Clemenceau remarked to a friend shortly after Armistice was declared.[5] Others, although hoping for the best, were similarly wary. If Clemenceau, "Father Victory," sees us through the minefield of what is to come, Helen Pearl Adam mused, "he will be doing to France almost as great a service as he did in bringing her through endurance to victory."[6]

President Wilson arrived in France in mid-December, and seldom had Parisians greeted anyone with such acclaim. Just as America's entry into the war brought the interminable conflict to a close, so Wilson's arrival signaled the reassuring imminence of a lasting peace. The French port of Brest welcomed him with a huge banner proclaiming him "the benefactor of mankind," and Paris was just as adulatory. His promise that this war would make the world "safe for democracy" resonated with French citizens from all walks of life, and one American resident of Paris called it "the most remarkable demonstration of enthusiasm and affection on the part of the Parisians that I have ever heard of, let alone seen."[7]

The City of Light was growing accustomed to its role as virtual capital of the world, and as the new year opened, Paris, already filled to brimming, was daily inundated with the arrival of yet more diplomats and their retinues (the British delegation alone totaled almost four hundred), along with multitudes of petitioners for endless interests and causes. These multitudes were there to address the great issues of the day, but the issues were complex and not easily resolved. Expectations were great, as were the possibilities for failure.

The peace conference officially opened on January 18, but several days earlier, on January 12, the first meeting took place between the Allied heads of state: Prime Minister Georges Clemenceau, President Wilson, Prime Minister Lloyd George, and Italy's prime minister, Vittorio Orlando. From the outset, the participants regarded informal meetings such as these as preliminary meetings, in preparation for the formal peace talks to come. But as the days and weeks passed, these informal meetings—at first including Japan as a major power and then reduced to Lloyd George, Clemenceau, Wilson, and Orlando—became the Council of Four, the inner core of the peace talks.

Even these came to a halt for a long month between February and March, following an assassination attempt on Clemenceau by a young anarchist. The plucky old man survived the attempt, although the bullet remained lodged between his ribs (the doctors decided against the risk of extraction). Within ten days he went back to work, and it was at this point—and Wilson's return from the United States—that Clemenceau, Lloyd George, and Wilson began to dig into the major questions. Now, in an informal atmosphere—either in Wilson's private residence, or in Clemenceau's room at the Ministry of War, or in Lloyd George's Paris apartment—came the discussions, disagreements, and hard bargaining that ultimately decided the major components of the peace settlement.

In March, the Allies refused to support the French franc any longer, leading to its immediate decline in foreign exchange markets. In April, despite huge war debts, a falling franc, and a shaky economy, the French government provided compensation, at prewar values, for every property owner who had suffered war damage. It was a remarkable step, supported by the general belief that war reparations from Germany would more than underwrite the expense. Unfortunately, those receiving compensation were paid in francs that were rapidly losing their value. In addition, the belief that the Germans

Manufacturing the first models of Citroën Type A cars at the Citroën factory, Paris, circa 1922. Photo © Tallandier / Bridgeman Images would pay, and that it was patriotic to overvalue one's property, led to an epidemic of overvaluation.

Despite this, reconstruction began to move forward, with farmland reviving at surprising speed, and whole towns and villages rapidly rebuilding. Industrial reconstructing was especially swift, with many firms taking advantage of the compensation to upgrade their equipment. In addition, thanks to a clause in the coming peace treaty, French industrialists, especially in the chemical industries, were now able to encroach freely on German patents without payment.

The war that had given French industrialists such as Renault and Citroën virtually unlimited markets for war materiel had also encouraged their move into mass production. At the war's end, many of these armament and aircraft firms were reconverting, largely to automobile factories—encouraged by reconversion possibilities as well by the war's huge slaughter of horses, which effectively diminished that form of transportation. At first there were many small auto factories in France, but three giants soon emerged: Renault, Peugeot, and a newcomer to the industry, André Citroën.

The struggle between Renault and Citroën began in January 1919, shortly after the war's end, when Citroën, who had made his name and fortune in the gear business, made the startling announcement that he was about to manufacture automobiles. Not just any automobiles, either, but the French equivalent of Henry Ford's Model T. Citroën's auto, the heralded Citroën Type A, appeared soon after—the first mass-produced car in France. As Citroën assured the public, it was lightweight and sturdy, and it sold for far less than other French-made automobiles. Earlier, he had rejected the design for a large and luxurious high-performance automobile and had sold the design to Gabriel Voisin, a leading aircraft manufacturer. Voisin, in the war's aftermath, went into the automobile business, producing his fast and stylish Type C1, which became the darling of fashionable celebrities such as Rudolph Valentino and Josephine Baker. Voisin produced this car and variations of it (including an aerodynamic, lightweight, all-aluminum racing version) throughout the decade.

But Citroën was not interested in creating a plaything for the rich. He wanted to make a useful car for the middle class, and his mass-produced Type A came fully equipped with tires, electric lights, and self-starter at an attractive all-inclusive price. In addition, the Type A was relatively inexpensive to run. In time, it would come in a wide variety of body styles, but these would all be based on a standard chassis, engine, and transmission. Citroën was onto a good thing, and he knew it.

Not only was Citroën establishing a new vehicle for an entirely new kind of market; he was also establishing procedures and practices for driving that would become standard throughout the auto world. The Type A Citroën was the first car in Europe with its steering wheel mounted on the vehicle's left side. Early manufacturers of luxury autos placed the steering wheel on the right, next to the curb, so that the driver (more typically the chauffeur) could see the edge of the road. But Citroën positioned the Type A's driving seat so that the driver could operate the gearstick with the right hand and have better visibility when passing.

A master salesman, Citroën also provided a number of thoughtful assists for the Type A owner. Rejecting the practice of other European auto manufacturers, who viewed the sale as the end of any further dealings with either the car or its owner, Citroën was determined to expand the market for his products as well as increase product loyalty. With this in mind, he set up a network of dealer franchises that sold and serviced Citroëns exclusively throughout France (he had two hundred of these at the outset, in 1919, and rapidly expanded these to five thousand by 1925). He offered purchasers a driver's manual and a list of approved Citroën repairers, along with standard service charges and standardized factory-made replacement parts. He also set up chemistry and physics labs at his factory to test materials and components, and he invented what is now called direct-mail marketing (carried out in those days via vast card-index files). "As soon as one sale ends," he said, "another more important sale commences. It is the after-sales service offered to the customer when he has already parted with his money that will decide whether he returns to buy from us a second time."[8]

Much to Citroën's gratification, although not to his surprise, the Type A was a huge success. Even though the falling franc meant that he had to raise prices, Citroën's reconfigured wartime factory on Paris's Quai de Javel (now Quai André Citroën) was by late spring 1919 turning out thirty cars a day. Soon this increased to more than fifty a day, until, within a year, thousands of Citroëns were on the road.

Admittedly the roads were still bad, but there were more of them, especially in the Paris area. Paris and the region around it had grown rapidly during the war, and it was continuing to grow—largely on the outskirts, where industries had taken root and flourished, in close proximity to government, government money, and transportation hubs. This trend did not show any sign of stopping at the war's end. Wartime factories were converting to peacetime manufacture, and as they did, Paris continued to attract masses of industrial workers, who settled near the factories where they worked, in a vast ring that circled the still-walled city.[9] Even within the confines of the city itself, things were changing. The fine artisan handwork for which Paris had been known since the time of Louis XIV was on the decline, while skilled and semiskilled workers could now be found in fields such as engineering, electrical equipment, and dyeing.

Still, the Paris to which Maurice Ravel returned that spring was regaining its cultural vigor. Ravel, who had not yet recovered his own personal vigor, exclaimed at the sheer number of "concerts, rehearsals, auditions." "Three quarters of the concert halls are empty," he wrote his good friend, Ida Godebska, "but they still insist on arranging new performances."[10] One of these was his first postwar public appearance, at an April 11 Société Musicale Indépendante (SMI) recital at which Marguerite Long premiered his *Le Tombeau de Couperin*. According to Madame Long, it was "the first appearance in public . . . of the man who, since the recent death of Debussy, had become the uncontested and glorious champion of our [French] music."[11] The audience cheered Ravel at length and applauded each section of *Le Tombeau de Couperin* so enthusiastically that Long happily encored the whole thing.

Meanwhile, Fernand Léger, who once said that he had "a lifelong desire to ignore the romantic point of view,"[12] succumbed delectably to romance one morning as he sat with companions in the long-established Montparnasse café, the Closerie des Lilas. Along came an amazing sight—a young woman in full bridal dress on a bicycle, her veil streaming behind her. Her name was Jeanne-Augustine Lohy, and she was due that very day to marry the son of a notary. But one of the wedding gifts had been this bicycle, and, well—how could she resist a short ride? Unfortunately the short ride had turned into a much longer one, and now she was many kilometers from where she should be getting married. What a disaster! But all was not lost, as Léger was quick to assure her, and she tremulously agreed. After all, Léger was a handsome man as well as a very nice one. Before long, all was well, and she became Madame Léger.

That spring, the newspaper *Paris–Midi* asked Jean Cocteau to write a weekly article on the Paris scene, a series (appearing between March and August) that Cocteau called *Carte blanche*. It was while Cocteau was writing *Carte blanche* that he met the fifteen-year-old poet Raymond Radiguet. It would be an understatement to say that Radiguet was precocious: his poetry was astonishingly mature, as were his relations with an ever-growing number of Paris's avant-garde. In the effort to publish his poetry, Radiguet had found his way into the newspaper offices of *L'Intransigeant*, where An-dré Salmon was an editor. Salmon introduced him to Max Jacob, who in turn sent him to Cocteau. Cocteau, who later said that he "sensed his star," fell madly in love with him.[13]

Cocteau's colleagues nicknamed Radiguet "Monsieur Bébé" behind his back, but none dared to treat him dismissively in person, least of all Coc-teau. "He was hard," Cocteau later said. "It took a diamond to scratch his heart." Radiguet's father tried to intervene, but with little effect. Cocteau assured the father that the young man was a prodigy and that "his literary future is of primary consideration with me." Radiguet *père* backed off, but this probably was due less to Cocteau's assurances than to the son's basic callousness and cruelty, which made people of any age think twice before crossing him. Salmon noted that young Radiguet's "cool insolence" made others "hesitate between hating him and admiring him," and another of Cocteau's friends, Jean Hugo, called Radiguet "silent, sulky, arrogant, amazingly mature in his judgments, certainly not affectionate." But Coc-teau was in love, even though he saw into the black depths of Radiguet's psyche. Soon the relationship went topsy-turvy, with Cocteau seeking Radiguet's approval even in literary matters. Cocteau styled himself to Radiguet as "Your adoptive father," but he also told him that he was "the only person who intimidates me, you stone-ager."[14]

Cocteau naturally brought Radiguet to the Groupe des Six's Saturday dinners, where the young man practiced his intimidation techniques to perfection. "Radiguet was like a young chess prodigy," Cocteau later wrote. "Without opening his mouth, simply by the scorn conveyed by his near-sighted glance, . . . he beat us all. Remember: the very finest players were sitting around that table."[15]

By winter, Radiguet had become a full-fledged member of the Saturday dinners and went everywhere with its members, writing publicity articles for Satie, for the Groupe des Six, and for Cocteau's new book of poems, *Poésies*. With the publication of his own volume of poems, *Les Joues en feu*, the literary avant-garde hailed Radiguet as the greatest young prodigy since Rimbaud.

Despite his aura of bored insolence, it must have been a heady experience for a young man still in his teens.

Like any good poker player, Clemenceau had been careful not to commit himself in public to any particular proposal or set of demands before the peace conference convened. Peace, he told the Chamber of Deputies that December following Armistice, "must be a compromise between all the Allies."[16] Well aware of the dangers that an isolated France would face if she lost American or British support, he was determined to maintain the entente between them—including necessary compromises. As for Wilson's League of Nations, it was perhaps a noble idea but could not, in Clemenceau's view, take the place of old-fashioned alliances and diplomacy. Concluding that it could provide little in the way of security for France, he consequently gave it little serious attention. As he put it, "I like the League, but I do not believe in it."[17]

The higher echelons of France's foreign ministry (known in shorthand as Quai d'Orsay, after the ministry's Left Bank address) early projected that France's interests would best be served by the military neutralization of the Rhine's industrial left bank as well as the return to France of Alsace-Lorraine (taken in 1871) and the Saar (an important source for coal, iron, and steel, lost in 1815). Further, a strong anti-German and anti-Bolshevik Poland would be in France's interest, as would a federal German republic—although the French were willing to let the Germans decide their own domestic political system.

These proposals were far more moderate than those that Marshall Ferdinand Foch, former commander-in-chief of the joint Allied armies, put forward. At a minimum, Foch's proposals would have given military control of the Rhineland to the Allies. But the proposals for which Clemenceau fought in March and April 1919 were far closer to those of the Quai d'Orsay. His primary goal was to protect France from future German invasion by surrounding Germany on the east (Poland) as well as the west with strong anti-German entities. A secondary goal was to require Germany to pay reparations for the full cost of the war—an enormous sum, including even the cost of military pensions.

Unquestionably, the French public was fiercely in support of taking tough measures with Germany. Even Marcel Proust, who "never liked or approved of the 1914 war, though he wanted France to win it," wrote to Madame Straus that "even I, who am such a supporter of the Peace because unable to bear men's suffering, believe that if total victory and a hard Peace was what we wanted, it had been better to make a still harder Peace."[18] The war had ruined France: it has been estimated that close to eight million acres had been reduced to desert, her mines flooded, her coal production drastically reduced, and other industries, as well as major portions of the transport system, virtually destroyed.[19] The French government had financed the war with enormous loans as well as the issue of paper money. In addition, it now had the burden of supporting orphans, widows, and the wounded. But increased taxation? No, French opinion resoundingly chorused that Germany should pay. In addition, the French—given the disproportionate amount of suffering that they and their nation had undergone—firmly believed that England and America should write off a major portion, if not all, of France's debts.

Unfortunately, reparations on the scale the French envisioned were economically impossible: Germany herself was now ruined and in no position to pay such astronomical sums. Plus, the Americans and the British were unenthusiastic about writing off war debts. In March, they had stopped supporting the franc, which promptly fell, causing economic havoc. The French regarded their allies' position as selfish, while the Americans and the British regarded any other as commercially unviable and even immoral.

In the end, the treaty had to limit itself to requiring Germany to pay a much smaller interim sum, with the grand total to be decided sometime in the future.[20] In the absence of full reparations, the treaty compelled Germany to admit its responsibility for starting the war—the famous, or infamous, war-guilt clause. What this amounted to was that, in lieu of extracting full payment, the treaty forced Germans to admit their liability for the full cost. Guilt and condemnation, however, were unmarketable currencies that gave the Allies, especially the French, little more than a temporary salve, while they accrued an interest of bitter resentment in Germany for years to come.

Despite much grumbling, the French in the end had to accept an increase in taxation (both income and indirect taxation), and this, along with stricter budget policies, would within several years significantly decrease the nation's deficit.[21] But in the meantime, life was tough.

Except, of course, for those foreigners, especially the Americans, currently enjoying themselves in Paris.

One of those Americans most enjoying herself during the peace talks was that irrepressible dynamo Elsa Maxwell. By this time Maxwell had gravitated to Paris, which enchanted her. She later wrote that it was "difficult to describe the exhilarating atmosphere of Paris during the peace negotiations. Every day was like a sparkling holiday." Blessed with unflagging enthusiasm and energy, she soon found her way into serving the well-to-do and the well connected, especially as the number of parties and entertainments escalated in a city packed full of important delegates and their staffs. She began by helping to plan parties, select guests, "and in general kept the ball rolling once the festivities began."[22] She was especially adept at keeping the ball rolling, and soon her ability to turn dismal receptions into triumphs led to parties of her own—brilliant and amusing occasions at which she often played and sang songs written by her talented young friend Cole Porter.

How did she manage to pull it off? After all, she had no money of her own ("At that time," she later wrote, "I couldn't afford to give a taffy pull in a telephone booth"). But she had wealthy and well-placed friends, and as it turned out, these friends needed her. "Most rich people are the poorest people I know," she observed. "I brought to them a capacity for friendship and gaiety that offered escape from plush-lined boredom."[23]

Another who was adept at entertaining the rich and bored was Count Etienne de Beaumont, the wealthy French aristocrat who found his own escape from boredom by funding avant-garde art and throwing lavish parties and costume balls for the most elite members of Parisian society and the artistic world. During the war, Beaumont had served his country by forming and funding a private ambulance service. This was no lightweight operation: during the war's early years, he (and, for a time, his wife) took his moving hospital units to numerous hellholes along the front, bringing with him a coterie of Parisians otherwise exempted from military service, included Jean Cocteau (who showed up for duty wearing an impeccable uniform designed by Paul Poiret).

Following the war, Beaumont turned his talents to entertaining Paris's upper crust, including those in the performing or visual arts who made the grade. At the first Beaumont ball following the war, Beaumont invited the guests to come in a potentially hazardous way, leaving exposed that part of their body they considered most interesting. Cecil Beaton, who still was a student but would in time gain admission to Beaumont extravaganzas as a fashion photographer and theatrical designer, later wondered whether this occasion might not have been fairly boring, since "even to that society the theme offered rather limited possibilities."[24]

Beaumont's ruthlessness in excluding those he felt unqualified most memorably extended to Coco Chanel, who advised him on decorations for the next spring's ball but did not receive the sought-after invitation because Beaumont considered her a tradesperson. By this time Chanel was a prominent figure in the Paris fashion world. She also was a friend of Misia Natanson Edwards, the longtime patron of Sergei Diaghilev and the Ballets Russes, who in her own exalted realm was as powerful, opinionated, and wealthy as Beaumont. Misia took Chanel's exclusion as a personal insult—after all, "she was *my* friend"—and decided to boycott the Beaumont ball. Instead of attending, she and Chanel, along with Picasso and Misia's husband-to-be, the painter José-Maria Sert, amused themselves by standing with the chauffeurs in front of the Beaumont mansion to watch the invited guests enter. Misia did not mention in her memoirs whether or not they heckled or otherwise disrupted the guests' entrances, but she seemed quite satisfied with her little escapade. "Rarely," she wrote later, "have I been so amused."[25]

Paul Poiret was on the defensive. Before the war, he had ascended to the pinnacle of Paris fashion—in his own words, the undisputed king of fashion. Not only did he set the styles in women's wear and accessories, but he also manufactured and marketed his own fragrances (produced by his perfume house, Les Parfums de Rosine) and related cosmetics lines. By 1914 he had moved with authority into the realm of interior design, producing furniture, carpets, and glassware, and he signed some of the first licensing agreements, enabling him to reach the lucrative American market. But the war virtually shut down his widespread businesses, and he returned from long years of designing uniforms for French soldiers to pick up the pieces.

After spending several restorative weeks in Morocco, Poiret stormed the Paris barricades by taking up his role as party giver *extraordinaire* (and by extension, leader of fashion) with a splendid post-Armistice bash. He then planned a summer of fêtes that were intended to secure his position against all comers. By this time Poiret had become a collector of modern art, and many of those whose works he collected were friends who collaborated with him on fashion designs and other projects. The most productive of these collaborations was with Raoul Dufy, who designed fabrics for Poiret's 1920 summer collection and helped to create Poiret's fabulous Oasis Theatre during the summers of 1919 and 1920.

The theater was yet another Poiret fantasy brought to life. He loved the garden of his residence, near the Champs-Elysées, and wondered how he might share it with other Parisians, complete with "subtle and refined entertainments that would appeal to the elite of Society."[26] The main obstacle, of course, was rain. But how to cover a garden blessed with large trees? Gabriel Voisin, the aircraft manufacturer turned automobile maker, was a friend of Poiret's and had an idea: why not construct a dome made out of the fabric used for airships? This dome, or envelope, would be double and stretch over the garden, sheltering it completely. Each evening a special motor would fill this envelope with compressed air, causing it to swell out and form a roof. As it turned out, Voisin's idea worked splendidly: this novel covering "had no weight and it was easy to raise it on a tackle," Poiret later wrote, "and set it above the garden at such a height that one was not deprived of the sight of the trees."[27]

It was a brilliant beginning to what unfortunately turned into a financial disaster. Poiret's ideas of what would entertain society's elite did not seem to jibe with what the postwar elite wanted. He envisioned his audience pleasantly relaxed in brightly colored armchairs, where they could lazily listen to the "choice pieces" that Poiret presented. These included "plays or farces of exceptional quality and curious interest," the reconstruction of a Parisian café concert, with performers acting out all the celebrated stars and songs of the past fifty years, and a series of themed fêtes. One of Poiret's favorites was the fête of the New Rich, to which all the women were asked to come dressed in gold or silver. Golden Louis d'Or pieces were "thrown in profusion on to the dining tables," and oysters containing pearl necklaces were distributed, while "golden rain and fireworks inundated the whole scene." It was a brilliant show, and as Poiret put it, "naturally, the guests could not tear themselves away from these charms." But in the end he had to acknowledge that "the 'Oasis' was a fiasco" in which he lost half a million francs.[28]

"It was my fault," he admitted. "I ought to have known that at that time of year there were not enough Parisians to make such a venture prosper. As for the foreigners, who in the months of July and August constitute the clientele of Paris, they could not understand the charm of the revivals to which I had devoted myself." Although a portion of the audience (the French) stood to applaud at the end of one especially moving performance, "the Americans went out, . . . in a hurry to get back to their cosmopolitan palaces, or to kick about in smart dancing places." Basically, to Poiret's chagrin, the Oasis was considered old fashioned.

"Bitter it was!!!" he concluded.[29]

In his memoirs, the society portrait painter Jacques-Emile Blanche had a few choice words to say about the influx of wealthy pleasure seekers who now were descending on the City of Light. "That cosmopolitan crowd which for four and a half years had been banished from the luxury of Paris was already swarming back," he wrote indignantly. But now it was even worse—a new crowd, whose entry ticket was wealth. Blanche was a snob, but he had a point. The *nouveaux riches* who were now storming the Ritz and the Rue de la Paix would never have been welcomed into the homes of Paris's prewar society. Proust was entirely correct in his epitaph for this prewar society, which in his words was "disappearing then and is now gone forever."[30]

Proust, however, word-painted with a more delicate brush than did Blanche, who was deeply offended by what he saw. Blanche took particular umbrage at the return of those who had sided with Germany. Olga de Meyer, for example—possibly the natural daughter of England's Edward VII, but married to the Baron Adolph de Meyer—reappeared without qualm, ready to be "the queen of fashion." Blanche had painted the lovely Olga as a young girl but was unimpressed with the woman she had become. Olga's many affairs, including a lengthy one with the Princesse Edmond de Polignac (the former Winnaretta Singer), did not figure in his disapproval; what appalled him was her avid support of Germany and the emperor, which she had strongly communicated to Blanche by letter from America, where she and her husband had holed up during the war. "She hated democracy," Blanche wrote. But since Germany had lost the war, and "pleasure and luxury were pre-eminently the attributes of victorious France," she now returned to Paris, having changed her name (to Mahra), although not her opinions. "Paris is the only place fit to live in, my dear," she told Blanche when they met again after the Armistice.[31]

Hand in hand with the return of those who hated democracy was the right-wing French political movement Action Française and its daily newspaper, *Action Française*, which by the war's end was thriving. Both the movement and its newspaper were assertively monarchist and Catholic in sympathies, but during the war it gained adherents having other points of view thanks to its full-throated nationalism. Joan of Arc was Action Française's heroine, and every year in May its supporters crowded around her golden statue in the Place des Pyramides to honor her.

May was also a time for demonstrations from the other end of the political spectrum, as socialists and members of the General Confederation of Labor (Confédération Générale du Travail, or CGT) participated in street demonstrations on May 1 to protest the plight of workers caught between rising prices and stagnant wages. There was fear throughout Paris that Bolshevism was spreading, especially when some of these demonstrations turned violent. But although social unrest and membership in the Socialist party and the CGT had increased dramatically in the months following Armistice, no general strike followed.

Protected from these eruptions of social discontent, Proust nonetheless was laboring under a different form of anguish as his moving date grew closer.

According to his devoted housekeeper, Céleste Albaret, death "began for him with our leaving boulevard Haussmann."[32] The move was killing him, he told anyone who would listen. "I am dreadfully ill, dying," he assured Anna de Noailles.[33] Only the need to complete his book kept him alive.

By contrast, Sarah Bernhardt—in her seventy-fifth year and with one leg partially amputated—was doing her considerable best to steer clear of the grave. She had returned to France from yet another lengthy and demanding American tour (her last, as it turned out), and she was full of plans. The deaths of her dear friends, the playwright Edmond Rostand and the painter Georges Clairin, brought sadness, but she soldiered on, continuing to spend money and energy extravagantly and giving dramatic readings of Victor Hugo and Rostand throughout France.

Picasso and his wife were planning to summer on the Mediterranean, after a difficult late spring in London with Diaghilev, who had been preparing his first postwar ballet season, including the London premiere of *Parade* and the world premiere of *The Three-Cornered Hat* (the latter with music by Manuel de Falla and costumes and sets by Picasso, with choreography for both ballets by Massine, who danced the lead role of the Miller). Picasso had dragged his feet and not arrived in London until the last minute, which added unneeded tension to Diaghilev's list of preperformance miseries. Still, both ballets went off well—especially *The Three-Cornered Hat*. Next came the Paris premiere for the following winter season, and Diaghilev was crossing his fingers that the Parisians would succumb to the rhythms of a Spanish ballet with just as much enthusiasm as they had greeted the exoticism of his prewar oriental ballets.

On May 4, Clemenceau presented the peace treaty to his cabinet, which unanimously gave its approval. Three days later, Allied terms were presented to Germany's representatives. On June 28, after initially recoiling from the terms, Germany signed the treaty in Versailles' great Hall of Mirrors—the very spot where, in 1871, Bismarck had capped his crushing defeat of the French with the formal creation of the German Empire. Harold Nicolson, who witnessed the 1919 event, noted the grandeur and magnificence of the occasion, and the contrast made by the two very ordinary-looking German delegates—"isolated and pitiable, . . . deathly pale." It was, Nicolson concluded, "most painful."[34]

For Clemenceau, though, the occasion was deeply emotional. Congratulated by an old friend as he passed down the aisle, the old man simply said,

"Oui, c'est une belle journée." Nicolson noticed that "there were tears in his bleary eyes."[35]

Clemenceau would have to defend the treaty the following autumn in France's Parliament, which he did with special eloquence. Still, since Parliament (at Clemenceau's insistence) was only able to vote for or against the entire treaty, rather than clause by individual clause, the outcome never was in doubt. The prime minister, with popular opinion staunchly behind him, carried the day.

In practical terms, then, France's victory celebration that July 14 was free from any shadow of hesitancy or doubt. As Helen Pearl Adam put it, "Five years of war, of loss, of endurance, of hardship, of political crises, sickening when they were small and disquieting when they were great, . . . above all, of waiting for letters and praying against telegrams—they were all wiped out." In an unusual but appropriate decision, a group of wounded soldiers led the parade. And so, instead of the usual prancing horses and glittering uniforms, the first to come down the Champs-Elysées from the Arc de Triomphe were "men on stretchers, men on crutches, blind men, one-armed men."[36] They then were followed by the marshals and generals and the armies with their trumpets and their banners.

Given the parade's many admirable qualities, it was unfortunate that the work of art meant to commemorate the war's fallen soldiers at the Fêtes de la Victoire came to a bad end. The privilege of creating a memorial for the war dead had gone to three men: the painter André Mare, along with his associates, architect Louis Süe and designer Gustave Jaulmes, all three former members of wartime camouflage units at the front. Their creation, a huge gilded cenotaph, or tomblike monument, thrust upward in the form of a gigantic bier, its sides decorated with Winged Victories, each backed by a pair of real wings from French warplanes. It had been a mammoth undertaking[37] and was unquestionably meant to be patriotic, but critics fiercely derided it as Germanic or "Boche" art. Mare was known for his Cubist style—indeed, he had been painting French artillery with Cubist designs when he was badly wounded at the front—and "l'affaire du cénotaphe" was immediately perceived by Mare's supporters as an attack by traditionalists on Cubism.

Yet rather than an expression of Cubism, the cenotaph's designers were reaching for what soon would be called Art Deco, a style in which Mare and Süe would lead the way. Still, the name hardly mattered; the public was not ready for whatever it was that Mare and friends were delivering, and the cenotaph was doomed. Responding to public outcry, Clemenceau had it demolished.[38]

It would not be until the following year that France would commemorate its dead with a Tomb of the Unknown Soldier at the Arc de Triomphe. With this gesture of honor and remembrance, the French came closer to putting the raw emotions of the war behind them. Yet despite this step toward closure, there still would be too many wounded, too many empty places at the table, and too much that had disappeared of life as it once was, ever to forget.

Sylvia Beach and Ernest Hemingway outside Shakespeare and Company, March 1928. [Hemingway's head injury is discussed in chapter 13]. Photo © Tallandier / Bridgeman Images

CHAPTER FOUR

~

Making Way for the New
(1919–1920)

To Marie Curie's delight, her beloved Poland was among those nations whose sovereignty received the peace conference's blessing. In the conference's aftermath, schoolchildren and their elders suddenly had new geographies and boundaries to learn: Poland, Czechoslovakia, and Yugoslavia (at first called the Kingdom of Serbs, Croats, and Slovenes); Finland, Latvia, Lithuania, and Estonia; a redistribution of Germany's overseas colonies to the victors; and a general land grab around the globe, especially in the Middle East.

But peace did not mean tranquility. Unsettled times spawned fear and fear's accomplices—anger, hate, and cruelty. While the Bolsheviks were fighting anti-Bolshevik forces in the east and to the west, Benito Mussolini was forming the first fascist organization in Milan. In France, the right-wing Action Française continued to thrive, fed by fears of Russian Bolshevism abroad and France's own workers at home. Léon Daudet seemed perfectly serious when, one evening at dinner, he told the Abbé Mugnier that Daudet's coleader of Action Française, Charles Maurras, resembled Napoleon Bonaparte "and would make a perfect president of the Republic."[1] A president or a dictator? Some would not have cared.

The poet Paul Valéry, emerging from an almost twenty-year silence, wrote that August in the *Nouvelle Revue Française* that "two dangers unceasingly menaced the mind: order (thought and reason) and disorder (the multiplicity of points of view called modernism)."[2] Valéry saw the dangers in both, but in a world that sometimes appeared to have lost its bearings, the perils of compensating for disorder with order would become increasingly marked.

For the French that November, the Bolsheviks represented an especially threatening source of disorder. In response to warnings of the Bolshevik danger, the French elected the most right-wing Chamber since the 1870s.[3] Clemenceau, too, had moved rightward since his younger days as a radical republican and remained enormously popular. But he now made the mistake of letting it be known that he would allow himself to be elected president of the Republic, where he would make better use of the office's powers than had preceding presidents. As this rumor circulated, his enemies (who pitched their appeal to Roman Catholics who resented Clemenceau's staunch anticlericalism) found foothold for accusations that Clemenceau was secretly aiming at a dictatorship. As if this were not enough, late in the year, Clemenceau was heard to recommend a program of financial austerity based on a more just tax system, which signaled a rising scale of income tax.[4]

In January, the National Assembly responded to the underground campaign against Clemenceau and elected someone else as president of the Republic.[5] Clemenceau immediately handed in his resignation and that of his cabinet. Most of the new government's members were connected with business, and—freed from any threat from the much-weakened political left—this group now proceeded to run the country as it saw fit. Clemenceau's last remarks to his cabinet were, "Poor France. The mistakes have begun already."[6]

One Monday morning in November 1919, Sylvia Beach opened the doors of her new bookshop on Rue Dupuytren. She had named it Shakespeare and Company, and it would change the lives of an important group of Anglo-American writers living in Paris, as well as those of generations of future readers.

Sylvia Beach had first visited Paris at the turn of the century, in the company of her parents and two sisters. The daughter of a well-connected Presbyterian minister, she had come because her father was embarking on a three-year ministry at the American Church in Paris. Her mother, who adored art, music, and anything French, was thrilled, and the rest of the family quickly became enthusiastic Francophiles.

Sylvia, then known as Nancy (she would change her name), was fourteen at the time and impressionable. Paris impressed her, as did the France she got to know through well-to-do family friends who owned a château in the Touraine. After the Beaches' return to the States, when the Reverend Beach was called to the important pastorate in Princeton, New Jersey, the family continued to visit France. "We had a passion for France," Sylvia later recalled.[7]

She also had a passion for books. As a child, she had been sufficiently frail that she was kept at home and received little formal education. In its absence, she gravitated to books and was fortunate that she found well-stocked libraries in her own home and those of friends to nourish her. Poetry, philosophy, languages, history—they all filled a mind eager to explore mental landscapes and to learn. In addition, she studied languages and the violin. She also traveled with a female friend for a year in Italy and spent the first years of the war with her mother in Spain.

It was a comfortable life, but she desperately needed to make her own way. As early as that first trip to Paris, she had begun to resent and resist her parents' overprotectiveness: "I never seemed to get anywhere near the living Paris," she later wrote.[8] Her parents feared for her health as well as for her supposedly delicate feminine sensibilities. At the same time, her father took pride in his three daughters' determination to be independent—a determination that by the war's height brought one (Holly) to work with the Red Cross in France, and another (Cyprian, originally named Eleanor) to study voice and work in films in Paris, where Sylvia joined her.

Although listing her profession as *journaliste littéraire*, Sylvia went to Paris to read French poetry and to escape home, where her parents' marriage had disintegrated. The Easter 1918 bombing of Saint-Gervais during its Good Friday service, in which eighty-six worshippers died and many others were wounded, prompted her to join the war effort, and she spent two grueling months harvesting in the fields of Touraine—helping to free up men for fighting. Much to her delight and her parents' surprise, her health had never been better.

She had also begun to dream about opening a bookstore, one that would stock "good English and American books and a supply of French and others."[9] Her mother dismissed the idea and pressured her, as well as her sisters, to return home. The parental marriage had become unbearable, and at their mother's behest, Cyprian would eventually sacrifice her budding film career and sail home. Sylvia opted to keep her distance.

She had already met Adrienne Monnier, who would become her life partner—a rich and rewarding companionship that contrasted starkly with the senior Beaches' bleak marriage. Adrienne and Sylvia met when Sylvia entered Adrienne's bookstore and lending library on Rue de l'Odéon (soon named the Maison des Amis des Livres), looking for a particular review. Adrienne greeted her warmly, and after an episode full of laughter, in which the wind carried Sylvia's hat into the street, they settled down for a long talk. They discussed French and American books and authors as well as Paris and that all-important topic, food. As the German guns boomed closer and closer, Sylvia returned again and again to this little bookshop, where French authors, including Valéry and Gide, "were always dropping in—some of them from the front and in uniform—and getting into lively discussions with [Monnier]."[10]

At the war's end, Sylvia joined her sister Holly in Belgrade with the American Red Cross, distributing supplies "among the valiant Serbs," who were suffering from widespread devastation in the aftermath of the fighting.[11] By July 1919, she was back in Paris, a confirmed feminist ("the [male dominated] Red Cross has made a regular feminist of me"),[12] a socialist, and an opponent of war. But she still dreamed of opening a bookshop—possibly in New York or London, although both seemed too expensive and not especially receptive to the French literature she planned to feature. In any case, she had already decided that she wanted to stay in Paris, and her mother's sudden willingness to risk her savings on this venture made it possible for Sylvia to consider a Paris location, especially as the falling franc made rents and the cost of living more affordable. She planned to stock and lend books in English by English and American writers, to complement Adrienne's French bookshop, and opened her little bookstore in a former laundry at 8 Rue Dupuytren, a small street in the Latin Quarter near Rue de l'Odéon (the more famous location, at 12 Rue de l'Odéon, would follow). As for living quarters, she slept on a daybed in the back room.

After four months of hard work, she opened Shakespeare and Company on Monday, November 17, 1919. Would anyone come? she wondered. She needn't have worried. The shutters on the little shop were scarcely removed when the first friends arrived. "From that moment on," she later wrote, "for over twenty years, they never gave me time to meditate."[13]

⌒

Georges Clemenceau later reminisced that his good friend Claude Monet "sometimes doubted his hand, but never his eye."[14] Yet what to do as Monet's eyesight rapidly deteriorated? All the many hours that Monet had spent beside his lily pond at Giverny had worsened his already-deteriorating eyesight. He had attempted to shield his eyes from the light reflected off the pond by painting beneath a parasol, but this had done little good. In November, Clemenceau—a doctor by training—strongly recommended an operation, but Monet resisted. He feared that "an operation might be fatal, that once the bad eye has been suppressed the other eye will follow."[15]

Age was catching up with the original Impressionist painters. Morisot, Sisley, Pissarro, and Cézanne had died many years earlier, and Degas died in September 1917. Monet was approaching eighty, and Pierre-Auguste Renoir had been ailing for years. Still, the news of Renoir's death, on December 3, 1919, came as a shock. "You can imagine how painful the loss of Renoir has been to me," Monet wrote a friend. "With him goes a part of my own life." Contemplating his own mortality, he added, "It's hard to be alone."[16]

Clemenceau, about to depart on journeys to Egypt and the Far East, visited Monet regularly to encourage him, but Monet remained morose. "For some while I've been in a state of utter despair," he wrote his good friend, the art critic Gustave Geffroy. "I'm disgusted with all I've done. Day by day my sight is going and I can sense only too well that with it comes an end to long-cherished hopes to do better."[17]

But no matter what sadness accompanies a death, youth is ever ready to move on. Upon Renoir's death, his three sons—Pierre, Jean, and Claude—divided his paintings and other possessions. It was a rich trove, and there were no disputes. In the end, Pierre-Auguste left each of his sons financially independent for life, allowing them to live as they wished. This meant that the eldest, Pierre, could (despite a serious war wound) return to his acting career. The middle son, Jean, and the youngest, Claude, were less decided on what they wanted to do with their lives. Their father, who mistrusted intellectual pursuits, had wanted them to work with their hands. Accordingly, Jean Renoir set up a pottery studio at Les Collettes, the family's light-washed farm and olive grove at Cagnes-sur-Mer, on the Mediterranean near Nice.

Renoir *père* had always detested winter weather and loved Les Collettes, which inspired him to continue painting, despite the arthritis that crippled his hands and, in time, his legs. In particular, the warmth at Les Collettes made it possible for him to continue painting until the day he died. Henri Matisse, now also located near Nice, visited Les Collettes regularly throughout 1919, and it pained him to see Renoir paint with "his poor, twisted, deformed, bleeding paw." But Renoir was undisturbed. "The pain passes, Matisse," he told his younger colleague, "but the beauty remains."[18]

Jean Renoir shared his father's enchantment with Les Collettes. He also was enchanted with his father's last model, a red-haired beauty named Andrée Heuschling, known as Dédée. A few weeks after the senior Renoir's death, Jean and Dédée married, but they remained for a time in Les Collettes' idyllic atmosphere, where they had no need to make a living, and where tough realities, such as the falling franc and memories of the war, could not touch them.

By his own self-effacing account, Jean had been a "spoilt child," enclosed in a "protective wall" of family life that was "softly padded on the inside." His father's paintings, which covered the walls of their various apartments, were "an essential part of the background of [his] small life." He grew up in Montmartre, but also in Burgundy and southern France, dictated by the senior Renoir's constant search for "new qualities of light."[19] Despite this semiperipatetic existence, Jean's small world was comfortable and secure. It became even more pleasant as he reached his teens and young adulthood. He was blessed with a genial disposition, sufficient money, plenty of friends, and a secure position as son of one of the greatest living painters. Undisturbed by more serious matters, his chief interests were horses, cars, and women.

This carefree existence vanished with the coming of war. Long afterward, Jean Renoir remembered how the Great War "divide[d] the chronicle of our time into two stages—before and after 1914."[20] The war was not kind to him or to his older brother, Pierre, both of whom fought in the trenches. After a German bullet smashed Pierre's arm, a noted surgeon tried to restore partial use of the right hand by a painful process of bone grafts, but was not successful. Pierre continued his acting career but henceforth used a prosthesis to support his arm while learning to avoid any movements that might betray his infirmity.

Jean was badly wounded in the leg, and by the time he was evacuated by mule, gangrene had set in. The doctors wanted to amputate, but his mother, who had raced to his bedside, begged them to reconsider. At this critical moment, the hospital's chief physician was replaced by a professor of medicine who had recently invented a procedure that could and did eradicate Jean's gangrene. It was a close call, but Jean kept his leg and was sent back to Paris to recuperate. His father joined him, but his mother, who had hidden her serious condition of diabetes from the family, died before Jean even emerged from the hospital.[21]

He had a limp for life and knew he could get himself discharged. But he was determined to reenter the fighting and signed on for aviation duty, where a bad leg was less inhibiting. After flight school, he went with a squadron that carried out reconnaissance missions, where he became interested in photography, using novel techniques such as a wide-angle camera to get the kind of results he wanted. He managed to stay out of the way of German artillery, but "a bad landing put an end to my career as a pilot," he later wrote. "French aviation lost little by this," he added wryly. "I was not a very good pilot."[22]

Back in Paris, Jean Renoir spent time—a lot of it—at the movies. The war had taught him "the creed of man for himself, man starkly naked,

Jean Renoir (in uniform) with his father, Pierre-Auguste Renoir, circa 1916, photo by Pierre Bonnard
© 2015 Artists Rights Society (ARS), New York / ADAGP, Paris. Musée d'Orsay © RMN-Grand Palais / Art Resource, NY

stripped of all romantic trappings." But he never completely broke with his childhood attachment to Alexandre Dumas' dashing musketeers, and while in Paris, he fell in love with the cinema, especially American melodramas and the films of Charlie Chaplin ("Charlot," in French). Soon he was going to three films a day—two in the afternoon and one in the evening. He "dreamed of Pearl White, Mary Pickford, Lillian Gish, Douglas Fairbanks and William Hart," although it never occurred to him at the time that these actors and actresses "were the living embodiment of the musketeers and grenadiers of my childhood."[23]

And then Dédée entered his life. Jean's mother had been "the soul of gaiety," and with her death, "the gaiety had fled."[24] But Dédée's arrival restored happiness to Les Collettes. Renoir adored her, and Jean fell madly in love with her. Jean and Dédée married in early 1920 and remained at Les Collettes until shortly after the birth of their son Alain in 1921, when they moved to a house and grounds in Marlotte, at the edge of the forest of Fontainebleau. It was beautiful, and it had memories connected with Jean's father, who had painted there. But there was another attraction: it was near Paris and its movie theaters, and both Jean and Dédée had become avid cinema fans.

For Modigliani, everything was secondary to his art—even his common-law wife, Jeanne Héburterne, and the daughter she bore him in late 1918. "He had no other attachments," according to his friend and drinking buddy Léopold Sauvage.[25] Yet according to other sources, Modigliani was thrilled by the birth of his daughter, also called Jeanne, and tried to straighten out his life on her behalf, drinking less, taking better care of his health, and working faster and with more purpose than ever before. According to this version, he had dreams of a normal family life and of making his name in the art world, starting with a large submission (fifty-nine works) to a major exhibition in London that August, in 1919.[26]

The exhibition indeed brought Modigliani rave reviews and his first major recognition. But he was unable to enjoy the triumph firsthand: he had come down with yet another severe case of influenza and was unable to attend. He was still battling the tuberculosis that had dogged him since childhood, and this, plus the destructive life he had been living for so many years, exacerbated his vulnerability to a wide range of afflictions. His art dealer immediately put all sales on hold, in the expectation that the artist's death would double or triple the prices his work could command, but Modigliani did not die—not immediately, anyway.

For the remainder of the year, his health and behavior deteriorated, but Modigliani continued to work, citing his favorite saying—"Life is a gift."[27] He drank and caroused, often with the gifted painter Maurice Utrillo, another notorious alcoholic. But Modigliani also seemed desperate to see his baby daughter, if not his lover, who by this time was expecting their second child. Despite his talk of marriage, Modigliani and the mother of his children did not wed.

He died on January 24, 1920, at the age of thirty-five. Thanks to his brother, who directed that he be buried "like a prince," Modigliani was buried in grand style in Père-Lachaise. But Jeanne Héburterne was not there to witness either the procession or the burial. Distraught at his death, she had hurled herself out of a sixth-floor window and fallen to her death. Her unborn child died with her.

Shocked and shamed by their unmarried daughter's suicide, Jeanne's family quietly buried her far from Modigliani, in a cemetery on the other side of Paris. But Modigliani's family worked to override their resistance, and after the death of Jeanne's father, Jeanne finally was moved to Père-Lachaise, to share Modigliani's grave. Her tombstone (in Italian) reads, in part, "The Devoted Companion of Amedeo Modigliani until Death."[28]

As for their little girl, Modigliani's aunt adopted her, and she became what her mother never officially was—Jeanne Modigliani.

⌒

Another shocking death took place that winter in the south of France. On December 22, Coco Chanel's lover, "Boy" Capel, died in a fiery car crash en route from Paris to Cannes. "He is the only man I have loved," she told her friend Paul Morand years later. "I have never forgotten him."[29]

Despite Chanel's devastation, it had been a relationship riddled with betrayal. Capel, son of a well-to-do English family with French connections, had lived what seemed like two or even three separate lives: one, as a wealthy playboy and polo player; another, as a shrewd businessman, who made a fortune in coal and shipping, especially during the war. In addition, as a friend of both Clemenceau and Lloyd George, he had served in a delicate diplomatic capacity between the Allies during the war. If that was not enough to keep him busy, he wrote a great deal (without publishing) on topics ranging from foreign policy to theosophy. "Beneath his dandyism," Chanel told Morand, "he was very serious, far more cultured than the polo players and big businessmen." On another occasion she told Morand that Capel's "manners were refined, his social success was dazzling."[30]

Early on, Capel had financed and championed Chanel, and she had been his mistress since at least 1910. But other women frequented his life, and despite his early talk of marriage, he never had intended any such thing; he was on the rise, and as such, he needed a well-born wife, not one with Chanel's baggage. The one he chose, Diana Wyndham, was a well-connected aristocrat widowed early in the war, who had her own history of dalliances, especially with the equally aristocratic but insufficiently well-off Duff Cooper. Capel, who unquestionably was rich, had met Diana while she was driving an ambulance for the Red Cross in France, and soon she was pregnant with their first child. A wedding promptly followed, but Diana continued to see Duff (who in the meantime had married well), even as Capel continued his relationship with Chanel.

When word of Capel's death reached her, Chanel immediately set off with one of her friends, who drove her through the night to the Riviera. There, she asked to be driven to the scene of the accident. The wrecked car remained, and Chanel—who until now had remained stoically dry eyed—wept.

Capel bequeathed Chanel with a substantial financial legacy, which allowed her to expand her shop on Rue Cambon and buy a villa in Garches, to the west of Paris. Oddly enough, she and Diana Capel now became, if not exactly friends, then at least acquaintances who shared a private grief. Diana—who had endured a miserable marriage to Capel—even stayed for a time at Chanel's new villa in Garches and became a regular Chanel client.

After Capel's death, Chanel's friend Misia Sert[31] and Misia's third husband, José-Maria Sert, feared that Chanel was on the edge of a breakdown and took her with them on their honeymoon to Italy. It was not as if Chanel made an unwelcome addition: Misia had been living with José-Maria for years, and their marriage simply legitimized what was a recognized arrangement. In addition, Misia and Chanel had been friends since 1917. Chanel later called Misia "my only woman friend," but not without a deft twist of the knife: "We only like people because of their failings," she later told Paul Morand, adding that "Misia gave me ample and countless reasons for liking her." As for the Serts, whom Chanel conceded were "moved to see a young woman weeping her heart out in grief," even this had its downside. "Other people's grief lures [Misia]," she added, "just as certain fragrances lure the bee."[32]

It must have been an interesting journey. According to Chanel, the Serts altered their plans and did not go to Venice, "which was their fiefdom, where I did not wish to go,"[33] but Misia recollected that they took her to Venice, where Misia threw a huge dinner party to introduce her to the "gratin" gathered there—"in short, the smartest people I could find!"[34] In any case, whether in Venice or in Paris, Misia's patronage did introduce Chanel to high society as well as to Diaghilev and his circle—a fine comeback for the insult that the Beaumonts had delivered to Chanel and, from Misia's perspective, to Misia as well.

"You must realize that Misia has done for you what she has done for no one else," a mutual friend told Chanel. "It's true," Chanel conceded. "She craved my affection. This love comes from a great basic generosity mixed with a devilish delight in denigrating everything she gives."[35]

It was, without doubt, a friendship fraught with hazards.

⌒

Misia's husband, José-Maria Sert, was a wealthy Catalan who painted murals and frescoes on an epic scale, filled with a plethora of jungle beasts, gods, goddesses, and mythological scenes, which he executed in a grand Baroque style—chiefly in rich shades of dark red, gold, and black. Out of step with current artistic trends, but greatly pleasing to those with deep pockets and a penchant for traditionalism and display, Sert (with Misia's assistance) had expanded his list of patrons to include many of her wealthy connections and by this time was an international success.

In addition to decorating large private mansions, Sert received commissions for public buildings, which during the 1930s most notably included New York's Rockefeller Center and the grand ballroom of the Waldorf Astoria.[36] He lived as extravagantly as he painted: recalling her trip with him and Misia to Italy, Chanel remembered that "Sert, who was lavish by nature, ordered rare wines, and meals that made our table look like a painting by Veronese or Parmigiano." Another of his quirks was to carry in his inside pocket "crumpled thousand-franc banknotes. What he did with these," Chanel added, "has always been a mystery to me." Back in Paris, Sert painted in an opulent studio, while he and Misia occupied a grand suite of rooms at the Hôtel Meurice, overlooking the Tuileries, which he filled with precious objects—many of them large, all of them expensive. "You have to admit that Sert makes everything else seem rather drab," Misia told Chanel, and Chanel had to admit that it was true.[37]

Other painters despised Sert's work and envied his success. He was labeled a decorator rather than an artist, and an especially malicious quip making the rounds was that "Sert paints with gold and *merde*." Degas, who visited Sert's studio, was supposed to have commented, "How very Spanish—and in such a quiet street!"[38] But others, especially Paul Claudel, admired him (as Sert admired Claudel in turn). Claudel, who despaired of contemporary art's decadence, found in Sert (and especially in Sert's ongoing project at the Catalan cathedral of Vich) the return to religion and the Church that he found essential to great art, and which he believed made Sert the heir of the Baroque masters.

Sert, of course, was a man of many appetites and regularly feasted on food, wine, women, and drugs. Misia certainly was aware of this and learned to live with it. But Claudel either did not know or refused to acknowledge it. Proust, who claimed to admire Sert, was more circumspect about Claudel. "I am not devout enough for that sort of person," he told Céleste Albaret.[39]

Shortly after Misia's marriage to Sert, Marcel Proust wrote her a congratulatory note in which he expressed his good wishes and warm admiration for them both, adding that their marriage "has the awesome perfection of all wonderfully unnecessary things." There was more than a little irony here, as there was in his follow-up: "What wife could Sert have found, and you what husband, as . . . uniquely worthy the one of the other?"[40] Proust's perceptive but unflattering portrayal of Misia as Princess Yourbeletieff, as well Misia's contribution to certain characteristics of the unforgettable Madame Verdurin (both characters from *In Search of Lost Time*), gives an unmistakable singe to his congratulations.

By this time, Proust himself had begun to receive the honors and congratulations that were due him. In December 1919, much to his surprise, he received the prestigious Goncourt Prize for his second volume of *In Search of Lost Time*, titled *A l'ombre des jeunes filles en fleurs* (now translated as *Within a Budding Grove*). The response to this volume had surprised him in every way. "I never expected *A l'ombre des jeunes filles en fleurs* to be a success," he wrote his publisher. "If you remember, I told you that I was rather ashamed to bring out this languid interlude on its own. Yet by some extraordinary fluke, this book is a hundred times more successful than *Swann*."[41]

Still, the Goncourt Prize did not arrive without controversy. Another author's novel had been a close contender, and it was clear that Léon Daudet's presence on the jury had swung the prize to Proust. Proust's competitor (or at least the fellow's publisher) did not accept defeat gracefully and advertised "Prix Goncourt" above his name and book title, with "four votes out of ten" in small print beneath. Proust understandably found this "deliberately misleading" and was just as understandably annoyed.[42] But critics still railed about awarding an author who had not served in any capacity during the war. In addition, a furor arose over Proust's age: the prize was supposed to be awarded to promising young authors. At the age of forty-eight, was Proust too old to qualify?

Nonetheless, the prize was his, and more acclaim would follow, including the Legion of Honor, presented to him a year later by his brother, Dr. Robert Proust, a longtime Legion of Honor member. In the spring of 1920, bolstered by the Goncourt Prize, Marcel also considered presenting himself as a candidate for the Académie Française. But both the poet Henri de Régnier and *Nouvelle Revue Française* editor Jacques Rivière discouraged him from seeking election, at least at that time. De Régnier told Proust that he had waited too long to begin his campaign—Académie members were already committed to other candidates—but this may have been a put-off. In subsequent exchanges, Proust touched on the subject of his friendship with Léon Daudet, who had enemies among the people Proust most needed to court.

But there was another, more difficult, problem: the very nature of Proust's books. Most of the Académie members "cannot understand you," Jacques Rivière said diplomatically; "their slumber is too deep."[43] Not only was *In Search of Lost Time* difficult reading, but, as Proust was well aware, the problem for a conservative body such as the Académie was the prominence of homosexuality in its pages, which Proust knew would be even more pronounced in his forthcoming volumes (*Sodom and Gomorrah* would appear in bookstores in May 1921).

Proust pursued the possibility of Académie membership for a time but in the end was not willing to change the essence of his books for a seat among the immortals.[44] This particular honor would remain beyond his reach.

As soon as the war broke out in 1914, the Louvre had taken immediate steps to protect its treasures, especially from the danger of aerial bombing. Some of these masterpieces, including the *Mona Lisa*, went into hiding in the countryside. Those that were much larger and heavier received protection in place. The *Venus de Milo* spent the long years of the Great War in a steel room. Heavy iron plates protected the *Winged Victory*, while sacks filled with earth served to protect the Louvre's irreplaceable sculptures by Phidias. Because the Louvre's upper stories were quickly turned into hospitals, the flag of the Red Cross flew over the works that remained.[45]

It took more than a year after Armistice for the Louvre to bring its treasures back and dust them off, but by late 1919, it finally was ready to reopen. Step by step, Paris was moving on.

Xavier Sager, At the Bal Tabarin Nightclub, *Paris, 1920s. Kharbine-Tapabor / The Art Archive at Art Resource, NY*

CHAPTER FIVE

~

Les Années Folles

(1920)

In America, they call the 1920s the "Roaring Twenties." In France, they call these years *les Années folles*, or the "Crazy Years," giving the era a spin of madness instead of the zoom of the American version. Yet whether viewed as crazy, foolish, savage, or frenzied, these years flaunted a particularly unabashed rawness and boldness that formed the essence of the postwar modern movement that Parisians already were calling *l'esprit nouveau*.

This "what the hell" attitude that underlay so much of the postwar decade, whether in Paris or elsewhere, was a distinctly urban and upper-class phenomenon. Farmers trying to resurrect their war-torn fields, or small-town tradesmen trying to reestablish their occupations and their lives, did not have the time, money, or inclination for such foolishness. Demobilized soldiers had families to support and work to do. Fortunate were the ones who were not wounded, or who did not carry the psychic scars of war.

But for those fortunate enough to have money and leisure, it became the height of fashion to be witty, decadent, and bored. Looking for distraction, everyone who could—whether rich Americans, exiled Russian aristocrats, or millionaires from any number of locations—came to Paris. There they could mingle in endless parties and late-night jazz clubs, indulging in a heady mix of booze, drugs, and sex. The British journalist Sisley Huddleston, who witnessed a good share of these chic encounters, called it the "Cocktail Epoch,"[1] and indeed, the free flow of liquor was a definite attraction, especially for those Americans escaping Prohibition back home. But the absence of puritanical constraints covered far more than simply alcohol. Couples could uncouple and recouple without concern for what Aunt Madge might say, since Aunt Madge was far away in Dubuque, and their Parisian friends and neighbors simply did not care.

This was not a phenomenon that suddenly occurred in 1920. Many of the most colorful features of the Parisian twenties had roots going back to the war or even before, although the war unquestionably hastened the annihilation of so much that characterized prewar society.[2] The frivolity and excesses of *les Années folles* followed as a natural response to death and destruction, whether as a kind of doom-infused escapism or simply as a desire to have fun.

Yet, concurrent with flamboyant lifestyles, there was another story, that of extraordinary creativity. As John Dos Passos later put it, the very permissiveness that accompanied "the disintegration of victory" in Paris had furthered a "creative tidal wave."[3] Maurice Sachs went further: "perhaps," he speculated from the not-so-distant perspective of 1933, the mad gaiety during the decade following the Armistice was not of itself "sufficient to produce an intellectual richness." Instead, "different elements—still only nebulously defined for us who are so near—combined to form a tension of creation."[4] Perhaps Sachs was right, or perhaps, at its most basic, it was simply an attitude of "out with the old and in with the new" that fostered ingenuity and imagination. In any case, Paris of the 1920s was a hotbed of innovation on every front. During these years the City of Light enjoyed its reputation as the cultural center of the world, whether in literature, art, architecture, music, or fashion.

Along with creativity came tolerance, at least in certain circles. Racism, which remained a bitter fact in America, almost disappeared in a Paris in love with African-American jazz bands and Josephine Baker. Similarly, homosexuals and homosexual relationships were accepted, if not always with enthusiasm, at least with a shrug, in a Paris where homosexuality had not been banned since the Revolution and where the cultural world was enriched by lesbian women such as Sylvia Beach, Gertrude Stein, Natalie Clifford Barney, and the Princesse de Polignac, and gay men such as Cocteau, Proust, Gide, and Diaghilev.[5]

As the 1920s opened, *l'esprit nouveau* was already bubbling through Paris, and nowhere more so than that unsightly area to the south of the Latin Quarter known as Montparnasse.

"Never go to Montparnasse!" These were the words that Picasso's longtime friend, the poet and artist Max Jacob, once scrawled in chalk on his wall in Montmartre. Without being entirely literal about it, Jacob was convinced that the devil reigned in Montparnasse. Nevertheless, the place fascinated him—as it did so many others. Jacob, a Jew who had recently converted to Catholicism, would soon move to the Benedictine monastery at Saint-Benoît-sur-Loire to avoid the temptations of bohemian life. But with the end of the war, the rest of the world was streaming in the opposite direction.

Montparnasse had never been a distinctly defined quarter in the sense that Montmartre was, and it certainly lacked Montmartre's charm. The area owed its name to the inventiveness of long-ago students from the Latin Quarter, who named it Mont-Parnasse, or Mount Parnassus, after the mountainous slag heap left by the quarries below. Students and others came to drink and dance here, at *guinguettes* and cafés such as the Closerie des Lilas, which for years had stood at the intersection of the Boulevard du Montparnasse and Boulevard Saint-Michel, connecting Montparnasse with the Latin Quarter. Two other cafés, the Dôme and the Rotonde, stood only a few minutes away, at the intersection of Boulevard du Montparnasse and Boulevard Raspail, a crossroads then called the Carrefour Vavin and now called Place Pablo-Picasso.

The 1910 completion of most of the Métro's Nord–Sud line (No. 12) linking Montmartre to Montparnasse, along with the cut-through of Boulevard Raspail to Boulevard du Montparnasse, suddenly made the Carrefour Vavin a hot spot. Both the Dôme and the Rotonde benefited, and this intersection now became the quarter's focal point, where artists and their comrades could meet, drink, and talk. The more well-to-do Americans, Scandinavians, and—before the war—Germans hung out at the Dôme, while just about everyone else favored the Rotonde, with its congenial and down-at-the-heels mix that had "no regard for nationality, styles of painting, or schools of poetry."[6] Victor Libion, the Rotonde's owner from 1911 on, may have given Kiki and other suspicious-looking females a bit of a hard time, but Kiki enjoyed the Rotonde's "nutty crowd" as well as the special treatment she received from the Rotonde's cooks, who heated water for her so she could take her bath in the washroom. "It's just like home there!" she enthusiastically exclaimed,[7] and a host of others felt much the same way, even without Kiki's bathing privileges.

"Père Libion is the best of men," Kiki wrote, "and he loves them, his ragtag bunch of artists!" She fondly recalled how the huge loaves of bread delivered daily to the Rotonde were placed in a willow basket near the bar, with part of the loaves sticking out above the top—at least until Père Libion turned his back, when the tops of all the loaves regularly disappeared, "in the blink of an eye." After which, day after day, everyone sauntered out with a piece of bread in his pocket. Libion's "bums," as he fondly called them, stole from him, but he continued to feed them. According to Kiki, "you could go into any artist's studio at that time and you would always find a lot of souvenirs of La Rotonde: saucers, forks, knives, plates." One night, to celebrate Modigliani's sale of a work for several hundred francs,[8] he and his friends decided to throw a big dinner. Père Libion was invited with the rest of the crowd, but at the sight of him, Modigliani became edgy. The problem was that the chairs, the knives, the glasses, the plates, and even the tables had all come from the Rotonde, and Père Libion clearly realized this. Soon, he got up and left, and Modigliani berated his friends for bringing him. "I love him as much as you do," he told them, "but if I did not invite him, it is because of all these dishes which I have taken from him." The party fell silent, when suddenly the door opened and Père Libion returned, his arms filled with bottles. "Only the wine wasn't from me," he told them, "so I went to get it. Let's go to the table, I am as hungry as a wolf."[9]

Victor Libion was for Montparnasse what the Lapin Agile's Frédé Gérard had been for Montmartre, and more, but there were other beloved characters as well. Among these, Rosalie Tobia, owner of Chez Rosalie on Rue Campagne-Première, figured large. Rosalie was an Italian model who had grown too old to pose in the nude, so she took over a small *crémerie*, where she fed "her" artists. Kiki went there to order soup, which sometimes earned her a bawling out for having the nerve not to spend more than six sous on a bowl of soup. Other times, "Rosalie would almost sob, and feed me for nothing." Modigliani was Rosalie's favorite customer, but they frequently fought—shouting insults in Italian, breaking dishes, and tearing drawings off the wall. Soon they would quiet down, embrace, and Modigliani would make new drawings for the walls.[10]

Modigliani's death in early 1920 left a marked gap in the Montparnasse scene, where he had become a legend. Victor Libion had become a legend as well, but a legend ready for retirement: in 1920, Libion sold his beloved Rotonde, which went on without him.

Kiki was still living hand to mouth, but she was doing some modeling for Montparnasse artists when she met the painter Moïse Kisling, who gave her a three-month contract. It wasn't a lot of money, but it was better than what she had been used to. In addition, she liked Kisling, even if he was "sort of hard-boiled." When they first met, Kiki overheard him ask the manager, "Who's the new whore?" This did not sit well with her. "I don't like that," she recalled thinking. But she said nothing about it, because she remained a little afraid of him until she began working for him. Then their relationship changed. "He yells at the top of his voice to make me laugh," she recalled, "or else—makes all sorts of funny noises, and we try to see who can outdo the other." Although Kisling had become successful, he was not snooty about it. "I swipe his soap and his tooth-paste," Kiki wrote, "and he never says a word. He's the swellest guy in the world!"[11] According to her, others were of the same opinion: Kisling was one of the most well-liked people in Montparnasse, and his studio was a popular gathering place.

～

Soon after his return to France, Milhaud—"haunted by my memories of Brazil"—composed a musical fantasy of Brazilian popular melodies interspersed with a rondo-like theme that he called *Le Boeuf sur le Toit*, or *The Ox on the Roof*.[12] Milhaud thought of this simply as a musical composition, but then Jean Cocteau decided to put it to better use.

Ever on the alert for the new and the outrageous, Cocteau appropriated Milhaud's musical score for *Le Boeuf sur le Toit* and turned it into a surrealistic pantomime-ballet by the same title, which aimed at being every bit as outrageous as *Parade*. "Cocteau has a genius for improvisation," Milhaud later acknowledged, perhaps ruefully. Cocteau changed the venue from Rio to a scene in an American bar during Prohibition. When this madcap production took place (in February 1920),[13] most in the audience as well as among the critics were baffled and treated it as a joke. After all, what could one say about a ballet whose climax calls for a bartender to decapitate a policeman with a large fan, after which a redheaded woman dances with the policeman's head and finishes by standing on her hands?

Milhaud gamely went along with the concept, but to his dismay, the public and critics henceforth forgot that he was a serious composer and "agreed that I was a clown." This was especially painful as he "hated comedy and . . . had only aspired to create a merry, unpretentious divertissement in memory of the Brazilian rhythms that had so captured my imagination."[14] That, of course, was before Jean Cocteau took charge.

As it happened, Milhaud's musical *Le Boeuf sur le Toit* would soon have another and more famous namesake. It all began with a problem: the Saturday-night dinners at Milhaud's apartment had become too large and successful, and he needed to move the party out of his living room. The solution came from an unexpected source. By Milhaud's account, he looked up Jean Wiéner, an old friend from Conservatoire days whom Milhaud had not seen since the war. Life had not been easy for Wiéner, Milhaud noted, adding that this talented pianist was now playing the piano in a small Right Bank night club called the Bar Gaya in Rue Duphot.

Darius Milhaud (far left), leaning on Raymond Radiguet, with Jean Cocteau (center), Jean Hugo (center rear), Paul Morand (far right), Valentine Hugo (between Morand and Cocteau), and (kneeling) Andrée Vaurabourg, the future Mme Arthur Honneger, Paris, 1921. Bridgeman Images

It was Wiéner who suggested that Milhaud's group transfer their Saturday-evening meetings to the Gaya. The new venue quickly became a success, and everyone who was anyone made a point of showing up at the Gaya to hear Wiéner play his brilliantly original mix of music, from jazz to Bach. Mindful of the ever-growing throng, which now included celebrities such as Picasso, Diaghilev, Ravel, Satie, Anna de Noailles, Maurice Chevalier, and Arthur Rubinstein, the Gaya's owner decided to move to larger and more attractive quarters, at nearby Rue Boissy-d'Anglas. But what to call the new place? In a stroke of brilliance, the fellow asked Cocteau and Milhaud to allow him to use the name "Le Boeuf sur le Toit."

And so the legendary Le Boeuf sur le Toit (the bar) began. As Jean Hugo put it, Le Boeuf, with its laughter and its tears, became "the crossroads of destinies, the cradle of love-affairs, the home of discords, the navel of Paris."[15]

While the Groupe des Six and their colleagues were reveling at the Gaya and the Boeuf sur le Toit, a movement of deliberate outsiders was thinking up a variety of pranks and figurative as well as literal stink bombs with which to bombard the cultural elite. Erupting in the midst of turbulent postwar Paris, Dada was an extremist movement born of bleak disillusionment with the war. It had begun in 1916 in Zurich, under the leadership of Rumanian-born Tristan Tzara—although the avant-garde French-Cuban painter Francis Picabia and the equally avant-garde Frenchman Marcel Duchamp (who had shocked attendees of New York's 1913 Armory Show with his fractured *Nude Descending a Staircase*) had already been moving in much the same direction in New York. Dada's founders declared that "Dada" meant nothing and that they had no intention of making it mean anything. In practice, as an extreme expression of disillusionment with the world and with life, Dada reveled in negativity, destructiveness, and the absurd, which its adherents embraced in intentionally incoherent manifestos, meetings, and nonevents.

In January 1920, Tzara arrived in Paris. By this time, André Breton, Philippe Soupault, and Louis Aragon had been meeting regularly in a café in the Passage de l'Opéra—quite a world apart from either Montmartre or Montparnasse, both of which they viewed with contempt. All had experienced the horrors of war—Breton, a first-year medical student, had served in a psychiatric center near the front; Aragon, also a medical student, had received the Croix de Guerre for his wartime service; and Soupault had been wounded in action. Others who joined them, including Paul Eluard and Pierre Drieu La Rochelle, also shared the war's traumas—Eluard having been severely gassed, and Drieu having been wounded three times, for which he, too, received the Croix de Guerre. By the war's end, they and other colleagues had bonded over a mutual antipathy to anything they believed deadened the spirit, including almost every aspect of current government and society—especially bourgeois morality and the rules and conventions governing art and culture.

In 1919, Breton, Aragon, and Soupault founded the radical review, *Littérature*, which took on the postwar world, especially its current literary movements. Even before Tzara arrived, the group that coalesced around *Littérature* was well aware of him and of Dada and demanded change through anarchy, chaos, and destruction. Even language itself was not immune to such an attack: early on, Breton and his colleagues embarked on experiments in automatic writing, which Breton later defined as "the dictation of thought, free of any influence exercised by reason, heedless of all moral and esthetic concerns."[16]

Tzara's arrival in early 1920, accompanied by Francis Picabia, set off sparks among the Paris group surrounding Breton. Soon they rented a hall where, among other acts of mingled nonsense and protest, Tzara read a speech by Léon Daudet, which Aragon and Breton immediately drowned out with rattles and clanging bells. Other events followed, in which, according to one spectator, "a dozen disillusioned men (and there was certainly plenty to be disillusioned about) would move to the front of the stage and groan: 'No art, no literature, no politics, no republic, no royalists, no philosophers, no nothing—Dada, Dada, Dada.'"[17]

Erik Satie may have been what one biographer has called "a born Dadaist,"[18] but Jean Cocteau got along with him (at least for a few more years),[19] even though Cocteau never managed to get along with Breton. Breton, who was uncomfortable about his modest rural upbringing and remained painfully antisocial, seems to have found Cocteau's elegance, wit, and social ease, not to mention his success, more than he could bear. Consequently, Dada would not provide a home to Cocteau if Breton had anything to say about it. Indeed, he later apologized that Cocteau's name "should ever come out of my pen."[20]

But Cocteau enjoyed Picabia, whose wealth, women, and cars (Picabia owned an impressive number of them, all expensive) added a certain charm to his undeniable talent and flair. With Picabia at his elbow, Cocteau for a time attempted to participate in Dada's odd and frequently disruptive displays. After all, Cocteau wanted to position himself at the knife-edge of the avant-garde, and Dada was the edgiest movement around. But too many unpleasant episodes began to add up, and finally Cocteau announced his break with Dada—a move that was greeted by the faithful with sarcasm and scorn. Soon after, at a Dada manifestation, Philippe Soupault plunged a dagger with the words "Jean Cocteau" into a large balloon.

Following Picabia's own break with Dada in 1921, he and Cocteau reestablished their friendship. But even after Breton finally broke with Tzara and founded Surrealism, he never could abide Jean Cocteau. As one of Picabia's friends put it, "How can you believe [Erik] Satie when he says that Breton and Cocteau are reconciled? That day, hell will freeze over."[21]

Igor Stravinsky was another whom Cocteau managed to infuriate. Cocteau's 1918 *Le Coq et l'Arlequin* had extolled the music of Satie and dismissed Stravinsky as "an octopus which you'd do well to flee or it will eat you." Although Cocteau conceded that *The Rite of Spring* was "a masterpiece," he waspishly added that "I find in the atmosphere surrounding its performance a religious complicity among adepts, that hypnotism of Bayreuth"[22]—a reference to Wagner as well as to the herd mentality that could not have pleased Stravinsky.

Yet Stravinsky had problems far larger than Jean Cocteau. His income had plummeted, thanks to the war and the Russian Revolution, while his family responsibilities had grown. He now supported a flock of destitute Russian in-laws as well as his own ailing wife and their four children. Diaghilev's financial woes with the Ballets Russes during the war years meant that Stravinsky could expect little help from that quarter. As late as 1919, with the exception of a single performance of *The Soldier's Tale*, Stravinsky had not enjoyed a major premiere since before the war.

Oddly, it was a combination of Diaghilev's postwar comeback and the support of Coco Chanel that now brought Stravinsky the help he so desperately needed. Diaghilev had originally turned to Manuel de Falla to arrange music by the eighteenth-century Italian composer, Giovanni Battista Pergolesi, for a commedia dell'arte–inspired ballet about the character Pulcinella (Punch). But de Falla was otherwise occupied, and so Diaghilev, despite a history of emotional arguments with his fellow Russian over money, turned in Stravinsky's direction. Even with the prospect of much-needed income, Stravinsky did not immediately jump at the offer: he did not think much of Diaghilev's choice of music ("I thought he must be deranged"). Moreover, he was not accustomed to taking on other people's projects on hire, still less what he termed a "rush-order commission." Still, once he looked at Pergolesi's music, he "fell in love."[23]

The great Diaghilev-Stravinsky partnership was once again in action, and in testimony to this, Diaghilev in early 1920 presented Parisians with a ballet version of Stravinsky's 1914 opera, *The Song of the Nightingale*, with Henri Matisse as set and costume designer and Paul Poiret brought in at the last minute to work with Matisse on the difficult costumes. Matisse had been a reluctant participant in this venture, but Diaghilev was an indefatigable persuader. Diaghilev was "charming and maddening at the same time," Matisse told his wife. "He's a real snake—he slips through your fingers—at bottom the only thing that counts is himself and his affairs."[24] Picasso, on the other hand, was stung by Stravinsky's collaboration with Matisse: "Matisse! What is a Matisse?" he demanded. "A balcony with a big red flowerpot falling all over it."[25]

Unfortunately, *The Song of the Nightingale* was not well received, largely because of Massine's choreography. But the May 1920 premiere of *Pulcinella*, with choreography by Massine and scenery and costumes by Picasso, was every bit the success that Diaghilev and Stravinsky had hoped for. The guests were therefore in a celebratory mood as they headed into the suburbs for the after-performance party, a memorably over-the-top affair given by Prince Firouz of Persia. According to the painter (and Victor Hugo's great-grandson) Jean Hugo, who regularly hung out with the in-crowd, it was held in an enticingly disreputable spot—a suburban dance hall run by an ex-convict friend of Cocteau's. The revelers, including the Picassos, the Serts, Cocteau, and young Radiguet (who memorialized the party afterward in his *Le Bal du Comte d'Orgel*), as well as Lucien Daudet, Poulenc, Auric, the Hugos (Jean and Valentine), and of course Diaghilev, Massine, and Stravinsky, arrived in a caravan of automobiles, guided by hired hands with flashlights. Prince Firouz, according to Hugo, was "un hôte magnifique," who generously lubricated his guests with vast quantities of champagne.[26] Not surprisingly, the party got a bit out of hand after a very drunk Stravinsky perched himself precariously on the balcony that ran around the huge dance floor and hurled cushions and bolsters from the adjoining rooms onto the guests below. This led to a pillow fight that lasted until three in the morning.

In a more sober state, Stravinsky was as pleased with *Pulcinella* as with its favorable reception. "It is a new kind of music," he told an interviewer, "a simple music with an orchestral conception different from my other works."[27] "*Pulcinella* was my discovery of the past," he later wrote, "the epiphany through which the whole of my late work became possible."[28] It marked, in fact, the beginning of Stravinsky's Neoclassical period.

⁓

As for the role Coco Chanel played in the Stravinsky story, two things are known: Chanel provided the funds for a December 1920 revival of *Rite of Spring*, and she provided a home to Stravinsky and his extended family after they left Switzerland for Paris. Beyond that, there is only rumor, conjecture, and Chanel's own vague account.

Switzerland had provided a refuge for the Stravinsky clan throughout the war, but in 1920, following the success of *Pulcinella*, Stravinsky moved his family to Brittany for the summer, hoping that he would be able to find lodging for them all by autumn. He had met Chanel somewhat earlier that year, probably through Misia and Diaghilev during rehearsals for *Pulcinella*. Chanel had recently moved to her large villa outside Paris, in Garches, and on hearing of Stravinsky's predicament, offered to share it with his family until they could find a place of their own.

Her new lover, the Grand Duke Dmitri Pavlovich, may have appeared on the scene as early as September, at about the time the Stravinskys arrived at Chanel's villa. Or, according to another account (from Stravinsky's close associate, Robert Craft, via Stravinsky's second wife), Chanel's affair with Dmitri Pavlovich did not begin until early 1921. This left plenty of time for an affair with Stravinsky, if indeed one took place, as Chanel herself (late in life) confirmed to her good friend Paul Morand.[29]

According to Chanel, at that time "the only man I felt attracted to [among the artistic set] was Picasso, but he was not available." Stravinsky, though, pursued her. When Chanel pointed out that he was married, he replied that his wife was well aware of his love for Chanel. "To whom else, if not to her," he demanded, "could I confide something so important?"[30] (In his own memoirs, Stravinsky simply said that Chanel "was a very close friend at the time, as well as one of Diaghilev's most generous supporters, and she had underwritten the December 1920 revival of *The Rite of Spring* at the Théâtre des Champs-Elysées.")[31]

The story, as Chanel told it, is vague and scarcely a story, except that the affair, if it was such, came to an abrupt end—due, Chanel says, to Misia's interference. Stravinsky went with the Ballets Russes to Spain, leaving Chanel alone. Grand Duke Dimitri then appeared. Misia sent Stravinsky a telegram to the effect that Chanel preferred grand dukes to artists, and Stravinsky exploded. Diaghilev then sent Chanel a telegram: "Don't come, he wants to kill you."[32]

And that was that. Except that, during those months when Diaghilev was in the midst of planning the December 1920 Paris revival of *The Rite of Spring*, with new choreography by Massine, he agonized at length with Misia about the usual lack of funds. Chanel, who so often accompanied Misia, overheard these deliberations and subsequently visited Diaghilev to hand him a large check.[33] Her only condition was that he not tell anyone—which of course Diaghilev promptly ignored. Was it a genuine attempt on Chanel's part to help, or a calculated move to establish herself in the Paris arts world? Chanel claimed the former, while Misia certainly understood it as the latter. With Misia now on the alert to protect her turf as queen of patrons, certainly of Stravinsky and the Ballets Russes, the stage was set for Misia and Chanel to become fierce competitors as well as the closest and most lethal of friends.

The December 1920 revival of *The Rite of Spring* was a huge success, with Stravinsky's music now accepted as a classic. Unfortunately, the choreographer for the revival, Léonide Massine, soon found himself without a job after having committed the unpardonable sin (in Diaghilev's eyes) of falling for a young ballerina, whom he eventually married. Having been dumped for a woman, first by Nijinsky and now by Massine, Diaghilev suffered a breakdown. Only the discovery of another handsome young lover, Boris Kochno, mended his broken heart—this young man having been graciously provided by Sergey Sudeykin, the bisexual husband of Vera de Bosset, who would shortly become Stravinsky's mistress.

In the meantime, Chanel's whirlwind affair with the glamorous but impoverished Russian exile, the Grand Duke Dmitri, was brief but, by her account, captivating. According to an unsubstantiated but persistent story, they were introduced by Dmitri's current lover, a friend of Chanel's, who is supposed to have told her, "If you're interested you can have him. He really is a little expensive for me." Chanel was interested, but not for long. Later, she recalled that "those Grand Dukes were all the same—they looked marvelous but there was nothing behind. . . . They were tall and handsome and splendid, but behind it all—nothing: just vodka and the void."[34]

Chanel was anything but vodka and void. By 1920 she not only had created the equivalent of an earthquake in women's fashion, sweeping away the old with a youthful, casual look that flaunted short pleated skirts, dropped waistlines, and hemlines raised to an unheard-of nine inches above the ground, but she was also beginning to venture into perfume. François Coty of course had preceded her, as had longtime perfumers such as Guerlain and Houbigant. Paul Poiret had even pioneered the concept of a *couturier* manufacturing and marketing his own fragrances. But Poiret had named his fragrances, Les Parfums de Rosine, after his daughter, not after himself or his establishment. Chanel would proceed quite differently, using her own name and finding a scent (Chanel No. 5) and a bottle (simple, square) that appealed to the modern woman.

Ernest Beaux, of the famed French perfume center at Grasse, became Chanel's perfumer and guide through this exotic world, although Chanel would later claim to have invented No. 5 herself. More likely, she responded to samples that Beaux had compounded, deciding what she did and did not like. Much like François Coty before him, Beaux had blended the relatively new discovery of synthetic aldehydes with a complex mixture of natural ingredients, in this case a blend that emphasized jasmine. Chanel's choice was light, clean, and floral without being cloying—a perfect scent for the modern woman. Chanel loved it and took samples to spray in her boutiques, piquing customer interest and preparing for department store sales (in Paris's famed Galeries Lafayette) as well as in her own boutiques. As for the name of her new perfume, there are many creation stories, but Beaux has the simplest: it was number five in the series of samples he presented to her. Chanel considered the number good luck and kept it.

While Chanel was latching securely on to fame and fortune, Cole Porter had fortune—his wife's and his own—in his pocket, but fame still eluded him. To his discouragement, he was floundering. After the honeymoon, he and Linda returned to Paris, where they first lived in her house near the Champs-Elysées before moving to their legendary address at 13 Rue Monsieur, in the seventh arrondissement, which became the center for some of the most glamorous parties in Paris. This reputation was perhaps predictable; Cole Porter had always majored in glamorous parties, in which he smoothly starred. More surprising was his enrollment at this time in Vincent d'Indy's Schola Cantorum, a rigorously conservative music school, for two years of intensive study in harmony, counterpoint, and orchestration.

Back in 1905, Erik Satie had startled friends by immersing himself in the same intensive curriculum, and Cole Porter's decision was no less unexpected. But with his musical comedy career going nowhere, Linda encouraged him to think of composing symphonies and serious music. D'Indy was a traditionalist, both politically and musically, but was remarkably open to supporting the work of contemporary composers such as Ravel, Debussy, and

Satie, even if he did not care for what they wrote. And so, Cole Porter found the doors of the Schola Cantorum open to him.

While there, he successfully orchestrated movements from Schumann's First and Second Piano Sonatas, but did not finish the course after discovering that what he was learning interfered with his own sense of rhythm. Schumann always remained a favorite with him, and the work he did at the Schola may have contributed to the extraordinary craftsmanship he demonstrated in his subsequent career. Yet Cole Porter, who excelled at giving parties, was still floundering.

At about the same time as Cole Porter, Maurice Ravel was also battling internal demons—in his case, the loss of creativity. Ravel's health had gradually recovered, but his morale remained frighteningly low. Depressed and unable to compose, he escaped Paris that winter of 1919–1920 for a friend's isolated country house, where he worked on smaller compositions until his creative impulses began to show signs of revival. He then tackled a long-abandoned project, a grand waltz that he had contemplated long before the war as an homage to Johann Strauss. Its original name was *Vienne*, or *Vienna*, and Ravel had written his friend, the music critic Jean Marnold, "You know of my deep sympathy for these wonderful rhythms, and that I value the *joie de vivre* expressed by the dance."[35] But by the time Ravel completed *Vienne* in early 1920, it had become *La Valse*, a distinctly postwar composition with far darker tones. Instead of expressing the *joie de vivre* of the dance, it evoked memories of a vanished world spinning out of control.

Diaghilev was interested in *La Valse* for his upcoming season and asked to hear it. Despite Ravel's disappointment over *Daphnis et Chloé*'s relatively unsuccessful prewar premiere with the Ballets Russes,[36] he was willing to try another venture with Diaghilev. That spring he gave *La Valse* a preliminary piano play-through (with Marcelle Meyer) at the home of Misia Sert. Present were Diaghilev, Massine (who still was on board), a very young Poulenc, and Stravinsky. According to Poulenc, Diaghilev was less than enthusiastic about the composition. "It's a masterpiece," he finally said, "but it's not a ballet. It's a portrait of a ballet; it's a painting of a ballet."[37]

Poulenc could not help but notice that Ravel was devastated, even though he made no protest. Instead, he quietly gathered up his music and left. Even more astonishing to Poulenc was that Stravinsky—once a friend of Ravel's—never said a word.[38]

It marked the end of any further association between Ravel and Diaghilev, as well as between Ravel and Stravinsky,[39] although Ravel remained on good terms with Misia, and he even dedicated *La Valse* to her. After all, he never forgot how Misia understood his anguish after his scandalous failure to win the Prix de Rome in 1905 and had generously invited him for a restorative summer cruise on her yacht.[40]

Quite possibly it was Ravel's memories of this unhappy Prix de Rome affair that prompted his refusal in early 1920 of the Legion of Honor, offered by some of the same official circles that had so famously snubbed him during his early career. His refusal created a fresh scandal, for one simply did not turn down the Legion of Honor. But Ravel, although a gentle man, was adamant. "Have you noticed," he asked his good friend Roland-Manuel, "that 'legionnaires' are similar to morphine addicts, who use any means, even deceit, to have others share their passion, perhaps in order to legitimatize it in their own eyes?"[41]

Ravel's brother, Edward, diplomatically told the press that Ravel had refused the decoration as a matter of principle, since he was opposed to all honorary awards. But despite this singular omission, Ravel would subsequently accept many other honors—just not this one.

Charles Jeanneret was struggling. He badly wanted to establish himself as a painter but, despite lack of official credentials, had become an architect, hoping to make enough money at it that he could at long last have the financial independence to paint.

He had been designing buildings since his late teens, including a luxurious house for his parents that (as he and they should have realized) they could not afford. He had traveled throughout Europe, worked in Berlin (where he first met the famed Mies van der Rohe), and spent formative time in Paris working for Auguste Perret, pioneer of reinforced concrete and architect of Paris's Théâtre des Champs-Elysées (and, like Jeanneret, a practicing architect without official credentials). In the process, Jeanneret had made a good start on developing an aesthetic, one heavily influenced by the "pure and honest architecture" of the monasteries of remote Mount Athos as well as the Charterhouse of Ema in Tuscany, which he described as an "earthly paradise," one that effectively combined community living and private spaces with access to gardens and nature.[42] In response to World War I's widespread destruction, he had also conceived of a major innovation that he called the Dom-ino system, a form of modular housing based on standardized low-cost elements that could be cheaply and quickly combined.

Jeanneret had expected that by this time he would have freed himself to do what he wanted, to paint, but now, at the age of thirty-three, he was still on the same old treadmill. His design for a major commercial project, a slaughterhouse modeled on the Taylor method of efficiency, lost out to a higher-cost plan. His parents were forced to sell the house he had designed for them, at a loss, taking a toll on their life savings. He had opened a factory to manufacture reinforced-concrete bricks, which at first sold well, but whose sales by late 1920 were lagging. Vision and ego he had aplenty, but where was he headed?

As a much-needed outlet for his creative energies, Jeanneret had begun work on *Towards a New Architecture*, which would in time become a classic, but he had already received verbal pummeling from a critic who had taken a look at Jeanneret's proposals for flat-roofed, cast-concrete structures and been appalled. To which Jeanneret famously replied that his proposed village would be "as lovely as a machine." He later explained that by this he meant "a machine for living," adding, "Is not the goal of a house to make life easy and agreeable?"[43] But he would spend much of his professional career explaining this to those unable to comprehend his underlying design, along with his intent to encourage rather than stifle rich and meaningful living.

Despite these setbacks, 1920 would become a major turning point for Jeanneret. That autumn, he and Ozenfant first published their magazine, *L'Esprit Nouveau*, in collaboration with the avant-garde poet Paul Dermée. Their goal was to promote "artistic balance and mathematical order" as a means toward human satisfaction, and they extolled the beauty and timelessness of "cubes, cones, spheres, cylinders, and pyramids."[44]

It was now, as a pseudonym for the new publication, that Charles Jeanneret came up with the name Le Corbusier. By his own account, he had derived it from the name of an ancestor, a Monsieur Lecorbesier, who had been one of the few truly successful and prosperous members of Jeanneret's family. Jeanneret may simply have liked the sound of the name and its association with *le corbeau* (the raven, or crow), given his own crow-like profile. Or perhaps it summoned up the verb *courber* (to bend) and the image of having others "bend" to his will.[45] Yet whatever the name's source, it gave Jeanneret the opportunity to reinvent himself. (The poet Blaise Cendrars, born only a month before Jeanneret in their mutual birthplace, La Chaux-de-Fonds, also changed his name, from Frédéric Sauser. The two would remain friends over the years.)

That year Le Corbusier's young second cousin, Pierre Jeanneret, reentered his life, arriving in Paris laden with prizes and accolades from his studies in Geneva to study architecture at the Ecole des Beaux-Arts. Initially, Le Corbusier was contemptuous of the young man but quickly grasped his abilities and potential. It would not be long before he would make Pierre Jeanneret his partner.

Others were also arriving in Paris, including the American poet Ezra Pound, who in turn convinced James Joyce to relocate to the City of Light. Originally from Dublin, Joyce had lived a peripatetic life, roving from Dublin to Paris and back again, then on to Trieste and Zurich, and then once more to Paris. Everywhere, he lived in poverty, accompanied by his partner, Nora Barnacle, whom he refused to marry—having rejected the conventions of marriage, the Church, and the home. Two children were born into this ragtag existence.

Joyce had come to Pound's attention before the war, while the latter was residing in London. Pound knew just about everyone who counted in his world and had been generous in his support of new names such as Robert Frost, D. H. Lawrence, and T. S. Eliot (Pound in fact would edit Eliot's *The Waste Land*). When Pound, looking for "markedly modern stuff," requested material from Joyce, Joyce sent him the first chapter of *A Portrait of the Artist as a Young Man*. Pound was hooked: "I'm not supposed to know much about prose," he wrote him, "but I think your novel is damn fine stuff."[46]

Joyce began to write his epic Irish Odyssey, *Ulysses*, at the beginning of the war and would not complete it until 1921, although in 1918 it began to appear in serialized form in the American avant-garde literary review, *The Little Review*. But *Ulysses* was far too provocative for America, certainly for the U.S. Post Office, which banned the January 1920 issue containing a section that especially enraged conservatives. With the case heading for trial, Joyce's prospects for publishing *Ulysses* were growing dim when he encountered Sylvia Beach.

They met at a Sunday dinner party in July 1920 at the home of the French poet André Spire. Adrienne Monnier invited Beach, who initially was afraid of Joyce—after all, despite his ongoing poverty, he already was a name to be reckoned with in the literary world, and she was in awe of him. But Beach quickly discovered that Joyce was a surprisingly gentlemanly and sensitive soul, with deep-seated fears that ranged from the ocean and heights to horses, dogs, machinery, and thunderstorms. During their first conversation, a barking dog sent him into a panic.

The next day, Joyce walked into Shakespeare and Company and joined Sylvia's lending library. He could only afford one month's membership.

∽

In March 1920, after a long debate that seemed to bring out the worst in just about everyone, the U.S. Senate rejected the Treaty of Versailles, falling short of the two-thirds majority that the Constitution required. At the heart of the problem were certain senators' fears that the League of Nations would entangle America in an unprecedented web of permanent transatlantic alliances. Defeat of the treaty meant that France, which had made significant concessions on establishing a protective military presence in the Rhineland, could no longer depend on Allied intervention in response to future German aggression.

Disillusioned by this unsatisfactory ending to their wartime suffering, the French had even more to complain about that year as the franc continued to fall and prices rose. By autumn, a worldwide economic crisis had begun to dampen inflation, but public opinion remained sour. In this atmosphere, strident nationalism, linked with fervent Catholicism, surged around the figure of Joan of Arc.

For years, France's nationalists and the Catholic Right had revered Joan of Arc, and throughout the war, French troops had carried her image into battle with them. The idea of a national day of remembrance to commemorate her martyrdom had been floating about for years, and Maurice Barrès had become its champion. Yet Barrès's campaign had never won enough support until the spring of 1920, when he attempted to broaden Joan's appeal to secularists (by portraying Joan as a down-to-earth peasant girl) and socialists (by portraying Joan as a champion of the poor), as well as to the usual array of monarchists, nationalists, and ardent Catholics. The Vatican (with which France had broken diplomatic relations fifteen years earlier) almost upset Barrès's chances by choosing this moment to canonize Joan, but despite resistance from anticlericals, the National Assembly agreed to set aside a secular holiday in May in her honor.

The first such celebration in Paris, held around Joan of Arc's gilded equestrian statue in the Place des Pyramides, turned out to be an exercise in flag-waving militarism and patriotism—much to the dismay of Parisian workers gathered on the city's outskirts to protest war, war profiteers, and the unholy union between the military and the Church. Fighting broke out between demonstrators and mounted guards, with one person killed and more than fifty wounded.

The protesters made no dent on public opinion, as the clash went virtually unreported, but they seemed to sense the danger in what Barrès and his supporters viewed as a triumph of civilization. For as Barrès's close collaborator, Charles Maurras, put it, "This national heroine was not the heroine of democracy." Instead, "in all earthly matters, she went straight to the essential thing, which was the prompt establishment of central authority and its swift recognition throughout the country."[47]

It would not be long before an upsurge of right-wing ideologues would make Joan of Arc their particular heroine.

Kiki of Montparnasse, photo by Man Ray © Man Ray Trust / Artists Rights Society (ARS), NY / ADAGP, Paris 2015. Musée National d'Art Moderne, Paris © CNAC/MNAM/Dist. RMN-Grand Palais / Art Resource, NY

CHAPTER SIX

~

Weddings, Breakups, and Other Affairs

(1921)

That spring, after a very proper and formal courtship, thirty-year-old Charles de Gaulle wed twenty-year-old Yvonne Vendroux.

Captain de Gaulle had spent much of 1919 and 1920 in Poland, where he served with the Polish general staff during that country's brief postwar tangle with Russia. Looking for something and someplace to bolster his stagnating career, de Gaulle had asked to be seconded as an adviser to the Polish army—although activity anywhere would do. In Warsaw, he served as a military instructor, the idea being to create a Polish army able to defend the newly independent nation's eastern borders against Soviet Russia and its western borders from future German aggression.

As it happened, many Poles were not satisfied with the eastern frontier their country received at the war's end, and, during 1919, Polish troops began to push eastward under an ambitious and charismatic general, Marshal Pilsudski, whose goal was to establish a Poland that stretched from the Baltic to the Black Sea. After a winter respite, during which the Allies tried to tamp down Polish fervor, Pilsudski resumed hostilities in 1920, during which the Poles broke through Soviet resistance all the way to Kiev. At this point, Russia entered the fray in earnest, and soon the Red Army recaptured the Ukraine and broke through the Polish line all the way to Warsaw. Sobered by the real possibility of becoming a Soviet satellite, Polish forces managed to extract themselves from this mess with a successful counterattack (the Battle of Warsaw, known as the Miracle of the Vistula) that ousted the Russians and fixed the Polish frontier somewhat to the east of what it had been before all this broke out.

De Gaulle did well during the fracas, having been authorized to join the Polish fighting forces as an adviser, and then becoming chief personal assistant to the head of the French mission. His conduct earned him some flattering accolades, which he knew would serve him well in the future. This was especially important now that he was about to wed.

Thanks to the machinations of both families, de Gaulle met Yvonne in the autumn of 1920 while on leave in Paris. Her father was a well-to-do Calais businessman, while her mother had earned a Croix de Guerre for wartime service as head of the Calais hospital—suitable family connections, indeed, for someone with de Gaulle's ambitions. In addition, both families were staunchly conservative Catholics.

The courtship was awkward but decorous. Six-foot-five-inch de Gaulle, clumsy as usual, managed to spill tea on Yvonne's dress (the details vary, as family stories so often do) and invited her to a ball at his alma mater, the elite military academy of Saint-Cyr. It seems that they did not dance (Charles de Gaulle did not dance), but they did talk at length, seated at a proper distance from one another. Still, he did not propose, and with the end of his leave approaching, both families grew anxious and stepped up their joint efforts. At last, on November 11, Charles and Yvonne became engaged, sealing their commitment with their first public kiss. The wedding was set for April, after de Gaulle returned from his last duties in Poland.

The civil marriage and subsequent church wedding took place in Calais, followed by a wedding celebration that included an eleven-course dinner. On this occasion, Captain de Gaulle waltzed with his bride ("I do not think life will provide me with any other chance of seeing my brother-in-law dancing," Yvonne's brother gleefully reported),[1] and then the newlyweds took the train for Lake Maggiore. Following this romantic interlude, which has remained completely off the record, they returned to Paris, where the captain took up his new posting.

Much to Charles de Gaulle's satisfaction, he was about to become an assistant professor of history at Saint-Cyr.

If Stravinsky ever was in love with Coco Chanel, by 1921 he had gotten over it. It was then that he fell deeply in love with Vera de Bosset Sudeykina, the ballerina who became his mistress until the death of his first wife in 1939, when Vera became the second Madame Stravinsky. Whether or not Chanel once had an affair with Stravinsky, for many years she continued her financial support.

That February, Picasso became a proud father when Olga gave birth to a baby boy, whom they christened Paul Joseph and called Paulo. Much to everyone's interest, Misia Sert rather than Gertrude Stein served as godmother: according to Stein, she and Picasso had quarreled, "neither of them never knew about what,"[2] and although they later were reconciled, they did not see one another as often as before. Another longtime Picasso friend and supporter, Max Jacob, was especially hurt that he was not asked to serve as godfather (Georges Bemberg, a wealthy patron with artistic aspirations, received the nod). Whether or not this disappointment contributed to Jacob's major change in lifestyle, as some have suggested,[3] the following June he left Paris for the monastery of Saint-Benoît-sur-Loire. There he would remain until 1928, in the attempt to steer clear of the sexual temptations of Montparnasse and Montmartre.

The birth of a Picasso son and heir accelerated Olga's social ambitions, and she and Picasso were seen at all the right places as they joined the increasingly frantic social swim (Max Jacob called it Picasso's "duchess period"). That meant stylish clothes, dress balls, and fashionable outings in Juan-les-Pins, Cap d'Antibes, and Monte Carlo, as well as Paris. It was expensive and distracting, in ways that Olga would only in time come to appreciate. Her preoccupation with their social life meant that Picasso had the opportunity for the kinds of affairs he had always conducted on the side, whoever his mistress was at the time.

Olga must not have understood the threat that Coco Chanel represented when she went to Chanel for her wardrobe. Chanel was Olga's favorite designer, but that summer, when the Picasso apartment was closed, Chanel offered her magnificent town apartment in the Ritz to Pablo (it is unclear where Olga was at the time). Already paired off by Cocteau with Chanel at the June 1921 opening of *Les Mariés de la Tour Eiffel* (*The Wedding Party on the Eiffel Tower*), when Olga was absent, Picasso does not seem to have required much urging to see more of Chanel, and they were rumored to have had an affair. After that, things settled into a close friendship. "I get along very well with strong personalities," Chanel later commented, adding of Picasso, "I liked the man."[4]

Unquestionably, both Picasso and Chanel got around. They also maintained their extraordinary professional output, with Chanel continuing to ramp up her *couturier* business (she would eventually have as many as three thousand women working for her) while successfully launching her new perfume, Chanel No. 5. Picasso's creative energy continued unabated, with summers on the Mediterranean influencing his emerging Neoclassicism, while continued partnership with Diaghilev and the Ballets Russes may well have encouraged his revived "concern with the natural and esthetic beauty of the human body."[5] In collaboration with Diaghilev once again that year, Picasso produced the scenery for *Cuadro flamenco*, and in 1924 he worked with the impresario for *Le Train bleu*.

By this time, Diaghilev was facing competition from an unexpected source—Rolf de Maré, a wealthy young Swedish impresario, and de Maré's Swedish Ballet. De Maré, who had arrived in Paris that winter, was quick to take on ballets that Diaghilev turned down and began to commission others, starting with a particularly unusual one thought up by Cocteau. By the time this endeavor emerged in June 1921, its title had changed to *Les Mariés de la Tour Eiffel*, and the music had become a group effort by all members of the Groupe des Six, with the exception of Louis Durey.[6] The story, such as it was, involved a series of hijinks and misadventures befalling a wedding party on the famous tower, including a photographer's camera that produces an ostrich, a baby, a bathing beauty, and a lion that eats one of the guests (a general), followed by the appearance of a dove of peace. Much like *Parade*, *Les Mariés* broke free of the constraints of classical ballet to invent something entirely new and wildly different. As Cocteau put it, "Before our very eyes a new theatrical genre is being born in France. . . . It expresses the modern spirit, and is still a world unmapped, rich in discoveries."[7]

The premiere took place at the Théâtre des Champs-Elysées and drew cheers from most of the audience, but also a significant anti-Cocteau demonstration by some irate Dadaists who had managed to get themselves evicted from their own event upstairs. Still, *Les Mariés* was deemed a success—enough so that Diaghilev, who now was looking thoughtfully at his new Swedish rival, commissioned Francis Poulenc to write an "atmospheric ballet" (*Les Biches*) for the Ballets Russes (premiered in 1924) and would soon extend commissions to Georges Auric and Darius Milhaud as well.

In the meantime, Diaghilev's new relationship with Boris Kochno was proving a happy one—personally for the impresario, and professionally for the Ballets Russes as a whole. Originally, following Massine's abrupt departure, Diaghilev had offered Kochno the job of personal secretary, and when the young man asked what this entailed, Diaghilev merely replied, "A secretary must be able to make himself indispensable."[8] Besides what this so clearly implied, Kochno quickly made himself a constructive influence with the company, ultimately providing scenarios for ballets, especially those of Diaghilev's last and most famous choreographer, George Balanchine.

～

Raymond Radiguet was proving a handful, even for Cocteau. This young man—unquestionably a genius, but at seventeen, still a hormone-addled teenager—was driving Cocteau wild with his drinking, difficult behavior, and frequent disappearances. In February, Radiguet turned up in the Mediterranean fishing village that Jean and Valentine Hugo had discovered over Christmas. According to Valentine, he ran off "to be away from Jean Cocteau for a while,"[9] but Cocteau trailed after him and spent several weeks of bliss with his protégé. "To me, Radiguet is a marvel," he wrote Valentine. "His poems are like peach-down, and they grow for him like violets, like wild strawberries."[10]

Cocteau's mother, who still supported him, was appalled by the company her son kept and wrote to tell him so. Cocteau was outraged: "Never again expect me to do anything in a conventional way," he shot back, but immediately relented and asked Valentine Hugo to intercede for him. Madame Cocteau, he told Valentine, "doesn't see that this child is a guardian angel for my work."[11]

But this particular guardian angel was becoming increasingly surly and difficult, and Cocteau knew it. They traveled together in the French countryside that summer, and Radiguet behaved badly. He drank too much and, according to Cocteau, "remained a lazy, moody schoolboy."[12] Cocteau finally had to lock him up to make him work, but then he took to escaping through the window. If pressed to write, he would scribble nonsense in an illegible hand. Still, there were moments when Radiguet's genius shone through, and somehow, despite the chaos, he produced his first novel, *Le Diable au Corps* (*The Devil in the Flesh*), the icy story of a self-absorbed teenager's involvement with a married woman whom he comes to dominate.

When the book was almost finished, Cocteau took Radiguet to Proust's publisher, Bernard Grasset, who accepted it on the spot and gave Radiguet a contract that included a substantial monthly stipend. With this, Radiguet no longer needed to maintain the pretense of living with his family and moved into a Paris hotel, where he continued to drink heavily and carried on a brief affair with the English writer Beatrice Hastings, who had once been Modigliani's mistress and was more than twice Radiguet's age.

Americans and other foreigners may have gravitated to Montparnasse for its cafés and freewheeling night scene, but artists and writers came for its cultural dynamism and the possibilities it offered for success. Montparnasse was a place where writers could publish works that were unpublishable anywhere else, and where artists could find buyers for their most avant-garde works.

Creative types, whatever their field of endeavor, found a wealth of support from a network of aspiring and similarly strapped Montparnasse comrades. Even the cafés contributed their bit: Victor Libion at the Rotonde was of course legendary, and the new Café du Parnasse, located next to the Rotonde, exhibited works (complete with printed catalogue) by Montparnasse artists on its walls.

In mid-1921, yet another American arrived in Montparnasse—a New York painter and photographer with the odd name of Man Ray. It really was his name, although he had altered it substantially from his birth name. His father, a tailor, had arrived at Ellis Island in the 1880s as Melach Radnitsky and had subsequently Americanized his first name to Max. Emmanuel, Max's oldest son, shortened the family name to Ray, and the rest of the family followed suit, although without legalizing the change. Emmanuel, known as Manny, began to sign his works as "Man," and his new identity as Man Ray began.

The name may have sounded a bit off-putting, but Man Ray was in fact quite approachable. A small, compact man, scarcely over five feet high, he had a pleasant way of getting along with everyone, no matter how prickly or explosive. Born in Brooklyn, he had shown talent in architecture before gravitating to the New York art world, with time out for experimental living in a rural New Jersey artist colony. While there he met and married the poet Adon Lacroix, the former wife of the poet Adolf Wolff.

Soon after his marriage, Man Ray encountered Marcel Duchamp, the French artist who in 1913 had set the art world on its ear with his notorious contribution to the equally notorious New York Armory Show. He called his painting *Nude Descending a Staircase*, although detractors (and there were many) derisively renamed it *Explosion in a Shingle Factory*. Man Ray's marriage did not last, but his friendship with Duchamp did: the two would remain friends and colleagues for fifty years.

With the outbreak of war, Duchamp, Francis Picabia, and the composer Edgard Varèse fled France for New York, where they gravitated to Man Ray's crowd, which was vigorously protesting any and all forms of tradition. After his arrival, Duchamp began work on the enormous *La Mariée mise à nue par ses célibataires, même* (*The Bride Stripped Bare by Her Bachelors, Even*, or *The Large Glass*), a work on two huge and heavy panes of glass with foil, wire, silvering, and a heavy accumulation of New York dust. Duchamp later cleaned off the dust, except for one area where he mixed it with varnish to create an effect "which I never would have obtained with paint."[13] Man Ray exposed Duchamp's bride to one hour of camera exposure, with the resulting image that Duchamp called *Elevage de poussière*, or *Breeding [Raising] Dust*. Many years later, Man Ray would write him, "Didn't we raise the dust, though, old boy!"[14]

While Duchamp was pushing the limits of what exactly constituted art, Man Ray was experimenting with the camera, drawing on exposed film or negatives of photographs, in addition to making mirrors that did not reflect and push buttons that did not work. Well before Dada hit New York, he and Duchamp, along with Picabia, had accepted its spirit of audacious anarchism, most notoriously in Duchamp's porcelain urinal, which he submitted as a sculpture to the new Society of Independent Artists under the title of *Fountain* (it was rejected).

By now, Man Ray was increasingly using his photography as a source of income (primarily portraits and record photos of paintings), but he was also using it to explore its artistic possibilities, photographing what, as he put it, he "did not wish to paint."[15] Still, he regarded himself primarily as a painter when he left New York for Paris in July 1921, preceded by Duchamp, who met him at the Gare Saint-Lazare and took him to a cheap hotel, followed by a meeting with leading Dadaists at the Café Certa in the Passage de l'Opéra.

Paris overwhelmed Man Ray: "Everything is gay and moving," he wrote his brother, "everyone is on the streets—it is a big Greenwich Village, but with wine and beer everywhere."[16] Food was cheap and remarkably good, jazz clubs were inexpensive, and café life was exhilarating, even though Man Ray spoke little French and had to trust to Duchamp for translation. He knew enough to step warily around the growing fissures between the Dadaists, especially those between Tzara and Breton, but his main challenge during his first months in Paris was poverty.

It was Picabia's wife, Gabrielle, who came up with a solution to Man Ray's financial difficulties. After all, the fellow was a whiz with the camera. Why not find employment for him with her friend Paul Poiret, the fashion designer, who was about to show his fall couture collection? Poiret was an avid collector of avant-garde art, which might make him sympathetic to an avant-garde American artist.

Entering La Maison Poiret on Rue d'Antin, Man Ray observed the brightly colored tables and chairs sheltered by the yellow canopy that marked Poiret's fabulous but ill-fated Oasis Theatre. After walking up marble steps and then a wide, carpeted stairway, the young American found himself in a richly appointed but otherwise empty salon. Soon a door opened, and a man carrying a bolt of cloth emerged and motioned for Man Ray to enter. There, the young American found an office filled with more bolts of silks and brocades scattered around a large desk. Behind this sat Poiret—imposing looking, with unsmiling eyes and an oriental-looking beard—carefully dressed in a canary-colored coat. Man Ray immediately thought of doing a portrait of the *couturier* in these surroundings, but at that moment Poiret was interested only in fashion photography. He wanted something different, something original. Could Man Ray manage this?

Equipped with a temporary studio, lights, and a darkroom—all available on the premises—Man Ray went to work. Finding an American model who understood him, he had her stand near Poiret's magnificent Brancusi sculpture of a golden bird, which "threw off beams of golden light, blending with the colors of [her] dress." This, he decided, was what he was looking for: he would "combine art and fashion." And then, noticing that Poiret's office door was open, with Poiret absent and the floor still littered with brilliant-colored bolts of material, he had the idea of asking his model to lie down on the pile. There was a practical as well as artistic reason for this pose: the room was dark, requiring a longer exposure, and he thought she would be less likely to move. In any case, the result was "ravishing, divine (as they say in fashion circles). There was line, color, texture, and above all, sex-appeal, which I instinctively felt was what Poiret wanted."[17]

Unfortunately, nothing came of these daring reclining shots, as Man Ray had forgotten to remove the holders before making the exposures; but the other shots came out well. And as he developed subsequent prints at home at night, something new and startling happened: he discovered what he would call his Rayograph process, or camera-less photographs. One sheet of unexposed photo paper had somehow gotten mixed with the exposed sheets in the developing tray, and while waiting for an image to appear, he placed a glass and other objects on the damp paper and turned on the light. "Before my eyes an image began to form, not quite a simple silhouette of the objects as in a straight photograph, but distorted and refracted by the glass more or less in contact with the paper and standing out against a black background, the part directly exposed to the light."[18]

Later, when Man Ray went to Poiret with his fashion prints, he slipped in a couple of the Rayographs, thinking that they might interest him. The young American explained that he was "trying to do with photography what painters were doing, but with light and chemicals instead of pigment, and without the optical help of the camera." Poiret did not quite understand, but nonetheless told Man Ray that he "might have the makings of a fine fashion photographer."[19] He also paid him what seemed like a lordly sum (several hundred francs) for the Rayographs. As for the fashion shots, Man Ray would have to negotiate his own fees from the fashion magazines.

It was a new world, but an enticing one. In addition to introducing Man Ray to Poiret, Picabia gave him an introduction to Jean Cocteau, whom he described as "someone who knew everybody in Paris."[20] Cocteau was predisposed to like everything and everyone American, and the two immediately hit it off. Man Ray invited him to pose for his portrait, and the results were such a success that soon Cocteau was bringing or sending musicians and writers to Man Ray's small hotel room. None of these paid for their prints (after all, as Gertrude Stein reminded him, most of those who came were artists and as hard up as Man Ray was), but the young American's reputation was growing.

Unfortunately his current location, in cramped quarters in the seventeenth arrondissement, cut him off from what he now realized was Paris's center of artistic activity, the colorful Montparnasse quarter. Late in 1921, bolstered by the uptick in his reputation and fortunes as a photographer, Man Ray made his move to the Hôtel des Ecoles (now the Hôtel Lenox) at 15 Rue Delambre, where his quarters were so small that they astonished Gertrude Stein when she visited. He also made one last effort to enter the art world, with a one-man show in Philippe Soupault's new bookshop, Librarie Six.

The exhibit opened on a cold and blustery December day, with a good crowd in attendance. Man Ray was hopeful, but nothing sold that day or during the remainder of the exhibit. But at the opening, a strange little man in a pince-nez, bowler hat, and umbrella approached him and, when Man Ray complained of the cold, took his arm and led him to a café, where he ordered hot grog for them both. The man, whom Man Ray thought looked like an undertaker or a banker, was in fact the aging but still unconventional composer Erik Satie—someone who, despite his appearance, was quite accustomed to upending the staid and the conservative. Leaving the café with Satie, Man Ray spotted a shop with household utensils and purchased a flatiron. With Satie's presumably gleeful help, he then glued a row of tacks to the iron's flat surface and titled it *The Gift*, adding it to the exhibition. It was his first Dada object in France.

By now, Man Ray had decided "not to bother with the art world as far as my painting was concerned."[21] He was working up a nice business taking record photographs of paintings for dealers and painters. It was not what he most wanted to do, but it was a living. And then there were the portraits, which were beginning to make money, especially those of aristocrats such as the eccentric Marquise Casati and the glamorous Count de Beaumont, who asked him to photograph the guests at one of his costume balls. It was a change of direction, and yet as the noted painter, collector, and art historian Roland Penrose observed, "since Man Ray is essentially a poet, the division between painting and photography becomes imperceptible in his hands."[22]

That December brought yet another major turning point in Man Ray's life, when he noticed an attractive woman and her friend at the Rotonde. The waiter had refused to serve them because they were not wearing hats.

The prettier of the two became irate and shouted that a café was not a church, and besides, "all the American bitches came in without hats."[23] The manager then arrived and tried to reason with her, telling her that since she was French, the fact that she was *sans chapeau* and unaccompanied might lead some to mistake her for a whore. This made the woman furious, but Man Ray's companion, the painter Marie Vassilieff, knew her and promptly invited her to join them. The waiter was all apologies—he did not realize that they were Man Ray's friends.

And that was how Man Ray met Kiki.

Late that October, Dédée Renoir gave birth to a son, Alain, and soon after, she and Jean moved to Marlotte, near Paris, where their close friends, Paul Cézanne (son of the painter) and his family, soon joined them. Although Jean Renoir loved to tear around in his high-performance Napier automobile, with which they regularly buzzed into Paris to see movies (they were "truly mad about movies"), he and Dédée still were occupied mainly with making pottery. They did not join other well-to-do young Parisians at trendy cafés or in various Montparnasse haunts where they would have been more than welcome. Nor did they contemplate entering the business of making movies. After all, Jean's older brother, Pierre, had told him, "Movies aren't for us. Our literary and artistic baggage is too heavy and slows us down. We should leave it to the Americans."[24]

Others continued to arrive in Paris, including the Spanish artist Joan Miró, who promptly settled in Montparnasse and, by winter, was joined by the Surrealist painter André Masson. And, late in the year, a young American by the name of Ernest Hemingway arrived with his bride in Paris, sent by Sherwood Anderson, who had spotted Hemingway's potential and promised that he would do well there. (Several years later, Hemingway would buy Miró's large painting, *The Farm*, which Miró completed that first winter in Paris and was unable to sell.)

While Americans were pouring into Paris at an unprecedented rate, at least one Parisian was heading to America. Marie Curie may have been initially hesitant about making the trip, but the idea of raising money from wealthy Americans for her institute was appealing. It was just that the whole thing snowballed into something that Curie never envisioned and, in truth, abhorred.

It all began with the Paris visit of Marie (Missy) Meloney, editor of an American women's magazine, who managed to snag a rare interview with Curie. In the course of their developing friendship, it became clear that Curie would welcome any help that interested Americans could provide in rais-ing funds to buy a gram of radium for her laboratory. Meloney immediately set to work on the campaign to raise one hundred thousand dollars to buy the desired radium, in the process creating for public consumption a breath-lessly hagiographic and socially conservative version of Curie that bordered on the ridiculous.

Marie Curie may have represented "the highest vision of womanhood" to Meloney, as Marie's daughter Eve charitably tried to explain,[25] but it was a distorted vision: ultimately, Meloney was uncomfortable with any woman's decision to leave the home for the workplace and could only understand Curie's formidable professional drive and scholarly quest within the context of dire necessity and supreme sacrifice on behalf of her children. Curie care-fully took issue with her: "I agree, of course," she wrote Meloney, "that it is not easy for a woman to bring up children and to work out of home." But she did not agree that entering the workplace poisoned the lives of a woman's children, as Meloney had strongly implied. What of "rich women who leave the children to a governess and give most of their time to visits and dresses," Curie asked. And what of "poor women, peasants or factory workers, who could not stop working, even if they wished ever so much."[26]

In addition to misrepresenting Curie, Meloney promoted the myth that, given proper assistance, Marie Curie could and would find a cure for can-cer. "Life is passing," Meloney wrote, "and the great Curie getting older, and the world losing, God alone knows, what great secret. And millions are dying of cancer every year!"[27] Marie Curie had never believed this and had never claimed it; in fact she underscored that her contribution to cur-ing cancer was and would continue to be an indirect one: she conducted pure rather than applied research. Still, Curie had taken a great interest in the medical applications of radium and from an early date promoted the establishment of a French institute for radium therapy. This was enough for Meloney to build on.

And so in May 1921, Marie Curie set off for America, in what she origi-nally intended to be a brief trip to receive the gift that Missy Meloney had so energetically raised. Curie's initial idea had been to come in the autumn, when the trip would least interfere with her work, and stay for two weeks, during which she would give few if any lectures. Meloney had other ideas, starting with a May–June itinerary that would make it possible for Curie to receive honorary doctorates in commencement exercises at a large number of prominent universities and women's colleges, as well as to meet with Presi-dent Harding at the White House, where she would receive that precious gram of radium.

The news that the American president was going to be involved shook even the French establishment into action. Previously it had ignored or denigrated Curie, most especially during the terrible drubbing she had received in the French press over her affair with Paul Langevin, as well as during her unsuccessful bid to join the French Academy of Sciences.[28] Now the president of France, Aristide Briand, and other luminaries gathered at the Paris Opéra to celebrate her accomplishments. As a highlight of this glittering affair, Sarah Bernhardt (another working mother and now grandmother) read a poem composed in Curie's honor.

Acceding to Meloney's plans, Marie Curie departed for America with her daughters, Irène and Eve, who were delighted to be included. A plethora of honorary degrees, medals, luncheons, dinners, assemblies, ceremonies, and receptions followed, along with extended travel and visits to famous sites such as Niagara Falls and the Grand Canyon. Eve and Irène loved it all, but Marie was overwhelmed by the hoopla and, as the tour progressed, became ill, forcing most of her official visits in the West to be canceled. She understood that her work with radium had damaged her health, but those around her refused to recognize this and instead attributed her illness to the trip's strenuous demands.

In the end, she got her gram of radium. But later, looking back on this "campaign of magnificent begging across a whole continent," her daughter Eve wondered whether it might not have made more sense for her parents to have taken out a patent on radium rather than having to suffer years of struggle. "How," she asked, "can one not be obsessed by the idea that a simple signature given on a patent years ago would have been altogether more effective?"[29]

Others voiced the same doubts, and shortly after Marie Curie's return from America, she addressed this question. Despite the years of hardship she and Pierre had endured, she concluded that they had made the right decision. What needed to change, she firmly believed, was society itself, which should assure to what she termed the "dreamers" the "efficient means of accomplishing their task, in a life freed from material care and freely consecrated to research."[30]

What mankind needed, to her way of thinking, was a world made safe for dreamers.

"History . . . is a nightmare from which I am trying to awake," Stephen Dedalus remarks early on in James Joyce's *Ulysses*,[31] and it pretty well summed up Joyce's own nightmarish situation in the spring of 1921, when he was trying

Marie Curie with her daughter Irène, 1925. HIP / Art Resource, NY

desperately to finish his mammoth work and unable to find a publisher, all the while battling deteriorating eyesight. In addition, Joyce was enmeshed in the censorship uproar that *Ulysses* had created for the brave editors of the New York–based *Little Review*.

Joyce's goal had never been to write a dirty book. Instead, he had proceeded from the assumption that the social order was based on lies and that it was necessary to smash through its web of deceit to show what life was really like. He chose for his protagonist a very ordinary and unheroic Jewish advertising salesman, Leopold Bloom, and sent him through the Dublin that Joyce knew so well in an odyssey that took place over the course of merely one average day, but which Joyce linked directly, though subtly, to the Homeric original. The book's complexity was and remains daunting, as Joyce crashed through conventions of style as well as content, removing quotation marks, complete sentences, linear narrative, and other traditional devices, as well as submitting the unmoored reader to an unprecedented amount of obscenity and vulgarity.

Joyce's Leopold Bloom is an earthy man with earthy drives, and it was the explicit description of Bloom's (and other characters') ordinary acts of bathing, eating, defecating, and sexual activity, complete with the crude language associated with these acts, that brought *Ulysses* to the outraged attention of the American morality police. Joyce described the human body in terms no one had dared to use quite so graphically before, and the Comstock Act made the publication of obscenity punishable by large fines and imprisonment. As head of the New York Society for the Suppression of Vice (NYSSV), Anthony Comstock and his successor, John Sumner, were widely and justifiably feared, especially when their crusade was reinforced by the wartime and postwar powers of the government to prohibit subversive speech.

The *Little Review* had serialized almost half of *Ulysses* by mid-1920 when the New York district attorney brought obscenity charges against the review's editors. The particular portion of *Ulysses* that infuriated the censors was a twilight scene on the beach, in which Bloom is sexually aroused while watching a young woman provocatively leaning further and further back to watch some distant fireworks, quite consciously exposing her legs and undergarments. The pathos of the scene is double: Bloom knows that he has been cuckolded that day by his wife, Molly, with whom he has not had sexual relations since the death of their son; the young woman, Gerty MacDowell, longs for a boyfriend and marriage but has placed her hopes on Bloom, who (unknown to her) is a married man. Worse, she turns out to be lame and, in her world at least, unlikely ever to wed.

The editors of the *Little Review* were fined and prevented from publishing anything further of *Ulysses*. In protest, Cocteau, Picabia, Ezra Pound, Brancusi, and others collaborated in an upcoming *Little Review* issue. But despite the support of many in the London and Paris literary communities, Joyce—by now embarked on writing the longest episode of *Ulysses*—could not find a publisher. No one wanted to take a chance of running afoul of obscenity laws either in Britain or America. "My book will never come out now," Joyce told Sylvia Beach "in a tone of complete discouragement." As Beach later recalled, it occurred to her that something indeed might be done, and she asked, "Would you let Shakespeare and Company have the honor of bringing out your *Ulysses?*" Joyce immediately and joyfully accepted, and "undeterred by lack of capital, experience, and all the other requisites of a publisher, [Beach] went right ahead with *Ulysses.*"[32]

Thus in late spring 1921, a major event in literary history officially began.

In October 1921, Claude Monet—about to turn eighty-one—contacted the art critic Arsène Alexandre to tell him that he was ready for "another talk about my gift to the State." Monet now frankly acknowledged that he wasn't "getting any younger" and that "it's important, indeed urgent, that this matter should be settled once and for all."[33]

In the meanwhile, the idea of placing Monet's grand paintings of water lilies in a pavilion at the Hôtel Biron (which by this time had become the Musée Rodin) had come to a dead end. The plan was too expensive and its architecture too modern for the authorities to swallow. In addition, Monet was becoming crotchety and difficult to deal with. Finally his longtime friend, Clemenceau, came to the rescue with the idea of using an existing building, either the Jeu de Paume or the Orangerie, both of which were allocated for use as museums or exhibition spaces. Upon investigation, the Jeu de Paume seemed too narrow, but the Orangerie appeared to provide a perfect fit, especially as it could accommodate Monet's demand for an oval-shaped room. Clemenceau advised Monet to accept immediately, even though the Orangerie's basement facilities (proposed for Monet's paintings) were out of the way and unattractive.[34] After numerous second thoughts, Monet at length agreed, even upping the number of donated panels from twelve to eighteen, so long as they could be hung in two oval-shaped rooms rather than one.[35]

In June 1922, the minister of education at long last signed the decree accepting Monet's donation. This news gave renewed impetus to the elderly painter, who wrote that he was "hard at work" and that he wanted "to paint everything" before his sight was "completely gone."[36]

⌒

In a similar vein, Marcel Proust was desperately trying to finish his own massive work before he died. Few quite believed that he was as ill as he claimed, and his frequent complaints in lengthy letters to friends that he could barely finish the page because he was dying only reinforced the image that he was crying wolf.[37]

That May of 1921, after *Sodom and Gomorrah* appeared in bookstores, André Gide seemed similarly skeptical about Proust's ill health. "Knowing how difficult it is for you to predict a day when you will be feeling better," he wrote, with thinly veiled sarcasm, "I sometimes wonder if it wouldn't be best to go and ring at your doorbell daily, in the hope that, for once, Céleste will say: 'Yes, M. Proust is better this evening, he can receive you for a moment.'"[38]

Proust was understandably reluctant to receive Gide. Readers had strenuously objected to the prominent role of homosexuals and homosexuality in *Sodom and Gomorrah*,[39] but Gide, himself homosexual, was instead angered by Proust's unflattering depiction of homosexuals. In a letter to Proust, he complained that Proust had "paint[ed] a picture of 'vice' that is more damning than any invective; by branding the subject [you speak] of, [you do] more to encourage entrenched attitudes than the most forceful moral tract."[40]

Gide preferred a depiction that was more flattering, and when he finally was able to visit Proust, they discussed the subject at length. Surprised by Proust's ready admission that he was exclusively homosexual, Gide nonetheless protested Proust's stigmatization of homosexuality. Later, Proust wrote to a friend and literary critic, "It's not my fault if M. de Charlus [a major character in *Sodom and Gomorrah* who is homosexual] is an old gentleman. I could not suddenly give him the appearance of a Sicilian Shepherd."[41] In any case, as Céleste later observed, Proust never especially cared for Gide or Gide's opinion anyway: "We always referred to him between ourselves as the 'fake monk.'"[42]

Despite the widespread objection and even anger that *Sodom and Gomorrah* aroused, there were those who congratulated Proust on his courage. The novelist Colette was especially effusive: "No one in the world has written pages such as these on homosexuals," she wrote him, "no one!"[43]

⌒

Colette, known for her scandalous lifestyle as well as for her success as a novelist, had begun her career during the height of the Belle Epoque, when she emerged on the literary scene with her Claudine novels, for which her husband, the writer and critic Henry Gauthier-Villars (known as Willy), shamelessly took credit. The Claudine novels—erotic stories of a rebellious teenage girl—became best sellers, and their true author, the young Burgundian by the name of Sidonie-Gabrielle Colette (who had by then dropped her first name and kept the last), eventually took proper credit for them—and dropped her husband as well. From there, contrary to the mores of her day, she lived the life she wanted, sexually fulfilled and free.

Colette proceeded from a brief affair with Natalie Clifford Barney to an extended one with the Marquise de Belbeuf (known as Missy), with whom she performed at the Moulin Rouge in an act that culminated in a scandalously erotic onstage kiss that created a riot. Colette engaged in affairs with men as well as women, becoming involved with the Italian writer Gabriele d'Annunzio as well as the wealthy playboy Auguste Hériot. By 1921 she had been married for several years to the editor of *Le Matin*, Henry de Jouvenel, with whom she had a daughter. But in an interesting turn, she had also entered into an affair with de Jouvenel's teenage stepson, which would lead to her divorce. In the meantime, she worked hard at her craft—not only as an independent writer, but also as literary and drama critic for *Le Matin*. Her fame (and notoriety) continued to grow, especially after 1920, when she published *Chéri*, the story of an aging courtesan and the pampered young man she loves. Many hailed it as a masterpiece, and Colette agreed: "For the first time in my life," she wrote to a close friend, "I felt morally certain of having written a novel for which I need neither blush nor doubt."[44]

It was ostensibly for her daughter that Colette wrote the libretto for the opera *L'Enfant et les sortilèges* (*The Child and the Spells*), for which she asked Maurice Ravel to write the music. They had known one another since the turn of the century, having met in the salons of Madame de Saint-Marceaux and Misia Natanson (eventually Misia Edwards Sert), and shared a love for nature and for animals. Indeed, Ravel, who was a tiny man with mischievous brown eyes, reminded Colette of a squirrel.[45] Because of wartime duties as well as poor health, Ravel was unable to do anything about her request until 1919, when he came up with several suggestions that captivated Colette: "Why certainly a ragtime!" she wrote him. "Why of course Negroes in Wedgwood! What a terrific gust from the music hall to stir up the dust of the Opéra!"[46]

Although Ravel sketched out the opening scenes of *L'Enfant* in 1920, he had now returned to public life and was involved in concerts and rehearsals in Vienna as well as in Paris. Musical gossip may have had it that Ravel's career was finished, but by 1920 the Swedish Ballet was successfully presenting a ballet in Paris set to his *Le Tombeau de Couperin*, and Paris's prestigious Orchestre Lamoureux was presenting the premiere of his *La Valse*. Although *La Valse*'s frenzied conclusion dismayed some critics, others praised its "inexhaustible verve" as well as its "dazzling orchestration."[47] It would become one of the most popular of Ravel's works.

By May 1921, Ravel was quite ready to move into his quiet villa in Montfort l'Amaury, not far from Paris. There, in what he called Le Belvédère (for its lovely views of the countryside), he would peacefully compose for the rest of his life.

⌣

Late in 1921, German count Harry Kessler returned to Paris for the first time since the war. Kessler had once been a welcome addition to any Parisian cultural gathering, but during the war he had served as a German officer on the western front, and Léon Daudet and others on the nationalist right had subjected him to considerable abuse in print. Kessler may well have wondered what kind of welcome he would receive, but although noting that Parisians in general had become "somewhat morose, less friendly," he otherwise felt "as though I was returning to the old familiar scene after but a brief absence." Jean Cocteau was especially friendly, emphasizing the need to "forge afresh the intellectual bonds between France and Germany." The following summer, Kessler paid his first postwar visit to the sculptor Aristide Maillol, who greeted him "with outstretched arms and tears in his eyes." Kessler, too, was "much moved" to see his longtime friend.[48]

Since late 1918, Germany had seen months of bloody street fighting and other manifestations of revolt and chaos, during which the monarchy collapsed and the fragile Weimar Republic emerged, buffeted by political riptides as well as by German hyperinflation following the defeated nation's first reparations payment in 1921. This economic collapse convinced the British that reparations had indeed been set too high, while the French would have none of it, holding that Germany still had its industrial base intact and was making excuses for foot-dragging.

There seemed no possible compromise between the two views, and when Prime Minister Briand at last agreed to revise the treaty to reduce Germany's reparations, French opinion was not behind him. Accused of being a toady to the British, he was additionally caught out by a united Anglo-American front on naval arms reductions, which ended by his having to accept a hierarchy of naval fleets that put France in the humiliating position of fourth in the world, next to Italy. Briand promptly handed in his resignation, leaving the position open for Raymond Poincaré.

France would recover from the falling franc, but it would take several years, and in late 1920 and early 1921, young Le Corbusier did not see what lay ahead. Caught in the vise of the postwar economic crisis, his business prospects had rapidly dwindled, leaving him depressed and ready to throw in the towel. Characteristically, his mood soon swung, and in 1921 he wrote his parents that he was "not the type to lie down and quit. If a storm today sweeps my business away it destroys money and nothing more. . . . This crisis may actually improve life for me by allowing me to undertake activities more appropriate to my skills."[49]

Over the course of several months, Le Corbusier was able to liquidate his failing commercial and industrial affairs, including his concrete brickworks on the outskirts of Paris. Perhaps more difficult for him was yet another setback on the artistic front, when his joint exhibition with Amédée Ozenfant at the prestigious Galerie Druet received a drubbing. "Our paintings are taxed with being mechanical," he wrote his staunch friend William Ritter. "Myself," he continued, "I am certain that they imply a dream, a dignified and austere dream."[50]

But he was right in realizing that these crises were pointing him in a more fruitful direction. Instead of changing the world as a painter, Le Corbusier now set out to do it through architecture. By 1921 he had begun to develop what he called the Citrohan housing type, which he called "mass-produced houses"—named partly after the Citroën automobiles because, like a car, "one needs to consider the house like a machine to live in or like a tool."[51] More sophisticated in concept than the Dom-ino structure, this house—cleanly shaped, like a shoe box—connected spaces of different heights with a glass wall in its two-story-high living room, through which sunshine flooded.

By now, Le Corbusier was finding Parisian admirers for his architecture, including Fernand Léger, with whom he spent long evenings talking at the Rotonde, as well as bicycled (they had met while Le Corbusier was bicycling through Montparnasse). Theirs was a friendship that would last.

While Le Corbusier was figuring out his life, another young man—a young American writer from Chicago—was settling into his seedy fourth-floor walk-up on Rue du Cardinal-Lemoine in the Latin Quarter. It was the bitter winter of December 1921, and Ernest Hemingway and his bride, Hadley, were about to discover a new world.

Ernest Hemingway in front of the apartment he shared with Hadley Hemingway on Rue Notre Dame-des-Champs in Paris, 1924. Bridgeman Images

CHAPTER SEVEN

~

The Lost Generation

(1922)

Ernest Hemingway was freezing. He had rented a room for writing, on the top floor of a small building near his scruffy Rue du Cardinal-Lemoine apartment, and he needed to build a fire. But it cost more than he could afford to buy the components—"a bundle of small twigs, three wire-wrapped packets of short, half-pencil length pieces of split pine to catch fire from the twigs, and then the bundle of half-dried lengths of hard wood."[1]

After looking out the window into the rain and contemplating the neighboring chimneys, none of which were active, he decided that his chimney probably would not draw and that the money rather than the wood would more likely go up in smoke. So he walked out into what he described as "the sadness of the city" to a welcoming café on the Place St-Michel. There he ordered a *café au lait* followed by a warming rum and took out a notebook and pencil. White wine and oysters followed. He saw a pretty girl and thought, "You belong to me and all Paris belongs to me and I belong to this notebook and this pencil."[2]

Hemingway's recollections of his Paris years may be more fiction than reliable memoirs, but they capture the essence of the city as he saw it, even as they created an image of himself that he wanted, and wanted others, to see. Born in 1899 into a strict middle-class family in the eminently respectable Chicago suburb of Oak Park, Hemingway spent his youth dreaming of Teddy Roosevelt–like heroics and of exploring wilderness frontiers. Family life became increasingly fraught as his father, a doctor with what turned out to be a growing mental disorder, retreated into paranoia-fueled seclusion while Hemingway's mother, a successful voice teacher and forceful champion for women's rights, came to dominate the household. In time, Hemingway's father would commit suicide, as would three, and possibly four, of Dr. Hemingway's five children.

America's entry into the Great War inspired teenage Hemingway, like so many other young Americans, to volunteer. Weak vision kept him out of the army, but it did not prevent him from becoming a Red Cross ambulance driver in Italy. There, he was wounded while handing out chocolate and cigarettes to soldiers in a forward observation post. The story would grow as he told it, until he transformed himself into a war hero and turned his tale into fodder for his fiction.

By the time he returned home, Hemingway had become acquainted with war, fallen in love with (and been rejected by) an older woman, and knew that he wanted to become a writer. Rather than go to college as his parents hoped, he opted for a newspaper job and moved to Chicago, where he expected to find work. Unfortunately Chicago, awash with postwar unemployed, provided no meaningful employment, but while there he did meet Hadley Richardson, a sweetly attentive and intelligent woman eight years his senior who had an appealing naiveté in addition to a substantial trust fund. Later, Hemingway would describe Hadley's "gently modeled face" as well as her eyes and smile that "lighted up at decisions as though they were rich presents."[3] Her controlling mother had recently died (her father had earlier committed suicide), and she was prepared to give Hemingway the attention and admiration he craved. He in turn provided her with the kind of strong masculine affection and support she had so long lacked. "I honestly think we have one of the best chances for out & out happiness I know of," she told him.[4]

They wed eleven months later, in the autumn of 1921, and late that year—influenced by Hemingway's new literary acquaintance, Sherwood Anderson—they made the move to Paris. Hemingway spoke no French, but Hadley had a schoolgirl's acquaintance with the language, and—bolstered by a position offered Hemingway as roving reporter for the *Toronto Star*—they decided to give the City of Light a try. After all, jobs in America remained scarce, and the cost of living in Paris was low. Of course, the newlyweds were drawn by the idea that Paris was the place for lovers, but it was the writers and artists that Anderson mentioned, such as James Joyce, Gertrude Stein, and Picasso, that roused Hemingway's interest. Anderson promised to write them all, and in addition promised that they would help.

And so, in early 1922, Ernest and Hadley Hemingway found themselves in a small, squalid apartment in a dark and bitterly cold corner of Paris's

Latin Quarter. "Home in the rue Cardinal Lemoine," Hemingway later wrote, "was a two-room flat that had no hot water and no inside toilet facilities except an antiseptic container."[5] He called it "a cheerful, gay flat," but there was no gas or electricity, and friends were appalled when they saw it, especially since the Hemingways did not need to live that way: Hadley had money, but Ernest (with macho pride) did not want to use it. Yet as Hadley later put it, for a Paris apartment, "it was kind of fun."[6] So while she tended to domestic chores, Ernest made the rounds, from Montparnasse's Café du Dôme (the Rotonde was temporarily closed for renovation) to Sylvia Beach's Shakespeare and Company in the Latin Quarter. He did not like Montparnasse, which he later called "a dismal place,"[7] but he enjoyed Sylvia Beach and especially enjoyed the opportunity to mend serious gaps in his education by borrowing from Beach's lending library—works from Turgenev and D. H. Lawrence, Dostoyevsky and Tolstoy, as well as the current literary magazines. Hadley, alone much of the time and (to Ernest's embarrassment) better educated than he was, also read avidly from books she borrowed from Shakespeare and Company.

But for the moment, the cold and the damp won out, as did the threat of Spanish influenza. Soon after they arrived, Ernest and Hadley abandoned Paris for the clean and healthful snows of Switzerland.

⌁

On February 2, as the Hemingways were preparing to return to Paris from Switzerland, Sylvia Beach was waiting on the platform of the Gare de Lyon for the express train from Dijon, which was bringing her the first two published copies of James Joyce's *Ulysses*.

Joyce had worked at fever pitch throughout 1921, trying—despite the terrible pain in his eyes—to finish the manuscript in time for its publication on February 2, 1922, the date of his fortieth birthday. He even managed to write the last two episodes simultaneously. It was a mammoth job for Beach as well. Joyce's manuscript produced panic in typists: several refused the job outright after seeing the manuscript, with its undecipherable handwriting and multiple arrows and inserts, and one, overcome by the manuscript's difficulty, threatened to throw herself out the window. Still another rang Joyce's doorbell and threw the manuscript on the floor, dashing away before he could pay her. At last, Sylvia's sister, Cyprian, typed it—waking before dawn to decipher Joyce's handwriting before heading for the movie studio, where she worked as a silent-film actress. A friend of Cyprian's, who took over when Cyprian had to film at locations outside Paris, gave up after forty-five pages, and the husband of yet another typist looked at part of the manuscript and, shocked by what he read, threw it into the fire. Fortunately, the typist had hidden the rest of the manuscript, but Beach had to retrieve the missing pages from the lawyer handling *Ulysses*' New York obscenity case, who reluctantly agreed to photograph the pages from his copy and send them with Beach's mother to Paris.

Not only had Joyce refused to capitulate in any way following the *Little Review*'s New York obscenity conviction, but he had gone on to write "Circe," the most bizarre and bawdy section of the entire book, which takes place in Nighttown, Dublin's slum-filled red-light district. Earlier, Ezra Pound, who read the chapters of *Ulysses* as they appeared, had begun to worry. Was Joyce all right? he wondered. Had he "got knocked on the head or bit by a wild dog and gone dotty?"[8]

But Sylvia Beach was undeterred. Although she had never published anything before, had no capital, and knew nothing about the publishing industry, she did not back away from the challenge. She found a master printer in Dijon who was undisturbed by the difficulties (and in any case could not read English), and she decided on a private edition of one thousand copies, with three versions of varying quality, the most expensive being printed on Dutch handmade paper and signed by Joyce. She then sent out a prospectus, mailed to likely recipients around the globe, and expected to receive orders by mail before publication with which to pay the printer. Soon numerous literary heavyweights subscribed, including Hart Crane, W. B. Yeats, William Carlos Williams, and Wallace Stevens, along with notables such as Winston Churchill, while a friend of Beach's rounded up more orders at Montparnasse nightclubs.

Joyce was not an easy author to work with. He finished the drafts of the last two chapters in late October 1921 and was still writing when the galleys began to come through, which he filled with inserts. He asked for multiple copies simultaneously, which he marked differently, and he subjected the page proofs to the same kinds of inserts as the galleys. It has been calculated that he "went through as many as four galleys and five page proofs for every page of *Ulysses*. He wrote almost a third of his novel . . . on the galleys and proofs."[9] Adding to the difficulty, Joyce insisted on a blue cover with white letters, with the blue being the precise shade of the Greek flag. To comply with this request, the printer had to go to Germany to locate the exact shade Joyce had in mind, and when this turned out to be on the wrong paper, the printer had to lithograph the color onto white paper. But Beach was willing to work with her difficult author, even with his most unreasonable requests, making the publication of *Ulysses* as close as possible to what Joyce wanted it to be.

By this time Beach had moved Shakespeare and Company to its final location at 12 Rue de l'Odéon, across from Adrienne Monnier's bookshop. When Beach brought the first two copies of *Ulysses* back from the Gare de Lyon on February 2, 1922, she presented the first copy to Joyce as his birthday present. Then she placed the other in the window of Shakespeare and Company, where a crowd formed to see it.

〜

Hemingway convinced Sylvia Beach, with whom he became great friends, that he had received his war wound from fighting in Italy, that "they thought he was done for," and that it had taken two years in a military hospital for him to recover. He also convinced Beach that his father had died "in tragic circumstances" while Ernest was still "a boy in short pants," leaving Ernest a gun as his sole legacy and forcing him to drop out of school to support his dependent mother and siblings by money earned in boxing matches.[10] It was a good story but a complete fabrication, including the death of Ernest's father, who was not doing well but was still alive. Yet Hemingway was convincing in his inventions, and may have convinced himself as well.

Early visitors to Shakespeare and Company were Gertrude Stein and Stein's partner, Alice B. Toklas. After that initial meeting, Beach saw the two of them often, either at Shakespeare and Company or at their Rue de Fleurus atelier, near the Luxembourg Gardens. According to Stein, "Sylvia Beach was very enthusiastic about Gertrude Stein and they became friends. [Stein] was Sylvia Beach's first annual subscriber [to Shakespeare and Company's lending library], and Sylvia Beach was proportionately proud and grateful."[11]

Gertrude Stein may have been an early subscriber to Beach's lending library, but certainly not the first: Stein did not show up at Shakespeare and Company until about four months after it opened, when the bookshop had already acquired about ninety members. In addition, despite Stein's conviction to the contrary, Beach's gratitude knew bounds: according to Beach, Gertrude Stein's "subscription was merely a friendly gesture," since "she took little interest, of course, in any but her own books." In addition, on their first meeting, Gertrude tried to put Beach on the spot by indignantly asking why she didn't carry titles such as *The Trail of the Lonesome Pine* and *The Girl of the Limberlost*—a humiliating experience for Beach, who had tried to stock all the works of Gertrude Stein she could put her hands on and, in any case, did not carry *The Trail of the Lonesome Pine*. Alice, in Beach's view, "was grown up: Gertrude was a child, something of an infant prodigy."[12]

Beach, according to Stein, "later stopped coming to the house."[13] It was not surprising. After the publication of *Ulysses*, Beach became, in the words of the writer and literary critic Eugene Jolas, "probably the best known woman in Paris."[14] Even if this was something of an exaggeration, Beach certainly had become as well known as Gertrude Stein—an affront that Gertrude Stein would not have taken lightly.

Worse yet, Beach had achieved her fame by publishing James Joyce's *Ulysses*, and Gertrude Stein emphatically did not care for James Joyce or *Ulysses*. After *Ulysses* appeared, Stein even came with Alice to announce that, as a consequence, they had transferred their membership from Shakespeare and Company to the American Library (then located across the Seine, near the Elysée Palace).

Stein's touchiness about Joyce may have stemmed, at least in part, from her irritation at being linked with him as a modernist writer, despite her conviction of their fundamental differences. But at the core, she seethed because she had been first, and because she had the unshakable conviction that she was better. Joyce "is a *good* writer," she condescendingly remarked on one occasion, adding that "people like him because he is incomprehensible and anybody can understand him." In case her audience (in this case, the American writers Samuel Putnam and Wambly Bald) missed the point, she asked, "But who came first, Gertrude Stein or James Joyce? Do not forget that my first great book, *Three Lives*, was published in 1908. That was long before *Ulysses*." And then, in a final dismissal, she pronounced that "his influence, however, is local. Like Synge, another Irish writer, he has had his day."[15]

"If you brought up Joyce twice, you would not be invited back," Hemingway wrote. "It was like mentioning one general favorably to another general. You learned not to do it the first time."[16] Perhaps the only one who managed it was the American novelist and journalist Elliot Paul, a shy and engaging fellow who somehow remained friends with both Stein and Joyce, and who even spoke favorably about Joyce within Stein's hearing. A friend of Paul's reported such an occasion with amazement, adding that "to talk about Joyce in Gertrude's salon was rushing in where angels feared to tread, but . . . if anyone else had dared praise Joyce to [Gertrude and Alice's] faces they would have read the Riot Act forthwith." Instead, Stein firmly but graciously brought the conversation to a close with the comment that "Joyce and I are at opposite poles, but our work comes to the same thing, the creation of something new."[17]

Much later, Sylvia Beach saw Joyce and Stein in separate corners at the same tea party. "They had never met," she explained, "so, with their mutual consent, I introduced them to each other and saw them shake hands quite peacefully."[18] Gertrude Stein described the occasion in especially flat terms: "We have never met," she told Joyce, "and he said no although our names are always together, and then we talked of Paris and where we lived and why we lived where we lived and that was all."[19]

As it happened, of all the modern writers, Gertrude Stein preferred Proust. But for reading enjoyment, she had no intention of sticking with Proust or any members of the literary set, past or present. She enjoyed detective stories.

It was Gertrude Stein who came up with the name the "Lost Generation," the phrase that came to describe the growing throng of literary and artistic expatriates in 1920s Paris. According to Hemingway's recollection, she decided on it after she had taken her old Model T Ford in for repairs and had not been satisfied with the attention that the repairman, a young former military man, had given it. It was his boss who first used the phrase, reprimanding the young man as one of a *génération perdue* (lost generation). In recounting the story to Hemingway, Stein told him, "That's what you all are. . . . All of you young people who served in the war. You are a lost generation."

Hemingway protested, but she insisted. "You have no respect for anything," she told him. "You drink yourselves to death." When Hemingway continued to protest, she retorted, "Don't argue with me, Hemingway. . . . It does no good at all. You're all a lost generation, exactly as the garage keeper said."

Afterward, Hemingway angrily thought of those who had suffered during and from the war, and just as angrily mused, "Who is calling who a lost generation?" And then he reminded himself of how good a friend Stein had been. Still, the conversation rankled: "The hell with her lost-generation talk," he thought, "and all the dirty, easy labels."[20]

After he got home, he told Hadley about it and then said, "You know, Gertrude *is* nice, anyway." When Hadley agreed, he added, "But she does talk a lot of rot sometimes."[21]

Early on, Hemingway had to decide what was useful in the advice that Gertrude Stein so readily gave, and what was not. He first met Stein in March 1922, after his return from Switzerland. He sent his letter of introduction from Sherwood Anderson, and she promptly responded, inviting him and Hadley to tea the following afternoon. As Hadley would soon learn, tea at 27 Rue de Fleurus meant tea for Ernest only, or at least tea with Gertrude; Alice took charge of all wives, in whom Gertrude had no interest whatever.

Yet it still was a remarkable occasion for both Hemingways. Gertrude no longer held her Saturday-evening salons, but her afternoon teas with smaller groups, held in her art-filled atelier, were still memorable. The paintings—

Gertrude Stein posing for Jo Davidson, photo by Man Ray, circa 1922 © Man Ray Trust / Artists Rights Society (ARS), NY / ADAGP, Paris 2015. National Portrait Gallery, Smithsonian Institution / Art Resource, NY

among them, early Picassos and Cézannes, but no longer any Matisses (Gertrude's brother Michael and sister-in-law Sarah were rival Matisse patrons, and besides, Gertrude had long before had a falling out with Matisse)—struck Hemingway as being in a fine museum, "except that there was a big fireplace and it was warm and comfortable and they gave you good things to eat." Gertrude and Alice seemed to like Ernest and Hadley, too, treating them, as Hemingway put it, "as though we were very good, well mannered and promising children."[22] Soon Gertrude and Alice returned the visit, sitting on the mattress that was on the Hemingways' floor, where Gertrude held forth her opinion on the writing samples that Hemingway gave her.

She talked, and he listened; that was the way she preferred it, whether in long walks together in the Luxembourg Gardens, or at 27 Rue de Fleurus. Gertrude found him "a born listener"[23] and dispensed advice, which in the main instructed him to throw out what he had written and start over. Hemingway may not have paid attention to all she said—after all, no one was publishing her prose, either, which rankled her endlessly (she had been forced to finance all her publications to date). But prompted by these sessions, Hemingway did begin to analyze his own prose and what worked and did not work. In the process, he absorbed something from Gertrude Stein's writing as well as from Ezra Pound, another major influence during Hemingway's early Paris stay.

Pound, born in Idaho when it was still Idaho Territory, and transplanted to Pennsylvania while still a young child, had acquired some cosmopolitan fine-tuning at the age of thirteen, when he traveled to Europe with his mother and aunt. Having already specialized in Latin at his military academy, he was admitted to the University of Pennsylvania at the age of fifteen, already determined to be a poet.

Years in London as foreign editor of several American literary magazines brought him into contact with some of the most up-and-coming young writers and poets of the day, and he took particular pride in his discovery of T. S. Eliot and James Joyce, all the while writing and publishing his own poetry and literary criticism. He also married the daughter of W. B. Yeats's former lover and became friends with Yeats.

But the war had left Pound disillusioned with just about everything, as it did so many of his generation, and in 1921 he left London for Paris, where he became part of the emerging Surrealist literary scene and spent much of his time building furniture—for his apartment and for the bookstore of his good friend Sylvia Beach. He also continued to publish his own poetry and help shepherd others' literature and poetry into publication, including T. S. Eliot's *The Wasteland* (published in the autumn of 1922), which Pound edited significantly, tightening and reducing it by at least a third.

Despite Ernest Hemingway's initial hesitation (he at first found Pound artsy and pompous), Pound soon became Hemingway's close friend and literary guide. "Ezra was the most generous writer I have ever known," Hemingway later wrote of his mentor. "He helped poets, painters, sculptors and prose writers that he believed in and he would help anyone whether he believed in them or not if they were in trouble."[24] Pound advised Hemingway on what to read (in what amounted to a three-year course in the classics) and helped him into print. Most importantly, he gave advice on Hemingway's writing—emphasizing tightness and precision—and introduced him everywhere as a promising young writer, a future literary star. Hemingway, in turn, followed Pound's literary advice and tried to teach Pound to box.

Hemingway's time with Gertrude Stein and Ezra Pound was brief: he and Stein only overlapped in Paris for about six weeks during Hemingway's first year and a half there, and he had only about six months with Pound, followed by brief visits and correspondence in subsequent years. During "these early restless years after the war," as Stein put it,[25] everyone was on the move. Pound soon left for Italy, and Gertrude departed with Alice for the countryside, where she remained for the rest of the year.

Hemingway was also on the move, always restless, leaving for Genoa in April (to cover the economic conference), Switzerland in May (where he and Hadley joined a friend in hiking over the St. Bernard Pass), Milan in June (where he interviewed Mussolini), and a Black Forest walking tour in August. In September, Hemingway left for Constantinople, to cover the Greco-Turkish War, and November brought him to Lausanne, where he reported on the conference renegotiating the treaty imposed on the Ottoman Empire (now Turkey) after the war. Hadley joined him in Switzerland for Christmas, after which came a dizzying succession of destinations in Italy and Germany, followed by their first trip to Spain. He would have gone to Russia and Ireland if he had had his way, but Hadley put her foot down.

All the while, Hemingway continued to write his fiction, even while he proved his physical prowess and established his image as a tough guy embarked on a never-ending round of sports, from skiing, hiking, and sledding to biking, fishing, and boxing. He went to horse races and played the ponies, and soon he would go to bullfights in Pamplona, which he would integrate into his first published novel, *The Sun Also Rises*. But this novel would not take shape in his head for a long while, and in the meantime Hemingway suffered rejection after rejection. Still, despite the rebuffs, he was making headway with his writing, tightening his sentences, shaping his paragraphs, and jettisoning formulas and sentimentality. By summer, he received his first acceptances—not for his short stories, but for several poems.

It was a start, however small. But the setbacks at year's end were enormous. First, Hadley lost his manuscripts—short stories, poems, and an unfinished novel. She was bringing them to Switzerland as a surprise so he could work on them there, but en route the suitcase containing them was stolen.

And then, early the following year, they learned that Hadley was pregnant. "I am too young to be a father," Gertrude Stein reported Hemingway telling her "with great bitterness."[26] Whether or not Gertrude could be entirely trusted on the subject of marriage and children, which she found tiresome, this is how she remembered the scene—including her attempt to console Ernest before sending him on his way.

That November, Proust died. He was fifty-one, and despite a long history of poor health, his death came as a shock. He had continued to work on *A la recherche* until his death, even though (according to his housekeeper, Céleste Albaret) he wrote "The End" on it early in the spring of 1922, and his biographer William Carter argues for a date falling somewhere between 1916 and 1919.[27]

One night, Proust told Céleste that he wanted his work "to be a sort of cathedral in literature. That is why it is never finished." Even after construction is complete, he told her, there is always something else to add.[28]

Proust had made one of his last public appearances at the Beaumonts' lavish New Year's Eve costume ball at the beginning of the year. Well before the event, he wrote the Count de Beaumont to ask if the house would be warm. On the day of the ball he followed this with a letter telling Beaumont that he was determined to come despite his weakened condition, and requesting "a cup of boiling-hot tea on arrival." He also requested that Beaumont not introduce him "to too many intellectual and fatiguing ladies."[29] Céleste also called ("for the tenth time," as Beaumont told Jean Hugo), to make certain that there would be no air currents in the room and that the tea (a tisane of *tilleul*) had been prepared properly, according to the recipe she had sent. Presumably Beaumont met all of these requirements satisfactorily, for after Proust's typically late arrival, he stayed for the duration. He looked ill, though, according to Hugo, who had not seen him since 1917 and was struck by his pale and swollen face.[30]

Cocteau was one of the earliest visitors to view Proust's body, and with the permission of Proust's brother, Dr. Robert Proust, he telephoned Man Ray to take a photograph—one print for the family, one for Cocteau, and a third for himself, if he wanted. Nothing for the press. As it happened, the picture unexpectedly appeared in what Man Ray called "a smart magazine," with another photographer credited. Man Ray demanded a correction, but instead, the editor merely said that Man Ray claimed the work as his.

Proust's funeral Mass (he had been baptized Catholic) was held in Saint-Pierre de Chaillot, and he was subsequently buried with his parents in Père-Lachaise cemetery. Among the mourners was James Joyce. Their one meeting, at a late-night dinner party the previous May, had merely resulted in a desultory exchange (Joyce complaining of his headaches and his eyes, Proust in turn complaining of his digestion) and a subsequent taxi ride in which Joyce, by this time drunk, horrified Proust by flinging open the window. It was something of a social disaster, but neither seemed to care one way or the other. Proust and Joyce had never shown any interest in the other, nor in the other's writing. Yet Joyce still came to pay his respects at Proust's funeral.

As for the deathbed photo, no one ever discovered who sent it.

Man Ray was photographing more and more celebrities that year, including James Joyce, whom Sylvia Beach herded into Man Ray's studio for an official author's photo just before *Ulysses* was about to come off the press. The photo, with Joyce looking downward, head on hand, was a success, but few at the time knew that Joyce was protecting his deteriorating eyes from the bright studio lights.[31]

Man Ray had already photographed Cocteau and Picasso, and now he photographed Picasso again, this time with his young son Paolo. He also photographed Henri Matisse (looking like a doctor, with his gold-rimmed spectacles) as well as Picabia, at the wheel of one of his fast cars. Soon other writers and artists, including Satie, Hemingway, Ezra Pound, Joan Miró, Georges Braque, and Juan Gris, found their way to Man Ray's studio, and in due course their portraits appeared on the walls of Shakespeare and Company, for whom Man Ray became the unofficial portraitist.

He had by 1922 established himself in commercial as well as artistic circles: *Vanity Fair* published his work and in April gave him a full-page spread, while Dada embraced him, as did the emerging Surrealist movement, which—under the breakaway leadership of Breton, Aragon, and Soupault—was beginning to take Dada's place. Man Ray designed the cover of the first (March 1922) issue of the revived *Littérature* review, which had briefly died and then reemerged as a Surrealist magazine, and it was for *Littérature* that, in 1924, he would take his memorable picture of a violin superimposed on Kiki's bare backside, titled *Le Violon d'Ingres*.

Gertrude Stein, of course, was curious about this new face, "a little man who sat in the corner" at a party given by American friends of hers. He seemed interesting, and so she and Alice visited him in his tiny studio, which impressed her with its organization. "He had a bed, he had three large cameras, he had several kinds of lighting, he had a window screen, and in a little closet he did all his developing."[32] He showed them pictures he had taken of Duchamp and others and asked if he might come and take pictures of Gertrude and of her studio. Gertrude agreed, and she was so pleased with the results (a photo of Gertrude and Alice at home, in their picture-filled atelier)[33] that more sessions followed. He would photograph Gertrude Stein for the next ten years, until they had a major falling-out over money (she expected a considerable discount in his fees, which were high; they were "all struggling artists," she curtly informed him).[34] The last photographs he took of her, where he told her to move all she liked, turned out to be, in her words, "extraordinarily interesting."[35]

Success had many benefits. Man Ray was now able to publish a limited edition of his Rayographs, which he titled *Les Champs délicieux* (*The Delightful Fields*). He also moved from his hotel room to a two-tiered combined studio and living space at 31 bis Rue Campagne-Première. The new place was still small, but the building was a treasure, covered with colored ceramic tile and a wealth of detail, and Man Ray was pleased with it, especially as he was soon sharing his space with Kiki.

He and Kiki had become lovers soon after they met in late 1921, shortly after Kiki agreed to pose for him. She had already become a popular model in Montparnasse, as much for her jaunty good humor as for her beauty, but now that she was with Man Ray, she would no longer pose for painters. Instead, she worked with Man Ray in more than forty photographic sessions over the coming years, their eight-year love affair and professional collaboration becoming a byword for 1920s Montparnasse.

While Man Ray was finding happiness with Kiki, Le Corbusier had begun to live with Yvonne Gallis, the woman he would eventually marry. He had met her at the couture house of Jove, where she was a saleswoman and model when he exhibited his paintings there in 1918. Yvonne was from Monaco, dark haired and vivacious—an essential balance for Le Corbusier's intellectualism, coldness, and zealotry. She embodied the Mediterranean spirit he yearned for, and he adored her. Of course he kept her existence a secret from his straitlaced parents, who would not have approved of a live-in girlfriend, but Yvonne would always remain out of the public eye, even after their marriage.

That same year, Le Corbusier altered his professional relationships as well, elevating his talented but once-disparaged cousin, Pierre Jeanneret, to the position of partner. It would never be an equal partnership: Le Corbusier would provide the genius and the imagination, while Jeanneret would contribute the necessary managerial skills. But the two worked well together, just as Yvonne and Le Corbusier complemented each other at home. "One day in 1922," Le Corbusier later wrote, he mentioned to Jeanneret the life-changing experience he had at the fifteenth-century monastery, the Charterhouse of the Valley of Ema, near Florence: "I believe I've never encountered such a joyous version of habitation," he recollected. Immediately he and Pierre were on the same wavelength. Responding jointly, "on the back of a restaurant menu we spontaneously sketched our 'villa apartments': the idea was born."[36]

That autumn, Le Corbusier exhibited at the Salon d'Automne the scheme for the mass-produced Maison Citrohan that he and Ozenfant had developed, with its shoe-box shape and two-story living room lit by sunshine streaming through a wall of glass. With this design in mind, Le Corbusier again likened a house to a machine, albeit "a machine to live in."[37] At the same exhibit, Le Corbusier presented the drawings, plans, and models for a city of three million, using glass, concrete, and steel to create a modern metropolis based on the vision he had first glimpsed at the Valley of Ema. He essentially agreed with those such as the Paris historian Jules Bertaut who complained of "an orgy of tumult and speed which makes it impossible to cross the street in safety."[38] Observing the impact of the automobile on Paris, Le Corbusier mused, "It is into this tight network, locked in, infinitely fragmented, that modern speeds, twenty and thirty times increased, are thrust. It's useless to describe the crisis, the disorder."[39] But while Bertaut was content to blame the postwar "desire to live rapidly,"[40] Le Corbusier sought solutions, envisioning limited-access expressways replacing traditional streets, and widely spaced high-rise buildings surrounded by park areas supplanting dense housing, murky alleyways, and dismal courtyards.

He was also designing and building a residence for Amédée Ozenfant, who had recently received a substantial inheritance and could now afford a five-story studio house on the southern edge of Montparnasse, between the Montsouris reservoir and Parc Montsouris. Creating a slim, upward-thrusting edifice topped by a double-peaked roof of angled skylights (the skylights are now gone), Le Corbusier incorporated the most modern of amenities, including a garage (an unusual provision in 1922) and a full-sized bathroom for the housekeeper as well as similar provision for the owner. An upward adaptation of the Citrohan plan to a corner site, the Villa Ozenfant was and remains clean lined, airy, and inviting.

The residence and studio designed and built by Le Corbusier for his partner, Amédée Ozenfant, Paris. © J. McAuliffe

That May, Isadora Duncan considerably startled the dance world by getting married. What astonished anyone who knew Isadora was her willingness to marry at all, since for years she had denounced marriage and had flatly refused to marry Gordon Craig or Paris Singer, the fathers of her two children.

Adding to the improbability of her marriage, the man she married, the brilliant young Russian poet Sergei Esenin, was eighteen years her junior and already well on his way to madness and alcoholic self-destruction. But Duncan, who saw in him a resemblance to the cherubic son she had lost years before in a freak auto accident in Paris, was immediately charmed and protective. She spoke no Russian and he no English, but that did not seem to matter—at least, not at first. Unfortunately, he soon began to treat her with contempt. Her foster daughter, Irma Duncan, recalled that "he was a wayward, willful, little child, and she was a mother passionately enough in love with him to overlook and forgive all the vulgar curses and the peasant blows."[41]

Isadora later explained that the marriage took place because she was about to embark on yet another tour of the United States and wanted to bring Esenin with her. "I am absolutely, unutterably and vehemently opposed to all legalized marriage," she wrote in her memoirs, but "was forced into marriage by the silly laws of the lands I had to travel through as an artist. I married my husband to get him past the customs officers."[42]

Unfortunately, disaster lay ahead.

That spring, much to his surprise, Stravinsky had a flop. *Mavra*, his opéra bouffe premiered by the Ballets Russes at the Paris Opéra, was one of his earliest Neoclassical works and may have represented an important stage in his development, but the public, which (according to Darius Milhaud) "had taken ten years to swallow *Le Sacre*, was scandalized by [*Mavra*'s] simplicity."[43]

Another scandal erupted earlier that same year when the pianist Jean Wiéner gave the first Paris performance of the complete *Pierrot Lunaire* by Arnold Schoenberg, with Darius Milhaud conducting. Due to the work's difficulty, it took twenty-five rehearsals to bring everyone up to speed, but even though *Pierrot Lunaire* was by that time a decade old and had been premiered in Berlin in 1912 (requiring forty rehearsals on that occasion), Paris audiences and critics alike were outraged. Not that anyone claimed that *Pierrot Lunaire* was easy listening: atonal and performed to instrumental accompaniment in *Sprechstimme* style (between singing and speaking), it clearly was a challenge, and Wiéner undertook to educate his audiences by multiple performances throughout the late winter and early spring. Adding to the difficulty, the criticism that boiled up in the press had a nasty chauvinist and anti-Semitic tinge (such as one critic's reference to "alien concerts" organized by "musical Dadaists" supported in their "intrigues" by "cosmopolitan fools")[44] and was quickly dubbed "l'affaire des poisons."[45] Schoenberg, after all, was Jewish, as were Wiéner and Milhaud. Ravel, Albert Roussel, André Caplet, and Roland-Manuel wrote a collective open letter of protest to *Le Courrier musical*, which had carried one of the most virulent of the reviews, and concluded with the hope "that patriotism err a bit less in an area where it has nothing to gain, but everything to lose."[46]

While Jean Wiéner was shaking up musical Paris, he continued his piano gig at Le Boeuf sur le Toit, which opened in January on the Rue Boissy d'Anglas under the gaze of a huge eye, Picabia's *L'Oeil cacodylate* (*The Poisonous Eye*), a Dadaist creation that Picabia's friends and associates completed by scrawling across its surface with graffiti-like comments. (Jean Hugo, who could think of nothing to say, simply signed his name and murmured, "Voilà!" At which, Picabia told him to add *Voilà!* to his signature.)[47] Le Boeuf, which had already achieved success at a different location and under a different name (Le Gaya), quickly became a sensation. "Two vast families were formed there," Maurice Sachs recalled, "the celebrated one, which occupied the tables and gave us a daily spectacle, [and] the obscure one of enchanted spectators who were modestly grouped about the bar."[48]

Shortly before Le Boeuf officially opened, an elite group of regulars, including the Picassos, Marie Laurencin, Cocteau, Radiguet, Brancusi, and the colorful Welsh artist and writer Nina Hamnett, gathered there to chat and drink champagne. According to Hamnett (who long before had established her bohemian bona fides by a liaison with Modigliani as well as with a number of other artists), the evening was "an enormous success." After the party broke up, she left for Montparnasse with Radiguet and Brancusi, who suddenly was struck with the idea of going to Marseilles—immediately.

Hamnett didn't believe him and went home, but as she tells the story, Brancusi and Radiguet, "the latter still in his dinner jacket, took a train for Marseilles a few hours later, without baggage, just as they were."[49] From there, they bought some clothes at a sailors' shop and went on to Corsica, where they remained for two weeks. Cocteau, who eventually received a telegram from the pair saying that they were having a splendid time and might or might not return, was upset by Radiguet's abrupt flight, although somewhat mollified by Hamnett's reminder that Radiguet was "quite safe" in Brancusi's care, since Brancusi's tastes ran to the heterosexual. Still, heterosexual adventures were just as possible and just as alarming, and when the runaway returned to Paris two weeks later, Cocteau received him coldly and never mentioned the incident again.

Despite tensions between the two, Radiguet proceeded to write most of his second novel (*Le Bal du Comte d'Orgel*) that summer and autumn, while Cocteau produced a volume of poetry (*Plain-Chant*), two short novels (*Le Grand Écart* and *Thomas l'Imposteur*), and an adaptation of Sophocles's *Antigone* (yet another manifestation of postwar Neoclassicism). His *Antigone* opened in late December at the Théâtre de l'Atelier in Montmartre, with music by Honegger, scenery by Picasso, and costumes by Chanel. Cocteau's range and sheer productivity, as well as the contrast between these works and the previous year's *Les Mariés de la Tour Eiffel*, was boggling. Maurice Sachs wrote that young men of the time "were so smitten by Cocteau's work and were so under his spell, that . . . one heard tales of some of them scaling the lamp-posts in the Rue d'Anjou to see Cocteau leave his house."[50]

Ravel, happily ensconced in his new residence in Montfort l'Amaury, was starting work on a commission he had received from Serge Koussevitzky to orchestrate Mussorgsky's *Pictures at an Exhibition*. Koussevitzky would soon replace Pierre Monteux as music director of the Boston Symphony Orchestra; but now, having only recently left the Soviet Union for Paris, he had organized the Paris Concerts Koussevitzky, specializing in presenting new works by composers such as Ravel, Stravinsky, and Prokofiev. Ravel's orchestration of *Pictures* would become the definitive version, a beloved staple in orchestra concerts for years to come.

Marie Curie, back from her exhausting tour of the United States, was once again at work in her laboratory, for which Sarah Bernhardt gave a benefit performance in the autumn—one of the last performances of her life. Although Curie was not a joiner, she did believe wholeheartedly in the mission of the League of Nations and accepted an appointment to its Commission on Intellectual Cooperation, on which she actively participated for more than a decade.

Reaching for new worlds to conquer, André Citroën had already demonstrated his cross-country Citroën-Kégresse half-track caterpillar car at a snow trial in the Alps, followed by a demonstration under the supervision of the French military. The value of a vehicle that could travel with low horsepower and equally low fuel requirements over sand, snow, or mud opened up dazzling military and trade possibilities, especially in France's new colonies in Africa and the Far East. To prove this conclusively, Citroën in late 1922 mounted the first crossing of the Sahara Desert by motor vehicle. Not surprisingly, the colorful four-thousand-mile crossing through trackless dessert, from Touggourt, in Algeria, to Timbuktu and back, captivated a worldwide audience.

Citroën may have been a gambler in his after-hours nightlife, but he was nothing but exacting in his preparations for this undertaking, which in his mind was an industrial rather than a romantic venture, in which nothing was left to chance. Twenty days after leaving Touggourt, ten intrepid men and their five strange-looking vehicles (painted white to resist the sun's heat, and bearing emblems taken from Egyptian mythology) triumphantly entered Timbuktu. With typical foresight, Citroën had equipped the expedition with its own filming equipment and cinematographer, in addition to a geographer and interpreter (the film, when completed, would be shown as a headline event in all the major capitals of Europe). Citroën also furnished the expedition with rifles and machine guns, with which the convoy protected itself by night, drawing up around a campfire—Wild West style—with its heavy guns pointing outward.

En route back, the party was met by Citroën himself and his equally fearless wife, who arrived in their own caterpillar cars and brought champagne. More than five hundred men on camels awaited the party in Touggourt, where the caterpillar cars arrived twelve weeks after starting out. In practical terms, Citroën had demonstrated that his cars could cross four thousand miles of sand in the same amount of time that it took a camel to cross merely one hundred. And in the process, he had created a bonanza of favorable publicity.

Renault would not allow himself to be left behind, and in early 1923 he mounted his own expedition, this one from Algeria to the Niger railway system. But instead of caterpillar-tracked vehicles, Renault used six-wheelers to cross the sands—a feat which he followed with a crossing by a single small six-horsepower Renault. Citroën responded with a five-horsepower car of his own making, and the competition between the two automakers continued to escalate.

Meanwhile, affairs between France and its allies had deteriorated further by year's end as France, under the leadership of Poincaré, and solidly backed by the right wing in Parliament, prepared to exact reparations by occupying Germany's industrial Ruhr, a move that Clemenceau roundly condemned.

The Germans declared that they were unable to pay, especially in the face of runaway inflation. Yet France was aggrieved when German industry, which unlike France's had suffered little war damage, regularly defaulted on its mandated shipments of raw materials, especially coal and timber. In addition, throughout 1922, France's allies refused to forgive its own war debts, while at the same time the growth of protectionism was closing American markets to French goods.

Poincaré may have preferred nonmilitary sanctions, but French right-wing anger and activism were growing. Throughout the year, Léon Daudet had denounced Bolshevism and what he called "Anglo-German-Jewish capital" to large, cheering crowds. It was Daudet who called the Treaty of Versailles "absurd"[51] and who, early in the year, helped to maneuver Briand (who had expressed willingness to reduce Germany's indemnity) out of the premiership and bring in Poincaré, whom Daudet and Maurras believed was more receptive to their views. Both certainly hailed Poincaré when, under his leadership, the French refused all concessions on disarmament and reparations.

Assisting Daudet and Maurras in their right-wing campaigns was François Coty, who in 1922 used a small portion of his by-now enormous wealth to buy the newspaper, *Le Figaro*. Coty, who yearned to play a major role in politics and countenanced no opposition within his organization, quickly changed *Le Figaro*'s name to *Figaro* and its political leanings from moderately conservative to far right.

It may have seemed an unusual step for a perfumer, but by now Coty had become an unquestionably wealthy and influential man. In 1922, despite challenges at home, especially from Chanel, but also from perfumers such as Guerlain and Lanvin, he formed Coty Inc., which would soon be listed on the New York Stock Exchange. The American press still called Coty the "king of perfumes." After all, Coty's factories were now producing one hundred thousand boxes of powder per day, and his clients numbered in the millions. Although he spent hugely, his fortune remained one of the largest in the world. As an impressively successful businessman, Coty now determined to shape public opinion in the direction he wanted.

While Coty was pursuing his right-wing vision, L'Oréal's by-now wealthy founder, Eugène Schueller—whose only child, Liliane, was born that same year—was developing a business model, and implicitly a world model, that was ostensibly benevolent and paternalistic, but fundamentally authoritarian. By the 1930s, this authoritarian streak would lead him to support a violent right-wing and fascist-leaning organization called La Cagoule.

It was a disturbing trend, especially as in late October, Benito Mussolini (whose National Fascist party by mid-1922 claimed more than half a million members) legitimately became prime minister of Italy, following his dramatic March on Rome—a historic event that was financed, at least in part, by Mussolini's great admirer, François Coty.[52]

The Boeuf sur le Toit, at its current Rue du Colisée location, Paris. © J. McAuliffe

CHAPTER EIGHT

~

A Death in Paris

(1923)

The year opened quite literally with a bang, when Germaine Berton shot and killed Marius Plateau, secretary of the League of Action Française and head of the Camelots du Roi, Action Française's division of young right-wing militants and street brawlers. Berton had in fact been looking for better-known targets, such as Léon Daudet or Charles Maurras, but settled for Plateau when she could not find either of the others.

The Camelots du Roi, formed to provide protection for Action Française and its activities, were widely feared bully boys. Blisteringly nationalist, anti-republican, and anti-Semitic, they could be quickly mobilized and unleashed, usually for violence. Berton, a young anarchist, returned violence for violence, and then turned the gun on herself—as it happened, unsuccessfully.

The Camelots du Roi had already spent several raucous days working over antigovernment protestors after French troops, with the support of Belgium, had marched on the Ruhr, seizing its industrial wealth. This military enforcement of reparations was temporarily effective but soon ran afoul of world opinion when the German mark went into free fall and French soldiers forcefully confronted thousands of German workers who were staging slowdowns. In the ensuing fracas, French soldiers shot more than one hundred resisting German workers.

Instead of becoming the bargaining lever that Poincaré had hoped for, France's occupation of the Ruhr soon became a millstone, especially since the heavily militarized occupation appeared to be an attempt to move back Germany's western border by establishing a French-controlled state there.

The United States was not interested in reducing France's debts or in providing capital for reconstruction, while the Bank of England went to Berlin's rescue, enabling Germany to set up a new currency and a more viable budget. In addition, although no one at the time may have paid much attention, in Munich, Adolf Hitler was stirring up crowds galvanized by France's occupation, which angry Germans viewed as imperialist expansion.

Action Française thrived in this overheated atmosphere. It now had three hundred chapters with thirty thousand members, and its journal, *Action Française*, had one hundred thousand subscribers, with additional numbers for its student and rural publications. French occupation of the Ruhr may have unsettled world opinion, but it struck a chord with nationalists at home, especially after the murder of Plateau, whose death *Action Française* blamed on German Bolsheviks. Germaine Berton seems to have been motivated by a stew of anger about everything from the 1914 assassination of socialist leader Jean Jaurès to what she termed "the new war in the Ruhr."[1] But her action resulted in widespread attacks on left-wing targets, including two newspapers whose premises were vandalized. And it certainly did not help the prospects of Marcel Cachin, founder (in 1920) of the French Communist party and communist deputy to the National Assembly. Subsequently, he was stripped of his parliamentary immunity and jailed on the grounds of plotting to overthrow the government.

While all this was going on, Count Harry Kessler returned to Paris and unexpectedly ran into Misia Sert and Diaghilev at a concert by Satie and Poulenc. It was their first encounter since the war, and they were all "deeply moved," he recorded in his diary, adding that "Misia could hardly speak." Two days later he went to see Misia and her husband, José-Maria Sert, and she again said how she was moved "nearly to tears" when she met Kessler so unexpectedly. "During the war," she told him, "you represented for us the image of the other side. We thought of you when one said: Germany." Later, Cocteau told him that Misia had not only been moved by the encounter, but also disturbed and embarrassed. In any case, Kessler noted, "it was a strange conversation."[2]

At Kessler's subsequent lunch with Cocteau, "there was of course a good deal of discussion about the Ruhr occupation." Cocteau deplored it, but Kessler was keenly aware that Cocteau "could not do much else, with myself present." On a subsequent occasion, Kessler tried to convince British journalist Henry William Massingham that many French "genuinely want reparations and real security (not imperialist expansion)" but was not able to persuade him.[3]

Kessler also visited the writer and poet Pierre Jean Jouve, who mused that "France's tragedy is to be a second-class nation which by every means wishes to move up to first rank." Intellectually, Jouve added, "it is still in the first rank, but it clings to tradition to a startling degree." As examples, he cited French poetry, which he thought was currently looking to the sixteenth century for inspiration, whereas current French fiction was turning to the seventeenth. At this, Kessler recalled Cocteau's attempts at modernizing the sixteenth-century poet, du Bellay. He also recollected Satie, "who preens himself on a return to eighteenth-century music."[4]

Neither mentioned Cocteau's adaptation of Sophocles's *Antigone*, Stravinsky's *Pulcinella* (based on music by an eighteenth-century Italian composer), or Picasso's newfound Neoclassicism.

The war's long years of brutality and destruction had created a need for and receptivity to serenity in the arts—"discipline and order, clarity and humanity," as art historian Alfred Barr put it.[5] This widespread movement, expressed in art and architecture as well as in theater, literature, and music, referenced antiquity from Racine and Poussin to Ingres, but it especially found inspiration in Greek and Roman mythology. Picasso's Neoclassicism was a part of this postwar search for calm and order, and although he continued to paint Cubist works, such as his *Three Musicians* (1921), his contribution to Neoclassicism proved especially important.

Picasso's explorations in Neoclassicism also proved lucrative, as works such as *Woman in White* and *The Lovers* went down more easily with wealthy American buyers than had his earlier adventures in Cubism. His current dealer, Paul Rosenberg, preferred art that sold, especially at high prices, and Picasso certainly enjoyed his own growing fortune. By 1923, among other accouterments of the good life, he had acquired a chauffeur-driven car, a luxurious Panhard. He was not the only one among his successful artist colleagues with expensive autos: Braque had an Alfa Romeo, Derain owned a Bugatti, and Picabia was notorious for the number of racing cars he owned. Braque painted his Alfa Romeo bright red and sold it to Blaise Cendrars, who was a terror on the road—especially since, as a war amputee, he had only one arm. But Picasso, for his part, refused to drive. Anyone rich enough to afford a luxury car was, in his opinion, rich enough to afford a chauffeur.[6]

By this time, Picasso had grown distant from his socializing and perhaps boring wife, as reflected in the portraits he now painted of her. More affection and possibly even passion emanate from those works of this same period for which the wealthy American expatriate Sara Murphy served as his model.

Sara and her husband, Gerald, had arrived in Paris with their three children in 1921, where they immediately gravitated to the in-crowd. Both were from wealthy families: Sara's father made his money in high-quality printer's ink and had already divided his fortune among his children, providing Sara with a considerable annual income. Gerald's father was the prosperous owner of Mark Cross, the purveyor of expensive leather goods. Gerald had been a friend of Cole Porter's since their Yale days, and the Murphys immediately found friends in the Porter set, in addition to the high-society world of the avant-garde in which the Picassos starred.

Gerald Murphy had artistic talent, which Picasso soon spotted, and Sara was beautiful, which Picasso was not alone in recognizing. She and her husband were attractive and elegant, warm and affectionate, in addition to being wealthy and cultured. Soon they gathered around them their own brilliant set, including Americans such as Ernest Hemingway, Cole Porter, F. Scott Fitzgerald, and John Dos Passos, as well as prominent European artists, musicians, and writers, including Picasso, Cocteau, and Stravinsky, all of whom they supported and surrounded with affection. Liberated from their own controlling and restrictive families, Sara and Gerald had found freedom in each other and created a life, as Gerald put it, "loaded and fragrant with everything that is beautiful." Moreover, they shared this gift with those around them. "There was a shine to life where they were," as Archibald MacLeish later said of the Murphys. "Not a decorative *added* value but a kind of revelation of inherent loveliness."[7]

Yet life was not perfect for this golden couple, especially as Gerald became increasingly aware of his homosexuality. But Sara, who was deeply in love with him, seems not to have succumbed to advances from Picasso or anyone else. Instead, the Murphys filled their lives with art and with artistic friends. Gerald's painting brought him a recommendation to Diaghilev, who hired him and Sara (who also had been taking art lessons) to repair the Ballets Russes's sets. This in turn gave the Murphys access to Diaghilev's world, including Picasso, Braque, and Derain, whose scenery they were repairing. Soon Fernand Léger entered their lives as well, as a mentor for Gerald, whose increasingly monumental paintings focused on machines and machine parts—prompting Léger to call him "the only *American* painter in Paris."[8] By spring 1923, Gerald was ready to submit four of his works to the Salon des Independents, where he received favorable attention.

While Gerald Murphy was finding himself as a painter, Jean Renoir was contemplating a fundamental change in his life from the one his father had envisioned for him as a potter.

Jean Renoir had long been fascinated by American movies, especially those with Charlie Chaplin. But it was in 1923, after seeing *Le Brasier ardent* (*The Blazing Inferno*)—a film made in France by the Russian émigré Ivan Mosjoukine—that he had the idea of making movies himself. His wife remembered events differently, but Jean was insistent on the role this film played in his own development. "The film astounded me," he recalled. "I must have seen it at least ten times." It made him realize that "instead of idly criticizing the [French] public's supposed lack of sophistication, I sensed that I should try to reach it through the projection of authentic images in the tradition of French realism." To reach the realism and authenticity he wanted, he decided "to make a study of French gesture as reflected in my father's paintings."[9]

He insisted that he "set foot in the world of the cinema only in order to make my wife a star." Dédée was beautiful and had long dreamed of being a film star. She dressed like one and took delight when people stopped her in the street to ask what film they had seen her in. She and Jean had even come up with a stage name for her, Catherine Hessling. The outcome was their first film together, a silent black-and-white one, as they all were then, called *Catherine, ou une vie sans joie* (*Catherine, or A Life without Joy*), which Jean financed and for which he shared writing duties for the screenplay. Naturally, Catherine starred. She played an innocent young servant who falls in love with her employer's son and is pursued by a villain. The whole thing was a "masterpiece of banality," Renoir recalled. Completed in 1924, it was, in his words, "a total failure" and never was shown in any theaters.[10]

But, he added, "the bug of film-directing had now taken root in me, and there was no resisting it."[11]

By this time, another bug—the bug of collecting—had taken hold of a wealthy American, Dr. Albert C. Barnes, and there were few who could resist his determined (many said relentless) passion.

Dr. Barnes, a forceful and often alienating personality, had made his millions by inventing and marketing an antiseptic called Argyrol that treated gonorrhea. Raised in a working-class family with little time or money for anything but the basics of getting by, Barnes became interested in art through a high school friend, William Glackens, who became a successful artist. In 1911, soon after Barnes became a millionaire, he gave Glackens a commission to go to Paris and buy contemporary French art for him. Those paintings that Glackens chose (including works by Cézanne, Renoir, Degas, Van Gogh, Monet, Gauguin, and Matisse) became the core of Barnes's collection.

Barnes soon visited Paris in person, where Glackens introduced him to a bevy of avant-garde artists and patrons. These included Gertrude and Leo Stein, through whom Barnes became acquainted with Matisse and Picasso. The voracious collector then acquired stellar examples of these painters' work, at prices he could and did boast about. After the war, Barnes continued his collecting spree. In addition to purchasing dozens of Renoirs, Cézannes, Picassos, and Matisses for the Philadelphia mansion he built specifically to display his collection, Barnes began to mop up works by Lipchitz, Kisling, Pascin, Marie Laurencin, and others.

And then, early in 1923, he spotted a painting by Chaim Soutine called *The Pastry Chef*. The painting hung in the gallery belonging to Paul Guillaume, who at the time was serving as Barnes's dealer and guide through the Paris art world. Intrigued, Barnes promptly bought all of Soutine's current work (at least twenty-five paintings). He could hardly have picked a more poverty-stricken and—until that moment—unknown painter.

Soutine, who had endured a childhood of grinding poverty just outside Minsk, had settled into more of the same in Paris, where he braved the rugged life at La Ruche before moving into a run-down atelier near the Gare Montparnasse—one that he shared, off and on, with his good friend Amedeo Modigliani. An acquaintance who once visited the two late one night recalled seeing them lying on the floor surrounded by a water-filled trench to ward off bedbugs. Each held a candle, by which Modigliani was reading Dante.

It was there in this studio that Kiki first met Soutine one freezing night, when he was burning what little furniture he had to keep warm. His prospects had not much improved by 1920, when the art critic Marcel Castaing and his wife Madeleine spotted his work and offered him one hundred francs for one of his paintings. The back room of the café where they met was dark, and Soutine—realizing that they could not have seen the painting clearly, and just as keenly aware that they knew he was impoverished—proudly refused the offer, retorting that he would have been happier if they had offered five francs.

The Castaings would eventually become Soutine's patrons and friends, but only after his fortunes had taken an abrupt turn for the better. In 1928, in fact, they would pay thirty thousand francs for a Soutine painting.

But it was Dr. Barnes who discovered Soutine, paying some sixty thousand francs (about three thousand dollars) for Soutine's total available output. According to stories that circulated soon after, Soutine celebrated this event by doing the first thing he could think of: he rushed into the street and hailed a taxi. "Where to?" the driver asked. "Why not the Riviera?" Soutine retorted. The driver was dubious, but Soutine flashed his wad of cash, and the taxi took off. In the end, the ride cost him only a fraction of the money he had received from Barnes.

Not surprisingly, word spread following the Barnes purchase, and Soutine's career took off. His paintings rose in price, and his story quickly became a legend, specifically a Montparnasse legend—one that had the additional charm of being at least partly true.

A highlight of that year's spring season was Stravinsky's ballet *Les Noces* (*The Wedding*). The composer—who had been working on the score of *Les Noces* for years—had decided on an unusual pared-down instrumentation of four pianos and six percussionists (drums, bells, and xylophone), along with a choir and four soloists, for his evocation of a primitive Russian wedding. Much to his approval, the choreographer, Bronislava Nijinska (Nijinsky's sister), focused on the corps de ballet rather than individual dancers, while the simple brown-and-white costumes and severe set were the creation of Natalya Goncharova (who was also the Murphys' art instructor, and who drafted them, along with their new friend, John Dos Passos, into painting the sets). Both audience and critics were enthusiastic; everyone agreed that *Les Noces* harkened back to the glory days of *The Rite of Spring*, and Stravinsky's *Mavra* now appeared, much to their relief, to be an aberration. Diaghilev himself was so moved when he first heard the music that he wept "and said it was the most beautiful and most purely Russian of all the creations of our Ballets Russes."[12] Stravinsky later said that it was because Diaghilev loved it so much that he dedicated it to him.

The Murphys' after-performance party was every bit as much of a success as the performance itself. After being rebuffed by the manager of the Cirque Medrano, which they originally thought would be the perfect place for the kind of relaxed modernist affair they wanted, Sara and Gerald settled on a converted barge located in front of the National Assembly. There, Sara—who had forgotten that because the party was on Sunday, no fresh flowers would be available—created a memorable substitute. Buying heaps of inexpensive toys at a Montparnasse bazaar, she arranged this cornucopia of dolls, trucks, and stuffed animals on the banquet table.

Picasso was enchanted with Sara's centerpiece and started to fiddle with the toys, rearranging them into a giant heap topped by a stuffed cow on the ladder of a fire truck. A variety of all-night escapades followed, lubricated by quantities of champagne, but Stravinsky definitely capped the evening by taking a running leap through the center of the huge laurel wreath held by *Les Noces* conductor Ernest Ansermet and Boris Kochno.

On a far more subdued note, Bronislava Nijinska's famous brother, Vaslav Nijinsky, had most surprisingly attended the opening performance of *Les Noces*. His doctors had thought it might bring him out of his long periods of silence. But Nijinsky, who had been institutionalized since 1919 as schizophrenic, gave no sign of recognition throughout the evening—even during the performance of *Petrushka*, in which he had once danced one of his most legendary roles.

~

There was a perfect crush of parties that spring. In late May, the Beaumonts gave one of their glittering costume balls, this one with the theme of antiquity in the era of Louis XIV. For entertainment, the Count de Beaumont looked to Cocteau, who came up with a divertissement that he called *La Statue retrouvée*, which he described as an imaginary supper party set in the world of Louis XIV–era fairy tales. Beaumont was able to summon the best of the best to carry out this frothy diversion: costumes by Picasso, choreography by Massine, and music by Satie. Stars included Olga Picasso and Winnaretta de Polignac's niece, the society belle Daisy Fellowes.

In addition to costume duty, Beaumont commissioned Picasso to paint four large panels to decorate the ballroom. Picasso, who envisioned an ensemble of classical scenes, only managed to complete one of these (his dealer, Paul Rosenberg, was unhappy about any commissions that brought little return to the artist and none to the dealer). But the one he completed was well worth all the evening's frivolity: a major Neoclassical work, his *Three Graces*.

Parties, especially at the Boeuf sur le Toit, continued almost nonstop throughout May and June, culminating in Milhaud's housewarming in early July, which everyone who was anyone attended, and where an array of trained birds provided diversion. The next night, Tristan Tzara presented an even more memorable event, his *Soirée du coeur à barbe* (*Evening of the Bearded Heart*)—an attempt to outshine the new Surrealist movement and revitalize Dada.

The evening began in deceptive calm, with the music of Stravinsky, Auric, Milhaud, and Satie, but began to get edgy with poetry readings, especially during some by Cocteau, during which someone continuously rang a bell. Peace was restored with the showing of an experimental film by Man Ray (*The Return to Reason*), in which images of Kiki's light-striped and nude torso appeared at the end of a series of moving Rayograph abstractions, such as "huge white pins crisscrossing and revolving in an epileptic dance, then again by a long thumbtack making desperate efforts to leave the screen."[13]

Man Ray recalled that the trouble began when his film broke, leaving the theater in darkness and leading to catcalls and fighting. Others remember that the heckling began during a performance of Tzara's Dadaist farce, *Le Coeur à gaz*. In any case, serious fighting did break out, leading to real injuries, and the theater was trashed. Lawsuits and countersuits followed, along with years of infighting. But majority opinion held that with this last great public manifestation, Dada had breathed its last, and Breton's Surrealists could now claim center stage.

At that, the *beau monde* left Paris for the summer. The previous summer, the Murphys had joined Cole and Linda Porter in Cap d'Antibes, a spot on the French Riviera that, until the Porters discovered it, was decidedly unfashionable and virtually deserted during the summer months. The Murphys returned, and soon the Picasso family joined them, as did Gertrude Stein and Alice B. Toklas.

Instead of Cap d'Antibes, the Porters headed to Venice for the summer of 1923, where they rented the glorious fourteenth-century Palazzo Barbaro on the Grand Canal. Their mode of travel had become equally luxurious: they reserved private compartments on the train for each of them, in addition to private compartments for Cole's valet and Linda's maid, with yet another for their own wardrobes and a sixth for a bar. Additional compartments were saved for guests, who traveled all expenses paid. By this time, Cole Porter had indirectly come into an inheritance from his grandfather. "True to his word," Porter later told an interviewer, "I wasn't mentioned in Grandfather's will. . . . But he left my mother over two million dollars, and she generously gave me half of it." In addition, his mother gave Porter another half when she inherited two million dollars more under the will's terms. Money may have been the bane of some people's existence, Porter later commented, but it certainly did not spoil his: "It simply made it wonderful."[14]

Unlike their friends the Murphys, whose Paris apartment overlooking the Seine was a clean-lined modernist expression of white walls and black floors, with modern furniture and minimal decoration, the Porters' new residence on posh Rue Monsieur—a twenty-room mansion built for the younger brother of Louis XVI—was unapologetically glamorous, with platinum wallpaper, zebra-skin rugs, and eighteenth-century furniture. But despite the Porters' increasing glamour, they mingled with the serious music crowd, especially Winnaretta de Polignac, whom they had met during their stays in Venice (she had purchased a palazzo there before the war) and had become frequent guests at her salon. It was Winnaretta who introduced Porter to Darius Milhaud, which led to a commission from Rolfe de Maré's Swedish Ballet.

De Maré had already given Milhaud the commission for an African-inspired ballet, *La Création du monde*, with costumes and set by Fernand Léger and scenario by Blaise Cendrars. Since the Milhaud ballet was short, de Maré was looking for another to go with it, and he had in mind one that was "American" (for the company's upcoming American tour) and shared *La Création*'s jazz influences. De Maré already had an idea for the subject: a young Swedish immigrant to America triumphs over difficulties and becomes a film star. Based on Léger's recommendation, De Maré signed up Gerald Murphy for sets and costumes. Murphy in turn proposed Porter's name for the score, and Milhaud (aware that Porter had "just the qualities that de Maré was looking for") introduced him to de Maré.[15] The result was *Within the Quota*, one of the earliest jazz-based compositions, which the composer Charles Koechlin orchestrated. It premiered to enthusiastic reviews in October at the Théâtre des Champs-Elysées, and the Swedish Ballet toured successfully with it that winter in America. Much to the delight of current-day Porter aficionados, *Within the Quota*'s jazz-based symphonic score preceded George Gershwin's *Rhapsody in Blue* by several months.

Despite the Porters' and the Murphys' discovery of the French Riviera as a summer destination, most of the fashionable avant-garde still spent the warm months relaxing along the coast of Normandy. That summer, Man Ray and Kiki joined a crowd at the Normandy villa that Peggy Guggenheim and her new husband, the sculptor and writer Laurence Vail, had rented.

Man Ray and Kiki were beginning to quarrel. In part, Kiki was bored with modeling ("Never again," she once cried to him, "will Kiki do the identical same thing three days running, never, never, never!").[16] But she also was upset with her lover's infidelity and his insistence that love played no part in their relationship ("We don't love, we screw," he reportedly told her).[17] Looking for a new life, she left for New York with an American journalist (or, according to Man Ray's memoirs, an American couple), with the hope of getting a movie contract. But after a few weeks, she wired Man Ray for return fare. According to one of Kiki's girlfriends, the American journalist left Kiki in New York and went elsewhere. According to Kiki, her meeting with Paramount (then located on Long Island) was a disaster. She got lost, couldn't speak English or find anyone who spoke French, and wanted to go home. Perhaps both happened; but in any case, on Kiki's return, she told Man Ray that she wanted to stay with him forever. And then she ran from café to café to let everyone know she was back, ending her victory lap at the Jockey Club, where she resumed her position as undisputed queen.

This famed nightspot—the first nightclub and cabaret in Montparnasse—owed its name, so they say, to the retired jockey who wandered into the place when it was still a simple zinc bar, liked it, and took it over. An American artist then decorated it with large painted figures à la the Wild West, in haphazard imitation of a Western saloon, and music and entertainment followed. Hence the name and the décor, where Americans soon flocked and where Kiki reigned.

Every night at the Jockey, Kiki sang her bawdy songs, delighting patrons with her cheerful vulgarity and sheer joy. Late each night, after the theater, long lines of limousines let out patrons at the Jockey's door, where they came to drink, talk, and revel in the ongoing party, to the accompaniment of American jazz and blues. "Everybody in Paris comes to the Jockey to have a good time," Kiki later wrote in her memoirs, "all the theatre and motion-picture stars, writers, painters." Best of all, she added, "we're just like one big family there. Everybody drinks a lot, and everybody's happy."[18]

Soon other nightclubs would open in Montparnasse, and after a few years, club-goers lost interest in the Jockey. But its quirky mix of sizzling music and raunchy fun set the tone for 1920s Montparnasse, which remained only a short distance and yet a separate world apart from the more fashionable and infinitely more sophisticated Boeuf sur le Toit.

Proust, in one of his rare outings during the last year of his life, had actually accompanied friends to the Boeuf sur le Toit, but he never would have dreamed of going to Montparnasse.

～

Jules Pascin was known as the Prince of Montparnasse. Born in Bulgaria of an Italian Serbian mother and Spanish Jewish father, he received a cosmopolitan education in Vienna and Munich before moving to the United States to avoid military duty in Bulgaria. After the war he gravitated to Paris, especially Montparnasse, where he became a legend—as much for his exploits as for his painting.

"He could have been someone who had stepped out of a Toulouse-Lautrec poster," Man Ray wrote, describing their frequent adventures together in the Paris demimonde.[19] Ernest Hemingway agreed, writing (in *A Moveable Feast*) of an evening he spent with Pascin at the Dôme. Hemingway had consciously avoided the Rotonde that evening and opted instead for the Dôme, because "there were people there who had worked."[20] There, he joined Pascin, who was sitting with two models. The conversation was suitably raunchy.

Several years later, Pascin evoked a typical Montparnasse evening: "Dined with the Salmons. Met [Othon] Friesz and went along to La Coupole. Bumped into Kisling who'd been looking for me . . . Man Ray, Kiki. . . . At one point, someone was talking about Derain and I said: 'Now there's someone I'd like to see again before going back to America.' Two minutes later, who turned up but Derain himself, totally drunk! I had a marvelous time!"[21]

"He looked more like a Broadway character of the Nineties than the lovely painter that he was," Hemingway remembered, "and afterwards, when he had hanged himself, I liked to remember him as he was that night at the Dôme."[22]

～

That year another nightclub, the Dingo (Madman), opened on Rue Delambre, across the street from Man Ray's first home in Montparnasse. Renowned for its all-night hours, its English pub atmosphere, and its pub-style bar snacks (especially Welsh rarebit), it quickly became popular with English and American artists and writers.

In the meantime, the Rotonde had expanded, absorbing the adjoining Parnasse, and had updated its décor in an effort to compete with the new club scene. Its big attraction was its large dance floor, which attracted crowds of young females on the lookout for men, although the Rotonde still had a strict policy about banning prostitutes. It also did not put up with drug dealing, which was common in other Montparnasse nightspots.

Drugs accompanied life in the fast lane of 1920s Paris, and by this time Raymond Radiguet, already a heavy drinker, had started taking opium. He and Cocteau starred in a constant round of parties that spring, and Radiguet had taken to repeating, "You have to *do* things," which he claimed originated with Apollinaire.[23] Still, during that summer, which he spent in the country with Cocteau, he seemed to have at least somewhat reformed. Although continuing to drink heavily, he became more orderly: according to Cocteau, Radiguet "slept, kept his papers in order, made clean copies."[24] Only later did Cocteau notice Radiguet's observation at the close of *Le Diable au corps*, where he writes that "a disorderly man who is about to die, and does not know it, suddenly begins to put everything around him in order. His life changes. He files his papers. He rises early and retires early to bed. . . . As a result his sudden death seems all the more unjust."[25]

Radiguet was finishing his second novel, *Le Bal du Comte d'Orgel*, loosely based on the classic seventeenth-century novel *La Princesse de Clèves*, in which the princess—devoted to her loving husband but infatuated with a dashing and insistent duke—resists the duke to the somber end, in which her husband dies of a broken heart and she retires to a convent. Radiguet's story, whose Count and Countess d'Orgel are modeled on the Count and Countess de Beaumont, has a different and more cynical ending. His Countess d'Orgel is firmly resistant to her suitor's advances, but her husband seems indifferent to her faithfulness. Instead, the count, who is absorbed with frivolity, reserves his passion for his elaborate parties.

Riding a huge wave of success, Radiguet showed no sign that danger might be imminent, even when he reverted to his old ways after returning to Paris that autumn. "Debts, alcohol, insomnia, heaps of dirty linen, moving about from hotel to hotel," Cocteau later wrote of Radiguet to Valentine Hugo, who had summered with them. On top of that, Radiguet was now threatening to marry a girl he had met, the beautiful Bronya Perlmutter—not because he loved her, but because he "refused to become a forty-year-old-man called 'Madame Jean Cocteau.'"[26]

It was driving Cocteau crazy, and if that was not enough, his dear friend Valentine Hugo had been unwell ever since her summer stay with him and Radiguet. No one yet realized that she—as well as Radiguet—had come down with typhoid.

That October, the French for the second time since 1916 refused to allow the showing of D. W. Griffith's motion picture, *The Birth of a Nation*. On one hand, the government was concerned that scenes showing the Ku Klux Klan's activities in the American South would be offensive to black residents and visitors from France's overseas colonies—holding "an entire people up to ridicule and hatred," as one deputy from Réunion put it.[27] Not only did these scenes undercut French ideals of equality, dating from the Declaration of the Rights of Man, but they posed a direct insult to the many soldiers from the French colonies, for whose significant contribution to the war effort the government was exceedingly grateful, and on whom it counted should war again arise.

Just as important to the government's response, though, was the impact of all those American tourists in Paris, most of whom came for a good time and brought their lifestyles and prejudices with them, including their insistence on segregation in public places. The French for the most part did not see things that way, leading to clashes when Americans in nightclubs and other public venues insisted on the ouster of black customers.

Americans had not made themselves popular in Paris during the postwar years, and their racism only exacerbated the resentment that many had already aroused by bad manners and flaunted wealth. America itself, for that matter, had not endeared itself to the French when it signed a separate peace treaty with Germany and insisted that France pay in full its wartime loans from the United States. Even before *The Birth of a Nation* appeared at the Salle Marivaux cinema on the Boulevard des Italiens, nasty incidents arising from white Americans' objections to the presence of blacks in nightclubs, restaurants, and bars had prompted the Ministry of Foreign Affairs to release a statement declaring that "some foreign tourists, forgetting that they are our guests and that, consequently, they should respect our customs and our laws, have recently, on numerous occasions, violently . . . demanded [black persons'] expulsion in offensive terms." If this continued, the statement went on, "sanctions will be taken."[28]

The Birth of a Nation did appear briefly at the Salle Marivaux and was greeted by throngs of eager ticket buyers as well as positive reviews by the critics. American films were popular in France, even if Americans were not, and for two days the film attracted record crowds. But on the third (August 19), prospective moviegoers found the cinema's doors blocked by gendarmes. The Prefecture of Police had banned the film as a threat to public order—after reportedly having received instructions from the highest levels of government (directly from Prime Minister Poincaré himself, according to *Le Matin*). The government offered to let the film run if all objectionable scenes involving the Klan were removed, but the film's owners strenuously objected.

Banning *The Birth of a Nation* may have been a largely symbolic gesture, but it vividly illustrated the potential minefields that existed in Franco-American relations as the decade progressed, especially as more and more Americans continued to pour into Paris.

A month after *The Birth of a Nation* was banned, Nazi party leader Adolph Hitler failed in his attempt to seize power in Bavaria, in a clash later known as the Beer Hall Putsch. At the time, Hemingway regarded the putsch as a joke, but four policemen died in the affair, as well as sixteen of Hitler's Nazi followers. As a backdrop to Hitler's attempted power grab, the German mark had fallen to two billion to the dollar, but the French were far more concerned about their own franc, which had continued to depreciate during the year. Whether or not any French noticed or cared, Hitler had seized his own nation's attention, even if he had not—for the moment—been able to seize actual power.

Closer to home, people were caught up in their own individual trials and tribulations. James Joyce underwent long-overdue eye surgery, while Claude Monet endured a series of operations on his right eye. Monet's first operations went well, but the third, in June, left him with impaired vision. "I think it's criminal to have placed me in such a predicament," he angrily wrote his doctor.[29] By August there was some improvement, although Monet told Clemenceau that "the distortion and exaggerated colours that I see are quite terrifying."[30] The painter now needed an operation for the other eye, which Clemenceau encouraged but Monet absolutely refused, resulting in a stalemate that fortunately did not break up their friendship. But then new remedial spectacles produced results that, to Monet's surprise, were unexpectedly good, and he plunged into his work again. In fact, as he told Joseph Durand-Ruel in November, he was having to make up for so much lost time that he could not receive visitors for a while at Giverny.[31]

Meanwhile, Le Corbusier had begun construction for his wealthiest client to date, the Swiss banker Raoul La Roche. Le Corbusier may have lectured other architects and the world at large about the need for a new kind of housing for the less well-to-do, but in practice he found (as did so many other architects) that it was housing for the rich that paid the bills. Situated on the outskirts of Paris's fashionable sixteenth arrondissement, the Villa La Roche was designed to showcase Raoul La Roche's art collection, including works by Léger and Lipchitz as well as several fine Picassos and a Braque that Le Corbusier and Ozenfant bought for him at auction from the collection of Daniel-Henry Kahnweiler, the German art dealer who fled France for Switzerland during the war.

As it happened, Le Corbusier's brother, Albert Jeanneret, had just married a well-to-do widow, who commissioned a Le Corbusier–designed house adjacent to La Roche's, where she and Albert and her two daughters would live. The site was a difficult one, consisting of a small plot at the end of a cul-de-sac, and construction of the twin houses took more time and far more money than originally envisioned. But when completed, both were revolutionary in materials (concrete and machined materials) as well as design. For the Villa La Roche especially, Le Corbusier created a magnificent space: a soaring interior atrium with balconies and a sloping ramp connecting the floors through a spacious gallery. A portion of the building rests on *pilotis*, or

Le Corbusier's Villa la Roche, now housing the Fondation Le Corbusier, Paris. © J. McAuliffe

pillars, and it culminates in a roof garden. In addition, Le Corbusier designed or selected all the furniture and interior fittings, including the curtains (a blend of flannel and cambric), the lighting fixtures (supplementing natural lighting), and floors made of special rubber instead of wood parquet.

But hiring Le Corbusier was not something to take lightly; the architect demanded a great deal from his clients. "You must renounce the things you have learned," he told them, "in order to pursue truths which inevitably develop around new techniques instigated by a new spirit born of the profound revolution of the machine age."[32] Unquestionably, Villa La Roche was a triumph, but it sorely tested relations between architect and client, especially when so much of the final product turned out to have flaws and needed to be redone.

It also led to the split, in 1925, between Le Corbusier and his friend and partner Amédée Ozenfant, after Le Corbusier discovered that Ozenfant had made substantial changes to the installation of La Roche's art collection that Le Corbusier had overseen. Contributing to the divide, Ozenfant had become enamored with Surrealism, which Le Corbusier thought ludicrous. Adding to the strain was the question of credit for their joint publication, *Towards a New Architecture*, an epic endeavor that attacked current architecture and forcefully proposed a totally new approach that the authors confidently claimed could and would solve social unrest. The book's first edition, which appeared toward the end of 1923, gave Ozenfant credit under his nom de plume, Saugnier. By the second edition, however, Le Corbusier claimed sole authorship, with a dedication to Ozenfant, and in the following edition, the dedication disappeared. The book is now widely considered to be Le Corbusier's alone.

Ozenfant later stated that "the clashes and the incidents between Le Corbusier and me—some childish, others offensive—multiplied. He wanted to be alone. I withdrew."[33] By the end of 1923, then, Le Corbusier was increasingly operating on his own and was doing so with considerable success. He had published *Towards a New Architecture* and begun the villas La Roche and Jeanneret. He also had managed to have his paintings shown at the Salon des Indépendants as well as in the gallery of the prominent art dealer Léonce Rosenberg (brother of Picasso's art dealer, Paul Rosenberg). Still, it was as an architect rather than as a painter that Le Corbusier was earning a reputation, as well as money, and he now made the decision to keep his painting a private matter. He had chosen architecture, and he was determined to be a success.

⌣

Erik Satie occupied a unique place in Paris music circles. Having for years firmly resisted any compromise in his simple but odd lifestyle, he had just as firmly resisted any compromise in his style of composition. Still, for the past decade, Satie's nonconformity had received staunch recognition from prominent composers such as Ravel and patrons such as the Princesse de Polignac, and since the war he had emerged as a kind of secular saint among younger composers, especially those known as the Groupe des Six.

Diaghilev, who by now had become uncomfortably aware of the Swedish Ballet's incursion on his Paris turf, had reached the conclusion that he had better incorporate more music from this new group of French composers, on whose behalf Satie was strenuously campaigning. The first to receive Diaghilev's nod was the relatively unknown Poulenc, whose ballet *Les Biches*, with choreography by Bronislava Nijinska and set and costumes by Marie Laurencin, would premiere to enthusiastic reviews in the Ballets Russes's spring 1924 Paris season.

Satie was determined to win Diaghilev's approval for Milhaud as well, but this was a harder sell. "Our friend Stravinsky was working [Diaghilev] up a bit against you, if I may say so," Satie wrote Milhaud in July 1923. Whether or not this was the case, Milhaud was convinced that Diaghilev did not like Milhaud's "usual kind of music." Satie went ahead and "pulled [Diaghilev's] leg a little about his ostracism of you" and thought that the impresario seemed "better disposed to you now." However, getting Diaghilev to relent was one thing, but persuading Milhaud to work with Diaghilev was quite another. "Once you get into the company," Satie assured Milhaud, "they will adore you, and Diaghilev will see for himself what a magnificent artist you are."[34]

The outcome was at first a small commission, to provide a musical setting for an opera by Chabrier. But this turned out to be the preface for a more interesting turn of events in early 1924, when Diaghilev came to Milhaud with a rush commission for a new ballet, *Le Train bleu*. By this time, Diaghilev could see competition rising from behind practically every tree—not only from de Maré's Swedish Ballet, but also from Count de Beaumont, who was devising a season of his own, most maddeningly by using the troupe of dancers headed by Diaghilev's former choreographer and lead dancer, Léonide Massine. As the new year opened, Milhaud was working with Beaumont, and Diaghilev was becoming edgy as he contemplated his rivals.

Fortunately for the Ballets Russes, Diaghilev's almost constant fears of financial ruin had recently been alleviated by a remarkable save on the part of Pierre de Polignac, nephew of the Princesse de Polignac and son-in-law to the new prince of Monte Carlo. Thanks to Pierre de Polignac, the Hereditary Princess of Monaco (his wife) now gave her patronage to the Ballets Russes, and Monaco became the Ballets Russes's home base. There it would perform, prepare for the new season, and receive a blessedly secure income during the winter months.

∿

It had been a hectic year for Hemingway. During the first months, he traveled to Italy, Germany, and Spain, with Hadley joining him at various locations in Italy before returning to Paris. Germany, specifically the Ruhr, was his editor's idea, but Ezra Pound—who was having an affair with the Cunard shipping line heiress, Nancy Cunard—was responsible for luring Ernest and Hadley to Italy during late winter and early spring. Wrapping up these peripatetic months, Ernest went with friends to Spain, while Hadley joined him in Pamplona for the festival, Ernest's first experience with the running of the bulls. He took notes—extensive ones—of everything in Spain that struck him as unusual or important. But he mostly took notes on the bullfights.

Early in August, his *Three Stories & Ten Poems* was published in Paris by Robert McAlmon's small Contact Editions, and Bill Bird's new Three Mountains Press (named for the Paris hills of Montparnasse, Montmartre, and Mont Sainte-Geneviève) would soon publish Hemingway's collection of short stories titled *in our time*. Not coincidentally, both McAlmon and Bird were fishing and bullfighting buddies of Hemingway's. In addition, prompted by Pamplona, the seeds of *The Sun Also Rises* were forming in his mind. But he and Hadley had little time left in Paris; they attended boxing matches, horse races, and a variety of social events before sailing for Canada in late August, where Ernest began full-time work with the *Toronto Star*. They expected to be back in a year or two, but as it happened, they only lasted four months.

On October 10, Hadley gave birth to a son—John Hadley Nicanor Hemingway, who would be known as Bumby ("Nicanor," from the name of the famed Spanish matador, Nicanor Villalta, was Ernest's idea). Baby Bumby came early, when Ernest was out of town covering a story. Ernest hated his job anyway, and he erupted when the editor lit into him for not filing his copy before visiting Hadley and his newborn son in the hospital. After that, his relationship with the *Star* abruptly ended.

Ernest visited his parents in Oak Park for Christmas, leaving Hadley and Bumby in Toronto: it would be several more years before the senior Hemingways saw their grandson. And then, in January of the new year, Ernest, Hadley, and Bumby sailed for France.

〜

That autumn, while Hadley Hemingway was giving birth to a son in Toronto, Marc Chagall was eagerly awaiting his wife and daughter in Paris.

It had been a long journey, all the way from Russia via Berlin, and Chagall had gone ahead, taking quarters in Montparnasse's Hôtel des Ecoles—until only recently Man Ray's address. Chagall was not new to Paris: he had lived there before the war, when he joined other impoverished Eastern European artists at La Ruche, spending night after night painting the homeland of his memories. Just before war broke out, he had gratefully accepted an invitation to exhibit his works in Berlin, from where he planned to return home to Vitebsk, to wed his fiancée, Bella. The Berlin show was a success, and he left his paintings there, intending to retrieve them on his return to Paris; but war and the Russian Revolution kept him for eight years in Russia. When he reappeared in Berlin in 1922, those who remembered him from the prewar years were amazed, having heard no word of him since 1914. They had presumed he was dead.

But Chagall was very much alive, despite much misery and deprivation. He had spent the intervening years first as head of an art school in Vitebsk and then (after losing the battle against party-approved socialist realism) as a stage designer for the State Jewish Chamber Theater in Moscow. After his unacceptably original work once again lost him his job, he resorted to a stint as art teacher in a shelter for Jewish orphans, victims of the pogroms then sweeping the Ukraine. Each year brought increasing hardship for him and his family, especially from the famine that gripped the land, and as Chagall fought to keep himself and his wife and daughter from starving, he feared that his artistic inspiration was dying as well. "Neither imperial Russia nor the Russia of the Soviets needs me," Chagall wrote in 1922. "They don't understand me." "Come back to Europe, you are famous here!" a friend told him,[35] and so in 1922, Chagall went ahead of his wife and daughter to Berlin, intending to sell the paintings he had left there.

To his shock, he discovered that his paintings had been sold—most of them at bargain prices—and the money deposited from their sale was worthless, thanks to German hyperinflation. "Everything [in Berlin] was colossal: prices, abuse, despair," another Russian émigré wrote, after landing there the year before.[36] The political climate was also threatening, especially for Jews, signaled by the rising strength of Hitler and the Nazis. Yet Chagall was welcomed by Berlin's avant-garde, and with his prospects looking considerably brighter there than in the Soviet Union, he sent for Bella and their daughter, Ida.

Bella, who spoke flawless German and who understood how best to present themselves to fashionable avant-garde society, stage-managed the family's public face, even as Chagall once again began to create. Yet despite the receptive community they found there, Bella—who loved everything French—insisted that they move to Paris. As it happened, the legendary art leader Ambroise Vollard had seen examples of Chagall's work and wanted to meet him; based on this, Chagall left for Paris in the spring of 1923.

After Chagall found a small single room at the Hôtel des Ecoles, he prepared for his family's arrival in a larger, although modest, apartment on Faubourg St-Jacques. But much as in Berlin, he soon learned that the paintings he had stored in his studio at La Ruche in 1914, for what he had expected to be a three-month absence, had disappeared. In a devastating repeat of the Berlin story, the dealer with whom he had signed a contract had helped himself, but none of the money went to Chagall. Chagall was distraught, even accusing his good friend Blaise Cendrars of participating in the plot to rob him—thus ending their friendship.

Vollard was precisely the dealer he needed at this moment—the same dealer who, early on, had exhibited Cézanne, van Gogh, Gauguin, Matisse, and Picasso. Gertrude and Leo Stein went to Vollard, as did Albert Barnes. Vollard agreed to Chagall's proposal to illustrate Gogol's *Dead Souls*, and with this financial assurance, Chagall sent for Bella and Ida. Bella arrived with the Russian paintings that Chagall had not sold in Berlin, plus a list of the best patisseries and dress shops in Paris. Ever the jeweler's daughter, she had no intention of living the impoverished refugee life any longer. And so, early in 1924, the family moved once again, this time to 110 Avenue d'Orléans (now Avenue du Général-Leclerc), where they resided in a much nicer and far larger apartment.

Fortunately, it now looked as though Marc Chagall would be able to pay for it.

⌒

Late in the year, Germaine Berton, the anarchist assassin of Action Française leader Marius Plateau, went to trial. Her attorney compared her to Charlotte

Corday, who had assassinated Marat at the height of the Terror, and told the jurors that she had killed the leader of a violent gang rather than a patriot. It was a crime of passion, he declared, and the jury agreed, deliberating only thirty-five minutes before acquitting her.

Action Française was horrified, but Léon Daudet was especially appalled. Not long before Berton's acquittal, his own son, Philippe—a fourteen-year-old who was a close friend of Raymond Radiguet—had told the anarchist newspaper *Le Libertaire* that he was prepared to kill for the anarchist cause and, without identifying himself, suggested his father as a possible target. Despite the precedent of Germaine Berton, the anarchists of the 1920s were a far cry from their bomb-throwing predecessors of the 1890s and gave him no encouragement. He then shot himself in the backseat of a taxi. Distraught, Daudet first blamed the Germans, then the police, for conspiracy to murder Philippe, with the taxi driver as an accomplice.

The taxi driver sued for slander—and won. In late 1925, Daudet was sentenced to five months in prison and a fine, but that was hardly the end of the story.

Late that year, Gustae Eiffel, father of the Eiffel Tower and of so much more, died peacefully in his sleep. He was ninety-one and had only recently retired from his active, productive life.

He was preceded by that incomparable divinity of the stage, Sarah Bernhardt, who died that March in her son's arms. For three days mourners filed past her body, which now lay permanently in that famous coffin, and thousands lined the streets, ten deep, to watch her funeral procession to Père-Lachaise.

For somber magnificence, Maurice Barrès's procession perhaps took top honors, with ten black horses drawing his hearse, followed by a huge cortège. En route to Notre-Dame, the procession stopped at the Place des Pyramides, in a symbolic tribute to the golden statue of Jeanne d'Arc.

But for sheer drama, nothing could top the funeral of Raymond Radiguet, who died on December 12. To begin with, he was young—only twenty years old—and his death was totally unexpected, at least until the very end. His typhoid, contracted late that summer, had developed over the long months of autumn. Valentine Hugo, who also contracted typhoid at the same time and place, survived. But Radiguet, weakened by his years of excess, did not.

Coco Chanel took charge of the funeral arrangements, filling the church of St-Philippe-du-Roule with white flowers, except for red roses on the white coffin. White horses pulled the white hearse through the rain to Père-Lachaise. "It was the most tragic sight that I have ever seen," Nina Hamnett later wrote. "Radiguet's father and mother were there, and then his four little brothers and sisters, the youngest being about six, stood in a row, their faces contorted with weeping."[37]

Cocteau, totally devastated, was too ill to attend.

René Vincent, Procession of Cars along the Champs-Elysées, *Paris, 1920s. Kharbine-Tapabor / The Art Archive at Art Resource, NY*

CHAPTER NINE

~

Americans in Paris

(1924)

American money, American influence, and American tourists—where could a Parisian look in 1924 without seeing the growing presence of America and Americans?

Thanks to American loans, Germany could now pay its reparations, which in turn made it possible for France to pay its war debts. At the same time, loans from American banks were directly helping to stabilize the French economy.

In addition, American intervention now enabled the French—by now sick of the costly Ruhr adventure, and reeling from its impact on the franc—to withdraw from the Ruhr under cover of the Dawes Plan, an international attempt to solve the huge problem of German reparations. Léon Daudet could cry "treason" all he wanted, but thanks to the Dawes Plan, France would now embark on a period of expansion and prosperity that, especially once the franc stabilized, would last until the end of the decade.

As for American tourists and expatriates, they were everywhere. By the time Ernest and Hadley Hemingway arrived back in Paris that January, more than thirty thousand Americans were living permanently in Paris, as well as twice that many British. Prices had risen in the few months since the Hemingways had left, and cheap places to live were scarce. They finally decided on a second-floor apartment over a lumberyard on Rue Notre-Dame-des-Champs—with no electricity, and at three times the rent they had been paying on Rue du Cardinal-Lemoine. But it was a larger space and had the definite advantage of being near the center of Montparnasse and its cafés.

One of the most popular of these, especially with Americans, remained the Dôme, which had been completely renovated during the Hemingways' absence, replacing its dingy décor with a sparkling new mirrored interior, accented in bordello red. Another, the Sélect, was a new and popular addition to the Montparnasse scene, with an American bar (serving cocktails), elegant décor, and all-night hours. The Dingo, not to be outdone in the bid for American patronage, now put in an American menu, including hamburgers and chicken-fried steaks, and even added English-speaking waiters. But most importantly, the Dingo brought in the barman, Jimmie Charters, who quickly became the place's main attraction.

Jimmie, a native of Manchester and Liverpool, had the ability to know exactly what his patrons needed and wanted, and the humanity to provide it. Most often, it was a cheerful demeanor and a listening ear, although Jimmie was adept at snuffing out impending fights, providing taxi money, and picking drunk customers up off the floor. But it was Jimmie's genuine caring that made him special. As Hugh Ford (an observant resident of Montparnasse) noted, the habitués of places like the Dingo were not achievers like Hemingway but, "more often than not, they were the ones who talked about writing and painting, drank, and talked some more."[1]

"I have always believed success behind the bar comes from an ability to understand the man or woman I am serving," Jimmie told Morrill Cody, who authored Jimmie's memoirs. "To enter into his joys or woes, make him feel the need of me as a person rather than a servant," while at the same time practicing diplomacy and tact, and knowing how "to keep my place."[2]

Jimmie's clients were mostly Americans (he estimated 70 percent), with British and a smattering of French, Italians, South Americans, and Swedes making up the rest. There were more women than men at his bar (he estimated that there were two or three women in Montparnasse for every man), and he guessed that women constituted almost three-quarters of those at his bar. This sometimes was a challenge: besides preventing fights and steering drunks into taxis, his big job was to diplomatically provide companionship for the lonely, especially for the single women who came to the Dingo looking for men.

This certainly did not apply to Kiki, who always was surrounded by men. Jimmie once saw her on the Dôme terrace "with thirty sailors and not another girl!" Nor did it include Sylvia Beach, who as far as Jimmie knew "never entered a bar in her life"—though she was good humored about it. He remembered that once she told him, "We have always served the same clients, you, Jimmie, with drinks, I with books."[3]

Hemingway came to Jimmie's bar frequently, and they would have long conversations about boxing or about bullfighting. "He has told me that he himself actually fought bulls at one time," Charters recalled, believing every word of it.[4]

~

Hemingway frequented the Dingo and a number of other Montparnasse cafés, but the place where he usually went to write was the Closerie des Lilas, just down the street from his apartment. He needed to escape the noise: Bumby was a baby, after all, while down in the courtyard, the lumberyard's huge saw hummed and screeched as it cut. Despite the name, the Closerie never had lilacs (they belonged to a long-gone rival establishment), but its terrace was peaceful. There, Hemingway "sat in a corner with the afternoon light coming in over [his] shoulder and wrote in the notebook."[5] After a long dry spell, he was writing again—eight short stories that spring, all of them good.

Yet he was making no money and constantly battling discouragement. Neither of his books of short stories and poems was selling, and in any case, both had been printed by tiny Montparnasse presses, which could barely cover their expenses. His parents were disapproving (which should not have mattered, but it did), and he continued to receive rejection after rejection from New York publishers. On top of all this, part of Hadley's trust fund turned out to have been badly invested, or misappropriated, with a significant loss of income.[6] He and Hadley were not destitute, nor (despite the stories) did he ever have to kill pigeons in the Luxembourg Gardens for dinner, but he was worried.

Still, Hemingway continued to eat oysters and drink good wine, and soon after Bumby's baptism (for which Gertrude Stein and Alice B. Toklas served as godmothers), he traveled alone to Provence, ostensibly to see the bullfights, but mainly just to get away. When he returned, Ford Madox Ford was about to leave for New York and left him in charge of editing Ford's *transatlantic review*, for which Hemingway had been working as an unpaid assistant editor. Earlier in the year Hemingway had encouraged ("forced, perhaps would be the word") Ford to publish Gertrude Stein's *The Making of Americans* in installments, and then had jointly done the retyping with Alice. In addition, he had read the proofs, "as this was a work which gave [Stein] no happiness."[7] But apart from Stein's contribution, Hemingway found the *transatlantic review* dull, and he took the opportunity to pep up the July issue, which was almost ready to print. "Goddam it," Hemingway wrote Ezra Pound, Ford "hasn't any advertizers [sic] to offend or any subscribers to discontinue, why not shoot the moon?"[8] Hemingway did not add much, but what he added managed to insult Tristan Tzara, Gilbert Seldes (editor of the *Dial*), and Jean Cocteau (who, according to Hemingway, "has a very good minor talent and a certain amount of intelligence").[9] Worse yet, in the August issue, Hemingway left out Ford's own contributions.

Surprisingly, Ford did not fire Hemingway, but perhaps Ford was more concerned about the transatlantic review's dire financial straits. In any case, Ford could deal with Hemingway later, since the impulsive assistant editor was about to leave for Pamplona.[10]

Tristan Tzara responded to Hemingway's insults with a quietly measured letter to the editor, which appeared in the transatlantic review's September issue. Cocteau did not respond, but perhaps he had other things to think about.

What chiefly preoccupied Cocteau was Radiguet. "Death would be better than this half-death," he wrote Abbé Mugnier soon after the young man's demise, adding that he suffered "night and day."[11] "I am suffering atrociously," he wrote Max Jacob, who remained at the monastery of Saint-Benoît-sur-Loire. "Yesterday and the day before I felt Raymond around me. Today I am alone."[12] He also appealed to Jacques Maritain, the Thomist philosopher whose conversion from Protestantism and then agnosticism to Catholicism, along with his eloquence and sensitivity to the arts, was drawing a number of artists and intellectuals. Radiguet's death, Cocteau told Maritain, had impacted on him like an operation without chloroform.[13] Maritain and his wife, Raissa, would have a decisive influence on Cocteau when they met that summer, but for the moment, Cocteau was beyond consolation. "I am in an excruciating state," he wrote Max Jacob in late January. "I would like to die."[14] Jacob sought to comfort him but feared for his health and stability, especially as Cocteau now was smoking more and more opium to blot out his pain.

Cocteau began his heavy use of opium in early 1924 on a trip to Monte Carlo. There he joined his friends and colleagues in Diaghilev's Ballets Russes, as well as Poulenc and Auric, who were there to attend rehearsals and premieres of their ballets (Poulenc's Les Biches and Auric's Les Fâcheux). Satie was also there, to work on Gounod's opera Le Médecin malgré lui (for Diaghilev's brief fling into opera). Much to Satie's dismay, another who was there at the time was the influential music critic Louis Laloy, a friend of Debussy's and champion of Debussy's music, who had been consistently hostile to the music of Satie and the Groupe des Six. Yet despite this history, Poulenc, Auric, and Cocteau were frequently seen in Laloy's company in Monte Carlo. Satie was furious, suspecting a deliberate campaign of flattery on Poulenc and Auric's part, and broke with them as well as with Cocteau, after which he abruptly returned to Paris. This left the four to enjoy themselves in Monte Carlo—which in Laloy's company meant opium.

Laloy was an authority on Chinese culture, especially opium, having written a guide to opium smoking called *Le Livre de la fumée* (*The Smoking Book*), which became a best seller among those in search of fashionable new stimulants. The four met daily in their hotel, where they requested absolute privacy. Laloy prided himself on having managed to control his opium smoking, allowing him to lead what he called a normal life, including what appeared to be a happy home as well as an illustrious career. Auric was reputed to use opium in moderation, although accounts differ, while Poulenc later attempted with difficulty to break his addiction, and Cocteau was hooked for life. Over the years he would ricochet from "cures" to dependence, somehow managing throughout to keep up his remarkable output as a poet and playwright while retaining center spotlight in the trendiest venues of Parisian nightlife.

During the months following Radiguet's death, Cocteau claimed that he was unable to work, and indeed, he produced far less than usual. His correspondence with Max Jacob certainly suffered. But he still was able to provide the libretto for Diaghilev's production of *Le Train bleu* (with music by Milhaud, choreography by Nijinska, costumes by Chanel, and an astonishing front curtain by Picasso, of two massive women in classical tunics dashing along a beach). Cocteau's concept for *Le Train bleu* was to portray a trendy beach on the French Riviera, where the fashionable Paris–Riviera express, called Le Train bleu (for the color of its sleeping cars), brought sun-starved members of the *beau monde* during the long winter months. Milhaud called the ballet "gay, frivolous, and frothy," and was not pleased that he could not produce his "usual kind of music, which [Diaghilev] did not like."[15] But its fashionable bathing beauties and gorgeous male lead (Diaghilev's new favorite, Patrick Healy-Kay, renamed as Anton Dolin) made it a success, even if Milhaud did not like it, and even though Picasso, who was tiring of the world surrounding the Ballets Russes, decided that this would be his last official association with Diaghilev.

Following Radiguet's death, Cocteau also managed to create his adaptation of *Romeo and Juliet* for the Count de Beaumont's newly launched Soirées de Paris, a six-week, May through June season of ballets and other entertainments at Montmartre's Théâtre de la Cigale, featuring Léonide Massine and his troupe of dancers (many formerly of the Ballets Russes). Inspired by the success of *La Statue retrouvée*, the divertissement that Cocteau dreamed up and Picasso executed for the Beaumonts' 1923 ball, the count had felt inspired to enter the lists with Diaghilev and become an impresario, using Diaghilev's former lead dancer and choreographer, not to mention lover, as his star. Beaumont also made good use of some of the same composers and artists that Diaghilev had come to rely on, including Braque and Picasso, Satie and Milhaud (although Diaghilev was able to head off the less-established Poulenc and Auric by warning that he would not produce their ballets in Paris if they worked for Beaumont).

Milhaud was in the middle of writing a choral ballet for Beaumont and Massine called *Salade* (with scenery by Braque) when Diaghilev asked him to come up with music for *Le Train bleu*. Milhaud by this time had sufficient standing that Diaghilev could not treat him as he had Poulenc and Auric, but the impresario did strongly advise him to break off all dealings with the Comte de Beaumont, "on the grounds that there was no future in the Soirées de Paris." Milhaud replied that he was under contract and would honor his commitments, but short of any clause forbidding him to undertake other work, he could do it. Milhaud then consulted Beaumont, who was "most understanding."[16] As a result, Milhaud (who had the reputation of working quickly) managed to compose the music for *Le Train bleu* in a three-week period following his completion of *Salade*, with both ballets produced in separate venues within a few days of one another (he later called these ballets his "twins"). The only hitch, according to Milhaud, was a musician strike ten minutes before the curtain was to go up for *Salade*, forcing him to play his own score by candlelight on the piano.

Beaumont also commissioned a ballet, *Mercure*, from Satie, with choreography by Massine and sets and costumes by Picasso (whose contribution, according to the Surrealist Louis Aragon, revealed "an entirely new style for Picasso, one that owes nothing to either cubism or realism").[17] Loie Fuller, who had made her name years before as a dancer who used electrical lighting, colored gels, and billowing silk to evoke images of fire, butterflies, and huge flowers, took charge of lighting. The result, a series of light and frivolous vignettes or tableaux that poked fun at Cocteau (the Mercury figure) as well as at Poulenc, Auric, and Laloy, left the audience in confusion, especially when several audience members, prompted by Auric and led by Breton, disrupted the performance by yelling, "Up with Picasso, down with Satie!" Unmoved, Satie merely left the theater to catch the last train for Arcueil, while Beaumont proceeded with his opening-night ball, as scheduled.

As for Cocteau's *Romeo and Juliet*, it was inspired by the vision of a woman trapeze artist he had seen soaring one night at the circus, her spangles and rhinestones sparkling against a black background. Based on this vivid memory, Cocteau (with the assistance of Jean and Valentine Hugo) created a visual version of the play. As he explained, "I had invented an entirely black set, in which only the colors of certain arabesques, costumes and props were visible."[18] In another tribute to his circus vision, Cocteau had the speaker of the first-act prologue "fly," like the trapeze artist he had seen. The stage set and costumes may have been a success, but the production as a whole prompted Hemingway to wonder, in that infamous issue of the *transatlantic*, "what school book edition of Shakespeare" Cocteau had used. "With this example," he added, "we expect a translation of Marlowe by Mr. Tzara who is also ignorant of English."[19]

It was now, in June, while the Diaghilev and the Beaumont seasons were coming to a close, that the first of two installments of Radiguet's *Le Bal du Comte d'Orgel* appeared in the *Nouvelle Revue Française* (NRF). Unfortunately, the NRF's editor, Jacques Rivière, prefaced the first installment with disparaging remarks about Radiguet's previous novel, *Le Diable au corps*, and gave his opinion that Radiguet had shown little promise of becoming a major writer. Cocteau was shocked and, for the book itself, appended a fulsome appreciation. Taking issue with Rivière, he wrote that "the literary tribunal has found [Radiguet's] heart arid," but this was untrue. "Raymond Radiguet's heart was hard," he explained, "and like a diamond it did not react to the least touch. It needed fire and other diamonds, and ignored the rest."[20]

So much for Rivière and other detractors, whom Cocteau clearly placed among those best ignored. He clearly took comfort that, during Radiguet's short life, he had supplied the requisite fire and diamonds that this young man's heart required.

Fire and diamonds were not on Coco Chanel's list of requirements. She scoffed at jewels, making light of them by turning her blatantly *faux* "costume jewelry" into a fashion. As for fire, she had long before wearied of her dashing Grand Duke Dmitri and his ilk when, in late 1923, she met another duke, the Duke of Westminster, in Monte Carlo.

The duke, or Bendor, as he was known to his family and close friends, was reputed to be the richest man in England and perhaps in all of Europe. Yet Chanel was hardly a fortune hunter, or at least by that time did not need to be. In addition to her hugely successful fashion business, she was building a burgeoning perfume empire. She had interested Théophile Bader, proprietor of Paris's elegant Galeries Lafayette, in Chanel No. 5, and he in turn had introduced her to Pierre and Paul Wertheimer, owners of a large cosmetics company. In April 1924, the Wertheimer brothers joined with Bader and Chanel to form the Société des Parfums Chanel, with the Wertheimers agreeing to fully finance the production, marketing, and distribution of Chanel's perfume. Eventually Chanel would argue for a larger share than the 10 percent she originally agreed to, but at the time, it seemed to her like an advantageous arrangement. And it was unquestionably profitable. Once again, Chanel had proven that she did not need a rich man to lead the kind of life she wanted.

So what was Bendor's appeal? The sheer lavishness of his lifestyle certainly was attractive: "He is far from knowing all of [his estates and properties]," Chanel later told Paul Morand. "Be they in Ireland, in Dalmatia, or in the Carpathians, there is a house belonging to Westminster, a house where everything is set up, where you can dine and go to bed on your arrival, with polished silverware, motor cars . . . with their batteries charged [Chanel recalled seventeen Rolls Royces in Bendor's Eaton Hall garage alone], small tankers in the harbor, . . . servants in livery, stewards."[21] Bendor bestowed special attention on his yacht, the *Flying Cloud*, one of the largest private yachts in the world, with a crew of forty. It was there that he entertained Chanel on their first evening together.

Bendor was at the time a rugged forty-four, an outdoor man and playboy with a history of two unsuccessful marriages and any number of mistresses. He was reputed to be kind and attentive, but also spoiled and prone to boredom and angry outbursts. Still, as Chanel told Morand, her years with Bendor were spent "very lovingly and very amicably." In addition, "beneath his clumsy exterior, he's a skillful hunter. You'd have to be skillful to hang on to me for ten years."[22]

Bendor and Chanel had become lovers by the spring of 1924, when he was seen at rehearsals for Diaghilev's production of *Le Train bleu*, for which she designed the costumes. Later, she joined him for cruises on the *Flying Cloud* as well as for house parties at some of the duke's numerous estates and hunting lodges.

During the coming years, rumors of their impending marriage circulated and recirculated. But there were insurmountable obstacles, especially Chanel's age (forty-one in 1924) and apparent inability to bear the heir that Bendor so desperately wanted. Not inconsequential was Chanel's own hesitation to give up her career and independence. Bendor's wealth may have dwarfed her own, but nonetheless, she was by now independently wealthy, with the ability to continue the flow of income that her own hard work and talent had brought her. And she was adamant about continuing the juggling act that maintaining her business required, even while she responded to Bendor's beck and call. On one occasion this even meant that the duke had to ship her seamstresses to England so that she could continue to work on her collection while remaining by his side.

Why, in her opinion, was Bendor so attracted to her? "Because I had not tried to lure him," she later explained. If you are famous and immensely rich, she added, "you stop being a man and become a hare, a fox. . . . In these sorts of situations, you can imagine how restful it is to live with someone you have pursued yourself, someone who the next day, probably, will dig a hole under the cage and run away."[23]

And that may have explained it. To whatever other attractions Chanel brought to their relationship, she added the undeniable allure of being, quite possibly, unobtainable.

⌒

While the unobtainable might possess an allure for some, Americans and others sought a more reliable form of glamour and excitement when they came to Paris and Montparnasse. As with the Jockey, the more unusual the clubbing experience turned out to be, the more "genuine" and appealing it became. By 1924, a new nightclub, the Bal Nègre, which began as a local dance hall for West Indians, quickly captivated an A-list of Parisians and Americans. Soon it began to draw crowds to its run-down quarters on the far side of Montparnasse, on Rue Blomet.

Although the Murphys and their good friends Archibald and Ada MacLeish now abandoned Paris for nearby Saint-Cloud (as well as Cap d'Antibes) in search of more peaceful lives, most Americans wanted the full Paris experience and continued to flock to Montparnasse. June brought a never-ending crowd of Americans, while during a single week in July, ocean liners (which had recently come up with more thrifty travel options)[24] disgorged some twelve thousand Americans onto French shores. Although most were looking for good times, a few had more serious objectives in mind. Edward Titus, for example, had left New York in the wake of his indomitable wife, Helena Rubinstein, to open what quickly became a renowned Montparnasse bookshop, At the Sign of the Black Manikin. Another, the poet William Carlos Williams, was taking time off from his medical practice to write, first in New York, then in Paris, much as F. Scott Fitzgerald would soon leave New York for Paris to complete *The Great Gatsby*. John Dos Passos, who had already published two novels (*One Man's Initiation: 1917* and *Three Soldiers*) and was working on another (*Manhattan Transfer*), returned that spring to Paris after travels throughout the Continent, Russia, and the Middle East (Sylvia Beach recalled that she met him "between *Three Soldiers* and *Manhattan Transfer*, but caught only glimpses of him as he raced by").[25] Dos Passos was well acquainted with Paris, having visited there during a precollege Grand Tour of Europe, and having lived there off and on during wartime, when based there (along with his friend E. E. Cummings) as a member of a volunteer ambulance corps. After Armistice, he lingered in Paris, studying anthropology at the Sorbonne. Now, returning once more to the City of Light, he became friends with Ernest Hemingway, whom he may have met briefly during the war, when both served in Italy.[26]

The Hemingways left for their second visit to Pamplona in late June, along with several friends, including Dos Passos. "It was fun and we ate well and drank well," Dos Passos later wrote, "but there were too many exhibitionistic personalities in the group to suit me."[27] By this, he meant Hemingway, who indulged in a variety of boneheaded feats to prove his courage. Hadley especially suffered, as Ernest's alarm that she might again be pregnant created a tense and miserable situation for them both. It turned out that she was not pregnant after all, but Ernest later blamed the entire unpleasantness on Hadley: the Pamplona festival was "a man's fiesta," he later complained, "and women at it make trouble."[28]

At the heart of Hemingway's malaise was his inability to publish successfully—or publish at all. From Spain he wrote Ezra Pound: "Now we haven't got any money anymore I am going to have to quit writing and I never will have a book published. I feel cheerful as hell."[29] Back in Paris, rejection followed rejection in discouraging staccato, while Bumby was cutting teeth and making his parents almost as miserable as he was.

Not far away, but in a far fancier part of town, Cole Porter was experiencing his own form of dejection. He wanted success badly and, as Kitty Carlisle Hart later put it, was trying to hide his longing by posing as "a playboy who incidentally wrote songs."[30] In Venice that summer, he wrote songs for a new musical called *Greenwich Village Follies*, but unfortunately they did not "set Broadway on fire," as Elsa Maxwell commented,[31] and were eventually dropped. In addition, he had fallen in love with Boris Kochno, who had progressed from being Diaghilev's secretary—and lover—to become a major collaborator in the Ballets Russes. Although Diaghilev's own affair with Kochno had by this time ended, Diaghilev managed to extract financial support from Porter for the Ballets Russes, to mollify the impresario's presumably wounded feelings.

Unlike Cole Porter or Hemingway, Marc Chagall was experiencing some welcome success. Late that year, Henri Matisse's youngest son, Pierre—who was starting out on what would prove to be a remarkable career as an art dealer—gave Chagall his first solo show in Paris, at the Galerie Barbazanges-Hodebert. Everyone who was anyone came, and Chagall was ecstatic: "What can I say about myself!" he wrote a friend in Moscow. "Only that now I am on the lips of all the contemporary French painters and poets. . . . The only thing worth having, is if masters such as Matisse acknowledge your existence."[32]

In actuality, the praise was mixed. Even though Germans in Cologne proved welcoming when the exhibit traveled there, some Paris critics still found Chagall alien and strange, and right-wingers took special umbrage at Vollard's subsequent selection of Chagall to illustrate La Fontaine's beloved

Fables. Chagall found this unsettling, especially in the context of the growing anti-Semitism in Germany and the Soviet Union. But he felt worthy of the La Fontaine project, so dear to the hearts of the French, since he was growing to appreciate French literature as well as the rural landscape around Paris. Still, he wrestled with the problem of identity: "Do I 'have to' become a French artist (never thought about it)," he wrote a friend in Russia. "It seems: I don't belong there." Yet he no longer belonged in Russia: "My paintings scattered all round the world, and in Russia they apparently don't even think and are not interested in an exhibition by me."[33] Vollard's support proved critical at this troubling moment.

Le Corbusier in 1924 was also experiencing some much-needed success, including the opportunity to lecture at the Sorbonne as well as in Prague and Geneva. He published *Urbanism*, setting forth his ideals for the city of tomorrow, and also began to record his achievements in *The Complete Work of Le Corbusier and Pierre Jeanneret* (there would be four volumes by 1938). His new office, located across from Bon Marché, already had twelve employees; soon there would be thirty. Inundated with work, he wrote a friend: "Existence continues to be exhausting but quite interesting, complex, impossible even to dream of such a thing as rest."[34]

Rest was out of the question for others as well that summer, especially the athletes congregated in Paris for the 1924 Summer Olympic Games. That year, the spotlight fell on the women's tennis competition, where Suzanne Lenglen was the favorite—having been wowing crowds at tennis matches since 1920, when she creamed the opposition at the Antwerp Olympic Games, after having demolished her rivals at Wimbledon. Not only was Lenglen the world's number-one female tennis player, but she also dressed for conquest in ways that would have been unthinkable just a few years before. While her opponents continued to wear long dresses that fully covered arms and legs, Lenglen shocked and delighted her audiences by wearing sleeveless silk dresses cut to above the calf, with white stockings rolled at the knee. Not surprisingly, this kind of outfit allowed Lenglen to leap gracefully from baseline to net, stretching for shots and winning handily. It also exposed her body in ways that made some gasp.

By 1924, Lenglen, now dubbed "La Divine," had become a celebrity in the mass media, where she fully embraced the "flapper" image by her daring clothes, her party-girl reputation, and her preference for sipping cognac between sets. She also was becoming a fashion icon, having hired the *couturier* Jean Patou to design her latest tennis togs. With Lenglen leading the way, sportswear now was emerging as a fashion market in itself, and in 1925 Patou took the next step by opening a boutique devoted to sportswear, with

Italian designer Elsa Schiaparelli following his lead. Naturally Coco Chanel, who achieved fame for her casual fashions, had a role to play in the Lenglen story. Earlier that year, Diaghilev's ballet, *Le Train bleu*, had featured a tennis player clearly based on Lenglen, and Chanel had designed the costumes.

Unfortunately, Lenglen disappointed her many followers by having to withdraw from the 1924 games due to illness, but her impact on the sport, as well as on fashion, remained. Her successor, the women's tennis champion of the 1924 Olympic Games, was an American, Helen Wills, a college undergraduate who swept to victory without dropping a set. Like Lenglen, Wills adopted a dress style that allowed for freedom of movement, although she was far less flamboyant than her predecessor. Instead of French *couturier* fashion, Wills wore a low-key outfit modeled on a sailor suit, with the practical addition of a sun visor.

Jean Renoir was in love with film—almost as much as he was in love with his entrancing wife, Catherine Hessling. His two loves of course went together, as he envisioned making films as a way of making Catherine a star. But something happened to him as he worked on their first venture together, and despite his disappointment with the film's commercial failure, he was, as he put it, hooked. Soon after, in 1924, he viewed Erich von Stroheim's film, *Foolish Wives*, which "astounded" him.[35] He returned to see it again and again, realizing that although Stroheim brought a Viennese sensibility to his film, there was much that a Frenchman could learn from it that Renoir could easily put on film. Indeed, "the way a washerwoman moves her arms, the way a lady combs her hair before a mirror, even a farmer selling his produce from a truck, each has its own sculptural value."[36]

Inspired by this insight, Renoir embarked on a new project, *La Fille de l'eau* (*The Water Girl*), using a friend's screenplay that he reworked. As it happened, the screenplay hardly mattered: the plot was "a secondary consideration, simply a pretext for purely visual imagery."[37] With this as his base, Renoir moved between fantasy and reality, juxtaposing details of daily life with dream sequences of Catherine on a white horse galloping through clouds and falling through the sky. The finished film did not generate much excitement among mainstream film distributors, but the dream sequence caught the attention of avant-garde film aficionados, one of whom cut the sequence and showed it in his movie house, to a standing ovation. Renoir, who was upset that someone had cut up his work and showed it to the public without his consent, was more than mollified by this response. "For the first time in my life," he noted, "I experienced the intoxication of success."[38]

Renoir was hardly the only one in Paris experimenting with film that year. Film had emerged as the newest vehicle for artistic expression, and artists such as Fernand Léger as well as Man Ray were beginning to explore its possibilities, focusing on the purely visual rather than the dramatic possibilities of the art. Léger, inspired by Man Ray[39] and working with filmmaker Dudley Murphy as well as with Ezra Pound, began to create *Ballet Mécanique*, an abstract film aimed at providing "percussion in pictures" by creating a juxtaposition of mundane objects such as wine bottles, a pendulum, egg whisks, and revolving saucepans with still-life shots of the closed and open eyes of Kiki, repeated and reflected in mirrors and special lenses to create a syncopated rhythm. Léger planned on a suitably avant-garde score as well, and he brought in the young American composer George Antheil to do the job. Antheil, who had recently arrived in Paris, was ecstatic about the project and boasted that his score "would exceed in discordance and tension Stravinsky's *Le Sacre du Printemps*."[40] But his music ended up being twice as long as the film, and for that and perhaps for other reasons, Léger presented the film at the International Exposition for New Theater Technique in Vienna that September without music.[41]

At almost the same time, the novice French film director René Clair had the opportunity to make a short intermission piece titled (appropriately) *Entr'acte*, for the Swedish Ballet's production of Picabia and Satie's ballet, *Relâche*. Satie wrote original music for *Entr'acte* as well as for *Relâche*, and the whole thing had the air of a Dadaist practical joke, since in the theater world *relâche* means "canceled," or "closed." Although what Picabia had in mind was a symbolic closing of the door on convention or tradition, the show's opening in fact was canceled due to the principal dancer's illness. But *Relâche* did go on at a later date and provided a certain amount of perplexing entertainment, including a dance with a wheelbarrow, a dance with a crown, a dance with a revolving door, and men plus one woman dressing and undressing on stage, all intended to be devoid of meaning and accompanied by Satie's deliberately provocative music, much of it set to well-known (and thoroughly bawdy) songs. Intermission brought the madly original *Entr'acte*, although Satie and Picabia had already appeared in a brief bit of film at the opening of *Relâche* that had them firing a cannon directly at the audience from the top of a building. *Entr'acte* itself brought brief appearances by well-known members of the avant-garde, including sequences where they run in slow motion, move in reverse, or disappear. A crowd of mourners follow a camel-drawn hearse, first in slow motion, then ever faster, as the hearse escapes the camel and the streets fill with racing cars. After a hectic roller-coaster ride, the coffin spills onto a field, where the corpse steps out as a ma-

Marcel Duchamp and Man Ray playing chess on the roof of the Théâtre des Champs-Elysées, in a scene from the film Entr'acte, directed by René Clair, 1924. The Museum of Modern Art Digital Image © The Museum of Modern Art / Licensed by SCALA / Art Resource, NY.

gician, who makes the mourners disappear one by one. In the midst of all this commotion, the camera catches Man Ray and Marcel Duchamp improbably playing chess on the roof of the Théâtre des Champs-Elysées.

Another experimental film project that year, *L'Inhumaine*, directed by Marcel L'Herbier and starring opera singer Georgette Leblanc, involved the collaboration of leading members of the arts, architecture, and music, including Darius Milhaud, Fernand Léger, Paul Poiret, René Lalique, and architect Robert Mallet-Stevens. Georgette Leblanc wanted a star vehicle and offered to partially finance it in return for a lead role as well as distribution rights in the United States. The plot itself was a melodrama with science-fiction-fantasy overtones, but it really did not matter: L'Herbier's primary goal was to bring together leaders in the arts, especially the decorative arts, in the hope that his vision of cinema as a synthesis of the arts would give his film a potentially profitable tie-in with the upcoming Paris Arts Décoratif exhibition in 1925.

Due to Leblanc's touring schedule, L'Herbier began shooting in late 1923, including a huge concert scene for his diva, set in the Théâtre des Champs-Elysées. There, exceptionally loud and jarring music by George Antheil set off what may have been a well-planned riot, which the film required and L'Herbier hoped for. In the audience, and presumably enjoying the scene, were Satie and Milhaud, Picasso and Picabia, as well as the ever-present Jean Cocteau. But whatever buzz the filming of *L'Inhumaine* created, the film itself did not impress audiences when it opened in November 1924. A few critics admired L'Herbier's remarkable technical innovations, but most thought these artsy gestures did not mesh with the film's entertainment function and blasted the actors' wooden performances as well as the melodramatic script. Audiences were similarly negative, and after a number of showings abroad, the film quietly disappeared. So did L'Herbier's production company, which did not survive the financial loss.

Relâche turned out to be a kind of swan song for Dada, for by now Dada had given place to Surrealism, a movement that assumed concrete form that autumn with its manifesto, written by André Breton, and its magazine, *La Révolution Surréaliste*, first issued on December 1. The basic Surrealist premise, according to Breton, was that art arises from the subconscious. Breton, who maintained that Surrealism freed the spirit from the chains of reason, took his followers into realms of dream narratives, automatic writing, and explorations of the unconscious. This in itself sounded fairly innocuous, but then he took his disciples a significant step further by his unrelenting attacks on reason-based Western literary culture, which he deemed sufficiently dangerous that extreme actions were justified in opposing it.

The Surrealists used their first public display of revolt to rail against Anatole France, whose success as a conventional man of letters offended them to the core. Not only was France a leading member of the Académie Française, but he also was revered for his support of Dreyfus and Zola during the height of the Dreyfus Affair (indeed, France had boycotted the Académie between 1902 and 1916 as a protest against his colleagues' anti-Dreyfusism). But Breton loathed everything Anatole France represented, "for it is made up of mediocrity, hate, and dull conceit."[42] He and his followers took the occasion of France's death on October 12 to publish a pamphlet, *Un Cadavre*, in which they wrote that France and his books should be thrown into the Seine. Although the *New Yorker*'s new Paris correspondent, Janet Flanner (pen name, Genêt), deemed Anatole France's sumptuous funeral procession "one of the biggest, most pretentious spectacles modern Paris has ever seen," she was not alone in her revulsion at the antics of the Surrealists, who followed the cortège through the streets and "shouted insults to his memory . . . every step of the way." She correctly believed that this was the first of "their sadistic street manifestations" and that they created a scandal, "since Paris has so long been noted as a great appreciator of its intellectual figures."[43]

Of course, a scandal was exactly what Breton wanted.

Not long after the death of Anatole France came the demise of yet another notable Parisian, the composer Gabriel Fauré. Until shortly before his death, Fauré had served as director of the Paris Conservatoire, shaking up that stodgy institution by broadening and modernizing the range of music taught within its walls. He also was an inspired teacher and, many years before, had recognized the talent of Maurice Ravel when so many others had not. In fact, it was due to the scandal surrounding Ravel's early elimination from the 1905 Prix de Rome competition that Fauré became head of the Conservatoire.[44]

Fauré remained a friend and colleague of Ravel's for life. "The techniques of Gabriel Fauré are as personal as they are subtle," Ravel told Roland-Manuel in a 1922 interview praising Fauré, which appeared in *La Revue musicale*. "He proposed no formulas to his pupils, urging them, on the contrary, to beware of stereotyped workmanship."[45] In a touching response, Fauré thanked Ravel with all his heart and then went on to say that he was "thinking of your growth, dear friend, since [your student days], and I am happier than you can imagine about the solid position which you occupy and which you have acquired so brilliantly and so rapidly. It is a source of joy and pride for your old professor."[46]

Another of Fauré's pupils was Nadia Boulanger, the prominent teacher, lecturer, conductor, and soloist (piano and organ), who had become the first woman to get as far as second place in the Prix de Rome competition (her younger sister, Lili, would be the first woman to win the Prix de Rome, shortly before her untimely death). After the war, Nadia Boulanger increasingly focused on teaching, and, thanks in great part to the wartime work she had done with Americans to support musicians on active duty, she began her remarkable teaching career at the American Conservatory in Fontainebleau. There, over the course of many years, she would instruct a stellar array of students from the Americas, one of the first being Aaron Copland.

As it happened, one of the founders (along with conductor Walter Damrosch) of the American Conservatory in Fontainebleau was Francis Casadesus, a member of the remarkable Casadesus family of musicians. Francis and his brothers and sisters were all fine musicians, but the most outstanding was Francis's nephew, Robert, whose narrow escape from life in an orphanage was all the more dramatic because of the renowned concert pianist he became. Born to Francis's brother and a young music student, the illegitimate child almost ended up on public assistance because his mother was so desperate to keep her family from finding out about him. But the child's father, who soon disappeared from his life, at least had the good sense and compassion to bring the baby home to his own family, where little Robert was warmly welcomed and his musical talents nurtured. In time, Robert entered the Paris Conservatory, where his considerable abilities as a pianist attracted the attention of numerous notables as well as that of another talented young pianist, Gabrielle (Gaby) L'Hôte, who was quite taken with the perfection of his piano playing—and his charm.

It was a touching love story as well as a remarkable success story. Robert and Gaby did indeed marry at the war's end and would celebrate fifty years together as partners in music making as well as in life. Early in their marriage, young Casadesus taught at the American Conservatory in Fontainebleau, and he would continue to teach and compose throughout his long life. But he had already begun to concertize, and, in a storybook turn of events, he caught the public eye when the Paris Opera called upon him at the last minute to substitute for an ailing soloist. From then on, Robert Casadesus's career skyrocketed.

Among those who took notice of the young pianist was Maurice Ravel, who in 1922 invited Casadesus to collaborate with him on a project to create piano rolls for several of Ravel's works (Ravel had heard Casadesus perform Ravel's fiendishly difficult *Gaspard de la nuit* and congratulated him on his interpretation). By 1924, the two were good friends, and Casadesus gave a recital that year entirely devoted to piano works by Ravel. The recital was broadcast on radio, a pioneering event, and in response, a typically reserved but pleased Ravel told Casadesus that "*Jeux d'eau* (among other pieces) has never been played so well."[47]

⌒

In late March, André Citroën made his second visit to the United States, where he traveled once again to Detroit to meet with Henry Ford, who by then had produced ten million Model T cars, lowered their price, and raised his profits to enormous levels. Based on Ford's interest in research and development, Citroën brought examples of his half-track system, which had carried his vehicles through the Sahara desert and, in his mind, were well suited to the vast expanse of America's many dirt roads. Much to his disappointment, neither Ford nor the U.S. military was interested.

Despite being hailed by the American press as the "Henry Ford of France," Citroën and Ford had little in common except for their automobiles and the scientific management ideas of Frederick Winslow Taylor. Unlike Citroën, who was a social progressive, a reformer, and a sophisticate who embraced the pleasures as well as the solid achievements of the Jazz Age, Ford was at heart still a country boy, with a puritanical mind-set and a deep mistrust of cities and the people who lived in them—especially African Americans, recent immigrants, and Jews. Citroën, who was Jewish, certainly did not strike up much of a friendship with the Detroit tycoon, whose anti-Semitism would become increasingly virulent in the coming years.

Ford's authoritarianism was becoming more rampant as well, as he sought to direct and regulate his workers' thoughts and leisure time as well as their work hours in an attempt to impose a new and better order on humanity—a vision that had far more in common with the views of L'Oréal's founder, Eugène Schueller, than with those of André Citroën. Schueller, too, thought that he could save the world, and he was beginning to develop a set of social as well as economic theories to do so. In time, much like Ford (whom he admired), Schueller would use his extensive businesses as a means of uplifting the race by modifying and controlling people's thoughts and lives in ways he thought fitting.

While Ford and Schueller were developing and putting into practice their particular forms of authoritarianism, François Coty was busy creating an ultra-right-wing newspaper empire, with the goal of influencing and forming public opinion on the largest scale possible. After all, Mussolini—whom Coty greatly admired—wrote in his autobiography that the newspaper was "that modern weapon, capable of all possibilities," and gave the credit to his own newspaper, the *Popolo d'Italia*, for being "an instrument for the making of me."[48] *Figaro* in Paris was merely the beginning: by 1924 Coty had bought or was creating a journal of finance, a women's daily, a student newspaper, regional papers, and morning, evening, and specialist papers, including one specifically targeted at electricians. Within several years he would have some forty newspapers at his command.

Concurrently, a new youth movement of the Right, Jeunesses Patriotes, was forming in Paris, inspired by Mussolini's fascism, while on the Left, the Communist party was taking root in France. Actively battling the communist threat, Coty corresponded with Mussolini and reprinted his tracts in *Figaro*. This did not sit well with the moderately conservative supporters of the paper, but Coty was fiercely anti-Bolshevik, having suffered extensive losses in his Moscow store following the Bolshevik Revolution. Besides, Coty was deeply anti-Semitic, and he flatly categorized all Bolsheviks as Jews.

Since Coty and others of his persuasion also equated socialists with communists, it was of particular pain to them when the French government (under the newly elected Cartel des Gauches, an alliance of leftist parties) laid out elaborate plans that autumn to honor socialist leader Jean Jaurès by transferring his ashes to the Panthéon. A decade had now passed since Jaurès's assassination, and Jaurès received a magnificent ceremony, in which his coffin, resting on an eighty-two-foot bier, was carried by twenty-two miners in working clothes. A huge cortège followed, in which leagues, cooperatives, and federations mingled—although in visual testimony to the complexity of the politics of the Left, the communists refused to join with their more moderate brethren and marched separately, behind the rest.

France, under its new prime minister, Edouard Herriot, had already recognized the Soviet Union, and members of the Right were horrified by what they envisaged as the revolutionary menace, with its unrelenting march westward. At the same time, Russians dismayed by life under Soviet rule were escaping to the West. Among them that year was a troupe of dancers from the Mariinsky Theatre in St. Petersburg, who landed first in Berlin and then London, where Diaghilev heard of them and invited them to Paris.

Their leader, a twenty-two-year-old dancer and choreographer by the name of Giorgi Balanchivadze, would soon become known as George Balanchine.

Josephine Baker in her famous banana skirt, circa 1927. Private Collection / Prismatic Pictures / Bridgeman Images

CHAPTER TEN

~

You've Come a Long Way
from St. Louis

(1925)

Josephine Baker hit Paris like a bombshell. Not only was she gorgeous, but she made an electrifying entrance—virtually nude, and slung over the shoulders of a muscular black dancer named Joe Alex.

Everyone who saw *La Revue Nègre* that night at the Théâtre des Champs-Elysées remembered her. How could they not? Baker was fabulous, utterly knockout fabulous, and the word soon spread. But her own most treasured memory of that unforgettable opening night in Paris was quite different from the one her smitten audience carried away: what Josephine Baker remembered was that, for the first time in her life, she was invited to eat with white people.

She was born in the slums of St. Louis and by the time she was fifteen had already discarded her first husband and her birth name (Freda J. McDonald) in a dogged attempt to make it in the theater. A second husband and a shot at fame followed, as an unstoppable Josephine went from road shows to big time in New York, and from there, in 1925, to Paris. Here, the girl who had been known to family and friends as "Tumpy" became the toast of the town, and although she went through many husbands and lovers afterward, Paris remained the one constant love of her life.

She was, of course, black, at a time when being black in America meant not only suffering the daily indignities of segregation, but also the dangers of racial hatred. Growing up black in St. Louis during the early twentieth century, Josephine Baker saw it all, including bloody race riots. It was through talent and determination that she managed to claw her way out, and it was through a stroke of luck that she found herself in Paris on the night of October 2, 1925.

Paris was already enamored with jazz and with the African Americans who made it. In response to this welcoming atmosphere, Caroline Dudley Reagan, the wife of an American foreign service officer stationed in Paris, decided to bring an all-black musical revue to Paris. She couldn't afford a star such as Ethel Waters, but while in New York she spotted nineteen-year-old Josephine Baker in the show Waters was headlining and decided that this young phenomenon would be her star.

What is generally forgotten is that at this stage in her career, Josephine Baker was primarily a clown. A dancer, too, but primarily a clown. From early childhood she had sent her family and friends into stitches with her cross-eyed chicken walk, which in time morphed into a comic Charleston routine. In fact, it was as a comic that she made her first appearance in *La Revue Nègre*. But the show's producers had concluded that the revue, as good as it was, needed something more to make it a smash hit. That is how, at the show's finale, Josephine Baker, clad only in a couple of pink feathers, came to be carried on stage draped across Joe Alex's shoulders. As Janet Flanner wrote, "She made her entry entirely nude except for a pink flamingo feather between her limbs; she was being carried upside down and doing the split on the shoulder of a black giant. Mid-stage he paused, and with his long fingers holding her basket-wise around the waist, swung her in a slow cartwheel to the stage floor, where she stood . . . in an instant of complete silence."[1] Pandemonium soon broke out as the amazed audience watched while the two slithered and jerked in a kind of frenzied mating ritual, accompanied by a pounding jazz beat.

Scarcely more than a decade before, Stravinsky had made the same sort of pounding impact in exactly the same theater with his ballet *The Rite of Spring*. Stravinsky and Josephine Baker may have had little else in common, but they both set off cultural fireworks at the Théâtre des Champs-Elysées, to the accompaniment of primal rhythms.

The other big story that year was the huge style-setting exhibition of the decorative arts called the Exposition Internationale des Arts Décoratifs et Industriels Modernes (International Exposition of Modern Decorative and Industrial Arts), a celebration of the new mode of design that would eventually be called, for short, Art Deco.[2] Lasting from April to October and spanning both sides of the Seine between the Invalides and the Champs-Elysées—including even the bridge between them, the Pont Alexandre III—the exhibition encompassed design in every form, from jewelry and fashion to furniture and architecture, and would leave its mark on taste and fashion during the decade and a half that followed. Maurice Sachs probably exaggerated, but he had a point when he wrote that, thanks to the exposition, "overnight the great boulevards of Paris were transformed. . . . All the shops changed face. . . . Nickel replaced wood, and an austerity which tried to be rich, an affected simplicity, and a severe arrangement replaced the sweet disorder of before the war."[3]

It did not happen quite that quickly or easily, but the new was in fact diametrically different from the old and was quickly edging its way into acceptance. Art Deco was clean edged and machine tooled, based on sleek and streamlined geometric forms rather than the organic shapes and sinuous lines of its turn-of-the-century predecessor, Art Nouveau. André Mare and Louis Süe, who had suffered undeserved ignominy in 1919 following the disaster of their war memorial,[4] were among the movement's French leaders, and together they designed the exposition's pavilion for contemporary art, one of many temporary exhibition structures that drew large crowds of curious and enthusiastic visitors—some sixteen million by the exhibition's end. Department stores such as Printemps and Galeries Lafayette mounted daring exhibits of the new style, which vaunted a look compatible with the modern machine age. Architect Pierre Patout designed the much-lauded Pavillon de Collectionneur containing Emile-Jacques Ruhlmann's Grand Salon, decorated by leading artists and designers. Other nations were represented as well, including Britain, Denmark, and Austria (which showed examples of the Viennese Secession movement), but it was France and especially Parisian taste and fashion that starred.

The movement's primary theme was modernism: Art Deco was the latest word in modernist chic, and those with the money to revamp their surroundings and their lives accordingly were encouraged by example to do so. Those with more modest means followed suit more modestly, but the idea behind the exposition clearly was the necessity of shopping and buying in Paris.

André Citroën, never one to miss an opportunity to publicize his name or his products, used the exposition to showcase his new all-steel B12 auto—with a version not painted in the usual dull black, but decorated by artist Sonia Delaunay in a multicolored Art Deco checkerboard motif and accompanied by models wearing an identical design.

Citroën's B12 itself was worth more than a second look. He had not come home empty-handed from his trip to America the previous year.

Detouring from Detroit to Philadelphia, he met with industrialist Edward Gowan Budd, who had developed a revolutionary process for constructing all-steel cars by welding together large preformed panels. Citroën immediately purchased the European rights and, along with a spray-painting process developed by another American firm, DuPont, was able to steal the spotlight with his B12 auto at the autumn 1924 Paris auto show. His new technique, which replaced a combined wood and metal body with an all-steel one, allowed him to build stronger, safer, and more weather-resistant autos than the old models, and by late 1925, the efficiencies these innovations introduced would allow Citroën to significantly increase output and reduce his prices.

Sales gimmicks like the checkerboard paint job drew attention to the B12, and Citroën had already marked the opening of an earlier Paris auto show with an airplane dramatically skywriting his brand name across the sky. But he entered a new realm entirely in 1925 by setting his name in electric lights on the Eiffel Tower. Between 1925 and 1934, "Citroën" appeared in letters one hundred feet high on the tower, the most distinctive landmark in Paris, using 250,000 electric lightbulbs that could be seen from sixty miles in every direction. Citroën switched on the signal lighting up his name on July 4, at the height of the Art Deco exposition.

It was an advertising feat of amazing audacity, but Citroën could point out that at least the name in lights was that of a Frenchman. He had heard that Henry Ford had expressed interest in the name-in-lights gimmick and had also considered buying the tower and bringing it back to Detroit.

The Eiffel Tower would now bear Citroën's name for a time, but at least it was staying put.

By late 1925, almost one-third of the cars on French roads were Citroëns. Within six years after starting his automobile business, he had overtaken older and more established European competitors such as Renault, Peugeot, and Fiat to become the fourth-largest auto company in the world, behind only the Americans—Ford, General Motors, and Chrysler.

Renault was fighting back, though. Working to secure control over his raw materials, he had bought his own steelworks and glass factory and established a hydroelectric plant as well as a tool factory, sawmills, a cotton-wool factory (for vehicle interiors), and a brick factory to make his own bricks for these various enterprises—a factory that would soon be supplying bricks, with the Renault trademark, to much of Paris, including a new workshop of Citroën's. In addition, he was setting up sales centers with Renault repair garages throughout France. He also was producing engines and machinery for the new battleships of the expanding French navy as well as for the growing aviation industry, and he would soon acquire a firm that made airplane fuselages so that he could control construction of engines and fuselages together.

As for trucks and buses, Renault now dominated this field more completely than ever, from vans and large carriers to ambulances and fire engines, and would soon have no rivals in the field of large limousines. And then there was agricultural equipment, where he converted the engines of his wartime tanks to use in tractors and financed an agricultural journal to persuade French farmers to move with the times.

By the war's end, Renault was confident that he had left his rivals well behind. But the unexpected emergence of Citroën confronted him with a far more serious competitor than ever before, one whose personality and approach to business, finance, and labor were almost diametrically opposed to his own. Challenges from Citroën appeared almost everywhere Renault looked, whether at the annual Paris auto show, on dueling intercity bus routes, or on cross-continent expeditions. It seemed that Citroën was everywhere, garnering publicity every step of the way. In 1925 alone, an expedition of Citroën's caterpillar cars completed an unheard-of north-to-south crossing of Africa, all the way to Cape Town, reported breathlessly by the international press.

Most people watching the Citroën saga thought that he would win the struggle between the two titans. By 1925, it seemed inevitable. But Renault was a fighter, and he was far from giving up.

A large number of dress designers took part in the great Exposition des Arts Décoratifs, but Paul Poiret was convinced that he could outshine them all. Resorting to his usual showmanship, he hired three barges near the Pont Alexandre III and equipped them lavishly. The one that he named *Délices*, featuring rare wines and elegant foods, was draped in red anemones; the second, *Amours*, done in blue carnations, starred a perfume piano that wafted Poiret's latest fragrances, while the third, *Orgues*, with a pipe organ and fourteen original frescoes by Dufy, was the showcase for Poiret's interior décor and couture collection.

Interior view of one of Paul Poiret's three barges, exhibited for the Paris Exposition of the Modern Decorative and Industrial Arts, 1925. Bibliothèque des Arts Décoratifs, Paris / Archives Charmet / Bridgeman Images

It was grand, it was glorious, and it was expensive—around five hundred thousand francs for each barge. Poiret certainly could not afford it, especially as his partners refused to share the expenses for this extravaganza. And by this time, Poiret indeed had partners: financial hardship had forced him to sell his business to a group of backers, who tried (unsuccessfully) to rein in his most grandiose schemes, forced him to provide exact records of his expenses (a requirement that devastated and insulted him), sold off his Parfums de Rosine to the Société Centrale de la Parfumerie Française, and made him move his grand salon to smaller quarters on Rond-Point, Champs-Elysées.[5] The problem was that by 1925, Poiret's fashions, which were every bit as over the top as his entertainments, appeared overly complex and outdated beside the easy and streamlined fashions of Chanel and others such as Jean Patou. As a result, Poiret's clients were steadily abandoning him for trendier alternatives.

Other expenses were also dragging Poiret down. Four years earlier, he had hired the modernist architect Robert Mallet-Stevens to design a country villa for him in Mézy, outside of Paris. It was a stunning house, with a view of the lake where the 1900 and 1924 Olympic boating events were held. But Poiret never occupied the main residence, which he could not afford to complete, and instead lived in the caretaker's cottage.

That autumn, in an attempt to pay off his debts, Poiret sold most of his extensive art collection. But even this was not enough. His binge for the Exposition des Arts Décoratifs turned out to be his swan song rather than his triumph, and its cost would continue to weigh on him for years.

⌒

Le Corbusier was happy. He was enjoying life with his mistress, Yvonne Gallis, and was experiencing a marked degree of professional success. Among the many projects now occupying him, he was completing a studio-residence for a good friend, the sculptor Jacques Lipchitz, and had been given preferential treatment by the influential avant-garde German architect Mies van der Rohe in a major Stuttgart exhibit of the modern home. But he was about to drop a bombshell, and the place he chose was the Paris Exposition des Arts Décoratifs.

To begin with, although Le Corbusier admired the exposition's intent of focusing on the era's "modern tendencies,"[6] he did not like Art Deco as a style and rejected the very concept of the decorative arts. Indeed, Le Corbusier's purist functionalism set out on quite a different path from Art Deco in its response to the mechanized age.

Inspired by the huge increase of automobile traffic in Paris, he declared that "surgery must be applied at the city's centre. . . . We must use the knife."[7] The outcome was his exhibit for the exposition, his Pavillon de l'Esprit Nouveau—a standardized single-family dwelling of moderate cost and avant-garde design, constructed much like a white concrete box, with an industrial-style window wall. As Le Corbusier later put it, his Pavillon de l'Esprit Nouveau "constituted in itself a document of standardization. All its furnishings were the product of industry and not of the decorators. The building itself was a 'cell' in a block of flats, a unit in a housing scheme, built on the 'honeycomb' principle"[8]—a principle that he had been developing ever since his Dom-ino system a decade before. Inside was an enclosed garden, and adjoining was a rotunda containing two large dioramas of the city's future—a generalized city, or the City for Three Million, and the Plan Voisin, which demonstrated Le Corbusier's solution for the center of Paris itself.

Much to Le Corbusier's dismay, his Pavillon de l'Esprit Nouveau was poorly situated, almost hidden within the garden of the Grand Palais. The exhibition's organizers, looking for something more elegant than a dwelling for everyman, had rejected Le Corbusier's initial proposal, and when they finally granted him a site, it was remote and complicated by trees. Worse, he received no funding to build it. Le Corbusier was angry but not surprised, and he proceeded to look for financing from automobile companies in return for a "naming opportunity." Jean-Pierre Peugeot and André Citroën turned him down, and the rubber-tire mogul André Michelin was out of the country. But Gabriel Voisin, the aircraft manufacturer with a division of luxury automobiles, agreed to become a sponsor. Le Corbusier consequently named his new plan for Paris the Plan Voisin.

The exhibition's building committee erected an eighteen-foot-high wall in front of Le Corbusier's pavilion, possibly to hide it while under construction, but more likely, as Le Corbusier thought, to hide it, period. In any case, the truly shocking elements of the exhibit were the City for Three Million and, especially, the Plan Voisin, which became in the minds of many a plan to destroy Paris. Having declared large sections of central Paris "antiquated . . . unhealthy . . . [and] overcrowded,"[9] Le Corbusier proposed to destroy hundreds of acres of the Right Bank, including much of the Marais.

Contrary to what his most livid opponents thought, Le Corbusier was not calling for a wholesale destruction of the past: he would have kept the Place des Vosges, the Louvre, the Arc de Triomphe, and the Palais Royal, with the intent of making them more visible by opening space around them. But for the rest, Le Corbusier envisioned a city of carefully spaced skyscrapers surrounded by parks and serviced by two limited-access expressways—roadways that he saw as dual backbones that channeled traffic east–west and north–south. In this way, the urban fabric would be opened to "air, light and greenery," and the Arc de Triomphe and the road leading to it "would be rescued from compromise, ambiguity, absurdity, and all of the traffic hastily thrust into the *cul-de-sac* of the Place de la Concorde would be re-absorbed."[10]

Le Corbusier does not seem to have intended his plan to be followed, at least not literally: "The 'Voisin' scheme does not claim to have found a final solution to the problem of the center of Paris," he wrote, "but it may serve to raise the discussion to a level in keeping with the spirit of our new age."[11] Some, like the poet Paul Valéry, understood what he was driving at—especially the necessity of thinking ahead and planning for the inevitabilities of the future. But most did not understand, and it would be this scheme that would permanently shape an outraged opinion of Le Corbusier as the man who wanted to destroy Paris.

Many of those scrutinizing the exhibits at the Exposition des Arts Décoratifs thought they could see a direct line from Cubism to Art Deco, and the British art historian and authority on Art Deco, Bevis Hillier, has written that "the influence of Cubism in Art Deco is undeniable."[12] But Picasso was having none of it. As he remarked, "What would Michelangelo have said if they had held him responsible for a Renaissance chest of drawers?"[13]

Fortunately, it never came to that, and Picasso, along with his wife and son, left Paris that summer for the Riviera, where they joined the Murphys and other interesting friends, including the Beaumonts, John Dos Passos, the Archibald MacLeishes, and the Picabias, along with the Scott Fitzgeralds, whose drunken exploits were becoming less and less amusing. But other than evenings with this crowd, it was a productive summer for Picasso, who had completed his masterful and starkly disquieting *La Danse* (or *Three Dancers*) just before he left Paris, and while in the south of France continued to focus on his painting rather than on socializing. Since 1920, Picasso had gone back and forth between Neoclassicism and a restrained Cubism, but *La Danse* moved decisively into more psychologically violent realms, and with it, Picasso moved beyond his Neoclassical phase. He continued his explorations that summer with still lifes that led him further into this realm.

André Breton, who saw *La Danse* shortly after its completion, promptly labeled it Surrealist and sent Man Ray to photograph it. Then he pressed

Picasso for the right to publish it in his journal, *La Révolution Surréaliste*. Picasso agreed to the picture's publication but did not agree to become the face of Surrealism. Breton continued to pursue him, but the painter kept his distance. As Picasso later told Roland Penrose, "We [Cubists] wanted to go deep into things. What was wrong with [the] Surrealists was that they did not go inside, they took the surface effects of the subconscious. They did not understand the inside of the object or themselves."[14]

Breton also tried to claim Chagall as a Surrealist, but Chagall did not fit into either the Neoclassical or the Surrealist mode and remained aloof from both. Breton would have more luck with Joan Miró, whose June exhibition—opening fashionably at midnight and attracting a crowd of Montparnasse regulars—was a great success, ending with everyone heading for the Jockey, where the diminutive Miró memorably tangoed with the much-taller Kiki. Picasso missed this occasion and the subsequent furor at the Closerie des Lilas, where Breton and his Surrealist followers created havoc at a banquet held in honor of the elderly Symbolist poet Saint-Pol-Roux. During the course of the evening, someone made a comment that angered Breton, and a food fight and shouting match quickly erupted into a riot, during which various Surrealists leaped onto tables, swung from the chandelier, and ripped a window off its hinges. Fortunately the poet was not injured, and the police soon put an end to the shenanigans. Cocteau correctly predicted that the next step in the Surrealists' break with society would be to join with the communists, and added to Max Jacob, "I no longer blame them—I pray for them."[15]

Picasso also missed the funeral of Satie, who died that July after a long illness. Satie had become incurably ill shortly after the performance of *Relâche*, which would be his last work. Etienne de Beaumont and Winnaretta de Polignac came to his aid, arranging for his admission to a private room in the Hôpital Saint-Joseph. There, surrounded by a small band of faithful friends—including Milhaud, Brancusi (who brought chicken soup), Valentine Hugo (who, at Satie's request, brought piles of handkerchiefs), Winnaretta, Braque, Derain, Jean Wiéner, and (before departing Paris for the summer) Picasso—Satie eked out the remaining months of his existence, often testing his friends' patience with odd requests and sudden rages. Poulenc and Auric were not allowed in, having joined the long list of those who had managed to affront Satie during the course of his life.

Milhaud, who had visited Satie daily for six months, left the dying man's bedside for good cause—marriage to Milhaud's cousin, Madeleine. By the time the newlyweds returned from their honeymoon, Satie had died. But

Milhaud was still involved in Satie's life, whether in locating Satie's brother, from whom Satie had been estranged, or in going through Satie's effects. This turned out to be a wrenching experience, as Satie had never allowed anyone into his tiny Arcueil apartment, and Milhaud was unprepared for what he saw. "It seemed impossible," he later wrote, "that Satie had lived in such poverty. This man, whose faultlessly clean and correct dress made him look rather like a model official, owned almost literally *nothing*." His belongings were "wretched" and included a half-filled wardrobe containing "a dozen old-fashioned corduroy suits, brand-new and absolutely identical."[16] Piles of old newspapers, old hats, umbrellas still in their wrappers, and walking sticks filled the room's corners (Satie never appeared in public without a bowler hat, a walking stick, and an umbrella). The piano was broken down, its pedals tied up with string, and behind it were compositions that Satie thought he had lost on a bus. Milhaud did not mention handkerchiefs, but when Valentine Hugo picked up Satie's laundry, as directed, she was astounded to find a total of eighty-nine.

Satie's funeral, held in Arcueil, drew a large crowd—not only from Montparnasse and the Boeuf sur le Toit, but from Arcueil itself, whose citizens remembered him with affection. In 1927, Diaghilev paid his tribute to Satie by mounting a production of *Le Mercure*, originally premiered by Beaumont's Soirées de Paris. Unfortunately it was not a success, and Diaghilev never restaged it.

By the middle of March, Cocteau's opium habit had become sufficiently debilitating that he entered a private hospital near the Place de l'Etoile, where he stayed for about six weeks, enduring a "cold turkey" cure accompanied by "showers, electric baths, nerves on edge, jerking legs that want to walk on the ceiling," as he wrote Jacques Maritain.[17] To help him through the ordeal, Max Jacob and other friends wrote him almost every day, and Valentine and Jean Hugo even managed to visit, although this was against the rules.

"Dear Max," he wrote the faithful Jacob in early April, "you are my doctor,"[18] and although both Maritain and Jacob were concerned about Cocteau's physical condition, they were far more concerned about the state of his soul. When, soon after his departure from the clinic, Cocteau decided to "convert" to Catholicism (it was a return to the Catholic faith, as he had been baptized in infancy), Jacob as well as Maritain were overjoyed. "Joy! Joy! Tears of joy!" Jacob wrote Cocteau, although he confided some concerns to the Princess Ghika, the former courtesan Liane de Pougy, who had turned to religion after the wartime death of her son. "Conversions have value only if they are complete," he wrote her, "and I fear that his has not changed his life."[19]

Several weeks later, Cocteau shared with Jean and Valentine Hugo his "plans for Catholic activity," which began with a pamphlet, *Letter to Jacques Maritain*, telling of his joyous return to the sacraments. His intent was to persuade others to follow in his footsteps, and soon one of his young followers, Maurice Sachs, enthusiastically renounced his Jewish roots and was baptized. Not long after, Sachs entered the Carmelite Seminary in Paris, with the intent of becoming a priest. The news was enough to amaze those who knew him: Jean Wiéner almost lost control of his automobile when he spotted Sachs near Place Saint-Sulpice in a cassock.

Unfortunately, Max Jacob was right: Cocteau's abstinence from opium lasted only five months. Sachs's vocation was similarly brief and ended disastrously.

While Parisians were trying to get on with their lives, tourists continued to stream into the City of Light, especially into Montparnasse. "Montparnasse is the center of the world!" declared the authors of a 1925 book on the quarter,[20] and tourists were as eager to have a drink at the Dôme and dance at the Jockey as they were to see the Venus de Milo. "Don't hesitate, come to Montparnasse!" was how the journalist Henri Broca put it. He added, "Go there two times rather than one, and after that, you will not leave."[21] It was even rumored that one could purchase a ticket in Des Moines that took one directly to the Dôme.

Among those who arrived that year was the future Spanish filmmaker, Luis Buñuel, who reported that the tune "On fait un' petite belote, et puis voilà" was everywhere (*belote* being a popular card game then sweeping Paris) and that the sound of accordions filled the city. Also arriving were an unknown American novelist by the name of William Faulkner as well as a successful one, F. Scott Fitzgerald. Fitzgerald had come to France the year before with his wife, Zelda, and his daughter, Scottie, but then traveled throughout Europe and summered on the Riviera (where Zelda had an affair with a young aviator) before settling in Paris that spring of 1925—shortly after his *The Great Gatsby* was published, to rave reviews. Fitzgerald was still in his twenties and a lauded author of *This Side of Paradise* and *The Beautiful and Damned* as well as two collections of short stories that pretty well summed up the Roaring Twenties' pleasure seekers: *Flappers and Philosophers* and *Tales of the Jazz Age*. Even before he and Hemingway met, he had passed along word to his editor at Scribner's, Maxwell Perkins, about the talented young midwesterner he had been hearing about.

Hemingway had in fact managed to establish himself as a literary person of promise among the cognoscenti of Montparnasse, even without much in the way of publication, but he was still on the defensive when he and Fitzgerald first met at the Dingo that afternoon in late April. Years later, after achieving fame, Hemingway still described that first meeting with a tone that seemed curiously out of place for someone talking about a friend, especially if that friend was by that time dead. Describing Fitzgerald's face, for instance, Hemingway wrote that "he had . . . a long-lipped Irish mouth that on a girl, would have been the mouth of a beauty. . . . The mouth worried you until you knew him and then it worried you more." According to Hemingway, Scott talked too much, even (especially) when he was complimentary, and he dressed too well. He was also too inquisitive. A few days later, though, when they met at the Closerie des Lilas, Fitzgerald was less drunk, and Hemingway liked him better. Still, Fitzgerald could be annoying, especially when drunk, and it took very little to get him drunk. After recognizing his alcoholism, Hemingway concluded "that no matter what Scott did, nor how he behaved, I must know it was like a sickness and be of any help I could to him and try to be a good friend."[22]

Throughout May and June, Hemingway and Fitzgerald saw a lot of one another—eating, drinking, and talking. Fitzgerald helped Hemingway to see that his short stories were not enough, and that he had to write a novel in order to make his reputation. Yet Fitzgerald was disappointed with the sales of *The Great Gatsby* and, despite his previous successes, seemed surprisingly insecure. Hemingway, who did not like Zelda, thought she was to blame for this, with her incessant attempts to undermine her husband's confidence. Despite Hemingway's own fixation on the negative impact of wives on their husbands—a lesson he had carried with him since childhood—he had a point: Zelda's mental instability was already apparent, and together, she and Fitzgerald would eventually destroy one another. But that still lay in the future, although hints of the tragedy were already evident.[23]

Two other women entered Hemingway's life that spring: Lady Duff Twysden and Pauline Pfeiffer. Twysden's most recent marriage to a British aristocrat had disintegrated and left her with a title but no money. Still, she had other resources: she was tall, slim, attractive, and could drink almost any man under the table. Hemingway adored her and was, like the many other men in her life, more than willing to pick up her bar tabs. After unsuccessfully attempting an affair with her, he turned her into a character in his novel, *The Sun Also Rises*. Tough and vulnerable, Duff Twysden would become the inspiration for Lady Brett Ashley.

He hadn't yet begun the novel; that would come after his third trip to Pamplona in June, preceded by a fishing trip with his buddies. In Pamplona, Hemingway went after Twysden, whose disinclination for an affair seemed to be the only thing keeping them apart (Twysden was supposed to have remarked that she liked Hadley too much to hurt her). Nonetheless, Hadley was deeply hurt, even while Ernest remained unrepentant. Soon after, he began the story that became *The Sun Also Rises*, basing it on what happened in Pamplona as well as on what he knew of Montparnasse and what Gertrude Stein insisted on calling the "lost" generation.

By now Hemingway had become quite taken with the many possibilities for love affairs in Montparnasse. As he wrote Fitzgerald, "To me heaven would be . . . two lovely houses in the town; one where I would have my wife and children and be monogamous and love them truly and well and the other where I would have my nine beautiful mistresses."[24] Duff Twysden may have withdrawn from the field, but Hemingway soon found another interesting woman, although this one, unlike Twysden, was not interested in mere affairs. Pauline Pfeiffer was trendy and lovely, but she was a devout Catholic, and that meant marriage. That winter, when Ernest headed once again for Austria with Hadley, Pauline joined them. Pauline, after all, was Hadley's friend. At least, that was how it started out.

It would be Ernest and Hadley's last Christmas together.

That spring, Edouard Herriot handed in his resignation as prime minister, after a bruising campaign in the press, largely financed by François Coty, that denounced Herriot's leftist administration and applauded Mussolini's fascist government in Italy.

Since the end of the war, Coty had been generously supporting the extreme right and between 1925 and 1926 alone provided a million and a half francs to Action Française, an amount that rose to a total of five and a half million francs during the next three years. Throughout 1925 and early 1926, backed by Action Française and the newspapers under his control, Coty and his supporters were able to inflame popular alarm over the falling franc, with which a series of cabinets were unable to deal effectively. Coty and the Action Française also spread alarm over the communist threat and, in a revival of old anxieties, renewed Catholics' fears of secularism and a general decline in morality.

It was against this backdrop, especially a rise in clashes between the communists and armed right-wing organizations such as the Camelots du Roi and the Jeunesses Patriotes, that the police began to enforce long-standing regulations about carrying firearms. This led to police raids and confiscation of firearms carried without a permit—an action that outraged members of these organizations, who threatened reprisals and protested that they were being left at the mercy of the communists.

Still, a reassuring measure of tranquility had appeared on the international scene following the previous year's Dawes Plan, which that autumn's Locarno Pact reinforced, settling Western Europe's territorial boundaries, normalizing diplomatic relations with Germany (especially Franco-German relations), and providing guarantees of peace. That the pact left Poland and Czechoslovakia open to German expansion did not concern the major Western European powers at the time, and it earned its lead negotiators, Aristide Briand and Gustav Stresemann, the Nobel Peace Prize. It also provided a large measure of relief to the French, who hoped for peace. In this spirit, in 1926 France would sponsor Germany's admission to the League of Nations.

While the franc continued to fall and prices to rise, those who could afford to party did so, whether in Montparnasse, the Riviera, or Pamplona. Fitzgerald called that summer of 1925 the summer of "a thousand parties and no work,"[25] and on a visit to Paris, the hugely successful novelist Sinclair Lewis (*Main Street, Babbitt*) took up this theme, angering the American expat crowd by writing an article saying that they were a bunch of useless drunks who never worked. The response to that came one night at the Dôme, when Lewis swore that he was a better stylist and psychologist than Flaubert and was greeted with, "Sit down, you're just a best-seller!"[26]

Some in Montparnasse worked, and some didn't. Jimmie Charters certainly knew the characters who hung out at the Dingo or at one of his subsequent bars and did little else. But the spirit of Montparnasse, which flowed on a river of coffee, alcohol, and chat, stimulated great works and small, launching—as Charters observed—an "organized rebellion against all in the world that is narrow and confining."[27]

Among those that year who were working rather than loafing was James Joyce, who had recovered from his exhaustion following the completion of *Ulysses* and had begun work on *Finnegans Wake*, which for the time being bore the title, *Work in Progress*. Still suffering from painful eye problems, Joyce nonetheless was no longer as poor as he once was—even though he still regularly complained to Sylvia Beach about the "dreadful struggle" he was having "to make ends meet."[28] His financial difficulties were not from poverty, as she so sympathetically supposed. By now the Joyce family was living well, and well beyond its means, including the series of large apartments in which they lived and the expensive restaurants where they dined. As Hemingway derisively noted, "the report is that he and all his family are starving but you can find the whole celtic [sic] crew of them every night in Michaud's," an expensive restaurant on Rue des Saints-Pères that normally was out of Ernest and Hadley's price range.[29] Joyce's favorite restaurant, Restaurant des Trianons, on the Place de Rennes, was similarly pricey, and his extravagant tipping brought him the kind of deferential service he believed he deserved.

No wonder that Joyce regularly outspent his income, in which case he just as regularly turned to his friends to make up the difference. Sylvia Beach was usually the first he turned to, and soon she noted with alarm that "the sums were going to but not fro," and "in fact, they were taking the form of advances on Ulysses."[30] "Living on the Joycean scale," she later observed, "while it matched his fame and talents was by no means adapted to his earnings."[31] Generously allowing that this was only natural, she responded by putting out a second edition—much of which was destroyed by censors in Britain and the United States. After that, she printed edition after edition—"Ulysses IV, V, VI, VII, and so on." Joyce told her that "it reminded him of the Popes."[32]

That autumn, at the same time that the Locarno Conference was convening, Jean Renoir began to film Nana, based on Zola's novel. He had been encouraged by the enthusiastic reception to the excerpted dream sequences of La Fille de l'eau and plunged ahead, with the cooperation of Zola's daughter, Denise Leblond-Zola. Catherine Hessling would of course play Nana, and the male lead was Werner Krauss, a well-known actor on stage and in German film. It was an ambitious and expensive undertaking, which led Renoir to shoot it in Germany—the first French film shot in Germany after the war, illustrating the possibilities of Franco-German reconciliation that the Locarno Conference embodied.

Despite have fought and been wounded in the war, Jean Renoir bore no grudges against Germany or Germans. He spoke and read German and was familiar with German literature. He had also vacationed in Bavaria with his father and greatly enjoyed the artistic renaissance that then was going on in Berlin. One of his friends there, the philosopher Karl Koch, turned out to have been commander of an antiaircraft battery near Reims, where Renoir had served as pilot in a reconnaissance squadron. "Koch and I concluded that this was his battery; we had made war together. These things form a bond. The fact that we had been on opposite sides was the merest detail," Renoir concluded, demonstrating the approach that made him friends wherever he went.[33]

Less inclined to make friends, and in fact delighting in making enemies, was André Breton, whose first exhibition of Surrealist art took place that autumn. Although at its inception Surrealism had primarily been a literary movement, Breton by now had decided to allow a place for painting along with poetry. The exhibition included several works by Picasso, but (thanks to Picasso's reluctance to become involved) these amounted to only three minor works from a private collection. Instead, the exhibition featured Miró's *The Harlequins' Carnival* and Max Ernst's extraordinary *Two Children Are Threatened by a Nightingale*. Soon the Surrealists would have their own showroom, near St-Germain-des-Prés, where their first show (the following spring) would be by Man Ray, including his early paintings.

Although Man Ray resisted Breton's attempts to claim him as one of Surrealism's own, he nonetheless agreed to participate in this exhibition under the Surrealists' auspices and had illustrated and provided cover photographs for the first ten issues of Breton's monthly, *La Revolution Surréaliste*. By this time Man Ray had become far more than an interesting member of Paris's avant-garde, having established himself in the world of the rich and famous as a fashion photographer (for *Vanity Fair* and *Vogue*, in addition to German art and fashion magazines) as well as a portrait photographer for international clients in Paris. Indeed, it was in recognition of his prominence that he received the commission to document that year's Exposition des Arts Décoratifs.

Not surprisingly, all this success was making him a wealthy man.

Charles de Gaulle was not looking for wealth when he responded to an invitation from General Pétain to join him in Paris. For all intents and purposes, de Gaulle had been in exile, following a bruising experience at the Ecole de Guerre, where he had been admitted after a year of teaching military history to officer-cadets at Saint-Cyr. An excellent report at the end of his term at the Ecole de Guerre, the training ground for champions (i.e., Bonaparte), would mean an open door to the illustrious career de Gaulle sought. But instead, he had serious differences with his instructors over fundamental strategy and tactics and came out with a humiliatingly low grade—which in his case meant virtual exile to Mainz, where he was attached to the staff of the army that accounted for supplies.

It was there that he published an article defying everything with which he had taken issue at the Ecole de Guerre (a place about which he subsequently remarked, "I shall never set foot in that hole again unless I go there as commanding officer").[34] It was a defiant and even dangerous article to publish for someone as intent on career advancement as Captain de Gaulle. But fortunately General Pétain (the hero of Verdun and now an inspector-general of the army and a marshal of France) remembered de Gaulle, who had served under him in the Thirty-third Infantry Regiment at Arras, and summoned him to his side. In particular, Pétain had taken note of de Gaulle's publications and was impressed with his writing. Pétain wanted an excellent writer to ghost a lengthy book on the French army, including a historical portrait of fighting France, with emphasis on the Great War and Verdun, and a program for the future. Pétain was "much pleased" with the beginning that de Gaulle made on the work while still in Mainz, and the summons to Paris promptly followed.

And there was more. Pétain also informed the Ecole de Guerre that Captain de Gaulle would be teaching there—the very Charles de Gaulle who had received such low marks from the Ecole that under normal circumstances he never would have been allowed to teach there. Pétain firmly believed that de Gaulle was "the most intelligent officer in the French army,"[35] and he planned to make good use of him.

It was a heady experience for Captain de Gaulle, but it was not long before disillusionment set in. He did not like the way Pétain undercut a rival while putting down a rebellion in Morocco, an act that in his eyes grossly diminished Pétain's character and honor. Later, he said that "Marshal Pétain is a great man: he died in 1925." On another occasion, he added, "I was present at this death, and since I was fond of him it made me very unhappy."[36] At the same time, de Gaulle was becoming keenly aware of fundamental differences between him and his patron on how to fight wars. After all, de Gaulle was a firm believer in flexibility of response, "the essentially empirical nature that the action of war must assume,"[37] while Pétain—facing the difficulties of large cuts in the military budget—had already dropped his hopes for a fast-moving and flexible tank and air force and was formulating a much cheaper system of fixed defense, one that would emerge as the Maginot Line.

Perhaps from disillusionment, but certainly not without ambition, de Gaulle now began to make other important connections, taking the bold step (for a military officer) of cultivating political figures, especially those with promising futures in fields that interested him—even while, on the surface at least, his relation to the childless Pétain continued to be much like that of a son.

It was an extraordinary relationship, especially given what would happen.

Eiffel Tower with "Citroën" in lights, Paris, July 1925. Bridgeman Images

~

CHAPTER ELEVEN

All That Jazz

(1926)

Jazz was the thing that year in Paris—*le jazz hot*, as the French called it—and Jean Renoir and Catherine Hessling now were spending their evenings in clubs featuring the new rage. Late at night, after the clubs closed, they returned to their house on the outskirts of Fontainebleau to listen to recordings, especially ones of Louis Armstrong and his Hot Five. Years later, Jean recalled that he and Catherine heard Armstrong that year in Paris as well as in Marseilles, where they followed him and his jazz band.

Renoir may have recalled another jazzman, or at least another occasion, since Armstrong would not tour France for several more years. But Renoir certainly got the feeling right. Jazz was the rage, and he and Catherine had become enthusiasts. They badly needed the diversion: *Nana* may have been the first movie Renoir made that he felt was "worth talking about,"[1] but its commercial failure left them with debts of more than one million francs. Renoir had to sell off some of his father's paintings to pay the creditors, and he vowed that henceforth he would abandon moviemaking.

Jazz, American movies, and sports cars soothed his spirits, and by autumn he was once again tempted into moviemaking, this time with a forgettable bit of fluff, *Charleston Parade*, in which Hessling and Johnny Huggins, a dancer who had come to Paris with *La Revue Nègre*, did a remarkable version of the dance. Jean thought of it as an homage to jazz, but the film's bizarre science-fiction plot and Catherine's seminude exhibitionism served to sink it.

⌒

"To preserve nature's remarkable equilibrium," Jean Renoir wrote years later, remembering his experience in filming *Nana* in Germany, "God grants conquered nations the gift of art. At least, that is what happened to Germany after its defeat in 1918. Before Hitler, Berlin was overflowing with talented people."[2]

There was of course another side to postwar Berlin, of which Renoir was well aware. "I can see now that, win or lose," he observed late in life, "no nation can escape the decadence engendered by war."[3] In 1926, Berlin was the most decadent city in Europe, and although many found this disconcerting, others—including Josephine Baker—adored it.

Josephine Baker arrived there on New Year's Eve 1925 with *La Revue Nègre* and quite typically held her audience spellbound. It was a triumph and, much as in Paris, she found herself the toast of the town, feted at one glittering event after another, completely oblivious to the dark undercurrents of racism that others in her troupe were encountering. Count Kessler had his first glimpse of her late one evening at a party where he found half a dozen nude girls, including Josephine, who "was also naked except for a pink gauze apron [loincloth]." The party went on until four in the morning, with Josephine dancing "like an Egyptian or archaic figure performing an intricate series of movements." By the evening's end, she was lying in the arms of one of the women, the two "like a rosy pair of lovers, between us males who stood around."[4]

Subsequently, Kessler held a dinner party at which Baker was to dance, and at which he also planned to discuss a ballet that he hoped to write for her. He had cleared his library for her to perform, but she "was not in the mood and sat for a long time in a corner, evidently embarrassed at exposing her nudity" in front of the women present, because, as Kessler understood it, "they are ladies."[5] But then he managed to interest Josephine in the story of his ballet, a fantasy about King Solomon and his love for a beautiful dancer. At this, Josephine "was as though transformed," imploring to dance the role, and then began to circle around Kessler's huge Maillol sculpture called *Crouching Woman*. She studied it intently—one genius addressing another, as Kessler saw it, "for she is a genius in the matter of grotesque movement"— and concluded that "one could see Maillol's creation was obviously much more interesting and real to her than we humans standing about her."[6]

Josephine Baker was enchanted with Berlin's nightlife ("the city had a jewel-like sparkle," she recalled, "especially at night, that didn't exist in Paris")[7] and considered staying, but the Folies Bergère was courting her. Despite her

Folies Bergère, Paris. © J. McAuliffe

contract, she jettisoned *La Revue Nègre*, which quickly sank without her, and returned to Paris with a salary of more than five thousand dollars a month to star at the Folies Bergère. There, she added a new element to her routine by donning a belt of bananas and continued to wow her audiences. Jean Cocteau later took credit for the costume, as did Paul Poiret, but it did not really matter who thought of it first. The skimpy skirt of bananas was supremely funny, as well as sexy, and quickly became Josephine Baker's symbol, which has endured.

In addition to her star turn, she had a protector, a handsome man who set her up in an apartment on the Champs-Elysées that she called "my marble palace."[8] They broke up, but others took his place. Still, despite all the lovers and her incandescent stardom, Josephine always felt on the defensive, aware that she did not know how to speak, eat, or dress properly—certainly not up to Parisian standards.

Then, sometime during that summer of 1926, Pepito entered her life. A small but dapper Sicilian whose real name was Giuseppe Abatino, he spoke several languages fluently, had served as an officer in the Italian army, and at one time was a minor bureaucrat in the Italian government. He was looking for a good way to live off wealthy women when Josephine Baker and a female friend encountered him one afternoon at a Montmartre club. They danced with Pepito and the other gigolos there, then hired him to give them private tango lessons. Soon Josephine invited him to escort her to a party, and shortly after, Pepito became her manager. "We all knew what Pepito was," an acquaintance of Josephine's later said, "but Josephine fell in love with him, it was just one of those things."[9]

It was with Pepito's encouragement that in late 1926 Josephine went into business for herself, opening her own club, Chez Joséphine, on Rue Fontaine in the Pigalle quarter. Both club and career flourished (two other clubs would follow), and as her voice improved, thanks to lessons, Josephine added singing to her repertoire. In time, her rendition of "J'ai deux amours" (I Have Two Loves) became almost as closely associated with her as her earlier banana dance.

There would continue to be many men in Josephine Baker's life, but the two loves of which she sang were Paris and her native land. And of these, Paris easily took first place in her heart.

〜

Could there be too many tourists? Jimmie Charters certainly thought so, and in his opinion, Montparnasse reached the pinnacle of its success in 1925, "the point where artists, tourists, and madmen mixed in equal parts in a gay abandon to the pleasures of the moment." After that, it was all downhill. "The number of tourists and onlookers became disproportionately high," he recalled. "Too much advertising had turned the spontaneity of 'la vie de bohème' into a huge commercial success." Even though the cafés and clubs continued to flourish, "the old-timers and the serious artists began to move out, not to any one quarter but to scattered and often outlying districts."[10]

One of the most prominent of those artists to pull up stakes was Foujita, who with his wife, Youki, first moved to fashionable Passy, then to a town house adjacent to lovely Parc Montsouris, where their neighbors included Georges Braque and André Derain. Chagall and his family had already moved out of Paris to a largely Russian neighborhood in Boulogne-sur-Seine, near the Bois de Boulogne. But other artists were still arriving, including Salvador Dali, on his first visit to Paris, and Alexander Calder, who planned on staying a while. Fresh from New York, Calder—an engineer with artistic aspirations—was enamored with circuses and managed to construct a miniature one of animated wire figurines that resided in a suitcase when he was not using them to entertain fellow artists. He had not yet discovered mobiles but was shortly about to—quite possibly inspired by a visit to Piet Mondrian and Mondrian's studio on Rue du Départ. "I was completely taken aback by his studio," Calder later recalled. "It was so huge, beautiful and irregularly shaped, its white walls split up by black lines and brightly colored rectangles, just like his paintings. It was extremely beautiful, . . . and right then I thought: if only everything could move!"[11]

Despite the arrival of newcomers like Calder, Montparnasse not only was becoming overtouristed, but the art that it produced in its glory days had become a market commodity—too late, certainly, for many of the artists themselves, such as the Douanier Rousseau, whose *The Sleeping Bohemian* sold that year at auction for half a million francs. "This is not art but commerce," a bearded old artist in shabby corduroy complained. "Rousseau," he added, "died in poverty."[12]

But there were enough living artists benefiting from the current collector's spree that few were complaining. Chagall had his first solo exhibit that year in New York, and collectors throughout Europe were anxious to acquire his paintings; his contract that year with the prestigious Bernheim-Jeune Gallery gave him financial security for the first time in his life. Derain certainly was doing nicely (that year, his *Self Portrait* went for forty thousand francs at auction), as was Soutine, who now could afford to rent an apartment on Rue du Parc-Montsouris, near Foujita, Braque, and Derain. Soutine's friends were astounded to discover that he now threw away brushes after one use and ordered pigments from around the globe. Completing the picture of prosperity, Soutine had shed his shabby clothes and was reported to be dressing like a dandy.

The Surrealists may once have hailed Joan Miró as "the only Surrealist painter," but by late spring Breton had broken with him. Miró had not been sufficiently Surrealist, having collaborated with Max Ernst on sets and costumes for Diaghilev's ballet, *Romeo and Juliet* (the score for this version by the twenty-year-old English composer, Constant Lambert; the Prokofiev ballet would come later). Diaghilev, in Breton's eyes, represented the "international aristocracy" and deserved all the trouble the Surrealists could give him—and they gave him plenty.

On opening night, as the orchestra began its introduction to the ballet's second act, numerous demonstrators started to howl and whistle, creating mayhem and drowning out the music. Diaghilev expected as much and had previously instructed the conductor to carry on, no matter what; he also called in the police. English members of the audience were especially outraged, as the composer was one of their own, and lit into the demonstrators. Prokofiev, who was seated in Diaghilev's box, had a close-up view of the ensuing rampage, which did not fare well for the Surrealists. "From my balcony seat," he wrote, "I saw incredible dandies in evening tails coming into action and giving fearsome blows . . . to the unfortunate demonstrators."[13] Soon the police arrived and mopped up the remaining protestors, leaving the audience to cool down and once again enjoy the ballet.

Another riot occurred that year when George Antheil's music for the *Ballet Mécanique* was finally performed at the Théâtre des Champs-Elysées, underwritten by an American patroness whom the composer had assiduously courted. Antheil decided to promote the affair by staging a disappearance, supposedly "in search of rhythms" in Africa, where his life reportedly was in danger (at least, according to Antheil's cooperative buddy, Sylvia Beach). He did not appear at the preview performance, held in a small room at the Salle Pleyel—an event that moved Janet Flanner to write that Antheil's creation sounded like three people doing different things at once, "one pounding an old boiler, one grinding a model 1890 coffee grinder, and one blowing the usual seven o'clock factory whistle and ringing the bell that starts the New York Fire Department going in the morning."[14] And that was without the drums and the airplane propellers, which were missing for this prefatory performance, leaving a player piano to do the heavy lifting.

Antheil turned up in time for the concert event, which was well attended by what Sylvia Beach termed "the Crowd." Despite the presumably avant-garde tastes of the audience, a riot soon erupted in response to the whistles, hammers, automobile horns, xylophones, electric bells, loudspeakers, and other noisemakers. "You saw people punching each other in the face," Beach wrote, "you heard the yelling, but you didn't hear a note of the *Ballet Mécanique*." Still, all the noise quickly subsided "when the plane propellers called for in the score began whirring and raised a breeze that . . . blew the wig off the head of a man . . . and whisked it all the way to the back of the house."[15]

Well, Beach concluded philosophically, at least George Antheil had a hearing, and an uproarious one at that. "From a Dada point of view," she added, "one couldn't have anything better."[16]

Man Ray was doing well. He owned an automobile, a powerful one, and he was acquiring a set of very wealthy friends. Among them was an American couple, Arthur and Rose Wheeler, who offered to put up the money for him to make a film, *Emak Bakia*, which he shot that summer at the Wheelers' villa near Biarritz (Emak Bakia being the name of the villa). Arthur Wheeler, a wealthy retired businessman, was not hesitant about giving advice, including his opinion that he thought Man Ray was wasting his time "photographing any person that came in who could pay," and that with his imagination and talent he should be doing bigger things. By "bigger things," Wheeler meant movies, which he considered "the future for all art as well as money-making," and he did not shy away even when Man Ray told him that he had no intention of making any concessions to the industry nor of using his own capital. Wheeler replied that he had "every confidence in me and my ideas, was sure I could do something sensational and give the movies a new direction."[17]

What Man Ray came up with was a short art film, "purely optical, made to appeal only to the eyes."[18] There wasn't a story, not even a scenario. One of the most interesting shots came when Rose Wheeler, driving him at high speed in her Mercedes, almost collided with a herd of sheep. This gave him the idea of filming a collision. He stepped out of the car, followed the herd while winding up the camera, then threw it high into the air and caught it again, giving the impression that the sheep had been hit and propelled in every direction. Other more carefully planned sequences also pleased him: a pair of legs doing a Charleston; the sea revolving so that it became the sky and vice versa; revolving crystals and mirrors interspersed with out-of-focus flashing lights. He finished the film with a close-up of Kiki, on whose closed eyelids he painted a pair of artificial eyes.

As Man Ray recalled, the film was short and was shown in the Théâtre du Vieux-Colombier along with one of Jean Renoir's early efforts.[19] The audience was enthusiastic, and the Wheelers were pleased with their investment, especially after the theater booked the film for an indefinite run. But the Surrealists in the audience were displeased. Man Ray was puzzled by this; he thought he had complied with the principles of Surrealism, including "irrationality, automatism, psychological and dreamlike sequences without apparent logic, and complete disregard of conventional storytelling."[20] Perhaps, he concluded, it was because he had not discussed the project with Breton and his followers beforehand and had not obtained their stamp of approval.

Perhaps, in Breton's view, Man Ray was becoming too independent. Or perhaps he simply had become too successful.

Another who was making a film that year was Le Corbusier, who used it to tackle the subject of urbanism. It was a busy time for him. In addition to his film project, his *Almanac of Modern Architecture* was in the bookstores, and a new German edition of *Towards a New Architecture* had quickly sold out. Despite his complaints about the falling franc, which "makes chaos of our budgetary forecasts,"[21] he was working on a large number of commissions.

These included a housing project in Pessac, on the outskirts of Bordeaux— a community of low-cost houses constructed out of reinforced concrete that Le Corbusier was building for a wealthy and idealistic patron, Henri Frugès, a sugar refiner, who envisioned them as life-enhancing experimental homes for low-income workers. Early in the process, Le Corbusier ran up against unrelenting hostility from local builders and authorities, who refused to issue the necessary permits to allow occupancy. As Le Corbusier was quick to point out, it took far longer to receive the necessary documents than it did to construct the buildings. Despite this, more than fifty of these open-plan houses would be completed by the decade's end—a remarkable achievement in town planning, although Pessac never achieved the kind of city-of-the-future status that Le Corbusier and his patron hoped for.

In addition, the Princess de Polignac (the former Winnaretta Singer) as well as the Michael Steins and the American journalist William Cook now approached Le Corbusier for significant projects. The princess requested plans for a villa in Neuilly-sur-Seine, as well as for a large addition to an in-town shelter for the homeless. Eventually, when the Salvation Army decided to build a much larger structure, Winnaretta would continue to serve as a patron and insist on Le Corbusier as the architect.

As for the Michael Steins, they along with their close friend Gabrielle de Monzie contacted Le Corbusier in late spring 1926, at about the same time as their friends Jeanne and William Cook. Michael Stein was the older brother of Gertrude and Leo Stein, and he and his wife, Sarah, had for almost two decades lived near Gertrude in Paris, where they played a similarly prominent role as patrons of avant-garde artists, especially of Matisse. Like the Cooks, Michael and Sarah Stein as well as Gabriele de Monzie were adventurous and attuned to the modern. It was not surprising that they were appreciative of Le Corbusier's radical ideas and clean-lined aesthetic.

Construction on the Cook villa proceeded quickly and was ready for occupancy before construction began on the Villa Stein-de Monzie, even though Villa Cook, in Boulogne-sur-Seine, was held back by numerous requirements from a neighbor, whose equally avant-garde structure had been designed by the prominent French architect Robert Mallet-Stevens. But Le Corbusier was able to satisfy these stipulations and arrive at a stunning house for the Cooks—one on posts, with a roof garden, an open internal plan, and a dramatic entrance at the top floor, overlooking the Bois de Boulogne. "The classical plan is reversed," Le Corbusier pronounced of Villa Cook. "One no longer is in Paris, one seems to be in the country."[22]

He was about to make a similarly bold statement for Michael and Sarah Stein, whose house—a larger and more complex structure than Villa Cook—went through several stages of design and redesign before construction could begin. The result (completed in late 1927) was even more dramatic. Located in Garches, outside of Paris, the Stein villa makes a prominent place for the automobile, but incorporates the garden and all outdoors into the whole, with bands of windows to draw in the sunlight and a large rooftop balcony to connect with the sky. The lines are clean, the proportions exact, and the heavy components, supported on *pilotis*, or posts, seemed weightless. The Steins, Gabrielle de Monzie, and their friends loved it. Le Corbusier was ecstatic: "These are the people," he wrote his mother, "who bought the first Matisses, and they seem to consider that their contact with Le Corbusier is also a special moment of their lives."[23]

Accolades for Le Corbusier were arriving from other quarters as well. The prominent German architect, Walter Gropius, director of the Bauhaus, honored Le Corbusier that year by a visit, and the Bund Osterreichischer Architekten made Le Corbusier a *membre correspondant*. Even though his father had died earlier in the year and his brother, Albert, had a breakdown, leaving Le Corbusier responsible for Albert's music school in Paris, life seemed good. "The painful hours have passed," he reassured his mother at the year's end. "There remains no more than what is agreeable: to make sure that it is beautiful."[24]

Most exciting of all, he had been invited to participate in the competition for the League of Nations' headquarters in Geneva.

That September, France sponsored Germany's admission to the League of Nations—the seat of "conciliation, arbitration, and peace," in the words of Aristide Briand, who once again was foreign minister of France, tirelessly working to put an end to war.[25]

By this time, Raymond Poincaré had returned to the premiership, aided by a strong wind from the far right, largely financed by François Coty, that had hammered away at France's eight-hour law and high wages, as well as a litany of democracy's shortcomings, blaming the lot for everything from moral decay to the undervalued franc. A series of governments had been unable to stabilize the economy, but Poincaré's return in July restored financial confidence, and the franc soon stopped its fall. Significantly, the new government increased a number of taxes, although with concessions to the rich, including a sharp drop in the rate of income tax. In his efforts to "right a foundering ship," Poincaré worked hand in hand with Coty, who lent large sums to the government to stabilize the French currency—a debt that Coty never collected and that he felt was never properly recognized.

Coty, whose belief system had been formed in the intensely Catholic and Bonapartist Corsica of his youth, was by now subsidizing a number of far-right organizations, including the Le Faisceau movement, a French Fascist political party, and its newspaper, *Le Nouveau Siècle*. Action Française was unhappy with Le Faisceau's success, correctly viewing it as a rival, and Coty became unhappy with it as well, withdrawing his considerable financial support when he proved unable to control its leader and when its chief of propaganda demonstrated an unacceptable leftward tilt.

In the meantime, Action Française had received a notable kick in the teeth from an unexpected quarter. Until the war, the movement had marched in close step with royalists and Bonapartists within the Catholic Church—an alliance blessed by Rome and fostered during the turbulent years of the Dreyfus Affair and France's bare-knuckle fight over the separation of Church and state. But by the 1920s, a new pope, Pius XI, was more concerned with world peace than with fighting battles, religious or otherwise, and found Action Française's belligerent nationalism off-putting—especially when served up by the unapologetically unreligious Charles Maurras, for whom politics ranked well above spirituality, and for whom the nation (preferably ruled by a monarch) constituted the highest moral authority.

In August 1926, Cardinal Andrieu, archbishop of Bordeaux, long a friend of Action Française and on record as praising it, sounded quite a different note in an article appearing in *L'Aquitaine*, the diocese's religious bulletin. In it, he accused Action Française of opportunism in its supposed support of the Church: "Atheism, agnosticism, anti-Christianism, anti-Catholicism, anti-moralism, both individual and social, . . . that, dear friends, is what the leaders of Action Française teach their disciples."[26]

Not surprisingly, the decision had already been taken in Rome to censure the organization, and Andrieu (historically responsive to the Holy See) had been chosen to open the campaign. Action Française begged to differ with Andrieu and made numerous declarations of loyalty to the pope, even while members expressed their disgust at such an injustice. "This will pass," one of its leaders wrote to friends. "Action Française is like the Church itself. Persecutions do it good."[27]

But more was to come. Even though Jacques Maritain helpfully suggested that Action Française create Catholic study groups to counter its more worldly side, Rome was not interested. In December, responding to escalating rhetoric from Action Française ("Our Faith from Rome, Our Policy from Home") and deepening divisions among the faithful, the Vatican placed seven of Maurras's works and the organization's crucial newspaper, *Action Française*, on the Index of Prohibited Books, branding the authors as men "who in their writings are alien to our dogma and morality."[28]

Angry and confused, Action Française's many followers, including those within the Church hierarchy, simmered resentfully, and there was considerable talk about betrayal and imminent danger to France, in addition to growls about an incompetent pope beset with bad advisers. At length, in March 1927, the Holy See responded with the demand for a collective declaration of loyalty: any seminarians refusing to comply would be considered unfit for priesthood, and those already priests would be prohibited from performing their sacred functions. In addition, any parishioners who insisted on adhering to Action Française, or even reading *Action Française*, would be denied the sacraments.

It was tough stuff and did some real damage to the movement, causing circulation of the newspaper and membership to fall. Still, anonymous donors increased, and many former readers found similar fare in other publications, especially in the provinces.

As it turned out, those who wanted to adhere to the letter of the condemnation managed to obey it while still harking to the spirit of Action Française, which would continue to be a force during the years to come.

It was about this time that Igor Stravinsky underwent religious conversion. Much like Jean Cocteau, he did not change his religion but returned to the faith of his fathers. In Stravinsky's case, this meant the Russian Orthodox Church.

Stravinsky had not grown up in an especially religious family and by his late teens had stopped attending church altogether. For the next two decades he showed little evidence of religious devotion, but by the mid-1920s he had changed. By then, he was back in touch with Jean Cocteau, from whom he had distanced himself following Cocteau's clever and very public 1918 denunciation of Stravinsky's music in *Le Coq et l'Arlequin*.[29] They reconciled four years later, after Cocteau praised Stravinsky's *Mavra*, which other critics largely ignored or panned, and Poulenc and Auric followed Cocteau's example, enraptured by *Mavra*'s Satie-like charms. After that, Stravinsky spent more time in Cocteau's company, especially during the summer of 1925, following Cocteau's conversion and at about the time of Cocteau's *Letter to Jacques Maritain*. The air was ripe for conversion that summer, and Maritain played a central role in it. Stravinsky would in turn meet Jacques Maritain, but not until several months after he wrote Diaghilev a letter of penitence, prior to taking his first communion in twenty years.

Stravinsky was taking this step, he wrote Diaghilev, "out of extreme mental and spiritual need."[30] There was no question that his life was stressful: he had taken a mistress, Vera de Bosset Sudeykina, with whom he was deeply in love; yet at the same time he keenly felt the devotion of his wife, Katya, who was ill and, as it turned out, slowly dying. In addition, he suffered from life as an exile from his beloved homeland. Religion offered much-needed solace, and Diaghilev responded to Stravinsky's heartfelt and penitent letter "with tears,"[31] although he did not go so far as following his friend to the confessional.

Soon after, Stravinsky composed a liturgical setting of the Lord's Prayer in Slavonic for the Russian church in Nice, where he then was living, and he and Katya provided a home for an Orthodox priest, in addition to planning for a small private chapel (although it never materialized). In Paris, Stravinsky gravitated, along with other Russian exiles, to the Russian Orthodox Cathedral of Saint-Alexandre-Nevsky, located near Place de l'Etoile, in the heart of Paris. He fondly remembered that "in the Paris of the 1920s, this church, with the cafés and restaurants nearby, was a focus of Russian life, for believers and non-believers alike."[32]

Picasso had married his Russian bride here, and Stravinsky worshipped here. He could remember "gathering birch twigs in a forest near Paris to help deck the church at the feast of the Trinity," and he remembered as well that on feast days, "the neighborhood would resemble an oriental fairground."[33] The world might seem crazy, but here, a sense of firmly rooted tradition comfortingly prevailed.

Comfort and stability seemed notably absent in a number of lives that year, most especially those of Hadley and Ernest Hemingway.

Their marriage was disintegrating. Hadley had accepted Pauline Pfeiffer's presence with them at their Austrian ski resort at Shruns, as an innocent third party, because, after all, Pauline was her friend. But it hadn't been all that innocent—or at least it became less innocent in a hurry. Suddenly Hadley was on the outside looking in, and she didn't understand what had happened. What had happened was that she had lost Ernest to Pauline, who was determined to be a wife, not a mistress.

Even while his marriage was falling apart, Ernest was revising the novel he now had named *The Sun Also Rises* and was working to free himself of his contract to Boni & Liveright so that he could sign up with Fitzgerald's editor, Max Perkins, at Scribner's. His means of extricating himself was a devastating satire of Sherwood Anderson called *The Torrents of Spring* that he hoped Liveright would refuse to publish, thus allowing him to move elsewhere. Hadley and Dos Passos did not approve of what he was doing, especially since Anderson had been an early mentor to Hemingway and had been one of those who made the Boni & Liveright contract possible in the first place (leading to the autumn 1925 publication of Hemingway's *In Our Time*).[34] But Pauline and Fitzgerald (who casually dismissed Anderson as a has-been)[35] egged Hemingway on. In any case, Hemingway was tired of being forever labeled as one of Anderson's protégés, and was even more tired of Anderson's success.

The ploy worked as Hemingway had hoped. Horace Liveright rejected *Torrents of Spring*, calling it "bitter" and "almost vicious."[36] This allowed Hemingway (who sailed for New York in February) to break his contract with Boni & Liveright and sign with Scribner's. Back in Shruns, he finished his revisions to *The Sun Also Rises* and sent it to New York. After a significant critique by Fitzgerald, who recommended cutting the book's entire opening section[37] (advice that Hemingway wisely took), Scribner's published the novel in October, to fine reviews. In the years to come, many would call it his greatest novel.

But there had been a price. Jimmie Charters remembered the anger of those on whom Hemingway based his characters: "At one time," Jimmie (or more likely his memoirs' author, Morrill Cody) recollected, with a knowing nod at Pirandello, "all Montparnasse was talking of 'six characters in search of an author—with a gun!'"[38] Janet Flanner put it a little less dramatically: "The appearance here of Ernest Hemingway's roman à clef, *The Sun Also Rises*, has stirred Montparnasse, where, it is asserted, all of the four leading characters are local and easily identifiable."[39] The *Paris Herald*'s gossip column reported that "several well-known habitués of the Carrefour Vavin are mercilessly dragged through the pages. Not very pretty reading, . . . but then Hemingway is noted . . . for not respecting the feelings of friends."[40] Whether or not the book incurred murderous rage, its frequently cruel depictions became a hot topic for gossip, which did not leave the easily identifiable subjects with kindly feelings toward the author. According to Hemingway, the day after *The Sun Also Rises* was published, he got word that Harold Loeb, the Robert Cohn character, was ready to kill him on sight.[41]

But the one who suffered the most was Hadley. By April, she fully realized what was going on and confronted her husband, who made it out as something that had just happened, and that somehow it was Hadley's fault for even mentioning it. From then on, things went spectacularly downhill, helped by miserable weather and a sick child. Their stays on the Riviera and at Pamplona that summer ("that awful summer," according to Hadley)[42] included Pauline, and by August, Hadley was desperate. On their return to Paris, she responded to Ernest's request for a divorce by asking for a separation, along with the stipulation that Ernest and Pauline not see each other for one hundred days, to think things over. If after that period of time Ernest still wanted a divorce, she would agree to it.

Yet even before the waiting period was over, Hadley had made up her mind. The separation had proved more useful to her than she or the lovers had anticipated, giving her a sense of peace and independence that she enjoyed. She now knew that she wanted a divorce. More than this, she wanted Ernest to take the legal steps to get one. "The entire problem belongs to you two," she wrote him in late November. "I am not responsible for your future welfare."[43]

That December, Ernest took the actions necessary to file for a divorce, with Hadley as the aggrieved party. The charge was desertion on his part. He would pay the lawyers' fees and the court costs.

Ernest also offered Hadley the royalties from his new book, *The Sun Also Rises*. Not inclined to go overboard with her thanks, she told Ernest that the gift of royalties "is very acceptable, and I can't see a reason right now why I should refuse it."[44]

Late that year, Sherwood Anderson made his second trip to Paris. His first visit had been a success, leaving him enraptured with the City of Light. The second was far less pleasant. Worried about money, and only recently recovered from a bout of depression, he came down with a bad cold that turned to flu and spent ten days in bed. The rest of his two months in Paris included alternating bouts of depression, illness, irritation, and writer's block, during which he and his wife managed to get completely on one another's nerves. Nothing went right. A dinner with James Joyce included oysters, even though Anderson found them repulsive but was too embarrassed to say so. An encounter with Hemingway was even worse. Hemingway had taken after him that year for no good reason that Anderson could think of, and Hemingway's *The Torrents of Spring* hurt. Just before it appeared, Hemingway had written, basically telling Anderson that he was a great writer, but that when a great writer writes something "rotten" (referring to Anderson's recent best seller, *Dark Laughter*), then it was the duty of a fellow writer to tell him so.[45]

This of course did not appease Anderson, who described the letter as "so raw, so pretentious, so patronizing, that it was amusing."[46] Toward the end of his Paris stay, he finally met up with Hemingway, sharing inconsequential small talk over their beer—occasions that Hemingway described to his editor, Max Perkins, as "two fine afternoons together." Hemingway told Perkins that Anderson "was not at all sore about *Torrents*"—a conclusion so far from the truth that Anderson must have concealed his feelings remarkably well, or else Hemingway was remarkably obtuse.[47] As Anderson recalled, Hemingway had suddenly appeared in his hotel doorway. "How about a drink?" he asked, and Anderson followed him to a small bar. "What will you have?" "Beer. And you?" "Beer" "Well, here's how." "Here's how." And then Hemingway "turned and walked rapidly away. It was the sum of what happened between us, . . . after what I had thought of as an old friendship."[48] In giving a far more positive spin to the encounter, and making it into "two fine afternoons together," Hemingway may simply have been trying to reassure Perkins (who after all had published *Torrents of Spring*) that Hemingway's relationship with Anderson was not going to be a problem. But Anderson concluded that, despite Hemingway's great talent as a writer, "there are men who say that he is incapable of friendship."[49]

Gertrude Stein was another with whom Hemingway broke that year, and Hemingway's treatment of Anderson had a lot to do with it. Anderson had hit it off with Stein on his first visit to Paris, and after that they had corresponded regularly. The secret of Anderson's success with Stein was his admiration for her writing: "Sherwood Anderson came," she wrote in her *Autobiography of Alice B. Toklas*, "and quite simply and directly . . . told her what he thought of [Stein's] work and what it had meant to him in his development. He told it to her then and what was even rarer he told it in print immediately after."[50] In his introduction to her collection of short pieces, called *Geography and Plays*, he wrote that he had found Stein "a woman of striking vigor, a subtle and powerful mind, a discrimination in the arts such as I have found in no other American born man or woman, and a charming brilliant conversationalist." As for her writing, he said, "For me the work of Gertrude Stein consists in a rebuilding, an entire new recasting of life, in the city of words."[51] Later, though, Anderson would admit to an acquaintance that he actually did not understand much of what she had most recently written, although he deeply appreciated her efforts to revitalize language.[52]

Hemingway had been Stein's good friend and loyal supporter during his early years in Paris, when he persuaded Ford Madox Ford to publish *The Making of Americans* in Ford's *transatlantic review*. "Gertrude Stein and me are just like brothers," he jocularly wrote Sherwood Anderson soon after his arrival in Paris,[53] and from Stein's point of view, young Hemingway had learned a lot from his close contact with her manuscript, having "admired all that he learned."[54] According to her, he had even learned about bullfighting from her and Alice following their lengthy stays in Spain (Picasso also claimed this distinction). But following *The Torrents of Spring*, she sided with Anderson and, during Anderson's 1926–1927 trip to Paris, they spent a lot of time talking about Hemingway, none of it complimentary.

After all, Hemingway had satirized Stein almost as much as Anderson in *The Torrents of Spring*, and Stein felt the insult keenly. Hemingway later circulated several accounts of their break, the one silly and another, as told in *A Moveable Feast*, far less laughable, where he claimed to have overheard an unsettling exchange between Gertrude and Alice that graphically reinforced Alice's reputation as manipulative and domineering.[55] In addition, he seems to have become contemptuous of what he came to view as Stein's fundamental laziness—"a very great writer who had stopped writing because she was too lazy to write for other people because writing for other people is very hard."[56] He never made this particular assessment public, but in 1934, he filled his introduction to Jimmy Charter's autobiography with acid comments about certain unnamed women who hold salons, especially those who write their memoirs and use the occasion to denigrate those they have fallen out with ("The best way to achieve an exhaustive mention . . . is to have the woman be fond of you and then get over it"). "Surely," he remarked, "Jimmy served more and better drinks than any legendary woman ever did in her salon, [and] certainly Jimmy gave less and better advice."[57]

Of course, by 1934 it was time for a little payback. Gertrude Stein had only recently amused a large audience by shredding Hemingway in her *Autobiography of Alice B. Toklas*, her thinly disguised memoirs in which she recounted at considerable length her discussions with Sherwood Anderson on Hemingway's sad failings as a writer.

As 1926 rolled along, Ernest and Hadley Hemingway were not the only ones among the quarter's residents who were working out a variety of personal and professional problems. James Joyce was continuing to write *Work in Progress* (*Finnegans Wake*), but he was not finding the same adulation for this new work that he had found with *Ulysses*. Most of his friends found it thoroughly puzzling, and some were irritated or even mocking. Ezra Pound was typically frank: "I will have another go at it," he wrote Joyce, "but up to present I make nothing of it whatever." He then added, "Nothing so far as I make out, nothing short of divine vision or a new cure for the clap can possibly be worth all the circumambient peripherization."[58]

Still, Joyce had his loyal supporters. When an American publisher printed a pirated version of *Ulysses*, Sylvia Beach rounded up 167 leading writers and other distinguished personages around the world to sign an International Protest that Beach cabled to hundreds of Western newspapers on Joyce's birthday (February 2, 1927).[59] As for *Finnegans Wake*, the Franco-American critic and writer Eugene Jolas and his wife, Maria, decided to publish *Work in Progress* serially in their new review, *transition*. Jolas was determined to foment a revolution of the word, as he announced in his manifesto ("The writer expresses. He does not communicate"),[60] and Joyce's *Finnegans Wake* was an ideal vehicle for Jolas's revolution.

Change, or at least transition, was in the air. While James Joyce was gravitating to a new and more supportive group of friends (most especially to Eugene and Maria Jolas), the photographer Berenice Abbott was in the process of leaving as Man Ray's assistant to set up a studio of her own. When Abbott first came to Man Ray in Paris in 1923, she had been desperate for work. An aspiring journalist and sculptor whom Man Ray had known from Greenwich

Village, she had not done well in Paris. Man Ray agreed to take her on, and for fifteen francs a day she learned to do everything from developing and printing to mounting. Soon she started taking her own pictures and turned out to have real ability. Not surprisingly, a certain amount of tension grew between the two as Abbott matured as a photographer and became increasingly sought out by the same crowd that lionized Man Ray. Her talent was undeniable, but in addition, she charged less than Man Ray—a sore point between them. She had learned from him, but it was time to go—especially as her prorated share of the studio rent and materials amounted to more than he was paying her. Leaving Montparnasse as well as Man Ray, Abbott set up her studio on Rue du Bac, in the seventh arrondissement. In June 1926, she had her first solo exhibition, where she received rave reviews.

At the same time, Coco Chanel's little black dress was making headlines (Vogue called it "the shape of the future").[61] Chanel later observed that its success was no accident: "I have said that black had everything. White too. . . . Dress women in white or black at a ball: they are the only ones you see." Yes, she agreed, she was a revolutionary ("I have used my talent like an explosive"), and yet there was something else at work as well: "Fashion," she observed, "should express the place, the moment."[62] Chanel expressed the place and the moment to an extraordinary degree in mid-1920s Paris and beyond, as her vision of fashion began to encircle the globe.

Others thought of globe circling in more literal terms. This was the year when four Renaults left Beirut for India, by means of Persia. Later, Renault vehicles crossed the Andes to Chile. Not to be outdone, Citroën (who had already sent cars through the jungles of South America) followed with his first trip through Alaska and opened his first foreign factory in England.

Meanwhile, Edouard and André Michelin, whose considerable success in the rubber-tire industry relied to a great extent on auto travel, had begun to put a price on their Michelin guides—after observing that free handouts did not draw the same sort of attention as ones that cost something. The American market for rubber tires was proving difficult to crack into, but in France, the brothers continued to build business by making auto travel safer and easier. This included a push for better road signs, especially at crossroads, where anarchy typically reigned, as well as regional guides that indicated with light or dark lines which routes to follow. At the same time, the brothers—who had made their fortune with the detachable pneumatic tire—introduced the low-pressure or balloon tire and campaigned extensively for its use. They also continued their widely publicized presence in the airplane industry, subsidizing air races as they had before the war.

But it was in mid-decade that the Michelins introduced what became the most successful of their many forays in public relations: the Michelin star system for restaurants. "For a certain number of important cities in which the tourist may expect to stop for a meal," the guide stated, "we have indicated restaurants that have been called to our attention for good food." These they graded in five categories, from "simple, but well run" (one star) to "restaurants of the highest class" (five stars).[63] From the outset, Michelin never explained its choices, and it never identified its reviewers. In addition, to assure its impartiality, it never accepted paid advertising from hotels or restaurants in any of its guides.

André Michelin, the brother in charge of advertising and hence of this particular endeavor, was based in Paris (the factory itself was based in Clermont-Ferrand). As a wealthy man with a discriminating palate, he quite naturally would have taken a great interest in the Paris restaurant listings, which from their early days included the still-extant La Tour d'Argent, a grand restaurant holding three out of a possible three stars starting in 1933[64] (the system had by then evolved into a three-star rather than five-star system). Yet then as now, Michelin's reviewers remained anonymous, and whether or not André's gastronomic interest extended to La Tour d'Argent's renowned pressed duck remained a tightly guarded secret.

In February, Colette and Ravel's opera, *L'Enfant et les sortilèges*, with ballet sequences choreographed by Balanchine, opened in Paris. The previous year it had premiered successfully in Monte Carlo, but Paris was a different matter. As had happened all too frequently in his career, Ravel once again encountered the stalwarts of tradition, who resisted what one critic called "a work of incomparable enchantment." Although the opera played before packed houses, "the partisans of traditional music do not forgive Ravel," Colette wrote her daughter, "for his instrumental and vocal audacities." The cat duet in particular elicited "a dreadful uproar."[65] More performances followed, in Copenhagen and other major European cities, but *L'Enfant et les sortilèges* was performed infrequently after that and would mark Ravel's last venture into opera.

Ravel and Colette were still at the peak of their careers, but Claude Monet was by now reaching the end of his. At the age of eighty-six he had at long last completed his great work, the water-lily panels that he had promised to the French nation, but he did not want to let them go. Always striving to perfect his masterwork, he wrote Clemenceau in September that he was "preparing my palette and brushes to resume work." But his frequent relapses prompted him to add, "If I don't recover my strength sufficiently to do what I want to my panels, I've decided to offer them as they are."[66]

Clemenceau, despite health problems of his own, continued to encourage his dear friend. Calling Monet his "abominable old hedgehog" and "poor old crustacean," Clemenceau exhorted him to "stand up straight, hold your head up, and kick your slipper into the stars."[67]

Yet no amount of encouragement could alter the fact that Monet's life was drawing to a close. By now his health was failing rapidly, and despite his continued popularity and eminence, his longevity had carried him into an era far different from the one in which he had forged his style and reputation. He looked with disapproval at the direction art was taking: he had seen reproductions of Cubism in reviews, and it annoyed him. "I don't want to see it," he told friends; "it would make me angry." Yet he acknowledged that he did not understand modern painting and could well remember "those who didn't understand my own paintings and who did say: 'That's bad.'"[68]

He now was willing to give detailed information to intimate friends about his technique, "his rejection of black, ochre and earth tones, and the importance he placed upon drawing and the layout of the composition."[69] And he told an admirer that "the only merit I have is to have painted directly from nature with the aim of conveying my impressions in front of the most fugitive effects." In recollecting the early days of Impressionism, he added that it still upset him that he was "responsible for the name given to a group the majority of whom had nothing of the impressionist about them."[70]

Always working to perfect his art and his beloved garden, Monet returned again and again to the role that Clemenceau had played in his life: "Several times I wanted to tear [the water lilies] all down and give up completely, [and] it was Clemenceau who stopped me."[71] As he lay dying, the only visitor allowed to see him was Clemenceau, who spoke with him about flowers and about his garden. And at Monet's funeral, it was Clemenceau who removed the black flag draped over the coffin and replaced it with a flower-patterned material, exclaiming, "No black for Monet!"[72]

Monet died on December 5, 1926, as the year came to a close. He had left instructions that there be no speeches or religious ceremony, and not even flowers, as "it would be a sacrilege to plunder the flowers of my garden for an occasion such as this."[73] Only a few family members and close friends were allowed to attend the funeral, although crowds of onlookers lined the roadside.

Later in the month, arrangements were made to transport Monet's water-lily panels to Paris, and in spring 1927, they were installed in the Orangerie. These were his legacy—along with the words that he told a small group of friends who visited him toward the end of his life at his beloved home in Giverny: "Come back soon. For you, I will always be here."[74]

Coco Chanel, 1920. © SZ Photo / Bridgeman Images

CHAPTER TWELVE

~

Sophisticated Lady

(1927)

Of course Josephine Baker's friends were worried when she made her new lover, Pepito, her manager. Pepito had hit the jackpot with Josephine, snaring a sizzling star plus control over her income. But soon it became clear that Pepito was a help rather than a hindrance, managing Josephine's business interests far more sensibly than she ever had. He also undertook to make a lady of her—hiring the right people to teach her manners, culture, and proper French.

Josephine clearly understood the importance of Pepito's schooling. Determined that the banana belt would not define her, she began the hard work of making herself into an elegant and sophisticated woman—a credit to Pepito's tutelage as well as to her own innate sense of drama and style. She lost weight, worked out (despite her claims that she never did such a thing), dressed glamorously, and famously took her diamond-collared pet leopard for walks along the Champs-Elysées—a dazzling addition to the brilliant City of Light.

Upping the glamour quotient, she agreed to star in a 1927 silent film called *La Sirène des Tropiques*, in which she costarred with Pierre Batcheff, one of the leading men of early French cinema. Supposedly en route from a tropical island to a destination somewhere in Europe, in pursuit of a young man with whom she had fallen in love, her character falls into a coal bin, turning her black, and then into flour, turning her white, before she takes a bath (in a well-calculated nude scene) to restore her own skin color. Of course, once on dry land, she becomes a huge success by teaching a new dance (the Charleston) to the Europeans. And then, having discovered that her true love is betrothed to another, she sends him back to the arms of the woman who loves him.

Her dancing was predictably fabulous, even if her acting (or overacting) was not. But it was her behavior on the set that brought Josephine her worst reviews, even if these were entirely in-house. She and Pepito made pests of themselves, constantly imposing new story lines and disrupting production. And her diva outbursts so "appalled and disgusted" the film's young assistant director, Luis Buñuel, that he quit. Buñuel, who had only recently arrived in Paris from Spain, had begun his notable cinema career by working for Jean Epstein as well as for Mario Nalpas, the director of *Sirène*. "Expected to be ready and on the set at nine in the morning," he later recalled of Baker, "she'd arrive at five in the afternoon, storm into her dressing room, slam the door, and begin smashing makeup bottles against the wall."[1] Of course she had been up virtually the entire night before, starting with her act at the Folies Bergère and then dancing at her own club from midnight until dawn. But more important as far as she was concerned was that the directors had imposed their own set of rules on her and had "neglected to . . . take into account my nature."[2]

"She lived by whims," one acquaintance recalled of Josephine. "She could be jealous, tender, passionate. She would scratch [Pepito], bite him, and beg forgiveness on her knees." But Pepito seems to have had his own way of dealing with her. "He used to beat the hell out of her," according to her friend Bessie Allison. "She just wanted to do what pleased her," recalled Maurice Sauvage, her collaborator on the first of her autobiographies, "but Pepito would lock her in her room until she had learned a song, or whatever he wanted her to learn."[3]

Still, despite the methods Pepito chose to discipline Josephine, and however many lovers she took on the side while living with him, the two suddenly agreed to get married. The occasion was Josephine's twenty-first birthday, on June 3, 1927. She announced that they had been married by the American ambassador at the American consulate and that they planned to honeymoon in Italy. Her in-laws were enchanted with the news, she added. So was the rest of the immediate world, as the news spread across the Atlantic to Harlem, where she was given the title of "Countess" (Pepito claimed to be a count).

And then reporters discovered that there was no record anywhere of the wedding. The police were concerned about the couple's taxes, and things became far more complex than Josephine had anticipated. It was only a joke, she explained, but black Americans were upset by the revised news, as were reporters, who had played along with Josephine's tall tales until then—including her story that she had arrived in Paris by accident, having been put on a boat in Argentina and awakened only to find that she was en route to France.

It had all been fizzy fun, but with fame, it became more difficult to out-run the myths—although Josephine certainly did her best. Of course she was not alone in mythmaking. One of her earliest lovers in Paris, Georges Simenon—a young writer who would achieve fame as the creator of the Inspector Maigret mysteries—later claimed to have slept with ten thousand women, Josephine among them. Simenon had recently arrived in Paris from Belgium, where he worked the seamier parts of Liège as a journalist. Attracted to Josephine and to her new nightclub, located in the color-ful Pigalle quarter, he soon began to help her run the club at night—an unpaid position, although his relations with Josephine may have served as sufficient compensation. After rhapsodizing about her rear end, which he described as "the world's most famous butt" as well as "a laughing butt," he described Josephine herself as "a burst of laughter, from her comically lacquered hair to her nervous legs, whose curves we cannot see because they are never still."[4] Simenon may well have had an affair with Baker, as he later claimed, but running the club took too much time from his pay-ing work, and there also was his wife to consider. He soon would move on. Still, he credited Josephine as being one of his great loves, and after it was over, he and Josephine remained friends.

Ernest Hemingway also claimed a connection to Josephine, although his claim was far more dubious. Hemingway maintained that he had danced with Josephine one memorable evening when she had been wearing noth-ing whatever beneath her fur coat.[5] The outfit sounds vintage Josephine, but there is no evidence that Hemingway—a habitual storyteller—ever had such an encounter. After all, among his other tales, Hemingway claimed to have had an affair with Mata Hari, who was executed in Paris well before he ever reached Europe. Still, a comment attributed to him about Baker sounds about right: Josephine Baker, he told the journalist A. E. Hotchner, was the "most sensational woman anybody ever saw. Or ever will."[6]

"Tough talk is only talk," Hemingway biographer Michael Reynolds has concluded, "a product of Hemingway's imagined version of himself, the man he wanted to be."[7] Reynolds, who included an index entry for "Fabrications" in his last volume on Hemingway, says that Hemingway "went to many wars, but was never a soldier; saw many bullfights, but never killed a single bull."[8]

And he never had an affair with Mata Hari or danced with a fur-clad but otherwise nude Josephine Baker.

Life was sufficiently complicated for Hemingway as it was, that spring of 1927, without further embroidery. He had shed one wife and was about to acquire another, a far more sophisticated lady than the first. Pauline Pfeiffer, a lithe 1920s "flapper," worked for *Vogue* and looked it. But she was also a devout Catholic—at least sufficiently devout to insist on marriage after an affair—and the two wed in May, after Hemingway converted to his new wife's faith. Not all of his friends approved: Ada MacLeish later said she had been "completely disgusted with Ernest's efforts to persuade the Catholic Church that he had been baptized by a priest who walked between aisles of wounded men in an Italian hospital—therefore Ernest was a Catholic and Hadley never had been his wife and Bumby was a bastard. To see this farce solemnized by the Catholic Church was more than we could take."[9]

And so Ada and Archibald MacLeish did not attend the wedding, although they did not break with Hemingway and in fact provided a luncheon for the wedding party. Soon after, the newlyweds departed for their honeymoon in a small fishing village at the mouth of the Rhône. There, they were insulated from the headlines of the day, including the miraculous flight of a lone pilot, Charles Lindbergh, from New York to Le Bourget Field in Paris. Although Ernest and Pauline did not notice, Lindbergh's feat with his airplane, the *Spirit of St. Louis*, captivated much of the rest of the civilized world.

Thirty-three hours and thirty minutes was what it took Lindbergh to fly his single-engine plane nonstop from New York to Paris on that historic flight, and the impact of his feat was far reaching—"an epochal achievement," as the normally reserved U.S. State Department put it, and the "most audacious feat of the century," according to France's own Chamber of Deputies.[10] Others had died in the attempt, including Captain Charles Nungesser and his navigator, François Coli, who took the reverse course—from Paris to New York—less than two weeks before Lindbergh's flight and disappeared somewhere over the Atlantic. More would try to duplicate or outperform the *Spirit of St. Louis*, but Lindbergh—"Lucky Lindy," as they now called him—had done it first. Despite the considerable dangers that transatlantic flight still presented, the two continents were suddenly that much closer, giving everyone from travelers to military strategists something to think about.

But first came the celebrations. In Paris, an enormous crowd greeted Lucky Lindy as he stepped down from his plane in the evening darkness of May 21, and in one form or another the cheering kept right on for days. Americans in Paris practically bathed in Lindbergh's popularity, with the Stars and Stripes flying throughout the City of Light, and expressions like *le boy* and *le handshake* suddenly appearing in speech and print. French friends inundated Sylvia Beach with congratulations—after all, Lindbergh was a fellow American, was he not?—while the president of France made the bashful boy from Minnesota a member of the Legion of Honor.

According to the story that soon circulated, and that André Citroën was quick to promote, Lindbergh had spotted Citroën's huge advertisement on the Eiffel Tower as he approached Paris and used it as a beacon to guide him through the darkness. And so Citroën, never one to miss an opportunity for publicity, invited the aviator, accompanied by Citroën's good friend, the American ambassador to France, to a grand reception at Citroën's headquarters on Quai de Javel. Some ten thousand excited employees looked on as their boss welcomed Lindbergh in the name of all the engineers and autoworkers of France, who (he said) applauded their American colleagues for building "the marvelous engine that made this epic flight possible."[11] He then managed to segue into automobiles, praising Detroit and pointing out that almost every American worker now owned a car. The publicity for this grand event was even better than it had been for the Prince of Wales's visit to Citroën's factory the month before.

It was difficult to find an opportunity for promotion that Citroën had overlooked. For example, when he presented Josephine Baker with a B14 Sport cabriolet, she responded by changing the words of "J'ai deux amours" (I Have Two Loves) to insert "Citroën" as one of them. Was he one of her many lovers? Probably not. More likely, she simply was giving a flashy thank-you, in publicity-garnering terms he would best appreciate. After all, Citroën— although a champion gambler and fond of nightlife—was not a womanizer.

∿

Josephine Baker may have been transforming herself into a sophisticated lady, but Coco Chanel already was one—and had been, for many years. Having left her modest roots well behind, and having become the companion—and possible future wife—of one of the most sophisticated aristocrats on the planet, she was not pleased by the prospect that either of her two brothers could suddenly surface, reminding the world of what and where she came from. Both lived far from Paris, but one never knew what unwelcome information someone might dig up, and she certainly did not want it known that her one brother, when working, sold cigarettes, newspapers, and lottery tickets at a small-town *tabac*, while the other sold shoes in the market of

Clermont-Ferrand (the home of Michelin tires). It took some persuading, in the form of generous gifts and money, to get these embarrassing relatives quietly out of the way, but in the end, she managed it.

Chanel also continued her role as Lady Bountiful in Paris, underwriting Diaghilev productions, entertaining brilliantly, and paying for Jean Cocteau's frequent detox visits. By now, Cocteau was living at Chanel's lavish Rue du Faubourg-St-Honoré residence with his new lover, Jean Desbordes—paid for in part by the sparkling wit with which he enlivened Chanel's dinner parties. But the main idea behind Cocteau's residency seems to have been Chanel's effort to impose some constraints on him and get him off drugs—a not very successful effort, it turned out, since he spent much of his time with Desbordes smoking opium.

While Chanel spent her money in ways that suited her, the perfume and *couturier* empire that she founded continued to prosper. In 1927, she opened a boutique in London's Mayfair district and added two more buildings to her Rue Cambon headquarters in Paris. Her generosity among those in her acquired social set was well known, even if she was discreet about it. Discretion, in fact, was essential, given her *couturier* business, which in the eyes of some (such as the Count de Beaumont) made her little more than a glorified seamstress. Discretion made her philanthropy easier to swallow and gave it the kind of elegance that was appreciated among those whose opinion counted.

Elegance had long been a defining trait of Coco Chanel, but her generosity knew bounds. Unlike André Citroën, who was deeply interested in his workers' welfare and had recently become the first employer in France to give his employees an extra month's pay at Christmas, Chanel was cavalier on the subject. She paid her models a pittance and was indignant when asked for a raise: "Increase their salaries, are you out of your mind?" she demanded, adding, "They are gorgeous girls, why don't they find lovers. They should have no trouble finding rich men to support them."[12]

Despite the low pay, Chanel had no difficulty in finding talented and capable women willing to work for her. She personally designed and adjusted the prototypes of her concepts on live models, but she delegated the task of actually making the clothes to skilled supervisors, who oversaw as many as three thousand workers. This gave Chanel the flexibility to go salmon fishing in Scotland and sailing on the Mediterranean while running her empire and turning out two major collections a year. Not only was it the kind of life she enjoyed, but it had its commercial benefits. It was not lost upon her clients that Coco Chanel traveled in the most exclusive circles, a fact that gave her fashions an extra cachet.

But how could marriage fit with her lifestyle? There was evidence that Chanel wanted marriage with Bendor, and that she badly hoped for (and consulted doctors about) a child—Bendor's child. The duke and his second wife had divorced in 1925, leaving him free to remarry. But although Bendor clearly adored Coco, what he wanted was a male heir. Could Coco, at the age of forty-four, still bear a child? And for that matter, was she even the kind of woman that a man, most especially a duke, would marry?

While these questions preoccupied the gossipmongers, and presumably prompted a certain amount of thought on the part of the principals themselves, Chanel in late 1927 spotted La Pausa, a five-acre property on the French Riviera overlooking the Mediterranean. The house that she built there was "one of the most enchanting villas that ever materialized on the shores of the Mediterranean," *Vogue* enthused in 1930, when work was completed. It was also expensive, with a multitude of private apartments and bathrooms as well as handcrafted building and decorating materials. Money was not an object, and although popular opinion had it that the duke bought the land and financed construction, Chanel purchased the land in her own name and by now was sufficiently wealthy to underwrite the entire project. It was her villa, and if Bendor contributed to its creation, it was in a distinctly backstage role.

Theater continued to play a significant part in Chanel's life. The previous year, she had created the costumes for Cocteau's *Orphée*, dressing Orpheus and Eurydice as if out for a country walk, and (according to Cocteau's instructions) draping Death, cast as a beautiful young woman, in a bright pink evening gown. All the fashions, especially Chanel's informal wear, set off new trends in the coming season.

With *Orphée* itself, Cocteau did not exactly set new trends, but he certainly presented a novel take on the Orpheus legend.[13] Unlike the tragic love story of Greek mythology, Cocteau chose to begin his tale after Orpheus has rescued Eurydice from death. But rather than a happily-ever-after scenario, he gives the lovers a less-than-blissful life. Eurydice, in Cocteau's version, is an insipid modern housewife, with whom Orpheus is annoyed and bored. He now loses her again, this time over a stupid argument, and Death appears—elegantly attired (à la Chanel) in an evening dress under a surgeon's gown and rubber gloves. Surrealist elements pop up, including table-tapping messages that Orpheus receives from a horse (probably a send-up of the Surrealists' preoccupation with automatic writing), which somehow leads to a batch of female furies who behead Orpheus. There is also an angel in the form of a glazier, which allows this character to appear as if haloed by the glass he is carrying.

Orphée did not win Cocteau plaudits among the critics: it was too much the circus to mix well with tragedy, and its irreverent take on miracles created some unease among the Catholics who had sheltered him. It also, probably to his satisfaction, made the Surrealists despise him even more. But it did reinforce Cocteau's credentials as a kind of prince among young homosexuals, who appreciated his wit and formed an ever-larger coterie around him. "What a strange lot, our disciples!" he wrote Max Jacob around this time, adding, "The suicide variety, or, 'Give me back my photographs!' or, 'I'm giving up literature.' You know the types."[14]

In fact, by 1927, Cocteau was seeing much less of Jacques Maritain and far more of Jean Desbordes, whom he had met on Christmas Day 1926. Desbordes, a very young twenty-year-old who was doing his military service in the Naval Ministry, was one of those many young men who wanted to write and who requested Cocteau's help. He had been wearing what Cocteau described as "the most charming uniform in the world," and Cocteau was ecstatic. "A miracle has happened in heaven," he wrote a friend; "Raymond has come back in another guise." But there was a dark side to this miracle. "I will never forget how uneasy this innocent boy's starry gaze made me feel as I gave my first advice," Cocteau recalled.[15] Soon, they were smoking opium and living together. Desbordes quickly became an addict.

Somehow, despite his opium addiction, Cocteau kept up his typically prodigious output, which that spring included his contribution to Stravinsky's *Oedipus Rex*, billed as a surprise present for Diaghilev on the anniversary of his twentieth Paris season (omitting 1918, when the Ballets Russes did not perform in Paris). Highlights of this 1927 season were the Ballets Russes premiere of *Le Mercure* (music by Satie, choreography by Massine, sets and costumes by Picasso), which Diaghilev programmed as a tribute to Satie, and *La Chatte* (choreography by Balanchine, with sets and costumes by the constructivist Russian sculptor Naum Gabo). *Le Mercure* fizzled and was dropped from subsequent seasons, but *La Chatte*, with its innovative choreography and avant-garde plastic forms, was more successful and continued in the Ballets Russes repertoire.

It has been speculated that Stravinsky was nervous about the nature of his upcoming work, since *Oedipus Rex* was no ballet or visual spectacle of the sort that Diaghilev prized, but rather a virtually static opera-oratorio with a Latin text. Quite possibly Stravinsky waited as long as he could before springing this austere gift on Diaghilev, which meant that the composer had to do his own fund-raising. Misia Sert, preoccupied with the dissolution of her current marriage, offered up Chanel as a possible source, but prefaced her communication to Chanel with a poisonous "they're waiting for you, my dear, you're the moneybags."[16] Not surprisingly, Chanel dexterously avoided a commitment, leaving for Spain and depositing all financial responsibility on the Princesse de Polignac, who was unwilling to underwrite a large enough sum for a full stage production.

By this time Diaghilev was well aware of what was afoot—keeping secrets from him was almost impossible, especially with Misia and Cocteau in on the supposed surprise. Cocteau had been collaborating with Stravinsky as lyricist on the work, and his irresistible urge to gossip, as well as Misia's equally irresistible urge to make trouble, was creating a mess. At this point, Stravinsky turned to Diaghilev to do his magic and rescue the production.

Diaghilev was not enamored with Stravinsky's gift, calling it "a very macabre present."[17] But he engineered a concert performance of the work, which premiered on May 30, after an *avant-première* held in the Princesse de Polignac's salon. He also removed Cocteau from the prime spot of speaker, which Cocteau coveted. Diaghilev had never much liked Cocteau, and with this difficult "gift," he found a convenient opportunity to take Cocteau down a peg.[18]

Presented as the second half of a double bill following *Firebird*, Stravinsky's *Oedipus* did not fare well. Stravinsky himself conducted, none too skillfully as it happened, and he later recalled that his "austere vocal concert, following a 'romantic' and colorful ballet, *Firebird*, was a greater failure than I had anticipated. The audience was hardly more than polite, and the [critics] were a lot less than that."[19] As one critic wrote, "This is . . . a soporific oratorio with people singing in evening dress and in Latin. The patrons of the dance festivities were not amused."[20]

Few at that Paris premiere recognized *Oedipus* for the revolutionary work it was, renouncing (in one critic's words) "what is known as inspiration, fantasy, all artistic spontaneity, . . . in order to resolve . . . problems of pure form."[21] Performances were rare during the next two decades, but Otto Klemperer conducted a staged performance in Berlin—an event that Stravinsky recalled made him "wince," even though Klemperer prepared the singers well.[22]

In the meantime, Sergei Prokofiev had become a name to reckon with, and his *Le Pas d'acier* (*The Steel Step*)—a celebration of Soviet industrialization performed only a week after Stravinsky's *Oedipus Rex*—was a big hit. Diaghilev now told reporters that Prokofiev "stood beside Stravinsky at the forefront of contemporary Russian music[23]—a judgment with which Stravinsky begged to differ, even though he claimed that he and Prokofiev "were always on good terms." The problem, as Stravinsky put it, was that Prokofiev's "musical judgments were usually commonplace and often wrong."[24] Nonetheless, Diaghilev thought differently and continued to send commissions to Prokofiev—not only *Le Pas d'acier* but especially Prokofiev's wildly popular 1929 ballet, *The Prodigal Son*.

⌒

That year La Coupole opened in Montparnasse and quickly became a smash hit. This new café-restaurant was huge—far bigger than either the Rotonde or the Dôme—and attracted absolutely everyone. With a restaurant on its first floor, dancing below, and another restaurant on the open-air roof, it could accommodate multiple cliques and clans without anyone feeling out of place or intruded upon. Local artists, including students of Léger and Kisling, decorated its pillars and walls, and an American bar (serving cocktails), accessible from the main room, skillfully cushioned roominess with an aura of coziness.

From the outset, La Coupole was fun—of the sort in which Montparnasse specialized. On its legendary opening night, in December 1927, crowds downed one thousand cakes, three thousand hard-boiled eggs, and fifteen hundred bottles of champagne, and that was just the beginning of a long and festive run. Located near its rivals the Dôme, the Rotonde, and the Sélect, the Coupole (now listed as a landmark) continued to serve more than one thousand customers a day right through the Depression.

Not all the other neighborhood establishments could survive such competition, and it was around this time that the famed original Jockey Club closed its doors after four years of high times. Kiki would remain the Queen of Montparnasse, but she would not hold court at the Jockey.

Kiki was not at a loss for things to do. She had begun to paint, primarily landscapes and scenes from her childhood, and in 1927 the Galerie au Sacre du Printemps held an exhibition of her works that drew substantial crowds and sold well. In addition, Man Ray took her along on his first trip back to America since arriving in Paris. The occasion was the New York screening of his film *Emak Bakia*, which did not do as well there as it had in Paris, London, and Brussels. Still, it gave him an opportunity to visit his family in Brooklyn and introduce Kiki, who charmed them—especially his father when she sat on his lap for a photograph. A classic Kiki moment followed when the family group moved on for dinner with Man Ray's sister-in-law, who called to ask them to bring a soup ladle. Kiki grabbed the ladle, held it like a baton, and led the procession down DeKalb Avenue, singing the Marseillaise at the top of her lungs and leaping over a fire hydrant en route. They—and probably most of Brooklyn—loved her.

Despite the lack of interest in *Emak Bakia*, Man Ray's paintings and Rayographs received agreeable recognition in the Société Anonyme's exhibition at the Brooklyn Museum. He had made it big in Paris, and now his work was coming home.

⌒

That same year, Man Ray took a photo of André Derain in Derain's pale blue racing car, which according to the painter was "more beautiful than any work of art."[25] Another artist, Francis Picabia, who over the course of his life owned more than one hundred fast automobiles, certainly agreed. Their sleek beauty was one attraction; their speed was another (the 1927 land-speed record was just under 180 miles per hour). With speed came danger—an attraction in itself for some. And with danger came death. During a land-speed record attempt that year, a driver was killed, decapitated by the whiplash of his auto's broken driving chain.[26]

It was a bad year for auto fatalities, probably the most spectacular being the death of Isadora Duncan. Her life had ricocheted dramatically since the tragic death of her children in 1913, and a decade later she told a friend that she still thought constantly about them: "Do you know that I see them every night? That is why I'm afraid of the night."[27] In recent years she had suffered abuse from her young husband, followed by the heart-stopping news of his suicide. She told her adopted daughter Irma that she had "wept and sobbed so many hours about him that it seems he had already exhausted any human capacity for suffering."[28] Shortly before her own death, she was heard to announce that "there are only two things left, a drink and a boy."[29]

By early 1927, Isadora had once again taken up residence in Paris, this time at 9 Rue Delambre in Montparnasse—not far from Man Ray's and Chagall's early apartments in the Hôtel des Ecoles, and across the street from the Dingo Bar. She was trying, in haphazard fashion, to write her memoirs—after all, she needed the money. But she took time out to join the throngs on May 21 who greeted Charles Lindbergh at Le Bourget airfield. When he landed, she was "suddenly overcome by patriotism" and tossed her hat into the air (according to William L. Shirer, who at the time was a foreign correspondent for the *Chicago Tribune*).[30]

Isadora's sudden surge of patriotism was only temporary. For years she had found much to dislike about her native land, and this feeling intensified during that spring and summer as she took up the cause of Sacco and Vanzetti, Italian anarchists convicted of murder during an armed robbery at a shoe factory near Boston. Their conviction set off widespread protests, based on evidence of their innocence, and as appeal after appeal for a new trial failed, outrage spread around the globe. Now, as the August 1927 date for their execution was drawing closer, Isadora had become a passionate defender of both men: "The Sacco-Vanzetti case is a blot on American justice," she told a visiting American judge, adding that "it will bring down a lasting curse on the United States, a curse deserved by American hypocrisy."[31] Their execution, on August 23, set off protests in Paris—where according to Luis Buñuel, "the city was in chaos"[32]—and throughout the world.

Isadora's dear friend Mary Desti Sturges had already turned up in Paris, and together the two partied endlessly and expensively around town. By this time Isadora's finances were hopelessly depleted, and Mary's were little better—although her indulgent former husband, Solomon Sturges, continued to come to her rescue, as he had throughout her colorful career. Still, even Mary was worried about Isadora's abandon: "She won't try to economize," Mary wrote her son, Preston (who, having been raised in his mother's flamboyant social circles, would in time become a famed Hollywood writer and director of screwball comedies). Isadora "refuses to eat except at the best restaurants, and wants to drink the most expensive wines," Mary went on. "She feels the world owes it to her—well I guess it does."[33] But still, Isadora's friend was distraught that she could find no way to "stop this sheer slide to destruction."[34]

Isadora now decided to return with Mary to Nice, declaring that she "refuse[d] absolutely to be poor. I will die first. I hate shoddy, shabby poverty."[35] It was there that she was unexpectedly reconciled with Paris Singer, the father of her second child. Singer had endured Isadora's faithlessness and recklessness for years before breaking with her. Now he was older and, if not completely wiser, certainly less wealthy than he had been during the height of their affair, having taken a huge financial loss with the Florida land bust. Still, he was willing to underwrite Isadora one more time.

It was then that Isadora, having spotted an attractive young man with a fast car, arranged to go for a ride with him. Singer appeared and, seeing the young man, understood the situation completely and left. It was the same old story, and even though Singer promised to return, bearing a check, Isadora was not convinced that he would. She went to dinner that evening draped in a six-foot-long red batik shawl that Mary had brought her and that Isadora refused to go anywhere without. Despite Mary's vague premonitions of disaster, Isadora went for another ride with the young man, flinging the shawl around her neck and crying, "Adieu, mes amis. Je vais à la gloire!" (Adieu, my friends. I go to glory!).[36]

The story has been told and retold—how Mary cried out, "Isadora, your shawl! Pull up your shawl!" But those eighteen-inch fringes had caught in the spokes of the left rear wheel, and before Isadora could retrieve them, the car had abruptly accelerated, breaking her neck.

Could anyone have exited more dramatically? Many certainly thought that Isadora had staged her suicide. According to Cocteau, "Isadora's end is *perfect*—a kind of horror that leaves one calm."[37] But few who knew her were calm—including Paris Singer, who was too devastated to make the trip accompanying Isadora's remains to Paris.

There, her dearest friends gave her a huge funeral, with heaps of the flowers she so loved. Thousands awaited her body in Père-Lachaise, where as many as could fit crammed into the crematory chapel. Following the service, her ashes went to the columbarium, where they still reside, beneath those of her much-adored children.

As Janet Flanner wrote in her tribute, "She inspired people who had never been inspired in their lives before. . . . It was not for nothing that she was hailed by her first name only, as queens have been."[38]

Isadora's was not the only automobile fatality of the year, although it certainly was the most dramatic. That spring, Jean Renoir, another aficionado of fast cars, barely survived an auto accident that killed his friend, Pierre Champagne. Pierre had just bought a Bugatti Brescia and took Jean along for a fast ride. They were going at top speed on a hillside in Fontainebleau's forest when the car skidded on an oil slick. Pierre died immediately, but Jean—found unconscious in the wreckage and taken to a hospital—most fortunately survived.

He and Pierre had been making a new film, *Marquitia*. After the financial disaster of *Nana*, followed by the failure of *Charleston Parade*, Jean Renoir had vowed not to make another film—except in the unlikely event that someone offered him a commercial film of which he was not also the producer. But this unlikely event did occur, the outcome of older brother Pierre Renoir's marriage to Marie-Louis Iribe, niece of fashion illustrator and set designer Paul Iribe. Marie, who was well connected, had started a film-production studio of her own and wanted to star in a film she had in mind. She had already lined up a distributor and several theaters but still needed a director. The obvious answer was her new brother-in-law, but Jean hesitated. He badly needed the money, but he did not want to make a film without Catherine. At length, he capitulated, and the lightweight *Marquitia* was the result—filmed during the winter of 1926 and first shown in commercial cinemas the following September, where it did well.

After directing *Marquitia*, Jean took an acting role in *La P'tite Lili*, with Catherine Hessling in the lead and Alberto Cavalcanti directing. Catherine would star in three Cavalcanti films that year, but it was *La P'tite Lili* that drew the most attention when it was shown in an avant-garde Left Bank movie house, Studio des Ursulines (Darius Milhaud would provide a soundtrack for the film in 1930).

Renoir then teamed up with Jean Tedesco to produce and direct a version of Hans Christian Anderson's *The Little Matchgirl*. It was the first time he made use of panchromatic film, which (to his delight) provided a variety of shades of gray rather than stark black and white—conveying the presence of a range of colors, if not the actual colors themselves. But panchromatic film required more elaborate lighting for indoor shots, prompting Renoir and his buddies to construct their own studio for this kind of film. They did all the work themselves, from cutting reflectors out of tin to using rheostats fed by a generator attached to an old automobile engine that they cooled by hooking it to a water faucet. They also developed their own film (in the kitchen), using wooden vats and hanging black curtains on the windows. "In my whole life," Renoir later told François Truffaut and Jacques Rivette, "that was my only attempt at true craftsmanship, and we were a group of technicians who thought the problem was fun. . . . It was wonderful, it was exciting, it was even more exciting since the results were actually very beautiful."[39]

It would be the last film he made with Catherine.

"A Paris *couturier* once said woman's modern freedom in dress is largely due to Isadora," Janet Flanner observed. Which *couturier* Flanner had in mind, we do not know, but from the outset Isadora favored Paul Poiret, and he in turn doted on Isadora, naming one of his earliest designs for her. Isadora, in Flanner's words, may have "arrived like a glorious bounding Minerva in the midst of a cautious corseted decade,"[40] but it was Poiret who actually freed women from their corsets, bustles, and projecting busts.

Yet while Poiret called himself the King of Fashion, by late 1926 his kingdom was sadly diminished and his finances in disarray. It was now that his longtime friend, Colette, invited him to play a lead role in the adaptation of her novel *La Vagabonde* for the theater. Ever ready for new artistic experiences, Poiret joined the cast, and the troupe opened in Paris early in 1927, having already performed in the Riviera. Unfortunately, this opening was not especially memorable: "His Parisian debut proved that M. Poiret is not a bad actor," Flanner conceded, "Nor is Mme. Colette. However, an efficiency expert could point out that Poiret might have a greater talent for, let us say, dressmaking, and that Colette was wasting her time at being anything except a novelist." In a final flattening comment, Flanner predicted that *La Vagabonde* "should not run long."[41] Which it did not.

While Robert Mallet-Stevens's villa for Paul Poiret remained unfinished in Mézy-sur-Seine, thanks to insufficient funds, Le Corbusier's dramatic villa for Sarah and Michael Stein was completed in late 1927 and ready for occupation by early 1928. It was not an inexpensive undertaking: Villa Stein-de Monzie was the most expensive single house that Le Corbusier built in the 1920s and 1930s. And yet there was little disagreement as the work proceeded. Le Corbusier wrote his mother that these three clients were "the best we have had, having a carefully established program, many requirements, but these being satisfied, having a total respect for the artist."[42]

That summer, Le Corbusier and Yvonne vacationed with the sculptor Jacques Lipchitz and his wife, for whom Le Corbusier had recently built a combined studio and residence just outside Paris in Boulogne-sur-Seine.[43] In the autumn, Charlotte Perriand joined Le Corbusier's by-now bustling atelier, where she introduced furniture design using tubular steel—a concept conceived by Bauhaus but shaped by Perriand into new and streamlined forms, especially her chaise longue. Le Corbusier had hoped that Perriand's chairs and tables would appeal to Sarah and Michael Stein for their new villa, but the Steins preferred to keep their Renaissance tables and eighteenth-century armchairs.

"This was a heroic, pioneering age," Perriand later recalled, "with no money and very few resources—all those architectural projects and urban schemes that were so painstakingly drawn up never panned out."[44] Still, it was an exhilarating experience working for Le Corbusier, and as she put it, "enthusiastic young men from the best schools the world over came here, not only for architecture but for Le Corbusier, for his way of reconsidering all problems, for his aura."[45] Not at all intimidated by the fact that she was the lone woman in the office, Perriand stayed for ten years, during which her designs slowly found acceptance.

It was a thrilling time to be working with Le Corbusier, especially now that he had been invited to participate in the competition for the League of Nations' headquarters in his native Switzerland—a dream commission. Students flocked to his atelier, where they contributed to the drafting of the competition drawings. The edifice that Le Corbusier and his cousin envisioned was meant to embody the high ideals of the League, incorporating comfort and the latest in acoustics and technology into a design aimed at inspiring community and cooperation within an atmosphere of serenity, nobility, and peace. It was a tall order, but it seemed likely to succeed, especially

Le Corbusier (left) and Charlotte Perriand (center), at the Bar Saint-Sulpice, photo by Pierre Jeanneret, 1928 © 2015 Artists Rights Society (ARS), New York / ADAGP, Paris. Banque d'Images, ADAGP / Art Resource, NY

as it was the only proposal that stayed within budget. The Le Corbusier/ Jeanneret plan became the jury's choice, and the president of the jury recommended that it be awarded the commission.

And then the fighting began. First the director of the Ecole des Beaux-Arts in Paris complained that the Le Corbusier/Jeanneret plan had not been submitted in the proper ink. After some haggling, this demoted their plan to the short list. Then word came that there was more money to spend on the project than had been originally planned. This meant that more designs qualified, and the battle intensified. "We are in fact the only moderns," Le Corbusier wrote his mother, "the others being notorious academics. So that the field is clearer than ever: *modernism or academicism?*"[46]

The opposition continued to mount, and in December 1927, the jury for the League of Nations headquarters declared another plan as winner—one submitted by four academics (two French, one Italian, and one Hungarian). Still, Le Corbusier was not about to give up, and as the new year began, he was already coming up with a second set of plans—this time in the correct ink.

⌐

It was while lecturing on urbanism in March that Le Corbusier met with Jacques Arthuys, a militant nationalist and one of the founders, with Georges Valois, of the French Fascist party, Le Faisceau. Le Corbusier (prompted by a friend, Pierre Winter) had inaugurated Le Faisceau's headquarters with a slide lecture in 1925, leading its founders to think of the architect as one of their own. As Georges Valois wrote in 1927, "I said then [on the 1925 occasion] how his grand conceptions expressed the deepest thought of Fascism. . . . Now, Fascism is precisely this, a rational organization of the entire national life, . . . Le Corbusier's work expresses this with genius."[47] Yet Le Corbusier at this point had no particular politics, and certainly no ideology, apart from the precepts of Purism that absorbed his life. As he wrote his mother, he was "received [by Arthuys] with open arms and much cordiality . . . and a clear proposition to appoint me minister of urbanism and housing. In short, you can bet your life I am not involving myself in politics."[48] This, however, would prove difficult in the years to come.

André Breton had already joined the Communist party, drawing many of the Surrealists with him—although some objected to the attempt to mix political and social action with their artistic and literary challenges to the bourgeois world. Moreover, the communists were suspicious of them—"If you are Marxist, you have no need to be surrealist," one party official told Breton. It was a rocky relationship from the start, but Breton gamely pressed on, trusting that these rough spots would eventually disappear.

In the meantime, Surrealism was flourishing, with its members producing books and paintings as well as publications, including a vigorous defense of Charlie Chaplin, whose nasty divorce, including Mrs. Chaplin's allegations of "indecent sexual demands," led to attempts in America to ban his films. The Surrealists eagerly jumped into this fray, but when not producing tracts of this sort, they took to the streets of Paris, where they wandered alone or in groups, looking for signs and revelations. They preferred certain locations, including the Passage de l'Opéra and the Tour Saint-Jacques, from where they believed the forces of the city's unconscious emanated.

Breton's 1927 Surrealist manifesto first appeared (even before it was published in *La Révolution Surréaliste*) in the fledgling *transition* magazine, where it was translated into English by Nancy Cunard. That year alone, *transition* published work by Gertrude Stein, Max Ernst, André Gide, and Man Ray, as well as the opening pages of James Joyce's *A Work in Progress*. Unfortunately, Gertrude Stein's contribution, "An Elucidation," was printed in a scrambled version, nullifying her attempt to explain her style. Although the printer could offer a solid defense based on the difficulty of the manuscript, Stein was upset and pressed *transition* to print the work as a separate pamphlet.

Gertrude Stein's style was unquestionably daunting, but William Carlos Williams committed the unforgivable sin by remarking, in the sanctity of Gertrude's salon, that "things that children write have seemed to me so Gertrude Steinish in their repetitions," and asked whether she was "sure that writing is your métier?"[49] Williams's remarks stung, and he was not invited back. Nonetheless, others continued to worship at her feet, and her salon continued to be regarded as a pinnacle in the expatriate world. As the social historian Lloyd Morris noted, "A summons to her home was an invitation to present oneself to Mont Blanc."[50]

Stein had by now become acquainted with Virgil Thomson, who was less inclined than the others to worship at her—or anyone's—feet. "She expected to be granted the freedom of a man," he commented, "without allowing anyone to sacrifice the respect due her as a woman."[51] Thomson nevertheless genuinely admired Stein and had, early on, put some of *Tender Buttons* to music. He would soon begin work on his opera score for *Four Saints in Three Acts*.

By now, Chagall had discovered the Côte d'Azur and was embarked on his popular flower paintings as well as his circus-themed gouaches and oil paintings, while Picasso had moved away from Neoclassicism and become close to several of the Surrealist painters, especially Paul Klee and Joan

Miró—although, according to his biographer John Richardson, he never embraced Surrealism.[52] As Picasso later told Daniel-Henry Kahnweiler, "the surrealists never understood what I intended . . . something more real than reality." To another friend, Picasso added, "Resemblance is what I am after, a resemblance deeper and more real than the real, that is what constitutes the sur-real."[53]

It was a time of ongoing discovery for the artist, now forty-five, who early in 1927 also discovered the lovely young Marie-Thérèse Walter, who became his mistress and muse for the next nine years.

Discovery, but also loss: that May, Juan Gris died at the age of forty, after a long period of poor health. This relatively young man, who had been Picasso's pupil before forging his own way, had been a friend (with interruptions) ever since their Bateau Lavoir days. Despite Gertrude Stein's sniping after the funeral, Picasso mourned Gris's loss deeply. "You have no right to mourn," Stein pronounced, to which Picasso retorted, "You have no right to say that to me." But Stein was not to be put off: "You never realized his meaning because you do not have it." Picasso quietly replied, "You know very well I did."[54]

An even more dramatic episode occurred that May when the police besieged the offices of *Action Française*, Action Française's newspaper, where Léon Daudet had barricaded himself. Daudet had been convicted two years earlier for slandering the taxi driver in whose vehicle Daudet's son had shot himself, and now Daudet faced prison time. But he protested in this dramatic fashion until, after three days, the prefect of police (who was known to be sympathetic to Daudet and his colleagues) persuaded him to surrender. Daudet emerged, surrounded by a guard of Camelots du Roi, and was taken by limousine to Santé prison. There he lived comfortably for several weeks until he escaped, thanks to a colleague impersonating a ministry official and a gullible (or accommodating) warden. From there, Daudet skipped to Belgium, steering clear of France until his pardon in 1930, when his native land had to deal with him once more.

By spring 1927, the Vatican had placed *Action Française* on its Index of Prohibited Books and denied the sacraments to anyone reading it or adhering to its parent organization. Action Française reeled from this blow but did not disappear. Many of its most militant supporters now gravitated to Pierre Taittinger's Jeunesses Patriotes, whose military wing was directly inspired by Mussolini's fascism. Soon it would claim nearly three hundred thousand members. In addition, in late 1927, Maurice Hanot d'Hartoy—with the encouragement and financial backing of François Coty—formed another extreme-right organization, this one an elite group of former combatants called the Ligue des Croix-de-Feu. Nationalist, anticommunist, and authoritarian, members of the Croix-de-Feu believed themselves more than qualified by their heroism on the field of battle to defend their country, especially in the field of politics.

In 1927 Georges Clemenceau at last published his *Au Soir de la pensée*— a two-volume tome in which, amid what amounted to a virtual history of everything, he condemned both Mussolini's fascism and Soviet communism, which he believed demonstrated "to what point of intellectual disarray nations can be brought when led by popular oligarchies."[55]

Yet neither Mussolini nor the Soviets seemed to dismay most French at that moment. Even Germany's revival and the growth of the Nazi party did not cause consternation. The French remained largely complacent, so long as Poincaré, known as a champion of security by force, was heading the government and the economy was behaving decently, which it continued to do. In 1927, military service in France was further reduced, from eighteen months to one year, which provided for an entirely defensive army. The military was almost in complete agreement on this step, which was the spirit in which the Maginot Line was about to be built; only Marshal Foch strenuously disagreed.

Briand continued his quest for peace, proposing a pact outlawing war between all the signatories. He would achieve his goal the following year, when fourteen nations, including Germany, signed the so-called Kellogg-Briand Pact, which "condemned recourse to war for the settlement of international differences" and outlawed it "as an instrument of national policy" except in the case of legitimate defense.[56]

There were causes for concern along France's colonial periphery, where anti-imperialism was beginning to rise, including Ho Chi Minh in Indochina and l'Etoile Nord-Africaine in Algeria. But these movements were systematically put down, prompting little further thought or anxiety. Most French believed, or chose to believe, that a new era was dawning.

It was in this atmosphere that Captain Charles de Gaulle began to lecture at France's elite Ecole de Guerre in the spring of 1927. He was facing leaders of an army that had forgotten the role played by tanks and aircraft in 1918 and that refused all innovation—a maddening attitude for someone like de Gaulle, but probably not an untypical response for a nation that had just won a war. Unfazed by the rank and importance of the members of his audience, de Gaulle unhesitatingly addressed the subject of military leadership and told them that "our days are not very favorable for the education of military leaders, [for] . . . in time of peace mechanically formed minds triumph over those that possess feeling and outstanding gifts." His own gifts were evident: he quoted freely and by heart from a roster of greats, from Plato to Tolstoy and Henri Bergson, leaving his audience stunned by his brilliance but furious at his arrogance. For his part, de Gaulle did not appear to have been aware of the depth of hostility he aroused. As he wrote his father, "Those on my side are delighted, the neutrals smile, and the sharks who swim around the ship waiting for me to fall in so that they may devour me have moved off to a considerable distance."[57]

Soon after, Henri Boegner, organizer of the far-right Cercle de Fustel de Coulanges, invited de Gaulle to repeat his lectures at the Sorbonne. Fustel de Coulanges had been a historian of ancient and medieval France, whose writings appealed to monarchists and far-right nationalists who wanted to return France to the glory of the Caesars; indeed, the leaders of Action Française gave Fustel a special place in their pantheon and, in 1926, blessed the circle of intellectuals, including Charles Maurras, that invited de Gaulle to speak. De Gaulle, flattered, agreed to come.

Pétain continued to be an important backer of the young de Gaulle, most especially his lecturing stint at the Ecole de Guerre, but a rift had begun between them. This became more evident that autumn, after de Gaulle's promotion to major and transfer to Germany to command an elite unit of light infantry (the 19th Chasseurs à Pied).[58] Their subsequent exchange of letters reveals a growing tension over the book that de Gaulle had been ghostwriting for Pétain. De Gaulle learned that, during his absence, Pétain was having another officer take over writing the work. De Gaulle was furious and with "respectful insistence" asked Pétain "not to hand over to any other pen that which I delivered to you alone."[59] He also requested that Pétain publicly acknowledge de Gaulle and his work in a preface or foreword. One of Pétain's right-hand men warned de Gaulle to withdraw the potentially offending letter if he did not want to endanger his career. Characteristically, de Gaulle ignored the warning and went ahead; rather than encounter any more difficulties with his subordinate, Pétain preferred to put the manuscript aside.

De Gaulle's career was not disrupted by this incident, and indeed, his reputation for future greatness was growing, even though pretty closely accompanied by a reputation for egotism and arrogance. When some raised eyebrows at his appointment to command the elite 19th Chasseurs à Pied, a notoriously crotchety director of infantry simply retorted, "I am appointing a future generalissimo of the French army!"[60]

Le Coupole, Paris, 1932. Bridgeman Images.

CHAPTER THIRTEEN

∼

Cocktails, Darling?

(1928)

"Cocktails! That is the real discovery of our age," enthused journalist Sisley Huddleston in 1928, as he directed his gaze at Bohemian literary and social life in Paris.[1]

The French preferred to make the name and the drink their own, spelling it "coquetèle," but in predawn hours at fashionable places, no one was very particular. In the course of Huddleston's extensive research, he encountered the painter Kees van Dongen, who declared, "Our epoch . . . is the cocktail epoch. Cocktails . . . contain something of everything. No, I do not merely mean the cocktails that one drinks. They are symbolic of the rest." A once-starving artist who had become wealthy as a portrait painter, van Dongen was now renowned for his fashionably edgy midnight parties, where he had plenty of opportunity to observe the local flora and fauna. "The modern society woman," he went on, "is a cocktail. She is a bright mixture. Society itself is a bright mixture."[2]

The modern society woman of 1928 dressed sleekly and casually by day (complete with low heels and cloche hat) and brilliantly by night, with drop-waist, knee-high fringed gowns intricately beaded in Art Deco patterns or interwoven with gold and metallic threads. Chanel, Lanvin, Patou, Molyneux, and Callot Soeurs were among the go-to names during the 1920s for sophisticated women of means, from Misia Sert to Marlene Dietrich and the Duchess of Kent. In addition, there were those, such as Marie-Laure de Noailles, wife of the Viscount Charles de Noailles, who preferred an even more adventurous side of fashion: in 1927, Man Ray photographed Marie-

Laure wearing a silvery sharkskin creation by the young interior designer Jean-Michel Franck—a full-skirted affair, anticipating 1950s Dior—that she wore to a Futurist Ball.

Those without sufficiently deep pockets to pay *couturier* prices could fall back on their own creativity and sense of style to enliven store-bought purchases. Eve Curie, Marie Curie's younger daughter, was one of these—an attractive and spirited young woman with a taste for fashion, which unfortunately brought her and her beloved mother into conflict. On the one hand, Madame Curie (to Eve's consternation) would pick the simplest dress and cheapest hat for her own use, which she would proceed to wear to tatters. Eve, on the other hand, loved style and (to her mother's distress) wore her fashionable clothes with panache. "Oh, my poor darling!" Marie would cry. "What *dreadful* heels! . . . And what sort of new style is this, to have the *back* of the dress cut out? Décolletage in front was bearable, just; but these miles and miles of naked back!" Marie Curie was willing to concede that, "apart from all this your dress is pretty." But then came the disagreement over makeup. Marie wore none and never had worn any; Eve, however, was a modern woman—which meant, in her mother's view, a lot of "daubing and smearing," which she thought was "dreadful."[3]

Still, the two loved one another, and after telling her daughter that she liked her better when she was "not so tricked out," Marie gently urged her on her way for the evening ahead. "And now you must run, my dear child. Good night."[4]

Taxi horns—specifically Paris taxi horns. They must have made a big impression on George Gershwin, for when he came to Paris in the spring of 1928, one of the first things he did was go hunting for them.

He had first glimpsed Paris, briefly, in 1923, and then again during a short visit in 1926, during which he began to sketch out the first bars of the "orchestral ballet" that he would eventually title *An American in Paris*. By early 1928 he had conceived the work's central motif: "I thought of a walk on the Champs-Elysées, of the honking taxi," and of "homesickness, the blues."[5] While in New York, he sketched out some of his major themes, but he still needed direct inspiration. In March 1928, he once again visited Europe, this time for more than three months.

After arriving in Paris, Gershwin went shopping for taxi horns on the Avenue de la Grande-Armée, which then was a center for auto shops. He was persistent, demanding horns that sounded precisely the right notes. He brought about twenty of them back to his hotel suite, where he piled them on top of the Steinway grand he had placed in the middle of the room.

There they were one day soon after, when the pianists Jacques Fray and Mario Braggiotti knocked on his door. They wanted to meet the famous American composer, and Gershwin, still in his dressing gown, was affable and gracious. Inviting them in, he noticed them staring at his unusual collection. No, he explained, this wasn't some new American fad. He simply wanted to capture the traffic sounds of the Place de la Concorde during rush hour for the opening section of *An American in Paris*. And then he invited them to help out, accompanying his piano with the taxi horns, squawking away in rhythm. Thrilled to have played a part in the creation of this particular piece of musical history, they departed on cloud nine.

A nice guy, as his many friends agreed. Also an intense guy, who managed to cram more into a twenty-four-hour day than most people would ever care to consider. This Paris trip was billed as a working vacation, a time out from the constant demands of Gershwin's many musical comedy hits in New York and London—a time during which he would rest, study, and compose. How much rest he got is certainly subject to question, but then again, Gershwin seemed to enjoy crowding his life with a million friends and activities.

In Paris, where he and his brother and collaborator, Ira, arrived at the Gare Saint-Lazare with their sister, Frances, the social whirl began immediately. A crush of visitors constantly surrounded him, vying for his attention and feting him all over town. One of the biggest bashes was the one Elsa Maxwell gave for him at the restaurant Laurent, in the gardens of the Champs-Elysées, following the European premier of his Concerto in F. There, he hobnobbed easily with a raft of celebrities. Of the lot, his encounter with Cole Porter was especially memorable. The two played piano together until late in the night, while Frances (known as Frankie) Gershwin sang. Porter was sufficiently impressed with Frankie's voice that he wrote her into a review on which he was collaborating, which was about to premier.

This review, *La Revue des Ambassadeurs*, appeared at the Café des Ambassadeurs and, together with the musical *Paris* of the same year, marked a major turning point in Porter's career. Later, after he achieved the fame that had been so elusive, he told a friend that by 1926 he had abandoned the idea that he would ever succeed on Broadway. Instead, he and Linda had focused ever more on parties, whether in Paris or in their Ca' Rezzonico palazzo in Venice. These, by all accounts, were extraordinary, but they were not enough to distract Porter very long from his flagging career.

As Elsa Maxwell later put it, "by 1927, Cole had such a reputation as a playboy that no producer would take a chance on him." It was then, according to Maxwell, that a Broadway producer by the name of Ray Goetz "went to Cole as a last resort."[6] Goetz had an idea for a musical as a starring vehicle for his wife, Irene Bordoni, but as yet had no suitable music. What Maxwell left out of her account was the role played by Irving Berlin. By now, Porter had met Berlin, and in the social swirl of New York and Paris, they and their wives had become good friends. Goetz was Berlin's brother-in-law by a previous marriage and wanted advice on his musical. Berlin took a look at Goetz's ideas to date and advised him to locate Porter and have a talk. In 1927, Goetz and Porter talked, and the result was the musical, *Paris*, for which Porter wrote the music and lyrics.

Paris, which included Porter's "Let's Do It," was a hit (the *New Yorker* was "ecstatic" about his songs),[7] while back in Paris, Porter's *Review* was equally successful.[8] It didn't hurt that for the review, Frankie Gershwin (backed by Fred Waring's Pennsylvanians) sang a medley of Gershwin songs, or that Gershwin himself accompanied his sister at the piano on opening night. Suddenly Cole Porter was a success on two continents, and in the next decade alone he would have eight smash musical comedies on Broadway.

Suddenly, after years of wandering in the proverbial wilderness, things were looking up.

～

Gershwin billed this trip to Europe as one of study as much as of gathering ideas for composition—"to benefit my technic [sic] as much as possible from a study of European orchestral methods."[9] His time in Paris (plus event-packed side trips to Vienna and Berlin) was certainly productive, and he even found occasion to seek out Nadia Boulanger to request lessons. He had already approached Maurice Ravel with the same request when both were in New York. Ravel was a friend—the two had spent several evenings together listening to jazz in Harlem, and Gershwin performed *Rhapsody in Blue* and other works, at Ravel's request, at a party given in honor of the French composer's fifty-third birthday. But Ravel declined Gershwin's request for lessons, telling Gershwin that studying with him "would probably cause him to write bad 'Ravel' and lose his great gift of melody and spontaneity."[10]

Ravel, however, did suggest that Gershwin consider working with Nadia Boulanger, who now was teaching American composers such as Aaron Copland, Virgil Thomson, and Walter Piston at the American School at Fontainebleau. Following up this suggestion, Ravel wrote Boulanger a letter in which he described Gershwin as a musician "endowed with the most brilliant, most enchanting, and perhaps the most profound talent." He added that Gershwin's "world-wide success no longer satisfies him, for he is aiming higher." But in teaching Gershwin the technical means to achieve his goal, "one might ruin his talent." Would Boulanger "have the courage, which I wouldn't dare have, to undertake this awesome responsibility?"[11]

By this time, Boulanger was well acquainted with Gershwin's music and reportedly enjoyed it. When she and Gershwin subsequently met in Paris, she told him that "what I could teach him wouldn't help him much . . . and he agreed. Never have I regretted the outcome." A third party at this interview later added that Boulanger turned him down "because he had a natural musical talent that she wouldn't dare disturb for anything."[12]

Gershwin also approached the composer Jacques Ibert, explaining that he wanted to know how to write "serious" music, including fugue and counterpoint. Ibert, too, backed off, after being "dazzled by [Gershwin's] prodigious technique and amazed at his melodic sense, at the boldness of his modulations, and by his audacious and often unexpected harmonic inventions."[13] Stravinsky was another whom Gershwin approached, but the Russian was notably less impressed than the others. When Gershwin inquired about lessons, Stravinsky allegedly asked how much he made a year and, upon hearing the sum, retorted that perhaps their roles should be reversed and Stravinsky should study under Gershwin.

Whether Gershwin was actually seeking instruction or simply looking for reassurance from leaders in a world into which he sought admission, it was abundantly clear that this once-unpromising son of Russian immigrant parents was already a marked success. George Gershwin (originally Gershovitz), a high school dropout who had not encountered a piano until he was twelve, had rousingly conquered Tin Pan Alley and Broadway, and then boldly ventured into concert music.[14] The times were right for such a move: Darius Milhaud and the Groupe des Six had already introduced jazz into their compositions.[15] Gershwin simply started from the other end, tenaciously acquiring the tools to express himself in the medium of Bach and Debussy, whose music he adored.

Somehow, even with everything else going on, Gershwin managed to complete about half of *An American in Paris* while he was in Paris, agreeing to let Walter Damrosch and the New York Philharmonic give the first performance. In December of that same year, Damrosch and the New York Philharmonic premiered *An American in Paris* at Carnegie Hall.

∽

George Gershwin may have lit up the lives of numerous people in Paris that year, but the big event for music lovers was the birth of a major new orchestra, the Orchestre Symphonique de Paris. This new orchestra was the complement to a new and very modern concert hall, the Salle Pleyel, a reinforced-concrete space that seated three thousand and eliminated the ornate decorations and other potential sound distorters that typified its more old-fashioned predecessors. The acoustics were excellent, but unfortunately fire broke out shortly after it opened, forcing the orchestra to play its first concerts in the Théâtre des Champs-Elysées.

Nonetheless, the Orchestre Symphonique de Paris represented a major step into a brave new world, providing salaries for its musicians and in return expecting regular and intensive rehearsals for its eighty-concert season. As part of the deal, the widespread practice of sending deputies in place of the regular musicians was now banned. The aim was to produce better music, and to this end, three conductors were appointed, including the young Swiss conductor, Ernest Ansermet. This represented a major opportunity for him, but not without its dangers: as he was about to discover, all the improvements in the world could not eradicate the web of backstage maneuvering and bureaucratic dealings of which such an organization was capable.

Within a few months the orchestra's board decided to replace Ansermet with Pierre Monteux—who had conducted *Rite of Spring* at its 1913 premiere and now was an international star. Still, when Ansermet conducted Stravinsky's *Rite of Spring* in late December, in one of the orchestra's early concerts in the newly reopened Salle Pleyel, the results were worthy of the rehearsal time he now was allowed to devote to it. Stravinsky was not present, but his mistress, Vera Sudeykina, attended and reported high praise for the young conductor, who in time would join Monteux in international prominence.

That spring, another American besides Gershwin was leaving Paris and going home. Ernest Hemingway and his new wife, Pauline, had already planned to return to America: after all, Pauline was pregnant and wanted her baby born there. But it was not until Ernest pulled a bathroom skylight down on his head (mistakenly grabbing it rather than the toilet chain) that he realized how much he needed to be in America to write his next book. Something about that accident—the taste of blood as it flowed down his face, and the memories it aroused of his own experience in the war—prompted him to abandon the novel on which he had been working and dive into another, this one a war story. In March, he and Pauline sailed for Havana and Key West, and then for Kansas City by way of Pauline's home in Arkansas. Their son, Patrick, was born in June. By then, Ernest had written almost three hundred pages of his new novel, *A Farewell to Arms*.

Hadley, on the other hand, went the opposite direction, returning to Paris from America, where she had gone with Bumby directly after her divorce became final. Back in Paris, she picked up her life, now as a single mother. "I knew how to live in France," she later recalled, "and I was the happiest I'd

ever been there." She had numerous friends (unlike Ernest, who had alien-
ated many), and despite the necessary adjustments, her life was good. In time,
she would happily remarry and live a quiet life with her second husband, the
journalist Paul Mowrer. Many years later, looking back on her marriage with
Ernest, Hadley told her son that their divorce "was a great relief, because as
much as I loved your father and he loved me, he was a very difficult man to
live with and it was a constant strain." For his part, Ernest would go on to two
more marriages, prompting Ada MacLeish to comment, "It would have been
better if he had just occasional ladies and didn't marry them."[16]

Others that year were picking up the pieces after failed relationships—or
attempting to do so. Paul Poiret's divorce was an acrimonious one (his wife,
to whom he had been married for many years, charged him with cruelty), but
he continued with his increasingly unrealistic ideas and dreams. A fine cook
(as Man Ray, one of his dinner guests, was quick to acknowledge), Poiret in
1928 published a cookbook, *Les 107 recettes ou curiosités culinaire*, as well as
a sumptuous advertising album, *Pan*, spanning (in his words) "every luxury
trade and industry."[17] *Pan* was the outcome of a series of weekly luncheon
meetings that Poiret held with a dozen leading designers, whose advertising
concepts Poiret published, in *Pan*, as "a bouquet of new ideas."[18] He also
worked with artists and designers to produce a collection of exquisitely illustrated books, in a limited edition of one copy each. Like so many of the ideas
he continued to hatch, neither project was financially viable and had to end,
although Poiret continued to believe that he was only going through a temporarily difficult time financially and that all would soon right itself. "One
day," he promised, *Pan* would be resumed "and will become the model for a
new magazine," while he "very much hope[d] to resume" his book-publishing
project "and go very far with it."[19]

Misia Sert was another who was attempting to recover from a failed marriage, in this case her third one. It had been an especially difficult breakup for
her, as she was still in love with her third husband, José-Maria Sert. Complicating matters, Misia was also more than a little in love with Sert's new wife,
Roussadana Mdivani, known as Roussy. The newcomer—a beautiful young
woman of Georgian ancestry who claimed to be a princess—was a sculptor
who had shown up at Sert's studio looking for studio space. Soon Sert made
room for Roussy in his bed as well as his studio. Misia decided on a clever
campaign to displace Roussy, but instead fell under her spell. She and Sert
and Roussy became a strange threesome, with Roussy as mistress to Sert and
as daughter to Misia—the daughter she had always longed for. Friends, especially Chanel, warned Misia that she was being an idiot, but it wasn't until
Misia realized that Sert planned to marry Roussy that Misia's world fell apart.

When Sert finally divorced Misia to marry Roussy, it devastated Misia, although she helped Sert pick out the ring as well as his wedding present to his new bride. Misia even managed to join the couple on their honeymoon cruise ("Alone, we three. Was that not wonderful?").[20] Chanel tried to help her unhappy friend, reversing the roles that she and Misia had played after Boy Capel's death. Now it was Chanel who invited Misia to join her and the Duke of Westminster for the summer at his country estates. Misia made the attempt but was miserable. In the end, she left Chanel and Bendor and continued, pathetically, to shadow Sert and his new wife.

It was the last year that Kiki and Man Ray would live together, and perhaps sensing the inevitable breakup, he gave her the starring role in his memorable Surrealist film, *L'Etoile de mer* (*Starfish*), whose distorted and out-of-focus scenes he took through glass or as reflected in mirrors. Inspired by a poem by one of the leading Surrealists, Robert Desnos, *L'Etoile de mer* has no dramatic action per se, but depicts a woman (Kiki) and a man in several repetitive encounters. In the longest, the woman is selling newspapers on the street, her pile of papers held down by a glass jar containing a starfish. A man appears and picks up the jar, and they enter a house together. Upstairs, the woman undresses and lies down on the bed while the man watches. He then takes her hand and kisses it, says adieu, and leaves with the starfish. At the end, the man and woman meet again, but a second man takes the woman from her lover, and a mirror with the word "Belle" cracks. Throughout this depiction of love and loss, images of departing trains, boats, and windblown newspapers are interspersed. As in the title, the starfish is central—the embodiment of lost love.

The film premiered in May, with Marlene Dietrich's *The Blue Angel*, at the small Latin Quarter cinema house, the Studio des Ursulines. It was a success, even though critics found it confusing. One thought the film's characters were "circulating in a kind of Milky Way . . . or appearing as if one had taken hashish. Everything dissolves and then is reborn, evolving arbitrarily."[21]

By now, the concept of lost love had become painfully real for Man Ray, as his public arguments and fights with Kiki grew louder and more frequent, accompanied by dramatically hurled bottles and chairs. It was now that Man Ray found a secluded location just outside of Montparnasse for an additional studio, on Rue du Val-de-Grâce, near the Luxembourg Gardens, where he could escape unwanted visitors and paint. Kiki, in turn, began to write her memoirs. And it was as she was looking for a collaborator on her memoirs that she met the journalist Henri Broca.

It would not be long before Kiki left Man Ray and moved in with Broca.

~

Early that year, Josephine Baker left Paris. Paris, she decided, had already left *her*. Her contract with the Folies Bergère had ended, and her Parisian audiences had grown increasingly blasé about her act. Even Baker's gala farewell performance at the Salle Pleyel was disappointing: the pianists Wiéner and Doucet (of Boeuf sur le Toit fame), who shared the bill with her, garnered a far more enthusiastic response than she did. Baker was annoyed at the fickleness of her Parisian audiences; plus she was bored with doing the same old thing. So she left Paris in January 1928 for a whirlwind European tour, bringing with her, in addition to Pepito and various members of his family, a secretary and a chauffeur as well as two dogs, 196 pairs of shoes, numerous dresses and furs, sixty-four kilos of face powder, and thirty thousand publicity pictures to hand out to fans.

This entourage entered Vienna with high expectations, but soon encountered a riptide of opposition denouncing her as the "black devil." This antagonism, rooted in the racism of the growing Hitler movement as much as in the forces of traditional morality, was not the sort of welcome she had anticipated. Yet despite newspaper articles branding her as a Jezebel, her performances sold out—doubtless helped by her daily drives through the streets of Vienna in a cart pulled by an ostrich.

In Prague and Budapest she encountered mobs, while in Zagreb the show closed after the audience began to hurl objects. Holland and Scandinavia were more placid, and in Oslo the crown prince was rumored to have invited her to the palace, where he covered her naked body with jewels. In Berlin, she opened a new Chez Josephine and encountered Nazi sympathizers—hostility that was repeated throughout Germany. It was time to return to Paris, where despite the racism she encountered from white Americans, she felt at home.

~

Anna de Noailles, lunching with Le Corbusier one day in 1928, described Josephine Baker as "a pantheress with gold claws."[22] It was an especially apt description, as Baker had already gained renown for taking her pet leopard, Chiquita, for walks on the Champs-Elysées. Le Corbusier would not meet Baker for another year, but when this encounter took place, he would find her as memorable as he could have possibly imagined.

In the meantime, he still was fighting the jury's decision on the League of Nations building, with one of his ardent supporters declaring the whole business "a second Dreyfus Affair"[23]—a startling comparison, but indicative of the depth of emotion on the part of the architect and his partisans, who regarded the outcome as the result of an evil conspiracy within the traditionalists' camp.

With this in mind, Le Corbusier and his cousin submitted an appeal demanding that the Council of the League of Nations overturn the jury's decision. His refusal to back down stirred up a hornet's nest, even in his hometown of La Chaux-de-Fonds, where the daily newspaper featured an article that accused Le Corbusier of "certain distinctly communistic tendencies, an arrant materialism, the abolition of thought and the triumph of action," and went on to describe his houses as "suicide crates."[24] This criticism burned, especially as it was something that Le Corbusier's mother and her neighbors would see. Enraged, Le Corbusier felt that his homeland had betrayed him—a belief that was reinforced when the jury considering his appeal decided definitively in favor of the other team of architects, but now with completely new requirements for the building. Le Corbusier and his cousin protested, along with supporters from numerous countries, but to no avail. Fifteen years later, Le Corbusier would still retain bitter memories from this experience: "Fair-minded people," he wrote, "along with the intellectual elite in every country, demanded that justice be done. Nothing of the kind occurred."[25]

Still, by now Le Corbusier had become prosperous and was finding an ever-widening group of supporters, including Fernand Léger, who visited the Villa Stein that July and called it a masterpiece. As a result of other major supporters, he became a founding member of the Congrès Internationaux d'Architecture Moderne (CIAM), while cities (Tunis and Buenos Aires) were hiring him to work on urban plans. In May, in another sign of his international recognition, he was asked to enter a design competition for the central office of cooperatives in Moscow, where he had an ardent following. Le Corbusier submitted his design, based on his Plan Voisin, and traveled to Moscow, where he was received at the Kremlin and feted around town. While there, he encountered Sergei Eisenstein, whose film, *The Battleship Potemkin*, he greatly admired. This led him to declare that "architecture and the cinema are the only two arts of our time."[26]

Yet all was not perfect in the Soviet Union, as Le Corbusier discovered one day when he began to sketch on a Moscow street corner and was abruptly told to cease and desist, as this was forbidden. Le Corbusier could not abide such restrictions and hid a sketchbook in his overcoat, in order to illustrate—hastily—some of the domes and monuments he saw. But when his proposal for the Moscow office of cooperatives was accepted, his delight immediately overcame his reservations—even when one of the leading Soviet architects proceeded to attack him for his "Bohemianism, isolation and inverted snobbery."[27] Even more scathingly, this architect, who had visited the Villa Stein, claimed to have spoken to a member of the Stein family who said the residence was far better to visit than to live in.

Still, as Le Corbusier promptly wrote his mother, the Soviet Union was the most promising place to attain his architectural vision: "here one of the most explicit designs of human evolution is being realized." His mother, alarmed, reminded him that "the Bolshevist leaders are usually Jews of rather low extraction, and the various massacres they have inflicted have certainly rendered them odious." But her son was unmoved: "The western world has shown itself to me under a rather shabby aspect," he reminded her. In contrast, "the sort of heroism, of inevitable stoicism, which exists in Russia . . . leaves a strong aftertaste."[28]

Le Corbusier had a reason for reminding his mother of the treatment he had received from Geneva: he was about to change his citizenship, from Swiss to French.

That year, rumors spread that the famed Montmartre cabaret, the Lapin Agile, was about to close—the result of its owner's inability to pay his taxes. As it happened, the reports of this colorful tavern's demise were greatly exaggerated, and the Lapin Agile continued its lively career under the ownership of Frédé Gérard's son, Paulo, who presumably came up with the requisite taxes or talked his way out of them.

The Lapin Agile's patrons had most famously included Pablo Picasso, back in the days when he was flat broke and lived in the tumbledown Bateau-Lavoir. But Picasso had not visited his old Montmartre haunts in years, and now he was middle aged, rich, and famous. He had recently acquired a nubile young mistress, Marie-Thérèse, and in 1928 he enlivened a dull summer in Brittany by stashing her nearby and painting her in secret. That spring he had already begun work in a new medium for him, tapestry (*Minotaur*), and had started to explore the possibilities of sculptures in metal.

His wife, Olga, was ill and in the autumn underwent two operations followed by lengthy recuperations. This meant that, even back in Paris, Picasso had the freedom to enjoy and paint Marie-Thérèse as often as he liked. Olga no longer provided the sexual inspiration he needed, and although he turned up regularly at her hospital bedside, he had long before abandoned her emotionally—as could be seen by the contrast in his paintings that year between those of Marie-Thérèse and those of his wife (the former filled with sexual references, albeit in radically distorted forms, while the latter was depicted as skinny and reproachful).

Picasso may have left his Bateau-Lavoir days far behind, but he was continuing his long-established pattern of burning through his numerous relationships with women, moving on to new conquests after casting his former lovers aside.

In June, France returned to the gold standard, fixing the franc at one-fifth of its prewar value. Poincaré had chosen a middle ground, between Germany's runaway inflation and Britain's brutal deflation, and France's undervalued currency immediately helped its foreign trade and wiped out the nation's debts to the Banque de France. But for those with property, especially those with considerable property, the state now became the great destroyer, to the benefit of what they viewed as the lazy working classes.

Still, prosperity continued to prevail, along with a huge amount of speculation. In late 1928, the Socialist party leader Léon Blum wrote about his surprise when his taxi driver stopped to buy a copy of *L'Information Financière*. He concluded that "nowadays everyone speculates, everyone gambles."[29]

One of the biggest gamblers was André Citroën. In addition to his expensive publicity campaigns, he was a frequenter of casinos, where he was losing ever-larger sums of money. His financial difficulties did not stem from declining auto sales: by then, there were almost one million autos in France (one for every forty-one inhabitants), of which one-third were Citroëns. The company's Paris factories could produce eight hundred cars a day—more than twice the output of Renault (although Renault produced far more trucks and commercial vehicles than any of his competitors). Yet Citroën's firm was an owner-managed company, and by 1928, his personal financial difficulties were sufficiently critical that he had to accept a takeover by Banque Lazard, a French banking syndicate that reorganized the company's finances and placed managerial control in the hands of a board of directors.

That August, fourteen nations, including Germany, France, and the United States, signed the Kellogg-Briand Pact renouncing war as an instrument of national policy (sixty-two nations, including the Soviet Union, would eventually sign). The signatories met in Paris, and as a consequence, Parisians were treated to the sight of a German minister for foreign affairs being officially received—a first since 1871, at the conclusion of the Franco-Prussian War.

The pact explicitly did not exclude the right to legitimate defense, and in this spirit, France began to construct the Maginot Line along its frontiers, as a defensive measure against the possibility of any future German invasion.

Such an event was regarded as unlikely, given the pounding the Germans had received during the recent war. Moreover, France's high command viewed the Maginot Line as invulnerable—or sufficiently so as to allow time to mobilize. Such optimism was hardly warranted, given the rapid rise of Hitler and his Nazi party. In addition, as few but Charles de Gaulle recognized, France's reliance on its infantry, while relegating tanks and air power to secondary support roles, was dangerously misplaced.

Yet France continued in its military illusions, while Raymond Poincaré continued to serve as head of a government that, despite the changing composition of its Chamber of Deputies, remained moderate and even static in its resistance to change. It was this moderation and complacency that François Coty was determined to upend—if not through *Figaro*, then through his new mass-circulation newspaper, *L'Ami du Peuple*.

"It is necessary," Coty proclaimed, "that the workers read something other than [the French communist newspaper] *L'Humanité*,"[30] and he sold *L'Ami du Peuple* for less than half the price of other newspapers, making it possible for the poorest workers to afford it. He aimed to reach a circulation of one million within six months, using advertising revenue to make up for any shortfall. In any case, he had his fortune to fall back on, and he believed it well worth the cost to turn *L'Ami du Peuple* into the most widely read journal in the world—a newspaper that would shape the French into the sort of people he believed would best serve their nation.

Coty used *L'Ami du Peuple* to spread his bitter opposition to a wide range of targets, from American films to France's income tax, which then was a modest 2 percent (he refused to pay any tax at all, and from 1926 he was in constant litigation with the Finance Ministry). He embraced extremist right-wing causes and, in particular, anti-Semitism: in an especially ugly incident, he published the virulently anti-Semitic *The Protocols of the Elders of Zion* in *L'Ami du Peuple*, after having it translated into French.

This no-holds-barred approach to content, plus the paper's modest price, had its appeal. When a consortium of other newspapers tried to shut him out of the newspaper-delivery infrastructure, Coty—infuriated—was able to circumvent all obstacles by establishing his own publishing and advertising company, printer, parcel service, newsstands, billboards, and newsboys. Within six months he had exceeded his circulation goal: an American journalist reported that in the first month, *L'Ami du Peuple* had sold eight million copies, with millions more thereafter. Delighted with his success, Coty decided to publish an evening edition of his new venture: "*L'Ami du peuple* represents the sole voice of Truth [in France]," he announced, "and the French people should not have to wait an entire twenty-four hours between editions."[31]

∽

Jean Renoir was not interested in politics and managed to distance himself from most of the newsworthy events of the day, whether Sacco and Vanzetti's execution or Lindbergh's transatlantic flight. He was thoroughly absorbed in his pleasures and his moviemaking, especially after being sued for plagiarism by Maurice Rostand (son of the playwright Edmond Rostand). At the heart of the dispute was Renoir and Tedesco's *The Little Matchgirl*: Maurice and his mother had written a comic opera several years before based on the same story. Although the suit would eventually fizzle, the process took two years, during which *The Little Matchgirl* was in limbo. Unfortunately, by the time the Rostand affair vanished the talkies had appeared, and *The Little Matchgirl* was a silent has-been. The distributor tried to update it but reissued it with a musical soundtrack and captions that Jean detested.

The Jazz Singer, the first feature-length talkie, starring Al Jolson, appeared in America in 1927 and upended the entire industry. In 1928, the vice president of Paramount came to Paris to announce this breakthrough and the death of silent film. But *The Jazz Singer* did not appear in Paris until early 1929, and in the meantime, Jean made the low-budget silent comedy, *Tire-au-flanc* (*The Lazybones*), a master-and-servant mix-up that Renoir later described as a "partly tragic, partly whimsical burlesque."[32] Although not a commercial success, it pioneered technical innovations and camera movements that François Truffaut later described as "unbelievably bold."[33] Nonetheless it labored under the fact that it was a silent film, as well as the perception that Renoir was merely a wealthy playboy and dilettante.

He and Catherine certainly lived up to their reputations as sparkling participants in *les Années folles*. They acquired an apartment in Paris near the Rue du Faubourg-Saint-Honoré, while maintaining their residence in Marlotte, where their son, Alain, continued to live with his nanny and grandmother. Jean and Catherine now spent much of their time in Paris, listening to jazz and enjoying themselves, especially with their new friends, Georges Simenon and Simenon's wife, Tigy.

Given his parents' preoccupations, Alain saw little of either. Jean seems to have loved his son, but Catherine found motherhood boring. Fortunately, Alain acquired a substitute mother, Dido Freire, a young Brazilian just out of boarding school who had played an extra in *La P'tite Lili*. Dido enjoyed Alain and took him to the zoo and other amusements. He loved her in turn, and in time she even took him on vacation to her own mother's home in England.

Catherine was relieved. For her, Dido was a godsend, a combination big sister and surrogate mother to a burdensome boy. What neither Catherine nor Jean realized, though, was that in time, Jean would also become enchanted with Dido, who would become the second Madame Renoir.

That June, Coco Chanel gave a magnificent party at her home to celebrate the closing of the Ballet Russes's 1928 Paris season. She then left for the Riviera, where she could oversee her emerging Mediterranean villa and join Bendor on his yacht.

Noël Coward, that razor-sharp observer of cocktail society, was about to immortalize this yacht in his frisky comedy of manners, *Private Lives*. The divorced lovers, Amanda and Elyot, stand on a balcony looking out to sea, and Amanda dreamily asks whose yacht they see in the distance. Elyot tells her that it is the Duke of Westminster's. "It always is," he adds pensively.

"I wish I were on it," Amanda says with a sigh.

"I wish you were too," Elyot murmurs.[34]

Kiki, Queen of Montparnasse, Paris, 1929. © Roger-Viollet / The Image Works

CHAPTER FOURTEEN

~

The Bubble Bursts

(1929)

When did the party end? According to one point of view—a view embraced by many, including Jimmie the Bartender—the party ended when Wall Street crashed in October 1929. But like most events of any significance, it was more complicated than that. For one thing, the crash did not affect France as quickly as it did America or Britain. For another, the party had been waning—or at least losing its fizz—for some time.[1]

"The good days are finished," Robert McAlmon pronounced at a New Year's Eve party on the last night of 1928.[2] McAlmon, the owner of Contact Editions and a friend of everyone from Hemingway to James Joyce, had seen 1920s Paris from the inside and rightly understood that *les Années folles* were over. At about the same time, Harry Crosby, founder of the Black Sun Press and another fixture in the Montparnasse expat community, declared more broadly that it was "The End of Europe."[3] Hemingway agreed, at least so far as Montparnasse was concerned, and abruptly stated in his introduction to Kiki's memoirs that "this is being written in nineteen hundred and twenty-nine and Kiki now looks like a monument to herself and to the era of Montparnasse that was definitely marked as closed when she, Kiki, published this book." From his viewpoint, when Montparnasse "became rich, prosperous, brightly lighted, . . . and they sold caviar at the Dome, . . . the Era for what it was worth, and personally I don't think it was worth much, was over."[4]

Hemingway by this time specialized in a tough-guy curl of the lip that showed his superiority to whatever he chose to denigrate, and now circumstances allowed him to denigrate Montparnasse. Many years later, he would write his love letter to Paris in *A Moveable Feast*, but now he was too close to painful events to allow sentimentality. The Montparnasse he had originally fallen in love with had changed on him, and he was giving it the back of his hand.

What many consider the last major Montparnasse fling of *les Années folles* took place during the spring of 1929, some months before the crash. The occasion was a raucous costume ball given by Madeleine Anspach at the Bal Nègre. Anspach was the mistress of André Derain, the colorful and by-now wealthy painter who adored race cars and who was fully capable of tearing up any bar he was in when sufficiently drunk. The theme Anspach chose was the character Ubu, from Alfred Jarry's bizarre and outrageous turn-of-the-century play, *Ubu Roi*, and partygoers came dressed in appropriate costume (Anspach came as Mère Ubu, and the painter Foujita as a whore). Soon the festivities settled into an all-night orgy, with Kiki obligingly doing a semi-topless cancan to the insistent beat of the jazz band, while another woman danced naked on a crate of champagne. Before it was over, one especially sozzled female was dragged screaming from the dance floor, where she had been conducting a frenzied attempt to seduce any or all of the players in the band.

Six weeks later, Madeleine Anspach was dead, a suicide—whether from drugs or depression, it is not known.

"Montparnasse has changed," Foujita wrote in his introduction to Kiki's memoirs, but "Kiki does not change."[5] Kiki may have been putting on weight, as Hemingway acerbically alluded ("Kiki still has the voice . . . and her face is as fine a work of art as ever. It is just that she has more material to work with now").[6] Yet she remained the same sweet, exuberant, and joyous woman she had been from the start. "We laughed, mon Dieu, how we laughed," one friend later reminisced.[7] And Samuel Putnam, who translated Kiki's memoirs into English, concluded that "Kiki is more like St. Theresa than anyone I know."[8] This was the woman who, at the end of her adventurous life, paid scant attention to the fact that she was broke and insisted on bringing candy to elderly patients at the hospital near where she lived. She loved laughter, and she loved giving joy.

Kiki gave a lot of joy during the course of her life, but by 1929 she had transferred her affections from Man Ray to Henri Broca. Man Ray and Edward Titus both took credit for encouraging her to write her memoirs, but it was Broca who collaborated with her on the manuscript and who published and publicized it. Broca included the first chapters in the April issue of his new magazine, *Paris-Montparnasse*, and published the actual book that spring in a deluxe signed edition as well as a standard one. In June, he organized a successful book-signing party, followed by another in October. The latter drew the attention of Wambly Bald in the *Paris Tribune* (the informal title of the European edition of the *Chicago Tribune*), who noted that Kiki was happily kissing all comers on Saturday night. "When the news swept the Quarter," Bald reported, "that for thirty francs one could get a copy of Kiki's *Memoirs*, her autograph, and a kiss in the bargain, men forgot their *demis*, dates and dignity, and scampered over."[9]

Broca adored Kiki and did his best to celebrate her, especially that spring, when he organized an afternoon performance to raise money for impoverished artists in Montparnasse (there still were some impoverished artists in Montparnasse; the rich ones had for the most part moved elsewhere). Many of those featured in Kiki's memoirs took part, and Kiki sang her famously bawdy songs. But the climax of the entire event was the election of Kiki as Queen of Montparnasse. The photo taken of her that day, with a rose in her teeth, sold thousands of copies as a postcard.

Kiki and Broca's love affair was a passionate one, as Wambly Bald noted in the *Paris Tribune*, after following the lovers in an "endurance kiss" that began at the Falstaff restaurant and "held until they came in front of the Coupole bar." There, Broca bought Kiki a flower, pinned it on her, and the two went inside.[10]

Unfortunately, Broca had begun to show strange and increasingly violent behavior, especially when drunk—an ever-more-frequent occurrence. Man Ray called Broca "a drinker and a drug addict, subject to hallucinations,"[11] and perhaps he was right. Before long, Kiki would have to commit Broca to the Hôpital Sainte-Anne, where—Kiki being Kiki—she regularly visited him. She would find other men, but she never again lived with Broca, even after he attempted a return to his life in Montparnasse. After several relapses, he left Paris and went back to his family in Bordeaux.

Kiki never returned to Man Ray, either. After she left, Man Ray took up with a stunningly beautiful American, who upon meeting him announced, "My name is Lee Miller, and I'm your new student." Man Ray curtly told her that he did not have any students, and that in any case, he was leaving shortly for the south of France. "So am I," the blonde beauty replied.[12] As it turned out, they would be lovers and partners for the next three years, during which Miller learned from Man Ray, worked by his side, and in time became a lauded photographer in her own right.

⌢

Earlier that year, during the height of winter, Man Ray received an invitation from the Viscount Charles de Noailles to spend some time with him and his wife, Marie-Laure, at their château on the Riviera. Noailles had an ulterior motive: he wanted Man Ray to make a film of his château, including his art collection and houseguests. Man Ray had by now become disillusioned with filmmaking, but he found an invitation allowing him to escape winter in Paris hard to resist.

Noailles was quite prepared for whatever Man Ray was about to give him, which was *Les Mystères du château de dés* (*The Mysteries of the Château of Dice*), inspired by imagery in Stéphane Mallarmé's poem, *Un Coup de dés jamais n'abolira le hasard* (*A Throw of the Dice Will Never Abolish Chance*). This twenty-minute film begins with two people, masked and tossing dice on whether or not to leave Paris. It then portrays their auto trip southward toward the Noailles' château, a striking modern structure designed by Robert Mallet-Stevens. In fact, it was the château's cubic form that originally made Man Ray think of Mallarmé's poem, which in turn inspired the dice theme.[13]

After the travelers depart, the film cuts to the mysteriously empty château, which it explores. People suddenly appear. Like the travelers, they too are masked, their identities hidden as they play with a large pair of dice on the floor. After a series of scenes highlighting light and shadows, shot in the château's swimming pool, the guests play on equipment and lie on the floor of the gymnasium, slowly throwing the dice until they fall asleep, accompanied by the caption, "A throw of the dice will never do away with chance." The film concludes with the two travelers at last arriving at the château and happening on a pair of large dice in the grass, which they roll, asking if they should stay or go. The dice answer that they should stay, and the travelers entwine and gradually become fixed and white, like a marble statue. The film then closes in on an artificial hand holding a pair of dice.

Noailles saw the finished film in June and was so pleased that he proposed a full-length film "with no strings attached." Man Ray staunchly resisted and even attempted to suppress any public showing of *Les Mystères*. Nonetheless, it appeared that autumn at the Studio des Ursulines, where the audience was polite but baffled. By this time Man Ray had resolved to stop making movies—in large part because the birth of the talkies meant the death of cinema as he believed it should be, with the entire focus on the visual. In addition, his fear of the new technology came into play: "Sound was now well established," he later wrote, "and the amount of work involved, collaboration with technicians, and all the details of production frightened me."[14]

Hôtel Martel, designed and built by Robert Mallet-Stevens, 10 Rue Mallet-Stevens, Paris.
© J. McAuliffe

It was a defining moment for Man Ray. As he later recalled, "my reaction to the hectic Twenties began in 1929," with the recognition that "my excursions into the film world had done me more harm than good." He had lost his enthusiasm, and "having terminated a love affair [with Kiki], I felt ready for new adventures."[15] More than anything, he wanted to reestablish himself as a photographer.

⌢

After Man Ray's rejection, Charles de Noailles made an offer to Luis Buñuel, who with Salvador Dali had recently completed *Un Chien Andalou* (*An Andalusian Dog*), a short film containing one of the most shocking scenes in any movie—a razor slicing through an eyeball. Other macabre scenes included a bloody hand crawling with ants and a bleeding calf on a piano. Buñuel and Dali's fundamental rule in making this film, one that appealed mightily to the Surrealists, was that "no idea or image that might lend itself to a rational explanation of any kind would be accepted." The filming took two weeks, and according to Buñuel, "there were only five or six of us involved, and most of the time no one quite knew what he was doing."[16]

Un Chien Andalou created a sensation at its preview (shown at the Studio des Ursulines along with Man Ray's *Les Mystères du château de dés*).[17] Breton and the Surrealists had by this time become enthusiasts of the film and staged a gala event around its autumn premiere (at Montmartre's Studio 28), triggering a nasty scene when members of the right-wing Jeunesses Patriotes and Camelots du Roi burst into the theater and disrupted proceedings, slashing paintings on their way out the door. This kind of publicity led to a nine-month run, as well as to an offer by Marie-Laure and Charles de Noailles for another Buñuel-Dali film, *L'Age d'or*, which would appear in 1931 (minus Dali, with whom Buñuel had by then split). *L'Age d'or* would cement Buñuel's reputation as a leading figure among the Surrealists, even as it created havoc in the Noailles' relations with the Church.

The Surrealists were flourishing on the tidal wave of such artistic events, but they were beginning to experience a deep division within the ranks, due in large part to Breton's decision to join the Communist party. On the one hand, there were the writers and artists who preferred to keep their focus on the purely aesthetic, while on the other, there were those—especially the Marxists—who preferred political action. Despite his awareness of what might follow, Breton (with the support of several stalwarts) decided to submit those who called themselves Surrealists to a general self-examination of the sort practiced by the Communist party.

Accordingly, in early 1929, Breton and his supporters sent out a large mailing asking for each recipient's ideological position and choice of colleagues in a collective revolutionary effort. Those (such as Picabia) who did not reply were quickly eliminated, while those who attended the subsequent meeting found that it soon degenerated into a harangue against those groups and individuals toward whom Breton held a grievance. The meeting rapidly collapsed, but Breton was undeterred and proceeded to issue a Second Manifesto of Surrealism, published in the December 1929 issue of *La Révolution Surréaliste*. This criticized the Marxists along with the heretics and demanded complete sacrifice on the part of Surrealism's adherents.

As the new decade opened, Breton's list of enemies was growing.

As if Breton needed any more enemies, he now antagonized Jean Hugo by making off with his wife, Valentine, who became Breton's mistress. The Hugos consequently separated, and Valentine continued her personal and artistic life with the Surrealists, her *"passage dans le Surréalisme,"* as she later called it.

Others whom Breton and his supporters held in contempt were Marie-Laure and Charles de Noailles, on account of their wealth and luxurious lifestyle. This did not stop the Surrealists from accepting patronage from the Noailles; it merely meant that they did so while not so secretly despising them.

This did not seem to bother either Charles or Marie-Laure, who continued to serve as patrons to a raft of avant-garde writers and artists. In addition to films from Man Ray, Luis Buñuel, and Salvador Dali, Marie-Laure and Charles would soon commission a film from Jean Cocteau, his celebrated *Le Sang d'un poète* (*The Blood of a Poet*)—the first of many Cocteau films to come.

Cocteau was now at his brilliant best. All of 1929 proved to be enormously productive for him, despite another lengthy stay in a clinic during the early part of the year. A number of people, including Stravinsky, wondered at the length of time he spent there. Stravinsky in fact suspected that Cocteau "must have chosen to prolong his stays in sanitariums for other reasons: remember, such institutions are nice quiet places to write books in."[18] Coco Chanel, who was footing the bill, finally told Cocteau that he now was perfectly well and should end what amounted to an expensive paid vacation.

She certainly had a point: after the first months in his Saint-Cloud clinic, Cocteau was able to receive visitors and make an automobile trip to the Comédie-Française, where he met with a committee to discuss his proposed

La Voix humaine (*The Human Voice*)—a one-act monologue in which a de-spairing woman speaks into the telephone to her longtime lover who has left her. (The committee immediately accepted *La Voix humaine* for production, and it would have the first of many performances in early 1930.) During Cocteau's Saint-Cloud respite, he also wrote his extraordinary and deeply disturbing novel, *Les Enfants terribles*. As he told André Gide, "The real benefit of my treatment: work has laid hands on me. I am producing a book that I have been wanting to write since 1912. It is emerging without a struggle."[19] It would be published with much acclaim the following year.

Jean Renoir did not much care for Buñuel and Dali's *Un Chien Andalou*, which was too cruel and brutal for him. In any case, he was greatly preoccupied with other matters, especially the gradual but unstoppable breakup of his marriage to Catherine. It was a long process, but during its course he evolved from a maker of films solely interested in featuring Catherine into an artist for whom film was as essential to his being as painting was for his father.

Although Jean had not yet had a success, he was learning new techniques and becoming increasingly immersed in the process of filmmaking. He welcomed the talkies "with delight, seeing at once all the use that could be made of sound,"[20] but he was unable to find sufficient backing to make one of his own. French film studios had already begun to respond to the new age by equipping themselves for sound, and Jean "would have liked to do as everyone else was doing, but I was classified once and for all as a director of silent dramas."[21] In addition, producers continued to regard him as a dilettante, and his business agent had not forgotten the financial disaster of *Nana*. Jean badly wanted to film the novel *La Chienne* (*The Bitch*) as a talkie, starring Michel Simon, but it would be two years before he had the chance.

In the meantime, he and a friend decided to film *Le Petit chaperon rouge* (*Little Red Riding Hood*), which Jean (against the advice of his business agent) once again self-produced. They filmed it during the summer of 1929 near the Renoirs' house in Marlotte, with Jean playing the wolf as a lecherous tramp in a definitely grown-up version of the tale.

Later, Jean admitted that in the early part of his career, "I went out of my way to repudiate my father's principles." But on looking back, he discovered that the influence of Renoir *père* had always been with him. According to Jean, his father "considered that the world is a whole, comprised of parts which fit together, and that its equilibrium is dependent on every piece." Jean added that it was his own "subconscious faith in the clear-sightedness of [Pierre-Auguste] Renoir that causes me to be attracted to those beings whom the world calls 'simple,' but who probably possess a small fragment of the eternal wisdom."[22]

⌒

That November, Georges Clemenceau died. He may not have fully sub-scribed to the worldview of Pierre-Auguste Renoir, who (according to Jean) "believed that in destroying an ant one might be upsetting the bal-ance of a whole empire."[23] Yet to a surprising degree for a man who had earned the nickname "the Tiger," Clemenceau possessed an unexpected amount of tenderness. His closest friends were artists, not politicians, and he valued his friendship with Claude Monet above all others. "I love you," he had once written him, "because you are you and because you have learned how to understand light." He added, "My eyes need your color, and my heart is happy."[24]

He had enjoyed good health until the end, but at the age of eighty-eight he had outlived most of his friends as well as his sisters and younger brother Albert, to whom he was especially close (Albert, a lawyer, had defended the managing editor of L'Aurore, which had published Zola's famous J'Accuse during the Dreyfus Affair). Clemenceau's instructions for burial underscored his essential modesty: rejecting any possibility for a state occasion, he requested simple burial beside his father at his birthplace, Le Colombier, in the heart of the Vendée. In addition, he wanted his body to be carried there without a cortège or any kind of ceremony. As for the grave, it was to be unmarked.

Inside the coffin, Clemenceau asked that certain small mementos be placed, including "two little bunches of dried flowers which are on the man-telpiece of the room by the garden."[25] These were the flowers that he had received from soldiers on the front in a touching scene at the war's height, when he was leading France through its darkest hours. He had promised that these flowers would go to his grave with him, and he kept his promise.

⌒

Another death that year was more unexpected and far more shattering. In August, Sergei Diaghilev died in Venice, setting off ripples throughout the cultural world that he had dominated and enriched for more than twenty years.

Only a short time before, Coco Chanel had given a splendid party to mark the close of the Ballets Russes's 1929 Paris season, as she had the previous year. The garden at her mansion on the Rue du Faubourg-Saint-Honoré had been brilliantly lit, with jazz musicians providing background music and the hostess providing duly expensive and exquisite food—most memorably, endless amounts of champagne, and soup tureens filled with caviar. "We drank torrents of champagne," Diaghilev's last star dancer and lover, Serge Lifar, remembered of that evening. Lifar had just danced the premiere of Stravinsky's *Apollo* brilliantly, and had danced Prokofiev's *Prodigal Son* to much acclaim only a few days before that. "Remember it, Seriozhka," Diaghilev told him, after ceremoniously kissing his leg and presenting him with a golden lyre pin. "Remember it for the rest of your days."[26]

Diaghilev had not been in good health. In Paris that spring, he had visited a doctor who sternly prescribed rest and a special diet, advice that the diabetic impresario completely ignored. Friends who had not seen him for a time were shocked by his physical deterioration, but he kept up his hectic pace through yet another triumphant season in London, taking time out only to bring a new protégé, the seventeen-year-old composer Igor Markevitch, on a strenuous cultural tour of the Rhine.[27] After that, he wearily departed for the Grand Hotel on the Lido in Venice, where he took to his bed. Lifar and Kochno nursed him around the clock.

Misia received a telegram from him, "Am ill, come at once," while cruising with Chanel and Bendor on Bendor's yacht, *The Flying Cloud*. At the time, the three were off the coast of Yugoslavia, and they raced to Venice.[28] There, Misia sent for a doctor and engaged nurses to relieve Lifar and Kochno. After a while, Diaghilev seemed to improve, and Chanel left on *The Flying Cloud* while Misia stayed behind. But now Diaghilev suddenly became worse. Misia, with Kochno and Lifar, stayed at his bedside. When it was clear that he was dying, Misia sent for a priest—who refused to perform last rites on a member of the Russian Orthodox Church until Misia screamed him into compliance.

Later that day she took a gondola to the island cemetery of San Michele to find a plot of ground for him in the Greek Orthodox section. "To choose a plot of ground for him," she later wrote, "was the last sad service I could render the friend who had dwelt in my heart for more than twenty years."[29] One more service she could perform: Diaghilev, as always, was in need of money, and Misia paid the hotel bill and the doctor. Chanel, who had returned to Venice, provided moral support and probably paid for the funeral.[30] After a funeral mass in the Greek Orthodox Church, a black funerary gondola carried the coffin to the cemetery island, escorted by priests, whose chants could be heard floating across the water.

Tomb of Sergei Diaghilev, Venice. © J. McAuliffe

The sense of loss among Diaghilev's wide circle of friends was enormous. "We are left without a magician," Misia sadly commented.[31] Stravinsky, who had quarreled with Diaghilev during the last months of the impresario's life, was heartbroken. Many years later, he would be buried at his request in Venice, near his friend.

⌒

Despite the impact that Diaghilev's death had on so many, life went on. Picasso was deeply moved by the unexpected loss, but continued to juggle his complicated private life with an ill wife and a toothsome mistress—a demanding situation that helped end his decadelong immersion in high society. The following spring, Count Kessler, ever an insider on social affairs in Paris as much as in London or Berlin, noted that some of Picasso's closest friends in the social set (among them, the Beaumonts) complained that they had not seen Picasso for a year—probably an exaggeration, but nonetheless an indication of where Picasso now was choosing to spend his time.[32]

While Picasso was enjoying Marie-Thérèse, Cole Porter was enjoying a career that at long last was taking off. After the success of *Paris*, he wrote the score for *Wake Up and Dream* (including "What Is This Thing Called Love?"), which opened in London to rave reviews in March and on Broadway in December 1929. There, despite the stock market crash, it enjoyed a long run. Best of all, Irving Berlin signed Porter up to write the music for *Fifty Million Frenchmen*, which opened on Broadway in November, with its memorable number, "You Do Something to Me." The 1920s were closing, and not only was Cole Porter being celebrated as a rising star, but New York—and Broadway—were drawing him ever more irresistibly from Paris, the city he would always adore.

Cole Porter's career was not the only one on the upswing: Edward Titus, husband of the cosmetics queen, Helena Rubinstein, was also beginning to enjoy professional success. During the spring of 1929, his tiny Black Manikin Press published D. H. Lawrence's *Lady Chatterley's Lover* (after Sylvia Beach turned down the opportunity),[33] and Titus was about to follow this with another big seller, the English translation of Kiki's *Memoirs*, for which he persuaded Hemingway to write an introduction.

Alberto Giacometti was another who was tasting success for the first time that June, when the Noailles attended his exhibition at a Montparnasse gallery and bought one of his sculptures. The eldest son of a Swiss family, Giacometti had arrived in Paris in 1922 to study with Antoine Bourdelle at the Grande-Chaumière Academy. The two had little in common artistically, but Bourdelle—a former *praticien* for Rodin—told Giacometti, as he had told all of his students, not to copy him but to "sing your own song."[34] Yet despite Bourdelle's encouragement, Giacometti found it difficult to discover his own individual form of expression and had spent much of the 1920s in his quest. Midway, his brother Diego joined him, and the two moved to a run-down apartment recently vacated by Marcel Duchamp. Two years later, in 1927, they moved to Rue Hippolyte-Maindron, an almost-rural block of Montparnasse studios where Alberto would stay in monk-like severity and simplicity for forty years, even after fame found him.[35]

In a busy studio not far from Giacometti's atelier—although in a significantly better neighborhood—another native of Switzerland, Le Corbusier, was doing very well indeed. He may have lost out on his dearly sought-after commission for the League of Nations, but he and his atelier were busier than ever. Even the new tubular steel furniture designs, the product of a collaboration between Le Corbusier, Charlotte Perriand, and Pierre Jeanneret, were shown publicly for the first time in that year's Salon d'Automne, marking the beginning of their acceptance and manufacture.

Le Corbusier began work that year on the Salvation Army's Cité de Refuge, a large multistoried homeless shelter underwritten by the Princesse de Polignac's gift of more than seven million francs. He had already completed an annex to the Salvation Army's dormitory, the Palais du Peuple, and— underwritten by the Princesse—he was also creating a floating dormitory designed as an ocean liner (the "Asile Flottant," or "Floating Refuge") from a Seine coal barge dating from World War I.[36] In addition, he received approval from Pierre and Emilie Savoye of his design for their country house in Poissy, near Paris. This was an important commission, as the Villa Savoye, completed in 1931, would embody the culmination of Le Corbusier's 1920s concepts for private housing, most especially his five points for the new architecture: *pilotis*, or posts, raising up and supporting the whole; roof gardens; an open interior plan; horizontal bands of windows; and a free, non-load-bearing façade. Adding to his rising number of commissions, a federation of Swiss universities now awarded him a consolation prize for his loss of the League of Nations commission—the commission for the Swiss Pavilion, a dormitory for Swiss students at the new Cité Universitaire Internationale de Paris.

Le Corbusier's Villa Savoye, Poissy, France. © *J. McAuliffe*

That September, Le Corbusier departed for Argentina and Brazil to give a series of lectures and develop urban plans for Buenos Aires, São Paulo, and Rio de Janeiro. By this time he was receiving large lecture fees, and the trip proved extremely lucrative. In a buoyant mood during the course of the tour, and not yet aware of the extent of the Wall Street crash, he anticipated similar success in the United States. "North Americans are strong and young," he wrote his mother on October 29. "Simple and not tricky. For them everything is action. In architecture they are completely backward. . . . I suspect my next voyage to the United States will be an important thing."[37]

As it happened, Le Corbusier was about to become intimately acquainted with one particular American, Josephine Baker, who was on tour in Latin America and was in Buenos Aires when she and Le Corbusier met. On this occasion she and Pepito asked the architect to design a house for them in elegant Passy, at the western edge of Paris, and also expressed interest in building a village for orphans from around the world.[38]

Josephine's architectural ideals—the houses were to be "charming, small and without pretension, amid all the flowers and all the green"—endeared her to Le Corbusier, who described her to his mother as "extraordinarily modest and natural. . . . Not an atom of vanity or pose."[39] She was also drop-dead gorgeous, and there seems to have been no question that he found her irresistible.

They met again en route from Buenos Aires to São Paulo, where they saw quite a lot of one another—including an episode (that he also reported to his mother) where Josephine sang to him, "I'm a little black bird looking for a little white bird." Josephine "reminds me of Yvonne," he informed his mother[40]—an observation that Yvonne might have received with a raised eyebrow. For his voyage back to France, Le Corbusier chose the *Lutétia*, the same ship that Josephine was taking.

Here they were inseparable, and spent much of the time in the privacy of Le Corbusier's stateroom, where he sketched Josephine in the nude, exaggerating her curves (he did not send these drawings to his mother).[41] If there ever was an unlikely combination of lovers, it was these two, but they chose to emphasize the ideal side of their relationship. For Le Corbusier, Josephine was "a little child, pure and simple," with "a warm heart." In her memoirs, Josephine described Le Corbusier as "a simple man and gay; we become friends." No private love nest for her: instead, "I amuse him with my little songs, which I sing for him as we walk around the bridge."[42]

Josephine's adopted son, Jean-Claude Baker, had a different take on the episode. Josephine, he believed, hated white men and preferred women (such as Colette) because of the abuse she had suffered as a child. Sex with white men was, for her, a form of revenge. Also, "for her, sleeping with men—beyond the revenge—was a way of getting a little security."[43]

It seems that Yvonne, Pierre Jeanneret, and Le Corbusier's mother were waiting at the dock to greet him when the boat arrived in Bordeaux. Whether or not Le Corbusier sashayed down the gangplank arm in arm with Baker, as stories have it, he certainly was ready enough to sing Baker's praises ("She slips into life's roughness. She has a heart of gold. She's a wonderful *artiste* when she dances").[44]

Whether or not it was an affair to remember, Charlotte Perriand for one concluded that Josephine Baker "had completely won him over."[45]

Although Le Corbusier was prospering, the year was proving difficult for others in Paris, especially for Gerald and Sara Murphy. The Murphys, who had been leading charmed lives, were suddenly devastated to learn of the illness of their second son, Patrick, who was diagnosed with tuberculosis. Within a few short years, even more misfortune would strike, turning their enchanted life to tragedy and inspiring Archibald MacLeish to base the main characters in his play, *J. B.*, not only on the biblical Job but on Sara and Gerald Murphy.

François Coty, whose golden life had seemed impervious to trouble, also found himself suddenly overwhelmed by disaster. The previous year, he had purchased the long-established Paris newspaper *Le Gaulois* and merged it with *Figaro*, managing to alienate the readership of both papers and sending *Figaro*'s circulation into severe decline. But even more devastating was that Coty's wife, Yvonne, now unexpectedly sued him for divorce. It was not as though Yvonne had been unaware of her husband's many mistresses (some accounts said twelve) and illegitimate children (five by one mistress alone). The press—at least those papers that Coty did not yet control—delighted in displaying the unabashedly debauched side of his life as well as his support of the ever-more-aggressive right-wing leagues. But by 1929, Yvonne had had enough. Encouraged by her lover, Léon Cotnareanu, she went for the jugular and received an enormous settlement—in large part by suing François in the courts of New York (made possible by Coty's thriving Fifth Avenue store), where Americans were especially appalled by Coty's behavior. *L'Ami du Peuple* went to Yvonne as part of the settlement. She then married Cotnareanu.

Cotnareanu was insistent about getting Yvonne's (and his) hands on as much of the Coty fortune as possible, certainly before François squandered any more of it on money-losing newspaper ventures and expensive political action. In large part, this was simply a question of money, but it was not the money alone: Cotnareanu was Jewish, and he was determined to end the anti-Semitic tirades of *L'Ami du Peuple*. In time, he would also engineer a takeover of *Figaro*, which under Coty's ownership had also become strongly anti-Semitic.

Coty was furious. Not only had his wife divorced him and mopped up much of his fortune as well as his most cherished newspapers, but she had married a Jew. This, for Coty, was unforgivable. He published a vituperative piece about Yvonne and Léon in *L'Ami du Peuple*, while it was still under his ownership, and promptly married Henriette Dieudé, the mother of his five illegitimate children. Unfortunately for Coty, Henriette just as promptly began an affair with Coty's friend, Maurice Hanot d'Hartoy, leading Coty to divorce her within a year of their marriage.

Paul Poiret's shop on the Rond-Point des Champs-Elysées closed in 1929, the remaining designs sold as scrap. Unable to afford his palatial town house, he sold most of his furniture and paintings and moved into an apartment above the Salle Pleyel concert hall. His sister, Nicole Groult, who by now had become a successful *couturière* in her own right, tried to help him, but he proudly refused. When friends collected forty thousand francs to help pay off his debts, he spent it on luxuries that sent him even further into debt. The previous year Jean Cocteau had sketched contrasting manikins, one an ungainly Poiret, the other a streamlined Chanel, with the caption, "Poiret Leaves—Chanel Arrives." By this time, the observation had been true for years.

While Poiret had become the victim of changing times, James Joyce had already succeeded in changing the literary landscape with *Ulysses*, although not with the kind of financial reward he so ardently desired. Picasso received "20,000 to 30,000 francs for a few hours' work," he complained, while Joyce's own current work was "not worth a penny a line."[46] As with Poiret, it never seems to have occurred to Joyce to moderate his style of living, and if anything, he was becoming ever more dependent on Sylvia Beach, who regularly worked to the utmost on his behalf in addition to looking out for a whole community of expats and running her own bookstore. Joyce regularly went on holiday in various locales in England and France, always staying in the best hotels, but he begrudged Sylvia's much-needed retreats to the weekend place she shared with Adrienne, and especially objected to her leaving town for the mountains in the summer. How could he possibly do without her?

Sylvia was exhausted, especially after the suicide of her mother in 1927, but she continued to act on Joyce's behalf, whether as publisher, agent, financial manager (she had his power of attorney), or personal errand runner. No bothersome matter was too great or small for Joyce to assume that Sylvia would take care of it, all the while giving him her complete allegiance. And Sylvia did all this, at least for the time being. But she was suffering from a growing variety of illnesses, and given her own difficulties, she found it increasingly grueling to give Joyce the total devotion he demanded.

Still, at Joyce's request, she (rather than Harry Crosby, the publisher) handled all the press copy for Joyce's publication of *Tales Told of Shem and Shaun* (later to become part of *Finnegans Wake*), and shortly afterward cohosted with Adrienne an elaborate celebration honoring the publication of the French translation of *Ulysses*, which Adrienne had shepherded. Among the leading French authors who attended were Paul Valéry, Léon-Paul Fargue, and Jules Romains, while the Irish portion of the entourage included young Samuel Beckett, who had quickly become virtually a part of Joyce's family, doing any number of tasks, including research, for the sight-impaired author.

In early October, at Joyce's behest, Sylvia arranged a twenty-fifth anniversary party for him and Nora, his common-law wife. Among the guests were the Hemingways, who had been traveling in Europe and arrived in Paris shortly before the September publication of Ernest's *Farewell to Arms*, which would soon become a best seller. The party was well attended and festive, lubricated by Irish whiskey and champagne. None of the participants realized it, but this marked the last time all of them would celebrate together in Paris.

⁓

Despite the troubles of a few, prospects for France's next decade appeared to be bright. Raymond Poincaré's retirement in July, due to illness, may have brought to a close the ministerial stability that had marked the two-plus years of his premiership, but as the weeks of autumn sped by, no one expected any problems. France as a nation had come out the other side of the Great War, and although victory had been bought at far too great a price—especially in terms of human lives—by 1929 the French as a whole were enjoying prosperity and looking to the future with optimism.

One of these optimistic Frenchmen was Maurice Ravel. Always interested in the future and in technological advances, Ravel entered his sixth decade by actively participating in efforts to record music. "Curious about everything," according to the musicologist Jean Dunoyer, "and passionately attentive to the exploration of sonorous phenomena, Ravel welcomed and followed the progress of recorded music."[47] In November 1929, he agreed to form a music committee of experts to assist engineers in the manufacture of records, and he was the first composer to have almost all of his major works recorded during his lifetime—recorded by himself or by his friends and colleagues. Not surprisingly, Ravel was an early owner of a phonograph, which he installed in his home at Montfort l'Amaury.

Another was Marie Curie, who may have disliked the ceremonial role in which she increasingly found herself, but nonetheless acknowledged the worthiness of the motives of those who hovered over her. After all, her second American trip, in the autumn of 1929, was prompted by the goodwill of a group of women who had raised enough money to buy a gram of radium for an institute in Poland, Curie's homeland. As Curie readily acknowledged, "what is beyond denying is the sincerity of all those who do these things and their conviction that they must do them."[48]

Although by 1929 the combative right-wing Jeunesses Patriotes claimed some three hundred thousand members, the widely shared goal of so many more individuals—whether expressed in the Kellogg-Briand Pact or the Cité Internationale Universitaire de Paris—was for peace, peace for all mankind. As Parisians went about their daily lives, stability, both economic and political, seemed assured.

And then an economic crisis of unprecedented proportions burst upon the world. It began in late October 1929 on Wall Street and quickly spread, although France at first was relatively immune to its devastation. Boom did not immediately turn to bust there, in part because of France's low unemployment and tight control of credit, as well as its relatively low level of investment in the stock market. But the Depression's effects would soon ripple outward, starting with all those American and British tourists and expats who suddenly had little or no money to spend and who either sought out cheaper locales in which to set up housekeeping or sadly returned to their native lands.

Wherever they landed, they brought with them memories of a decade that, in hindsight, appeared gloriously carefree and joyous, whether viewed as an amusing alcohol-fueled escapade or as a kind of Camelot. In memory, les Années folles sizzled and glowed, to the accompaniment of an insistent jazz beat. Ernest and Hadley's fourth-floor walk-up, impromptu gatherings at Shakespeare and Company, chance encounters with one another, whether at the Dôme, the Rotonde, or the Dingo—all this, and memories of Kiki's irrepressible laughter, fueled reminiscences that shaped the portrayal of these years.

And yet, looking back on les Années folles and the glory years of Montparnasse, two of its longtime residents, Hugh Ford and Morrill Cody, remarked on what they called "the distortion and romanticizing of the time, the place, and the inhabitants." It bothered them, as it did some others who lived in Paris during those years, that a couple of myths about Montparnasse had become entrenched: one, that the inhabitants were "a libidinous gang of immoderate drinkers and philanderers," and the other, that they were "a harmonious community of generous-minded artists congregating in cafés to discuss high art." It was neither one nor the other, Ford and Cody agreed—neither as "glorious nor as notorious as it has been made out to be."[49]

Then what was it? Kiki, ever upbeat but no romantic, had this to say about Montparnasse of the 1920s: "Montparnasse is a village that is as round as a circus," she wrote in her memoirs of 1929. "All the people of the earth have come here to pitch their tents; and yet it's all just like one big family." She conceded that it was too bad that "the little wine-shops where one used to be able to get so nice a meal have all disappeared." And "some evenings, I must say, they tried to turn me aside from the path of duty and take me to Montmartre."

Yet, characteristically, she then added that she "refused to be a deserter."[50] And she never did desert Montparnasse, even after the party was over.

Notes

1 Out of Darkness (1918)

Selected Sources for this and subsequent chapters are listed, by chapter, in the approximate order in which they informed the text: Helen Pearl Adam, *Paris Sees It Through: A Diary, 1914–1919* (New York: Hodder & Stoughton, 1919); Eve Curie, *Madame Curie: A Biography* (New York: Da Capo, 2001); Susan Quinn, *Marie Curie: A Life* (New York: Simon & Schuster, 1995); Abbé (Arthur) Mugnier, *Journal de l'Abbé Mugnier: 1879–1939* (Paris: Mercure de France, 1985); Marcel Proust, *Correspondance de Marcel Proust*, ed. Philip Kolb (Paris: Plon, 1989); Jean Cocteau, *The Journals of Jean Cocteau* (New York: Criterion Books, 1956); Francis Steegmuller, *Cocteau: A Biography* (Boston: Little Brown, 1970); Margaret MacMillan, *Paris 1919: Six Months That Changed the World* (New York: Random House, 2002); Nicholas Fox Weber, *Le Corbusier: A Life* (New York: Knopf, 2008); Jean Petit, *Le Corbusier lui-même* (Geneva, Switzerland: Editions Rousseau, 1970); H. Allen Brooks, *Le Corbusier's Formative Years: Charles-Edouard Jeanneret at La Chaux-de-Fonds* (Chicago: University of Chicago Press, 1997); Charles Jencks, *Le Corbusier and the Continual Revolution in Architecture* (New York: Monacelli Press, 2000); Deborah Gans, *The Le Corbusier Guide* (New York: Princeton Architectural Press, 2006); Claude Monet, *Monet by Himself: Paintings, Drawings, Pastels, Letters* (London: Macdonald, 1989); Daniel Wildenstein, *Monet, or the Triumph of Impressionism*, vol. 1 (Cologne, Germany, and Paris, France: Taschen/Wildenstein Institute, 1999); Valérie Bougault, *Paris, Montparnasse: The Heyday of Modern Art, 1910–1940* (Paris: Editions Pierre Terrail, 1997); Peter De Francia, *Fernand Léger* (New Haven, Conn.: Yale University Press, 1983); André Mare, *André Mare, cubisme et camouflage, 1914–1918* (Bernay, France: Musée de Bernay, 1998); H. G. Wells, *The War That Will End War* (New

York: Duffield, 1914); Siegfried Sassoon, *Sherston's Progress* (London: Faber & Faber, 1936); Raymond Radiguet, *Count d'Orgel* (London: Pushkin Press, 2001); Maurice Sachs, *The Decade of Illusion: Paris, 1918–1928* (New York: Knopf, 1933); Yvonne Deslandres, *Poiret: Paul Poiret, 1879–1944* (Paris: Editions du Regard, 1986); François Baudot, *Poiret* (New York: Assouline, 2006); Paul Poiret, *King of Fashion: The Autobiography of Paul Poiret* (London: V & A Publishing, 2009); Axel Madsen, *Chanel: A Woman of Her Own* (New York: Henry Holt, 1990); Paul Morand, *The Allure of Chanel* (London: Pushkin Press, 2008); Justine Picardie, *Coco Chanel: The Legend and the Life* (New York: itbooks, 2010); Jean Leymarie, *Chanel* (New York: Abrams, 2010); Kiki, *Kiki's Memoirs* (Hopewell, N.J.: Ecco Press, 1996); John Richardson, *A Life of Picasso: The Triumphant Years, 1917–1932* (New York: Knopf, 2007); Jean-Paul Crespelle, *La Vie quotidienne à Montparnasse à la Grande Epoque, 1905–1930* (Paris: Hachette, 1976); Billy Klüver and Julie Martin, *Kiki's Paris: Artists and Lovers, 1900–1930* (New York: Abrams, 1989); Dan Franck, *Bohemian Paris: Picasso, Modigliani, Matisse, and the Birth of Modern Art* (New York: Grove Press, 2001); Gertrude Stein, *The Autobiography of Alice B. Toklas* (New York: Vintage, 1990); Anthony Rhodes, *Louis Renault: A Biography* (New York: Harcourt, Brace & World, 1970); John Reynolds, *André Citroën: The Man and the Motor Cars* (Thrupp, Stroud, UK: Sutton, 1996); Alain Frèrejean, *André Citroën, Louis Renault: un duel sans merci* (Paris: A. Michel, 1998); Arbie Orenstein, *Ravel: Man and Musician* (New York: Dover, 1991); Maurice Ravel, *Ravel Reader: Correspondence, Articles, Interviews*, ed. Arbie Orenstein (Mineola, N.Y.: Dover, 2003); Jean Lacouture, *De Gaulle: The Rebel, 1890–1944* (New York: Norton, 1993); Charles Williams, *The Last Great Frenchman: A Life of General de Gaulle* (New York: Wiley, 1993).

1. Adam, *Paris Sees It Through*, 255–56.

2. Proust à Madame Straus, [le lundi soir 11 novembre 1918], in *Correspondance de Marcel Proust*, 17:448–50.

3. Apollinaire lived at 202 Boulevard Saint-Germain from 1913 until his death.

4. Cocteau, *Journals of Jean Cocteau*, 48.

5. Jeanneret lived at 20 Rue Jacob, where he would remain until 1934. The American expatriate writer Natalie Clifford Barney lived on the ground floor.

6. Petit, *Le Corbusier lui-même*, 52.

7. Monet to Clemenceau, 12 November 1918, in *Monet by Himself*, 252. Monet initially proposed that these be displayed in the Musée des Arts Décoratifs.

8. Geffroy quoted in Wildenstein, *Monet*, 1:410.

9. Monet quoted in Wildenstein, *Monet*, 1:422. See also Monet to G or J. Bernheim-Jeune, 24 November 1918, in *Monet by Himself*, 252.

10. Bougault, *Paris, Montparnasse*, 159. A slightly different translation is in De Francia, *Fernand Léger*, 40.

11. "This, the greatest of all wars, is not just another war—it is the last war!" (Wells, *The War That Will End War*, 14).

12. Kessel quoted in Bougault, *Paris, Montparnasse*, 159.

13. *New York Times*, 5 August 2014.

14. Sassoon, *Sherston's Progress*, 278. "My knight-errantry about the war had fizzled out . . . . How could I begin my life all over again when I had no conviction about anything except that the war was a dirty trick which had been played on me and my generation?" (278).

15. Radiguet, *Comte d'Orgel*, 107.

16. Sachs, *Decade of Illusion*, 9, 10.

17. Steegmuller, *Cocteau*, 214.

18. Madsen, *Chanel*, 4.

19. Morand, *Allure of Chanel*, 42–43.

20. Picardie, *Coco Chanel*, 70.

21. Kiki, *Kiki's Memoirs*, 75, 81.

22. Kiki, *Kiki's Memoirs*, 84.

23. Kiki, *Kiki's Memoirs*, 126. Other impoverished residents of Montparnasse recalled similar experiences (*Kiki's Memoirs*, 254).

24. Kiki, *Kiki's Memoirs*, 132.

25. Stein, *Autobiography of Alice B. Toklas*, 193.

26. Rhodes, *Louis Renault*, 42, 48.

27. Ravel to Lucien Garban, 8 May 1916, in *Ravel Reader*, 165.

28. Ravel to Mme René de Saint-Marceaux, 22 January 1919, in *Ravel Reader*, 186.

29. Lacouture, *De Gaulle: The Rebel*, 53.

30. Lacouture, *De Gaulle: The Rebel*, 54. This was an undated lecture, his last to his companions at Wülzburg prison.

2 Going Forward (1918–1919)

Selected sources for this chapter: De Francia, *Fernand Léger*; Blaise Cendrars, *J'ai tué* (Paris: G. Grès, 1919); Bougault, *Paris, Montparnasse*; Musée des Arts Décoratifs (Paris, France), *Fernand Léger, 1881–1955: [Exposition] juin–octobre 1956* (Paris: F. Hazan, 1956); Mary McAuliffe, *Twilight of the Belle Epoque: The Paris of Picasso, Stravinsky, Proust, Renault, Marie Curie, Gertrude Stein, and Their Friends through the Great War* (Lanham, Md.: Rowman & Littlefield, 2014); Nicholas Weber, *Le Corbusier*; Brooks, *Le Corbusier's Formative Years*; Petit, *Le Corbusier lui-même*; Jencks, *Le Corbusier and the Continual Revolution in Architecture*; Carol S. Eliel, *L'Esprit nouveau: Purism in Paris, 1918–1925*, with essays by Françoise Ducros, Tag Gronberg, and an English translation of *After Cubism* by Amédée Ozenfant and Charles-Edouard Jeanneret (Los Angeles, Calif.: Los Angeles County Museum of Art in association with Harry N. Abrams, 2001); Kenneth E. Silver, *Esprit de Corps: The Art of the Parisian Avant-Garde and the First World War, 1914–1925* (Princeton, N.J.: Princeton University Press, 1989); Kevin Birmingham, *The Most Dangerous Book: The Battle for James Joyce's Ulysses* (New York: Penguin, 2014); Amanda Vaill, *Everybody Was So Young: Gerald and Sara Murphy, A Lost Generation Love Story* (New York: Broadway

Books, 1999); Ernest Hemingway, *A Moveable Feast* (New York: Simon & Schuster, 1996); William McBrien, *Cole Porter: A Biography* (New York: Vintage, 1998); Elsa Maxwell, *R.S.V.P.: Elsa Maxwell's Own Story* (Boston: Little, Brown, 1954); Rhodes, *Louis Renault*; Ruth Brandon, *Ugly Beauty: Helena Rubinstein, L'Oréal, and the Blemished History of Looking Good* (New York: Harper, 2011); William C. Carter, *Marcel Proust: A Life* (New Haven, Conn.: Yale University Press, 2000); Céleste Albaret, *Monsieur Proust: A Memoir* (New York: McGraw-Hill, 1976); Marcel Proust, *Selected Letters*, ed. Philip Kolb (London: HarperCollins, 2000); Marcel Proust, *La Correspondance de Marcel Proust*, ed. Philip Kolb (Paris: Plon, 1989–1993); Alain Duménil, *Parfum d'empire: la vie extraordinaire de François Coty* (Paris: Plon, 2009); Ghislaine Sicard-Picchiottino, *François Coty: un industriel corse sous la IIIe République* (Ajaccio, France: Albiana, 2006); Roulhac B. Toledano and Elizabeth Z. Coty, *François Coty: Fragrance, Power, Money* (Gretna, La.: Pelican, 2009); Darius Milhaud, *Notes without Music* (New York: Knopf, 1953); Francis Poulenc, *Moi et mes amis* (Paris: Palatine, 1963); Rollo H. Myers, *Erik Satie* (New York: Dover, 1968); Alan M. Gillmor, *Erik Satie* (Boston: Twayne, 1988); Barbara L. Kelly, *Music and Ultra-Modernism in France: A Fragile Consensus, 1913–1939* (Woodbridge, Suffolk, UK: Boydell Press, 2013); Steegmuller, *Cocteau*; Arthur Gold and Robert Fizdale, *Misia: The Life of Misia Sert* (New York: Morrow, 1981); Sjeng Scheijen, *Diaghilev: A Life* (New York: Oxford University Press, 2009); Maurice Sachs, *Day of Wrath: Confessions of a Turbulent Youth* (London: Arthur Baker, 1953); Jean Cocteau, *Lettres à sa mère*, vol. 1 (1898–1918) (Paris: Gallimard, 1989).

1. Cendrars translated and quoted in De Francia, *Fernand Léger*, 34–35. The original edition of *J'ai tué* appeared in November 1918 with illustrations by Fernand Léger. A 1919 edition contains a portrait of Cendrars by Léger.

2. From a 1925 lecture. Léger translated and quoted in De Francia, *Fernand Léger*, 36.

3. Musée des Arts Décoratifs, *Fernand Léger*, 78.

4. The term *Tubism* was originally a derisive one, conferred by the critic Louis Vauxcelles, who also—with Matisse's unwitting help—gave Cubism its name (see McAuliffe, *Twilight of the Belle Epoque*, 180).

5. At Galerie Thomas, 5 Rue de Penthièvre, a temporary gallery that Ozenfant occasionally set up in Jove, the couture salon that he managed.

6. Nicholas Weber, *Le Corbusier*, 166.

7. For a detailed discussion of this point, see Nicholas Weber, *Le Corbusier*, 779–80n5.

8. Petit, *Le Corbusier lui-même*, 52.

9. From *Après le Cubisme*, in Eliel, *L'Esprit nouveau*, 133.

10. From *Après le Cubisme*, in Eliel, *L'Esprit nouveau*, 132, 142.

11. Birmingham gives these figures (*The Most Dangerous Book*, 163). Amanda Vaill gives similar figures, including six thousand Americans living in Paris in 1921, and thirty thousand by 1924 (*Everybody Was So Young*, 96).

12. Maxwell, *R.S.V.P.*, 119–20.

13. Maxwell, *R.S.V.P.*, 119–20.

14. McBrien, *Cole Porter*, 73.

15. He received numerous citations as well as the Croix de Guerre.

16. Nicholas Weber, *Le Corbusier*, 168.

17. Carter, *Marcel Proust*, 679.

18. Proust to Walter Berry, [21 January 1919], in Proust, *Selected Letters*, 4:65.

19. Walter Berry à Marcel Proust, 22 Jan[vier] 1919, in Proust, *Correspondance*, 18:55.

20. Milhaud, *Notes without Music*, 94.

21. Milhaud, *Notes without Music*, 13, 21.

22. Milhaud, *Notes without Music*, 17.

23. Milhaud, *Notes without Music*, 43, 44.

24. Milhaud, *Notes without Music*, 70, 75.

25. Milhaud, *Notes without Music*, 98.

26. Milhaud, *Notes without Music*, 225. Poulenc has written: "Never did we have an aesthetic in common, and our music has always been dissimilar" (Steegmuller, *Cocteau*, 238–39).

27. According to Poulenc, "Jean Cocteau, always attracted by every novelty, was not our theorist, as many have claimed, but our friend and our brilliant spokesman" (Steegmuller, *Cocteau*, 239).

28. Steegmuller, *Cocteau*, 207.

29. Steegmuller, *Cocteau*, 82.

30. Gold and Fizdale, *Misia*, 215.

31. Scheijen, *Diaghilev*, preface, 36.

32. Steegmuller, *Cocteau*, 214.

33. Sachs, *Day of Wrath*, 75.

34. Cocteau, *Lettres à sa mère*, 1:351.

3 Versailles and Victory (1919)

Selected sources for this chapter: Harold George Nicholson, *Peacemaking, 1919* (New York: Grosset & Dunlap, 1965); Adam, *Paris Sees It Through*; Nicholas Weber, *Le Corbusier*; Carter, *Marcel Proust*; David Robin Watson, *Georges Clemenceau: A Political Biography* (New York: David McKay, 1974); Margaret MacMillan, *Paris 1919: Six Months That Changed the World* (New York: Random House, 2002); Philippe Bernard and Henri Dubief, *The Decline of the Third Republic, 1914–1938* (New York: Cambridge University Press, 1988); Rhodes, *Louis Renault*; Reynolds, *André Citroën*; Frèrejean, *André Citroën, Louis Renault*; Ravel, *Ravel Reader*; Orenstein, *Ravel*; Roger Nichols, *Ravel* (New Haven, Conn.: Yale University Press, 2011); Marguerite Long, *Au piano avec Maurice Ravel* (Paris: Juillard, 1971); Bougault, *Paris, Montparnasse*; Steegmuller, *Cocteau*; Jean Hugo, *Avant d'oublier: 1918–1931* (Paris: Fayard, 1976); Albaret, *Monsieur Proust*; Proust, *Selected Letters*;

Maxwell, *R.S.V.P.*; McBrien, *Cole Porter*; Radiguet, *Count d'Orgel*; Gold and Fizdale, *Misia*; Misia Sert, *Misia and the Muses: The Memoirs of Misia Sert* (New York: John Day, 1953); Poiret, *King of Fashion*; Baudot, *Poiret*; Deslandres, *Poiret*; Russell T. Clement, *Les Fauves: A Sourcebook* (Westport, Conn.: Greenwood, 1994); Jacques-Emile Blanche, *More Portraits of a Lifetime: 1918–1938* (London: J. M. Dent, 1939); Michael de Cossart, *The Food of Love: Princesse Edmond de Polignac and Her Salon* (London: Hamish Hamilton, 1978); Frederick Brown, *The Embrace of Unreason: France, 1914–1940* (New York: Knopf, 2014); Eugen Joseph Weber, *Action Française: Royalism and Reaction in Twentieth Century France* (Stanford, Calif.: Stanford University Press, 1962); Arthur Gold and Robert Fizdale, *The Divine Sarah: A Life of Sarah Bernhardt* (New York: Vintage, 1992); Lysiane Sarah Bernhardt and Marion Dix, *Sarah Bernhardt, My Grandmother* (n.p., 1949); Richardson, *Life of Picasso: The Triumphant Years*; Scheijen, *Diaghilev*; André Mare, *Carnets de guerre, 1914–1918* (Paris: Herscher, 1996); Nicole Zapata-Aubé, *André Mare, cubism et camouflage, 1914–1918* (Bernay, France: Musée de Bernay, 1998).

1. Nicolson, *Peacemaking, 1919*, 6.
2. Adam, *Paris Sees It Through*, 266–67.
3. Adam, *Paris Sees It Through*, 269.
4. Adam, *Paris Sees It Through*, 270.
5. "We have won the war: now we have to win the peace, and it may be more difficult" (Watson, *Georges Clemenceau*, 327).
6. Adam, *Paris Sees It Through*, 259.
7. MacMillan, *Paris, 1919*, 16.
8. Reynolds, *André Citroën*, 58.
9. Paris's last remaining wall, the Thiers Fortifications, would not come down until after World War I. Paris's ring road, the Périphérique, follows its course.
10. Ravel to Ida Godebska, 24 May 1919, in *Ravel Reader*, 190.
11. Long, *Au piano avec Maurice Ravel*, 142.
12. Bougault, *Paris, Montparnasse*, 122.
13. Steegmuller, *Cocteau*, 249. Steegmuller notes that "Cocteau always minimized the extent to which Radiguet, young as he was, had been 'around' before they met" (249n).
14. Steegmuller, *Cocteau*, 276, 254, 249, 252.
15. Steegmuller, *Cocteau*, 249.
16. Watson, *Georges Clemenceau*, 336.
17. MacMillan, *Paris, 1919*, 86.
18. Albaret, *Monsieur Proust*, 204; Proust to Mme Straus, 12 November 1918, in *Selected Letters*, 4:61–62.
19. Bernard and Dubief, *Decline of the Third Republic*, 79.
20. The total German reparations debt, around 226 billion gold marks, was in 1921 reduced to a still huge 132 billion gold marks, with some of the payments in industrial raw materials. The Germans were to pay two billion marks annually, in

addition to a sum equal to a quarter of their exports (see Bernard and Dubief, *Decline of the Third Republic*, 109).

21. France's twenty-six billion franc deficit in 1919 was reduced to a ten billion franc deficit by 1922 (Bernard and Dubief, *Decline of the Third Republic*, 95).

22. Maxwell, *R.S.V.P.*, 135–36.

23. Maxwell, *R.S.V.P.*, 142, 9.

24. Steegmuller, *Cocteau*, 227n.

25. Gold and Fizdale, *Misia*, 199 (this is from a missing chapter in Misia's published memoirs).

26. Poiret, *King of Fashion*, 130. The residence was located at 26 Rue d'Antin, now Avenue Franklin D. Roosevelt. Neither it nor the garden remains.

27. Poiret, *King of Fashion*, 130.

28. Poiret, *King of Fashion*, 131, 133–34.

29. Poiret, *King of Fashion*, 135.

30. Albaret, *Monsieur Proust*, 155.

31. Blanche, *More Portraits of a Lifetime*, 8–9.

32. Albaret, *Monsieur Proust*, 315.

33. Proust to Madame de Noailles, 27 May 1919, in *Selected Letters*, 4:78.

34. Nicolson, *Peacemaking, 1919*, 368.

35. Nicolson, *Peacemaking, 1919*, 370.

36. Adam, *Paris Sees It Through*, 312, 314.

37. Seventeen meters high, and on a nine-meter-high base, it weighed forty tons (Zapata-Aubé, *André Mare*, 115).

38. This cenotaph, like its more conservatively designed companion in London, was constructed quickly with wood, clay, and other temporary materials and was not meant to be permanent. The British loved their cenotaph and promptly ordered up a permanent version in stone. The French cenotaph did not share this outcome.

4 Making Way for the New (1919–1920)

Selected sources for this chapter: Quinn, *Marie Curie*; Eugen Weber, *Action Française*; Mugnier, *Journal*; Brown, *Embrace of Unreason*; Max Jacob and Jean Cocteau, *Correspondance, 1917–1944*, ed. and intro. Anne Kimball (Paris: Paris-Méditer-ranée, 2000); Bernard and Dubief, *Decline of the Third Republic*; Mary McAuliffe, *Dawn of the Belle Epoque: The Paris of Monet, Zola, Bernhardt, Eiffel, Debussy, Clemenceau, and Their Friends* (Lanham, Md.: Rowman & Littlefield, 2011); Watson, *Georges Clemenceau*; Sylvia Beach, *Shakespeare and Company* (Lincoln: University of Nebraska Press, 1980); Noel Riley Fitch, *Sylvia Beach and the Lost Generation: A History of Literary Paris in the Twenties and Thirties* (New York: Norton, 1983); Birmingham, *Most Dangerous Book*; Georges Clemenceau, *Claude Monet: The Water Lilies* (Garden City, N.Y.: Doubleday, Doran, 1930); Wildenstein, *Monet, or the Triumph of Impressionism*, vol. 1; Monet, *Monet by Himself*; Célia Bertin, *Jean Renoir: A Life in Pictures* (Baltimore, Md.: Johns Hopkins University Press, 1991);

Jean Renoir, *My Life and My Films* (New York: Atheneum, 1974); André Bazin, *Jean Renoir* (New York: De Capo, 1992); Hilary Spurling, *Matisse the Master: A Life of Henri Matisse, the Conquest of Colour, 1909–1954* (New York: Knopf, 2005); Meryle Secrest, *Modigliani: A Life* (New York: Knopf, 2011); Ambrogio Ceroni, *Amedeo Modigliani, peintre: suivi des "souvenirs" de Lunia Czechowska* (Milan: Edizioni del Milione, 1958); Morand, *The Allure of Chanel*; Madsen, *Chanel*; Picardie, *Coco Chanel*; Leymarie, *Chanel*; Gold and Fizdale, *Misia*; Steegmuller, *Cocteau*; Albaret, *Monsieur Proust*; Proust, *Selected Letters*; Carter, *Marcel Proust*; Proust, *Correspondance de Marcel Proust*; Herbert R. Lottman, *Man Ray's Montparnasse* (New York: Harry N. Abrams, 2001); Roger Ingpen, *The Fighting Retreat to Paris* (New York: Hodder & Stoughton, 1914); Silver, *Esprit de Corps*.

1. Mugnier, 1 June 1919, in *Journal*, 355.
2. Anne Kimball, intro. to Jacob and Cocteau, *Correspondance*, 22.
3. On the politics of the 1870s, see McAuliffe, *Dawn of the Belle Epoque*, 44, 73.
4. The income tax, adopted by the Chamber of Deputies before the war, began operation after the war.
5. Paul Deschanel, who unfortunately went mad and had to be institutionalized.
6. Watson, *Georges Clemenceau*, 387.
7. Beach, *Shakespeare and Company*, 8.
8. Fitch, *Sylvia Beach and the Lost Generation*, [from an early version of her memoirs], 25.
9. Fitch, *Sylvia Beach and the Lost Generation*, 32.
10. Beach, *Shakespeare and Company*, 13.
11. Beach, *Shakespeare and Company*, 14.
12. Fitch, *Sylvia Beach and the Lost Generation*, 37.
13. Beach, *Shakespeare and Company*, 21.
14. Clemenceau, *Claude Monet*, 10.
15. Monet to Clemenceau, 10 November 1919, in *Monet by Himself*, 252.
16. Monet to Félix Fénéon, [about mid-December 1919], in *Monet by Himself*, 253.
17. Monet to Gustave Geffroy, 20 January 1920, in *Monet by Himself*, 253.
18. Spurling, *Matisse the Master*, 217.
19. Jean Renoir, *My Life and My Films*, 17, 22, 23.
20. Jean Renoir, *My Life and My Films*, 40.
21. Jean Renoir later wrote that the doctors said she died of diabetes, but he knew "that she had died of the nervous strain of a journey to the front after I had been seriously wounded" (*My Life and My Films*, 47).
22. Jean Renoir, *My Life and My Films*, 43.
23. Jean Renoir, *My Life and My Films*, 40, 44.
24. Jean Renoir, *My Life and My Films*, 47.
25. Secrest, *Modigliani*, 273.

26. This assessment of Modigliani comes primarily from Lunia Czechowska, a friend of Modigliani's agent, Léopold Zborowski, and Zborowski's wife. Czechowska frequently modeled for Modigliani (Ceroni, *Amedeo Modigliani, peintre*, 26, 28; see also Secrest, *Modigliani*, 279).

27. Secrest, *Modigliani*, 293.

28. Or, more literally, "Until the Supreme Sacrifice"—which on Italian tombstones generally means "until death." My thanks to Joseph Li Vecchi for the translation.

29. Morand, *Allure of Chanel*, 34.

30. Morand, *Allure of Chanel*, 54, 34.

31. By this time, the much-married Misia's full name was Misia Godebska Natanson Edwards Sert.

32. Morand, *Allure of Chanel*, 65, 59, 65.

33. Morand, *Allure of Chanel*, 59.

34. Gold and Fizdale, *Misia*, 199.

35. Morand, *Allure of Chanel*, 66.

36. The murals at 30 Rockefeller Plaza are still there. Sert's murals from the Waldorf Astoria were removed in the 1970s and subsequently sold in Barcelona. Paris's Musée Carnavalet (museum of the history of Paris) has Sert's ornate 1924 ballroom from the Hôtel de Wendel, on Paris's Avenue de New York.

37. Morand, *Allure of Chanel*, 61, 60.

38. Gold and Fizdale, *Misia*, 218–19.

39. Albaret, *Monsieur Proust*, 294.

40. Proust to Madame Sert, [1 September 1920], in *Selected Letters*, 4:149.

41. Proust to Gaston Gallimard, [shortly before 3 December 1919], in *Selected Letters*, 4:100.

42. Proust to Jacques Boulenger, [20 December 1919], in *Selected Letters*, 4:104.

43. "Ils ne peuvent pas vous comprendre: leur sommeil est trop profond" (Rivière to Proust, 29 May 1920, in *Correspondance de Marcel Proust*, 19:284).

44. Proust to Henri de Régnier, [14 April 1920], in *Selected Letters*, 4:138–39.

45. The Musée de Luxembourg, the repository for more contemporary works, moved many of its paintings and sculptures into hiding, while other public and private collections hid their collections underground or placed them behind heavy screens (Ingpen, *The Fighting Retreat to Paris*, 164).

5 Les Années Folles (1920)

Selected sources for this chapter: Sisley Huddleston, *Bohemian Literary and Social Life in Paris; Salons, Cafés, Studios* (London: G. G. Harrap, 1928); McAuliffe, *Twilight of the Belle Epoque*; Townsend Ludington, *John Dos Passos: A Twentieth Century Odyssey* (New York: Dutton, 1980); Sachs, *Decade of Illusion*; Shari Benstock, *Women of the Left Bank, Paris, 1900–1940* (Austin: University of Texas Press, 1986); Richardson,

Life of Picasso: The Triumphant Years; Crespelle, *La Vie quotidienne à Montparnasse*; Klüver and Martin, *Kiki's Paris*; Kiki, *Kiki's Memoirs*; Franck, *Bohemian Paris*; Lottman, *Man Ray's Montparnasse*; Milhaud, *Notes without Music*; Steegmuller, *Cocteau*; Hugo, *Avant d'oublier*; Brown, *Embrace of Unreason*; Gillmor, *Erik Satie*; Stephen Walsh, *Stravinsky: A Creative Spring; Russia and France, 1882–1934* (Berkeley: University of California Press, 2002); Scheijen, *Diaghilev*; Igor Stravinsky and Robert Craft, *Memories and Commentaries* (New York: Faber & Faber, 2002); Spurling, *Matisse the Master*; Radiguet, *Count d'Orgel*; Morand, *Allure of Chanel*; Picardie, *Coco Chanel*; Madsen, *Chanel*; Gold and Fizdale, *Misia*; Baudot, *Poiret*; McBrien, *Cole Porter*; Ravel, *Ravel Reader*; Orenstein, *Ravel*; Nichols, *Ravel*; Poulenc, *Moi et mes amis*; Nicholas Weber, *Le Corbusier*; Jencks, *Le Corbusier and the Continual Revolution in Architecture*; Peter Blake, *The Master Builders* (New York: Knopf, 1960); Gans, *Le Corbusier Guide*; Eliel, *L'Esprit nouveau*; Richard Ellmann, *James Joyce* (New York: Oxford University Press, 1982); Birmingham, *Most Dangerous Book*; Beach, *Shakespeare and Company*; Fitch, *Sylvia Beach and the Lost Generation*; Bernard and Dubief, *Decline of the Third Republic*.

1. Huddleston, *Bohemian Literary and Social Life in Paris*, 21.
2. See McAuliffe, *Twilight of the Belle Epoque*.
3. Ludington, *John Dos Passos*, 175.
4. Sachs, *Decade of Illusion*, 8.
5. Sheri Benstock notes that because the Code Napoléon "made no provision for punishment of homosexuality, . . . homosexual practices were not banned by law" in Paris of the Belle Epoque (Benstock, *Women of the Left Bank*, 47). This held true for Paris of the 1920s as well.
6. Klüver and Martin, *Kiki's Paris*, 63.
7. Kiki, *Kiki's Memoirs*, 138.
8. Possibly to Léopold Zborowski, who in 1916 became his art dealer.
9. Kiki, *Kiki's Memoirs*, 228–32. Critic and writer André Salmon once suggested that a statue of Libion should replace that of Rodin's Balzac, just outside La Rotonde (238, re p. 16).
10. Kiki, *Kiki's Memoirs*, 256.
11. Kiki, *Kiki's Memoirs*, 139, 142.
12. Milhaud, *Notes without Music*, 101–2.
13. A few months later, *Le Boeuf sur le Toit* received its London production, where it was subtitled *The Nothing-Doing Bar* (Steegmuller, *Cocteau*, 244).
14. Milhaud, *Notes without Music*, 104.
15. Hugo, *Avant d'oublier*, 131. Le Boeuf sur le Toit (the bar) opened in January 1922. Eventually it moved from Rue Boissy d'Anglas to Rue de Penthièvre and Avenue Pierre-1er-de-Serbie before arriving at its present location, 34 Rue du Colisée, near the Champs-Elysées. Les Six and their gang began to frequent Le Gaya in late 1920 or early 1921 (Steegmuller, *Cocteau*, 263).
16. Brown, *Embrace of Unreason*, 134.

17. Quote from Madame Gleizes, wife of the Cubist painter Albert Gleizes, in Steegmuller, *Cocteau*, 222n. Gleizes, who still championed Cubism, was a frequent target of Dada.

18. Gillmor, *Erik Satie*, 245.

19. See chapter 9 (1924).

20. Steegmuller, *Cocteau*, 227.

21. Steegmuller, *Cocteau*, 227.

22. Walsh, *Stravinsky: A Creative Spring*, 380.

23. Stravinsky and Craft, *Memories and Commentaries*, 126, 137. Much of the music in fact turned out to have been by composers other than Pergolesi (Walsh, *Stravinsky: A Creative Spring*, 622n55).

24. Spurling, *Matisse the Master*, 230.

25. Stravinsky and Craft, *Memories and Commentaries*, 113.

26. Hugo, *Avant d'oublier*, 67.

27. Walsh, *Stravinsky: A Creative Spring*, 312.

28. Stravinsky and Craft, *Memories and Commentaries*, 138.

29. Morand, *Allure of Chanel*, 127–29. Stravinsky's second wife firmly denied the possibility of any such affair (Picardie, *Coco Chanel*, 133–34).

30. Morand, *Allure of Chanel*, 127.

31. Stravinsky and Craft, *Memories and Commentaries*, 141.

32. Morand, *Allure, of Chanel*, 129.

33. Some accounts have it as three hundred thousand francs (Madsen, *Chanel*, 113), and Chanel gave conflicting accounts: "I'm only a French dress designer," she recalls telling Diaghilev, "but here is two hundred thousand." And then she tells Morand, "I wanted to hear it [*Le Sacre du Printemps*] and to offer to subsidize it. I don't regret the three hundred thousand francs that it cost me" (Morand, *Allure of Chanel*, 87–88).

34. Picardie, *Coco Chanel*, 128.

35. Ravel to Jean Marnold, 7 February 1906, in *Ravel Reader*, 80.

36. See McAuliffe, *Twilight of the Belle Epoque*, 188, 232, 375n14. See also Ravel's letter to Misia: "Poor *Daphnis* had a good deal to complain about from Diaghilev . . . even though it was not always his fault" (Gold and Fizdale, *Misia*, 226).

37. Poulenc, *Moi et mes amis*, 179; Orenstein, *Ravel*, 77–78. Contrary to Diaghilev's assessment, George Balanchine successfully turned *La Valse* into a ballet, although *La Valse* became especially popular in the concert hall (Gold and Fizdale, *Misia*, 228n).

38. "Mais ce qu'il y a eu d'extraordinaire, c'est que Stravinsky n'a pas dit UN MOT!" (Poulenc, *Moi et mes amis*, 179).

39. In addition to this unpleasant episode, Poulenc notes, Ravel did not like Stravinsky's music after *Les Noces*: "He did not like *Oedipus Rex*, he did not like any of that" (*Moi et mes amis*, 178).

40. McAuliffe, *Twilight of the Belle Epoque*, 111–13.

41. Ravel to Roland-Manuel, 22 January 1920, in *Ravel Reader*, 199.

42. Nicholas Weber, *Le Corbusier*, 88, 47.
43. Nicholas Weber, *Le Corbusier*, 170, 171.
44. Nicholas Weber, *Le Corbusier*, 177, 179.
45. Nicholas Weber, *Le Corbusier*, 178; Gans, *Le Corbusier Guide*, 30–31.
46. Birmingham, *Most Dangerous Book*, 55.
47. Brown, *Embrace of Unreason*, 91.

6 Weddings, Breakups, and Other Affairs (1921)

Selected sources for this chapter: Lacouture, *De Gaulle: The Rebel*; Williams, *The Last Great Frenchman*; Bernard and Dubief, *Decline of the Third Republic*; Walsh, *Stravinsky: A Creative Spring*; Picardie, *Coco Chanel*; Morand, *Allure of Chanel*; Richardson, *Life of Picasso: The Triumphant Years*; Alfred H. Barr Jr., *Picasso: Fifty Years of His Art* (New York: Museum of Modern Art/Plantin, 1951); Stein, *Autobiography of Alice B. Toklas*; Carl Schmidt, *Entrancing Muse: A Documented Biography of Francis Poulenc* (Hillsdale, N.Y.: Pendragon Press, 2001); Jacob and Cocteau, *Correspondance*; Steegmuller, *Cocteau*; Cocteau, *Lettres à sa mère*, vol. 2; Hugo, *Avant d'oublier*; Scheijen, *Diaghilev*; Milhaud, *Notes without Music*; Gold and Fizdale, *Misia*; Man Ray, *Self Portrait* (Boston: Little, Brown, 1988); Neil Baldwin, *Man Ray, American Artist* (New York: Da Capo, 2001); Lottman, *Man Ray's Montparnasse*; Roland Penrose, *Man Ray* (New York: Thames & Hudson, 1989); Kiki, *Kiki's Memoirs*; Bertin, *Jean Renoir*; Bougault, *Paris, Montparnasse*; Walter B. Rideout, *Sherwood Anderson: A Writer in America*, vol. 1 (Madison: University of Wisconsin Press, 2006); Quinn, *Marie Curie*; Eve Curie, *Madame Curie*; McAuliffe, *Twilight of the Belle Epoque*; James Joyce, *Ulysses* (New York: Vintage, 1993); Birmingham, *Most Dangerous Book*; Fitch, *Sylvia Beach and the Lost Generation*; Beach, *Shakespeare and Company*; Georges Clemenceau, *Georges Clemenceau à son ami Claude Monet: Correspondance* (Paris: Editions de la Réunion des Musées Nationaux, 1993); Wildenstein, *Monet, or the Triumph of Impressionism*, vol. 1; Monet, *Monet by Himself*; Proust, *Selected Letters*; Proust, *Correspondance de Marcel Proust*; Carter, *Marcel Proust*; Albaret, *Monsieur Proust*; Judith Thurman, *Secrets of the Flesh: A Life of Colette* (New York: Ballantine, 1999); Orenstein, *Ravel*; Ravel, *Ravel Reader*; Harry Kessler, *The Diaries of a Cosmopolitan: Count Harry Kessler, 1918–1937* (London: Weidenfeld & Nicolson, 1971); Laird McLeod Easton, *The Red Count: The Life and Times of Harry Kessler* (Berkeley: University of California Press, 2002); Nicholas Weber, *Le Corbusier*; Brooks, *Le Corbusier's Formative Years*; Eliel, *L'Esprit nouveau*.

1. Lacouture, *De Gaulle: The Rebel*, 63.
2. Stein, *Autobiography of Alice B. Toklas*, 190.
3. See Richardson, *Life of Picasso: The Triumphant Years*, 171–72.
4. Morand, *Allure of Chanel*, 96.
5. Barr, *Picasso*, 100.

6. Durey formally withdrew from Les Six in 1921, for reasons of health (Schmidt, *Entrancing Muse*, 94).

7. Steegmuller, *Cocteau*, 268n.

8. Scheijen, *Diaghilev*, 366.

9. Steegmuller, *Cocteau*, 270.

10. Steegmuller, *Cocteau*, 270.

11. Cocteau to his mother, 30 March 1921, in *Cocteau à sa mère*, 2:103; Steegmuller, *Cocteau*, 272.

12. Steegmuller, *Cocteau*, 275.

13. Baldwin, *Man Ray*, 72.

14. Baldwin, *Man Ray*, 72.

15. Baldwin, *Man Ray*, 70.

16. Baldwin, *Man Ray*, 83.

17. Man Ray, *Self Portrait*, 104.

18. Man Ray, *Self Portrait*, 106.

19. Man Ray, *Self Portrait*, 109.

20. Man Ray, *Self Portrait*, 99.

21. Man Ray, *Self Portrait*, 97.

22. Penrose, *Man Ray*, 76. During the early 1920s, Penrose (who would in time become Sir Roland Penrose) lived in Paris, where he knew everyone in the art world. Eventually he would marry Man Ray's mistress, pupil, and collaborator, Lee Miller.

23. Man Ray, *Self Portrait*, 116.

24. Bertin, *Jean Renoir*, 53.

25. Eve Curie, *Madame Curie*, 322.

26. Quinn, *Marie Curie*, 385.

27. Quinn, *Marie Curie*, 387.

28. See McAuliffe, *Twilight of the Belle Epoque*, 198–200, 209–12.

29. Eve Curie, *Madame Curie*, 336.

30. Eve Curie, *Madame Curie*, 336.

31. Joyce, *Ulysses*, 28.

32. Beach, *Shakespeare and Company*, 47.

33. Monet to Arsène Alexandre, 22 October 1921, in *Monet by Himself*, 257. See also Wildenstein, *Monet, or the Triumph of Impressionism*, 1:415.

34. Clemenceau à Monet, 31 mars 1921, in *Georges Clemenceau à son ami Claude Monet*, 87.

35. This is what eventually happened. Yet Monet was never satisfied with the areas designated for his water lilies, and recently, the Orangerie has completely redesigned the rooms, to much better effect.

36. Wildenstein, *Monet, or the Triumph of Impressionism*, 1:422.

37. For example, see Proust to Madame de Chevigné, [around September 1921], in *Selected Letters*, 4:257: "This futile letter, when I'm incapable of writing to anybody, is unfinished, but I haven't the strength to continue with it this evening."

38. Gide to Proust, 3 May 1921, in *Selected Letters*, 4:218.

39. See for example Léon Daudet to Marcel Proust, 18 juin 1921, 352, and Jacques Boulenger to Proust, in ed. note appended to Proust to Boulenger, 6 décembre 1921, 565n3, both in *Correspondance de Marcel Proust*, vol. 20.

40. Gide to Proust, 3 May 1921, in *Selected Letters*, 4:218.

41. Carter, *Marcel Proust*, 750.

42. Albaret, *Monsieur Proust*, 299.

43. Colette to Marcel Proust, [early July 1921], in *Correspondance de Marcel Proust*, 20:380. Colette added that she thought *Sodom et Gomorrah* "dazzling," "magnificent," and swore that no one except Proust could add anything to what he had written (20:380–82). See also Jacques-Emile Blanche to Marcel Proust, 9 May 1921, in *Correspondance de Marcel Proust*, 20:247–49.

44. Thurman, *Secrets of the Flesh*, 292.

45. Arbie Orenstein in *Ravel Reader*, 13.

46. Colette de Jouvenel to Maurice Ravel, [5 March 1919], in *Ravel Reader*, 189.

47. Orenstein, *Ravel*, 80.

48. Kessler, 11 December 1921, p.144; 22 December 1921, pp.145–46; 13 August 1922, p.192, all in *Diaries of a Cosmopolitan*.

49. Brooks, *Le Corbusier's Formative Years*, 502.

50. Nicholas Weber, *Le Corbusier*, 181.

51. Nicholas Weber, *Le Corbusier*, 183.

7 The Lost Generation (1922)

Selected sources for this chapter: Michael Reynolds, *The Young Hemingway* (New York: Norton, 1998); Michael Reynolds, *Hemingway: The Paris Years* (New York: Norton, 1999); Ernest Hemingway, *A Moveable Feast* (New York: Touchstone, 1996); Gioia Diliberto, *Paris without End: The True Story of Hemingway's First Wife* (New York: Harper Perennial, 2011); Beach, *Shakespeare and Company*; Ellmann, *James Joyce*; Birmingham, *Most Dangerous Book*; Fitch, *Sylvia Beach and the Lost Generation*; Stein, *Autobiography of Alice B. Toklas*; Jimmie Charters, as told to Morrill Cody, *This Must Be the Place: Memoirs of Montparnasse* (New York: Collier Macmillan, 1989); Samuel Putnam, *Paris Was Our Mistress: Memoirs of a Lost and Found Generation* (New York: Viking, 1947); Marianne DeKoven, *A Different Language: Gertrude Stein's Experimental Writing* (Madison: University of Wisconsin Press, 1983); John Malcolm Brinnin, *The Third Rose: Gertrude Stein and Her World* (Reading, Mass.: Addison-Wesley, 1987); A. E. Hotchner, *Papa Hemingway: A Personal Memoir* (New York: Random House, 1966); Albaret, *Monsieur Proust*; Carter, *Marcel Proust*; Proust, *Selected Letters*; Proust, *Correspondance de Marcel Proust*; Hugo, *Avant d'oublier*; Lottman, *Man Ray's Montparnasse*; Penrose, *Man Ray*; Man Ray, *Self Portrait*; Baldwin, *Man Ray, American Artist*; Kiki, *Kiki's Memoirs*; Klüver and Martin, *Kiki's Paris*; Nicholas Weber, *Le Corbusier*; Eliel, *L'Esprit nouveau*; Jules Bertaut, *Paris, 1870–1935* (London: Eyre & Spottiswoode, 1936); Norma Evenson, *Paris: A Cen-*

tury of Change, 1878–1978 (New Haven, Conn.: Yale University Press, 1979); Peter Kurth, *Isadora: A Sensational Life* (Boston: Little, Brown, 2001); Isadora Duncan, *My Life* (New York: Liveright, 2013); Irma Duncan, *Duncan Dancer* (New York: Books for Libraries, 1980); Milhaud, *Notes without Music*; Jean Wiéner, *Allegro appassionato* (Paris: P. Belfond, 1978); Kelly, *Music and Ultra-Modernism in France*; Sachs, *Decade of Illusion*; Steegmuller, *Cocteau*; Nina Hamnett, *Laughing Torso: Reminiscences* (New York: Ray Long & R. R. Smith, 1932); Quinn, *Marie Curie*; Gold and Fizdale, *Divine Sarah*; Reynolds, *André Citroën*; Rhodes, *Louis Renault*; Bernard and Dubief, *Decline of the Third Republic*; Brown, *Embrace of Unreason*; Eugen Weber, *Action Française*; Sicard-Picchiottino, *François Coty*; Duménil, *Parfum d'empire*; Toledano and Coty, *François Coty*; Brandon, *Ugly Beauty*.

1. Hemingway, *Moveable Feast*, 4.
2. Hemingway, *Moveable Feast*, 6.
3. Hemingway, *Moveable Feast*, 7.
4. Diliberto, *Paris without End*, 67.
5. Hemingway, *Moveable Feast*, 37.
6. Diliberto, *Paris without End*, 99.
7. Hemingway's introduction to Jimmie Charters, *This Must Be the Place*, 3.
8. Birmingham, *Most Dangerous Book*, 145.
9. Birmingham, *Most Dangerous Book*, 234.
10. Beach, *Shakespeare and Company*, 78.
11. Stein, *Autobiography of Alice B. Toklas*, 195.
12. Beach, *Shakespeare and Company*, 28, 27.
13. Stein, *Autobiography of Alice B. Toklas*, 196.
14. Fitch, *Sylvia Beach and the Lost Generation*, 41.
15. Putnam, *Paris Was Our Mistress*, 138.
16. Hemingway, *Moveable Feast*, 28. Man Ray observed that "her bitterness really showed up when the others [Hemingway, Joyce, the Dadaists, the Surrealists] got universal attention before she did" (*Self Portrait*, 147).
17. Brinnin, *Third Rose*, 289–90. It may have helped that at the time Paul was writing, or had just written, a series of articles on Stein's work for the *Paris Tribune*, "the first seriously popular estimation of her work," as Stein herself put it (*Autobiography of Alice B. Toklas*, 238–39).
18. Beach, *Shakespeare and Company*, 32.
19. Brinnin, *Third Rose*, 230.
20. Hemingway, *Moveable Feast*, 29–31. Later, Hemingway would emphatically tell his friend, the journalist A. E. Hotchner, "That was Gertrude Stein's pronouncement, not mine! . . . Well, Gertrude . . . a pronouncement was a pronouncement was a pronouncement. I only used it in the front of *Sun Also Rises* so I could counter it with what I thought. That passage from Ecclesiastes, that sound lost?" (Hotchner, *Papa Hemingway*, 49).
21. Hemingway, *Moveable Feast*, 31.

22. Hemingway, *Moveable Feast*, 13–14.

23. Brinnin, *Third Rose*, 249.

24. Hemingway, *Moveable Feast*, 110.

25. Stein, *Autobiography of Alice B. Toklas*, 206.

26. Stein, *Autobiography of Alice B. Toklas*, 213. Hemingway was twenty-three.

27. Albaret, *Monsieur Proust*, 335–37; Carter, *Marcel Proust*, 629–30.

28. Albaret, *Monsieur Proust*, 240.

29. Proust to Etienne de Beaumont, [31 December 1921], in *Selected Letters*, 4:283.

30. Hugo, *Avant d'oublier*, 127.

31. Man Ray later wrote that Joyce was "very patient, until after a couple of shots when he turned his head away from the lights, putting his hand over his eyes and saying that he could no longer face the glare. I snapped the pose, which has become the favorite one, although in certain quarters it was criticized as too artificial, too posed" (*Self Portrait*, 151).

32. Stein, *Autobiography of Alice B. Toklas*, 197.

33. According to Man Ray, this portrait "pleased her especially" (*Self Portrait*, 148).

34. Man Ray, *Self Portrait*, 148.

35. Stein, *Autobiography of Alice B. Toklas*, 198.

36. Nicholas Weber, *Le Corbusier*, 47, 48.

37. Nicholas Weber, *Le Corbusier*, 183.

38. Bertaut, *Paris*, 294.

39. Evenson, *Paris*, 51–52.

40. Bertaut, *Paris*, 293.

41. Kurth, *Isadora*, 430.

42. Kurth, *Isadora*, 439.

43. Milhaud, *Notes without Music*, 131.

44. Ravel, Roussel, Caplet, and Roland-Manuel to the editor of *Le Courrier musical*, c. March 1923, in *Ravel Reader*, 240n2. Barbara L. Kelly gives the letter a 1 April 1923 date, in *Music and Ultra-Modernism in France*, 73.

45. Milhaud, *Notes without Music*, 129; Wiéner, *Allegro appassionato*, 80; and Kelly, *Music and Ultra-Modernism in France*, 5, 73. In his memoirs, Wiéner stepped aside from the controversy and attributed the vitriol to the "shock produced by the revelation of Schoenberg and the Vienna School" (*Allegro appassionato*, 57).

46. Ravel, Roussel, Caplet, and Roland-Manuel to the editor of *Le Courrier musical*, c. March 1923 [1 April 1923], in *Ravel Reader*, 239–40.

47. Hugo, *Avant d'oublier*, 130. *L'Oeil Cacodylate* is now in the Pompidou's Musée National d'Art Moderne.

48. Sachs, *Decade of Illusion*, 17.

49. Hamnett, *Laughing Torso*, 196–97.

50. Steegmuller, *Cocteau*, 298.

51. Brown, *Embrace of Unreason*, 121.

52. Toledano and Coty, *François Coty*, 181.

8 A Death in Paris (1923)

Selected sources for this chapter: Brown, *Embrace of Unreason*; Eugen Weber, *Action Française*; Bernard and Dubief, *Decline of the Third Republic*; Kessler, *Diaries of a Cosmopolitan*; Easton, *The Red Count*; Alex Danchev, *Georges Braque: A Life* (New York: Arcade, 2012); Barr, *Picasso*; Richardson, *Life of Picasso: The Triumphant Years*; Silver, *Esprit de Corps*; Vaill, *Everybody Was So Young*; Bazin, *Jean Renoir*; Jean Renoir, *My Life and My Films*; Bertin, *Jean Renoir*; Howard Greenfeld, *The Devil and Dr. Barnes: Portrait of an American Art Collector* (Philadelphia, Pa.: Camino Books, 2006); William Schack, *Art and Argyrol: The Life and Career of Dr. Albert C. Barnes* (New York: T. Yoseloff, 1960); Bougault, *Paris, Montparnasse*; Walsh, *Stravinsky: A Creative Spring*; Stravinsky and Craft, *Memories and Commentaries*; Scheijen, *Diaghilev*; Ludington, *John Dos Passos*; Milhaud, *Notes without Music*; Schmidt, *Entrancing Muse*; Man Ray, *Self Portrait*; Lottman, *Man Ray's Montparnasse*; McBrien, *Cole Porter*; Cossart, *Food of Love*; Baldwin, *Man Ray, American Artist*; Kiki, *Kiki's Memoirs*; Crespelle, *La Vie quotidienne à Montparnasse*; Arlen J. Hansen, *Expatriate Paris: A Cultural and Literary Guide to Paris of the 1920s* (New York: Arcade, 1990); Steegmuller, *Cocteau*; Raymond Radiguet, *The Devil in the Flesh* [*Le Diable au corps*] (New York: Marion Boyars, 2005); Melvyn Stokes, *D. W. Griffith's* The Birth of a Nation: *A History of "The Most Controversial Motion Picture of All Time"* (New York: Oxford University Press, 2007); Melvyn Stokes, "Race, Politics, and Censorship: D. W. Griffith's *The Birth of a Nation* in France, 1916–1923," *Cinema Journal* 50, no. 1 (Fall 2010): 19–38; Richard Maltby and Melvyn Stokes, eds., *Hollywood Abroad: Audiences and Cultural Exchange* (London: BFI, 2004); Hemingway, *Moveable Feast*; Reynolds, *Hemingway: The Paris Years*; Diliberto, *Paris without End*; Fitch, *Sylvia Beach and the Lost Generation*; Ellmann, *James Joyce*; Monet, *Monet by Himself*; Wildenstein, *Monet, or the Triumph of Impressionism*, vol. 1; Clemenceau, *Clemenceau à son ami Claude Monet*; Nicholas Weber, *Le Corbusier*; Tim Benton, *The Villas of Le Corbusier: 1920–1930* (New Haven, Conn.: Yale University Press, 1987); Eliel, *L'Esprit nouveau*; Blake, *Master Builders*; Myers, *Erik Satie*; Gillmor, *Erik Satie*; Jackie Wullschläger, *Chagall: A Biography* (New York: Knopf, 2008); David I. Harvie, *Eiffel: The Genius Who Reinvented Himself* (Stroud, UK: Sutton, 2004); Gold and Fizdale, *Divine Sarah*; Lysiane Bernhardt and Marion Dix, *Sarah Bernhardt*; Hugo, *Avant d'oublier*; Gold and Fizdale, *Misia*; Hamnett, *Laughing Torso*.

1. Brown, *Embrace of Unreason*, 123.
2. Kessler, 4 January 1923, pp. 207–8; 6 January 1923, p. 209, both in *Diaries of a Cosmopolitan*.
3. Kessler, 8 January 1923, p. 209; 3 March 1923, p. 210, both in *Diaries of a Cosmopolitan*.
4. Kessler, 8 January 1923, in *Diaries of a Cosmopolitan*, 209–10.
5. Barr, *Picasso*, 115.

6. Eventually Braque would also acquire "a liveried chauffeur" (Danchev, *Georges Braque*, 159).

7. Vaill, *Everybody Was So Young*, 63, 6. Ernest Hemingway later noted sourly that "maybe [the Murphys] were fine and good . . . certainly [they] never did anything for their own ends. They collected people then as some collect pictures and others breed horses" (Diliberto, *Paris without End*, 222).

8. Vaill, *Everybody Was So Young*, 166.

9. Bazin, *Jean Renoir*, 15, 17.

10. Jean Renoir, *My Life and My Films*, 49, 50. *Catherine, or A Life without Joy*, was completed in 1924 but not shown until 1927 (Bertin, *Jean Renoir*, 56).

11. Jean Renoir, *My Life and My Films*, 50.

12. Stravinsky and Craft, *Memories and Commentaries*, 125.

13. Man Ray, *Self Portrait*, 212.

14. McBrien, *Cole Porter*, 85.

15. Milhaud, *Notes without Music*, 153.

16. Klüver and Martin, foreword to *Kiki's Memoirs*, 38.

17. Lottman, *Man Ray's Montparnasse*, 100.

18. Kiki, *Kiki's Memoirs*, 156, 152.

19. Man Ray, *Self Portrait*, 198.

20. Hemingway, *Moveable Feast*, 101. Shortly after arriving in Paris, he wrote, "The scum of Greenwich Village, New York, has been skimmed off and deposited in large ladleful on that section of Paris adjacent to the Café Rotonde. . . . The scummiest scum has come across the ocean, somehow, and . . . has made the Rotonde the leading Latin Quarter show place for tourists in search of atmosphere" (Hansen, *Expatriate Paris*, 123).

21. Bougault, *Paris, Montparnasse*, 129.

22. Hemingway, *Moveable Feast*, 104.

23. Steegmuller, *Cocteau*, 308.

24. Steegmuller, *Cocteau*, 310.

25. Radiguet, *Devil in the Flesh*, 125.

26. Steegmuller, *Cocteau*, 314.

27. Quote from Georges Boussenot, a black deputy from Réunion, who attended one of the film's opening performances and immediately wrote the minister of foreign affairs to complain. Gratien Candace, the black deputy from Guadeloupe, attended a performance and also seems to have protested (Stokes, "Race, Politics, and Censorship," 33).

28. Quoted in Stokes, "Race, Politics, and Censorship," 30.

29. Monet to Doctor Charles Coutella, 22 June 1923, in *Monet by Himself*, 261.

30. Monet to Georges Clemenceau, 30 August 1923, in *Monet by Himself*, 262.

31. Monet to Joseph Durand-Ruel, 20 November 1923, in *Monet by Himself*, 263.

32. Nicholas Weber, *Le Corbusier*, 203.

33. Eliel, *L'Esprit nouveau*, 64.

34. Milhaud, *Notes without Music*, 154–55, 159.

35. Wullschlager, *Chagall*, 274, 282.
36. Wullschlager, *Chagall*, 284.
37. Hamnett, *Laughing Torso*, 301.

9 Americans in Paris (1924)

Selected sources for this chapter: Bernard and Dubief, *Decline of the Third Republic*; Brown, *Embrace of Unreason*; Reynolds, *Hemingway: The Paris Years*; Diliberto, *Paris without End*; Hemingway, *Selected Letters*; Crespelle, *La Vie quotidienne à Montparnasse*; Lottman, *Man Ray's Montparnasse*; Charters, *This Must Be the Place*; Steegmuller, *Cocteau*; Jacob and Cocteau, *Correspondance*; Scheijen, *Diaghilev*; Milhaud, *Notes without Music*; Danchev, *Georges Braque*; Gold and Fizdale, *Misia*; Myers, *Erik Satie*; Gillmor, *Erik Satie*; Richardson, *Life of Picasso: The Triumphant Years*; Radiguet, *Count d'Orgel*; Madsen, *Chanel*; Picardie, *Coco Chanel*; Morand, *Allure of Chanel*; Sicard-Picchiottino, *François Coty*; Vaill, *Everybody Was So Young*; Fitch, *Sylvia Beach and the Lost Generation*; Beach, *Shakespeare and Company*; Ludington, *John Dos Passos*; McBrien, *Cole Porter*; Maxwell, *R.S.V.P.*; Wullschläger, *Chagall*; Nicholas Weber, *Le Corbusier*; Mike O'Mahony, *Olympic Visions: Images of the Games through History* (London: Reaktion Books, 2012); Jean Renoir, *My Life and My Films*; Bertin, *Jean Renoir*; Bazin, *Jean Renoir*; Richard Abel, *French Cinema: The First Wave, 1915–1929* (Princeton, N.J.: Princeton University Press, 1984); De Francia, *Fernand Léger*; Christopher Green, *Léger and the Avant-Garde* (New Haven, Conn.: Yale University Press, 1976); Man Ray, *Self-Portrait*; Hugh D. Ford, *Four Lives in Paris* (San Francisco, Calif.: North Point Press, 1987); Clifford Browder, *André Breton, Arbiter of Surrealism* (Geneva, Switzerland: Droz, 1967); André Breton, *Manifestoes of Surrealism* (Ann Arbor: University of Michigan Press, 1969); Janet Flanner, *Paris Was Yesterday: 1925–1939* (New York: Viking, 1972); McAuliffe, *Twilight of the Belle Epoque*; Orenstein, *Ravel*; Ravel, *Ravel Reader*; Jean Roy, *L'Intemporel: Robert Casadesus, Pianist et compositeur* (Paris: Buchet-Chastel, 1999); Gaby Casadesus, *Mes noces musicales: Gaby Casadesus, conversation avec Jacqueline Muller* (Paris: Buchet-Chastel, 1989); Caroline Potter, *Nadia and Lili Boulanger* (Burlington, Vt.: Ashgate, 2006); Reynolds, *André Citroën*; Brandon, *Ugly Beauty*; Duménil, *Parfum d'empire*; Toledano and Coty, *François Coty*; Benito Mussolini, *My Autobiography* (Westport, Conn.: Greenwood, 1970); Eugen Weber, *Action Française*.

1. Ford, in foreword to Charters, *This Must Be the Place*, xii.
2. Charters, *This Must Be the Place*, 9.
3. Charters, *This Must Be the Place*, 33, 27. Jimmie recalled that he used to pass by Shakespeare and Company almost daily when he worked at a nearby bar (34).
4. Charters, *This Must Be the Place*, 38.
5. Hemingway, *Moveable Feast*, 76.
6. It later became evident that the friend to whom Hadley entrusted her funds for investment embezzled the missing money (Diliberto, *Paris without End*, 171).

7. Hemingway, *Moveable Feast*, 18. "I made it clear [to Ford] it was a remarkable scoop for his magazine," Hemingway wrote Stein, "obtained only through my obtaining genius. He is under the impression that you get big prices when you consent to publish. I did not give him this impression but did not discourage it" (Hemingway to Gertrude Stein, 17 February 1924, in *Selected Letters*, 111).

8. Hemingway to Ezra Pound, 2 May 1924, in *Selected Letters*, 116.

9. Reynolds, *Hemingway: The Paris Years*, 200.

10. From where Hemingway wrote Ford two letters "and got no answer. I suppose he is sore at me though Christnose [sic] I tried to run his paper the way he would have liked to have it run" (Hemingway to Ezra Pound, 19 July 1924, in *Selected Letters*, 119).

11. Steegmuller, *Cocteau*, 316.

12. Cocteau to Jacob, Noël [1923], in *Correspondance*, 178.

13. Kimball, intro. to Jacob and Cocteau, *Correspondance*, 17.

14. Cocteau to Jacob, 29 January 1924, in *Correspondance*, 78.

15. Milhaud, *Notes without Music*, 159.

16. Milhaud, *Notes without Music*, 158–59.

17. Richardson, *Life of Picasso: The Triumphant Years*, 261.

18. Steegmuller, *Cocteau*, 328.

19. Reynolds, *Hemingway: The Paris Years*, 200.

20. Cocteau, in afterword to Radiguet, *Count d'Orgel*, 157.

21. Morand, *Allure of Chanel*, 162.

22. Morand, *Allure of Chanel*, 158.

23. Morand, *Allure of Chanel*, 163.

24. Possibly to replace income lost by the major decrease of immigrants to the United States imposed by the Immigration Act of 1924.

25. Beach, *Shakespeare and Company*, 111.

26. This meeting may not have taken place, although the principals seem to recall it clearly (Ludington, *John Dos Passos*, 159n).

27. Ludington, *John Dos Passos*, 233.

28. Reynolds, *Hemingway: The Paris Years*, 217.

29. Hemingway to Ezra Pound, 19 July 1924, in *Selected Letters*, 119.

30. McBrien, *Cole Porter*, 96.

31. Maxwell, *R.S.V.P.*, 124.

32. Wullschlager, *Chagall*, 323.

33. Wullschlager, *Chagall*, 324.

34. Nicholas Weber, *Le Corbusier*, 207.

35. Bazin, *Jean Renoir*, 152.

36. Bertin, *Jean Renoir*, 57.

37. Jean Renoir, *My Life and My Films*, 55.

38. Bertin, *Jean Renoir*, 60–61.

39. Man Ray later wrote that he backed out when he discovered that he was expected to provide financing as well as ideas (*Self Portrait*, 218).

40. Ford, *Four Lives in Paris*, 30.

41. It was first shown in Paris in November, still without music (Green, *Léger and the Avant-Garde*, 281).
42. Breton, *Manifestoes of Surrealism*, 6.
43. Flanner, *Paris Was Yesterday*, 4.
44. For more on this event, see McAuliffe, *Twilight of the Belle Epoque*, 111–12.
45. Ravel, *Ravel Reader*, 387.
46. Fauré to Ravel, 15 October 1922, in *Ravel Reader*, 230–31.
47. Ravel to Robert Casadesus, 18 June 1924, in *Ravel Reader*, 256.
48. Mussolini, *My Autobiography*, 38, 40; Toledano and Coty, *François Coty*, 181.

10 You've Come a Long Way from St. Louis (1925)

Selected sources for this chapter: Jean-Claude Baker and Chris Chase, *Josephine: The Hungry Heart* (New York: Cooper Square Press, 2001); Josephine Baker and Jo Bouillon, *Josephine* (New York: Harper & Row, 1977); Flanner, *Paris Was Yesterday*; Bevis Hillier, *Art Deco Style* (London: Phaidon, 1997); Sachs, *Decade of Illusion*; Emmanuel Bréon et Philippe Rivoirard, eds., *1925, quand l'art deco séduit le monde* (Paris: Cité de l'Architecture et du Patrimoine, 2013); Mare, *Carnets de Guerre*; Silver, *Esprit de Corps*; Reynolds, *André Citroën*; Rhodes, *Louis Renault*; Baudot, *Poiret*; Deslandres, *Poiret*; Poiret, *King of Fashion*; Nicholas Weber, *Le Corbusier*; Benton, *Villas of Le Corbusier*; Eliel, *L'Esprit nouveau*; Evenson, *Paris*; Blake, *Master Builders*; Le Corbusier, *The City of To-morrow and Its Planning* (London: J. Rodker, 1929); Richardson, *Life of Picasso: The Triumphant Years*; Barr, *Picasso*; Browder, *André Breton*; Wullschläger, *Chagall*; Bougault, *Paris, Montparnasse*; Jacob and Cocteau, *Correspondance*; Myers, *Erik Satie*; Gillmor, *Erik Satie*; Cossart, *Food of Love*; Milhaud, *Notes without Music*; Erik Satie, *Satie Seen through His Letters* (New York: Marion Boyars, 1989); Hamnett, *Laughing Torso*; Scheijen, *Diaghilev*; Steegmuller, *Cocteau*; Jean Cocteau, *Lettre à Jacques Maritain* (Paris: Stock, 1983); Kiki, *Kiki's Memoirs*; Gustave Fuss-Amore and Maurice des Ombiaux, *Montparnasse* (Paris: Albin Michel, 1925); Henri Broca, *T'en fais pas, viens à Montrnasse! Enquête sur le Montparnasse actuel* (Paris: 71 Rue de Rennes, 1928); Lottman, *Man Ray's Montparnasse*; Luis Buñuel, *My Last Sigh* (New York: Vintage, 1984); Jeffrey Meyers, *Scott Fitzgerald: A Biography* (New York: HarperCollins, 1994); F. Scott Fitzgerald, *A Life in Letters: F. Scott Fitzgerald* (New York: Scribner, 1995); Hemingway, *Moveable Feast*; Reynolds, *Hemingway: The Paris Years*; Hemingway, *Selected Letters*; Diliberto, *Paris without End*; Bernard and Dubief, *Decline of the Third Republic*; Sicard-Picchiottino, *François Coty*; Duménil, *Parfum d'empire*; Brown, *Embrace of Unreason*; Eugen Weber, *Action Française*; Fitch, *Sylvia Beach and the Lost Generation*; Sylvia Beach, *Shakespeare and Company*; Charters, *This Must Be the Place*; Robert McAlmon, *Being Geniuses Together, 1920–1930* (San Francisco, Calif.: North Point Press, 1984); Ellmann, *James Joyce*; Bertin, *Jean Renoir*; Jean Renoir, *My Life and My Films*; Baldwin, *Man Ray*; Man Ray, *Self Portrait*; Lacouture, *De Gaulle*.

1. Flanner, *Paris Was Yesterday*, xx.

2. Bevis Hillier notes that "the term 'Art Deco' was not current in the 1920s and 1930s" and first appeared in English publications in the 1960s (*Art Deco Style*, 8).

3. Sachs, *Decade of Illusion*, 19.

4. See chapter 3.

5. Now 6 Rond-Point. The wrought-iron grille that Poiret commissioned from Edgar Brandt for this spot still remains.

6. Nicholas Weber, *Le Corbusier*, 215.

7. Nicholas Weber, *Le Corbusier*, 215.

8. Le Corbusier, *City of To-morrow*, 231n2.

9. Nicholas Weber, *Le Corbusier*, 216.

10. Evenson, *Paris*, 52, 174.

11. Le Corbusier, *City of To-morrow*, 288.

12. *Art Deco Style*, 35.

13. Sachs, *Decade of Illusion*, 18.

14. Richardson, *Life of Picasso: The Triumphant Years*, 285.

15. Cocteau to Jacob, [early July 1925], in Jacob and Cocteau, *Correspondance*, 324.

16. Milhaud, *Notes without Music*, 176–78.

17. Steegmuller, *Cocteau*, 340.

18. Cocteau to Jacob, 3 April [1925], in Jacob and Cocteau, *Correspondance*, 231.

19. Jacob to Cocteau, 18 June 1925, in Jacob and Cocteau, *Correspondance*, 317; Jacob to the Princess Ghika, quoted in introduction to Jacob and Cocteau, *Correspondance*, 19.

20. Fuss-Amore and Des Ombiaux, *Montparnasse*, 12.

21. Broca, *T'en fais pas, viens à Montparnasse!*, 6.

22. Hemingway, *Moveable Feast*, 149, 176.

23. As in this 1925 letter from Fitzgerald to his editor, Maxwell Perkins: "You remember I used to say I wanted to die at thirty—well, I'm now twenty-nine and the prospect is still welcome (Fitzgerald to Perkins, 27 December 1925, in Fitzgerald, *A Life in Letters*, 131).

24. Hemingway to Fitzgerald, 1 July 1925, in *Selected Letters*, 165.

25. Fitch, *Sylvia Beach and the Lost Generation*, 183.

26. Charters, *This Must Be the Place*, 42. Robert McAlmon also tells this story (*Being Geniuses Together*, 33–34).

27. Charters, *This Must Be the Place*, 7.

28. Sylvia Beach, *Shakespeare and Company*, 74.

29. Hemingway to Sherwood Anderson, 9 March 1922, in *Selected Letters*, 62. See also Hemingway, *Moveable Feast*, 56, 36, and Ellmann, *James Joyce*, 529.

30. Beach, *Shakespeare and Company*, 75.

31. Fitch, *Sylvia Beach and the Lost Generation*, 230.

32. Beach, *Shakespeare and Company*, 97.

33. Jean Renoir, *My Life and My Films*, 161.

34. Lacouture, *De Gaulle*, 71.
35. Lacouture, *De Gaulle*, 81.
36. Lacouture, *De Gaulle*, 80.
37. Lacouture, *De Gaulle*, 72.

11 All That Jazz (1926)

Selected sources for this chapter: Bazin, *Jean Renoir*; Bertin, *Jean Renoir*; Jean Renoir, *My Life and My Films*; Abel, *French Cinema*; Jean-Claude Baker and Chris Chase, *Josephine*; Josephine Baker and Jo Bouillon, *Josephine*; Kessler, *Diaries of a Cosmopolitan*; Charters, *This Must Be the Place*; Bougault, *Paris, Montparnasse*; Lottman, *Man Ray's Montparnasse*; Crespelle, *La Vie quotidienne à Montparnasse*; Flanner, *Paris Was Yesterday*; Wullschläger, *Chagall*; Brown, *Embrace of Unreason*; Browder, *André Breton*; Scheijen, *Diaghilev*; Ford, *Four Lives in Paris*; Beach, *Shakespeare and Company*; Fitch, *Sylvia Beach and the Lost Generation*; Man Ray, *Self Portrait*; Penrose, *Man Ray*; Baldwin, *Man Ray*; Nicholas Weber, *Le Corbusier*; Benton, *Villas of Le Corbusier*; Blake, *Master Builders*; Bernard and Dubief, *Decline of the Third Republic*; Duménil, *Parfum d'empire*; Toledano and Coty, *François Coty*; Eugen Weber, *Action Française*; Walsh, *Stravinsky: A Creative Spring*; Stravinsky and Craft, *Memories and Commentaries*; Michael Reynolds, *Hemingway: The American Homecoming* (Cambridge, Mass.: Blackwell, 1992); Diliberto, *Paris without End*; Hotchner, *Papa Hemingway*; Harold Loeb, *The Way It Was* (New York: Criterion Books, 1959); Meyers, *Scott Fitzgerald*; Fitzgerald, *A Life in Letters*; Hemingway, *Selected Letters*; Sherwood Anderson, *Sherwood Anderson's Memoirs* (Chapel Hill: University of North Carolina Press, 1969); Rideout, *Sherwood Anderson*, vol. 1; Sherwood Anderson, *Sherwood Anderson/Gertrude Stein: Correspondence and Personal Essays* (Chapel Hill: University of North Carolina Press, 1972); Brinnin, *Third Rose*; Stein, *Autobiography of Alice B. Toklas*; Hemingway, *A Moveable Feast*; Ellmann, *James Joyce*; Picardie, *Coco Chanel*; Morand, *Allure of Chanel*; Madsen, *Chanel*; Rhodes, *Louis Renault*; Reynolds, *André Citroën*; Herbert R. Lottman, *The Michelin Men: Driving an Empire* (New York: I. B. Tauris, 2003); Orenstein, *Ravel*; Thurman, *Secrets of the Flesh*; Monet, *Monet by Himself*; Wildenstein, *Monet, or the Triumph of Impressionism*; Clemenceau, *Georges Clemenceau à son ami Claude Monet*.

1. Bazin, *Renoir*, 152.
2. Bertin, *Jean Renoir*, 62.
3. Jean Renoir, *My Life and My Films*, 96.
4. Kessler, 13 February 1926, in *Diaries of a Cosmopolitan*, 279–80.
5. Kessler, 24 February 1926, in *Diaries of a Cosmopolitan*, 283. Another account has her sitting "for hours in a corner sulking" (Jean-Claude Baker, *Josephine*, 128).
6. Kessler, 24 February 1926, in *Diaries of a Cosmopolitan*, 284. The ballet never took place.
7. Josephine Baker, *Josephine*, 58.

8. Josephine Baker, *Josephine*, 66.

9. Jean-Claude Baker, *Josephine*, 142.

10. Charters, *This Must Be the Place*, 4.

11. Bougault, *Paris, Montparnasse*, 155.

12. Flanner, *Paris Was Yesterday*, 9–10.

13. Scheijen, *Diaghilev*, 409.

14. Ford, *Four Lives in Paris*, 37.

15. Beach, *Shakespeare and Company*, 124–25.

16. Beach, *Shakespeare and Company*, 125.

17. Man Ray, *Self Portrait*, 219.

18. Man Ray, *Self Portrait*, 221.

19. Possibly *Nana* or even the dream sequences from *La Fille de l'eau*. According to Richard Abel, *Emak Bakia* was shown at the avant-garde Studio des Ursulines (*French Cinema*, 268).

20. Man Ray, *Self Portrait*, 222.

21. Nicholas Weber, *Le Corbusier*, 236.

22. Weber, *Le Corbusier*, 232.

23. Nicholas Weber, *Le Corbusier*, 266. The Villa Stein remains at Garches, but its interior has been divided into apartments and no longer is open to the public.

24. Nicholas Weber, *Le Corbusier*, 244.

25. Bernard and Dubief, *Decline of the Third Republic*, 120. This was from the speech in which Briand welcomed the admission of Germany to the League.

26. Eugen Weber, *Action Française*, 231.

27. Eugen Weber, *Action Française*, 232.

28. Eugen Weber, *Action Française*, 234.

29. See chapter 5; Walsh, *Stravinsky: A Creative Spring*, 380.

30. Walsh, *Stravinsky: A Creative Spring*, 431.

31. Scheijen, *Diaghilev*, 407.

32. Stravinsky and Craft, *Memories and Commentaries*, 170.

33. Stravinsky and Craft, *Memories and Commentaries*, 170.

34. At the time he signed with Boni & Liveright, Hemingway acknowledged his debt to both Anderson and Dos Passos with fulsome letters of thanks (Hemingway to John Dos Passos, 22 April 1925, and Hemingway to Sherwood Anderson, 23 May 1925, both in *Selected Letters*, 157 and 161).

35. Fitzgerald wrote Max Perkins: "I agree with Ernest that Anderson's last two books have let everybody down who believed in him—I think they're cheap, faked, obscurantic and awful" (Fitzgerald to Max Perkins, 30 December 1925, in Fitzgerald, *A Life in Letters*, 133).

36. Rideout, *Sherwood Anderson*, 1:636.

37. After telling Hemingway about those who helpfully edited his own work, Fitzgerald wrote, "Anyhow I think parts of *Sun Also* are careless + ineffectual. . . . Why not cut the inessentials in Cohn's biography? . . . When so many people can

write well + the competition is so heavy I can't imagine how you could have done these first 20 pp. so casually" (Fitzgerald to Hemingway, June 1926, in Fitzgerald, *A Life in Letters*, 142, 144).

38. Charters, *This Must Be the Place*, 38. Luigi Pirandello's *Six Characters in Search of an Author* first appeared in Milan in 1922.

39. Flanner, *Paris Was Yesterday*, 12. She names these as Lady Duff Twysden, Pat Guthrie, Kitty Cannell, and Harold Loeb.

40. Reynolds, *Hemingway: The American Homecoming*, 74.

41. Hotchner, *Papa Hemingway*, 47. Hemingway had already treated Loeb badly at Pamplona in 1925 and the day after had apologized for "the stinking, unjust uncalled for things I said" (Hemingway to Harold Loeb, 12 July 1925, in *Selected Letters*, 166; see also Loeb, *The Way It Was*, 297). Still, it would have been entirely out of character for Loeb to want to kill Hemingway—or anyone.

42. Diliberto, *Paris without End*, 219.

43. Reynolds, *Hemingway: The American Homecoming*, 79.

44. Diliberto, *Paris without End*, 237.

45. Hemingway to Sherwood Anderson, 21 May 1926, in *Selected Letters*, 205–6.

46. Anderson, *Sherwood Anderson's Memoirs*, 463.

47. Rideout, *Sherwood Anderson*, 1:662; Reynolds, *Hemingway: The American Homecoming*, 92.

48. Anderson, *Sherwood Anderson's Memoirs*, 465.

49. Anderson, *Sherwood Anderson's Memoirs*, 463.

50. Stein, *Autobiography of Alice B. Toklas*, 197.

51. Anderson, *Sherwood Anderson/Gertrude Stein*, 15, 17.

52. Rideout, *Sherwood Anderson*, 414.

53. Hemingway to Anderson, 9 March 1922, in *Selected Letters*, 62.

54. Stein, *Autobiography of Alice B. Toklas*, 217.

55. Hemingway, *Moveable Feast*, 118.

56. Reynolds, *Hemingway: The American Homecoming*, 84.

57. Charters, *This Must Be the Place*, 1, 2.

58. Ellmann, *James Joyce*, 584.

59. In October 1927, the pirated publication of Joyce's *Ulysses* stopped, but this was due to Joyce's legal action rather than to the international protest that Beach had organized (Ellmann, *James Joyce*, 587).

60. Ellmann, *James Joyce*, 588.

61. Picardie, *Coco Chanel*, 92.

62. Morand, *Allure of Chanel*, 155, 151, 146.

63. Lottman, *Michelin Men*, 146.

64. La Tour d'Argent now holds but one star, a decline in wattage that has caused considerable anxiety among its owners and its devoted following.

65. Orenstein, *Ravel*, 90.

66. Monet to Georges Clemenceau, 18 September 1926, in *Monet by Himself*, 265.

67. Wildenstein, *Monet, or the Triumph of Impressionism*, 437; Clemenceau à Monet, 6 août [August] 1926, in *Georges Clemenceau à son ami Claude Monet*, 182; Clemenceau à Monet, 4 juillet 1926, in *Georges Clemenceau à son ami Claude Monet*, 181.

68. Wildenstein, *Monet, or the Triumph of Impressionism*, 446, 448.

69. Wildenstein, *Monet, or the Triumph of Impressionism*, 446.

70. Monet to Evan Charteris, 21 June 1926, in *Monet by Himself*, 265.

71. Wildenstein, *Monet, or the Triumph of Impressionism*, 446.

72. Wildenstein, *Monet, or the Triumph of Impressionism*, 458.

73. Wildenstein, *Monet, or the Triumph of Impressionism*, 458. The authenticity of these instructions has been disputed, even though this particular phrase certainly is compatible with Monet's views.

74. Wildenstein, *Monet, or the Triumph of Impressionism*, 447.

12 Sophisticated Lady (1927)

Selected sources for this chapter: Jean-Claude Baker and Chris Chase, *Josephine Baker*; Buñuel, *My Last Sigh*; Pierre Assouline, *Simenon: A Biography* (New York: Knopf, 1997); Peter L. Hays, *Fifty Years of Hemingway Criticism* (Lanham, Md.: Scarecrow Press, 2014); Hotchner, *Papa Hemingway*; Reynolds, *Hemingway: The Paris Years*; Michael Reynolds, *Hemingway: The Final Years* (New York: Norton, 1999); Reynolds, *Hemingway: The American Homecoming*; Thomas Kessner, *The Flight of the Century: Charles Lindbergh and the Rise of American Aviation* (New York: Oxford University Press, 2010); U.S. Department of State, *The Flight of Captain Charles A. Lindbergh from New York to Paris, May 20–21, 1927* (Washington, D.C.: Government Printing Office, 1927); Fitch, *Sylvia Beach and the Lost Generation*; Reynolds, *André Citroën*; Madsen, *Chanel*; Picardie, *Coco Chanel*; Steegmuller, *Cocteau*; Walter A. Strauss, "Jean Cocteau: The Difficulty of Being Orpheus," in *Reviewing Orpheus: Essays on the Cinema and Art of Jean Cocteau*, ed. Cornelia A. Tsakiridou (Lewisburg, Pa.: Bucknell University Press, 1997); Jacob and Cocteau, *Correspondance*; Walsh, *Stravinsky: A Creative Spring*; Scheijen, *Diaghilev*; Cossart, *Food of Love*; Stravinsky and Craft, *Memories and Commentaries*; Flanner, *Paris Was Yesterday*; Crespelle, *La Vie quotidienne à Montparnasse*; Bougault, *Paris, Montparnasse*; Lottman, *Man Ray's Montparnasse*; Man Ray, *Self-Portrait*; Baldwin, *Man Ray*; Kiki, *Kiki's Memoirs*; Hugh Tours, *Parry Thomas, Designer-Driver* (London: B. T. Batsford, 1959); Kurth, *Isadora*; Mary Desti, *The Unknown Story: The Life of Isadora Duncan* (New York: Da Capo, 1981); Irma Duncan, *Duncan Dancer*; Bertin, *Jean Renoir*; Jean Renoir, *My Life and My Films*; Bazin, *Jean Renoir*; Abel, *French Cinema*; Deslandres, *Poiret*; Baudot, *Poiret*; Nicholas Weber, *Le Corbusier*; Benton, *Villas of Le Corbusier*; Charlotte Perriand, *A Life of Creation: An Autobiography* (New York: Monacelli Press, 2003); Browder, *André Breton*; Brinnin, *Third Rose*; Ellmann, *James Joyce*; Wullschläger, *Chagall*; Richardson, *Life of Picasso: The Triumphant Years*; Stein, *Autobiography of Alice B. Toklas*; Brown, *Embrace of Unreason*; Eugen Weber, *Action Française*; Duménil, *Parfum d'empire*; Watson, *Georges Clemenceau*; Bernard and Dubief, *Decline of the Third Republic*; Lacouture, *De Gaulle, The Rebel*; Williams, *Last Great Frenchman*.

1. Bunuel, *My Last Sigh*, 90.

2. Jean-Claude Baker, *Josephine Baker*, 151.

3. Jean-Claude Baker, *Josephine Baker*, 142, 146.

4. Assouline, *Simenon*, 74–75.

5. As Hemingway told his friend, A. E. Hotchner, "She turned her eyes on me—she was dancing with the big British gunner subaltern who had brought her—but I responded to the eyes like a hypnotic and cut in on them. The subaltern tried to shoulder me out but the girl slid off him and onto me. Everything under that fur instantly communicated with me. I introduced myself and asked her name. 'Josephine Baker,' she said. We danced nonstop for the rest of the night. She never took off her fur coat. Wasn't until the joint closed she told me she had nothing on underneath" (Hotchner, *Papa Hemingway*, 53).

6. Hotchner, *Papa Hemingway*, 53.

7. Reynolds, *Hemingway: The Paris Years*, 63.

8. Reynolds, *Hemingway: The Paris Years*, 63. The fabrications Reynolds discusses are on pp. 33, 151, 154–55, 168–69, 170, 204–5, 206–7, 221, 222–23, and 245 in *Hemingway: The Final Years*.

9. Reynolds, *Hemingway: The American Homecoming*, 124.

10. U.S. Dept. of State, *Flight of Captain Charles A. Lindbergh*, cover; Kessner, *Flight of the Century*, 108. In an especially French observation, France's minister of war called it "an aesthetic triumph, a thing so beautiful that it has gone to the heart of the world as only beauty, and beauty alone, can" (Kessner, *Flight of the Century*, 115).

11. Reynolds, *André Citroën*, 79.

12. Madsen, *Chanel*, 160.

13. Steegmuller notes that "Today the play is overshadowed by Cocteau's [much later] film of the same name" (*Cocteau*, 371).

14. Steegmuller, *Cocteau*, 370.

15. Steegmuller, *Cocteau*, 382, 383.

16. Walsh, *Stravinsky: A Creative Spring*, 444.

17. Walsh, *Stravinsky: A Creative Spring*, 448.

18. In subsequent productions, especially a Paris one in 1952, Cocteau would make the speaker "one of his most notable roles" (Steegmuller, *Cocteau*, 386).

19. Stravinsky and Craft, *Memories and Commentaries*, 163.

20. Walsh, *Stravinsky: A Creative Spring*, 447.

21. Boris de Schloezer quoted in Walsh, *Stravinsky: A Creative Spring*, 447.

22. Stravinsky and Craft, *Memories and Commentaries*, 163.

23. Scheijen, *Diaghilev*, 415.

24. Stravinsky and Craft, *Memories and Commentaries*, 71.

25. Man Ray, *Self Portrait*, 175.

26. John Parry-Thomas at Pendine Sands, Wales, on 3 March 1927 (Tours, *Parry Thomas*, 149).

27. Kurth, *Isadora*, 514.

28. Irma Duncan, *Duncan Dancer*, 266.

29. Kurth, *Isadora*, 517.

30. Kurth, *Isadora*, 539. The European edition of the *Chicago Tribune* was usually referred to simply as the *Paris Tribune*.

31. Kurth, *Isadora*, 539.

32. Buñuel, *My Last Sigh*, 91. A British actress in *The Siren of the Tropics*, the movie on which Buñuel was then working, told him that "someone had machine-gunned the foyer of her hotel. The damage to the boulevard Sébastopol was particularly devastating; ten days later, the police were still rounding up suspected looters" (91).

33. Kurth, *Isadora*, 540.

34. Desti, *Unknown Story*, 205.

35. Kurth, *Isadora*, 545.

36. Desti, *Untold Story*, 271.

37. Steegmuller, *Cocteau*, 387.

38. Flanner, *Paris Was Yesterday*, 30, 35.

39. Bertin, *Jean Renoir*, 71.

40. Flanner, *Paris Was Yesterday*, 29.

41. Flanner, *Paris Was Yesterday*, 17.

42. Nicholas Weber, *Le Corbusier*, 265–66.

43. The Villa Lipchitz is next to another Le Corbusier studio-residence, the Villa Miestchaninoff.

44. Perriand, *Life of Creation*, 24.

45. Nicholas Weber, *Le Corbusier*, 260.

46. Nicholas Weber, *Le Corbusier*, 248.

47. Nicholas Weber, *Le Corbusier*, 424.

48. Nicholas Weber, *Le Corbusier*, 269.

49. Brinnin, *Third Rose*, 274.

50. Brinnin, *Third Rose*, 269.

51. Brinnin, *Third, Rose*, 278.

52. Richardson, *Life of Picasso: The Triumphant Years*, 308.

53. Richardson, *Life of Picasso: The Triumphant Years*, 349.

54. Stein, *Autobiography of Alice B. Toklas*, 212.

55. Watson, *Georges Clemenceau*, 391n.

56. Bernard and Dubief, *Decline of the Third Republic*, 122.

57. Lacouture, *De Gaulle: The Rebel*, 83.

58. De Gaulle served with the Army of Occupation in the Rhineland. French forces continued to occupy the Rhineland until late 1930.

59. Lacouture, *De Gaulle: The Rebel*, 85.

60. Lacouture, *De Gaulle: The Rebel*, 88.

13 Cocktails, Darling? (1928)

Selected sources for this chapter: Huddleston, *Bohemian Literary and Social Life in Paris*; Man Ray, *Self Portrait*; Eve Curie, *Madame Curie*; Howard Pollack, *George Gershwin: His Life and Work* (Berkeley: University of California Press, 2006); Edward

Jablonski, *Gershwin* (Garden City, N.Y.: Doubleday, 1987); Robert Kimball and Alfred Simon, *The Gershwins* (New York: Atheneum, 1973); McBrien, *Cole Porter*; Maxwell, *R.S.V.P.*; Ravel, *Ravel Reader*; Walsh, *Stravinsky: A Creative Spring*; Reynolds, *Hemingway: The American Homecoming*; Diliberto, *Paris without End*; Poiret, *King of Fashion*; Deslandres, *Poiret*; Gold and Fizdale, *Misia*; Misia Sert, *Misia and the Muses*; Madsen, *Chanel*; Baldwin, *Man Ray*; Lottman, *Man Ray's Montparnasse*; Kiki, *Kiki's Memoirs*; Jean-Claude Baker and Chris Chase, *Josephine*; Flanner, *Paris Was Yesterday*; Nicholas Weber, *Le Corbusier*; Bernard and Dubief, *Decline of the Third Republic*; Reynolds, *André Citroën*; Rhodes, *Louis Renault*; Frèrejean, *André Citroën, Louis Renault*; Roy Church, "Family Firms and Managerial Capitalism: The Case of the International Motor Industry," in *Business in the Age of Depression and War*, ed. R. P. T. Davenport-Hines (Savage, Md.: Frank Cass, 1990); Lacouture, *De Gaulle: The Rebel*; Duménil, *Parfum d'empire*; Toledano and Coty, *François Coty*; Bertin, *Jean Renoir*; Bazin, *Jean Renoir*; Abel, *French Cinema*; Picardie, *Coco Chanel*.

1. Huddleston, *Bohemian Literary and Social Life in Paris*, 21.
2. Huddleston, *Bohemian Literary and Social Life in Paris*, 21.
3. Eve Curie, *Madame Curie*, 358–59.
4. Eve Curie, *Madame Curie*, 359.
5. Pollack, *George Gershwin*, 431.
6. Maxwell, *R.S.V.P.*, 124–25.
7. McBrien, *Cole Porter*, 121.
8. Despite its success, it quickly disappeared—eclipsed by *Paris*, which opened a few months later.
9. Pollack, *George Gershwin*, 139.
10. Pollack, *George Gershwin*, 119.
11. Ravel to Boulanger, 8 March 1928, in *Ravel Reader*, 293.
12. Pollack, *George Gershwin*, 120.
13. Pollack, *George Gershwin*, 121.
14. For about two years, sometime between 1927 and 1931, Gershwin studied with the avant-garde American composer Henry Cowell, and briefly during this period with the composer Wallingford Riegger (both at that time on the faculty of the New School for Social Research). He studied with Joseph Schillinger from about 1932 until the end of his life (*Ravel Reader*, 294n3; Pollack, *George Gershwin*, 127).
15. According to Gershwin biographer Howard Pollack, "The received wisdom presumes that both composers [Milhaud and Gershwin], similarly molded by American jazz and Jewish sensibilities, arrived at their related styles independently, but that, to quote Deborah Mawer, 'Milhaud got there first'" (*George Gershwin*, 140). The quote is from Mawer, *Darius Milhaud: Modality and Structure in Music of the 1920s* (Brookfield, Vt.: Ashgate, 1997, 163).
16. Diliberto, *Paris without End*, 245, 260, 230.
17. Poiret, *King of Fashion*, 172.
18. Deslandres, *Poiret*, 75–76.
19. Poiret, *King of Fashion*, 172.

20. Misia Sert, *Misia and the Muses*, 180.
21. Baldwin, *Man Ray*, 143.
22. Nicholas Weber, *Le Corbusier*, 302.
23. Nicholas Weber, *Le Corbusier*, 272.
24. Nicholas Weber, *Le Corbusier*, 272.
25. Nicholas Weber, *Le Corbusier*, 274.
26. Nicholas Weber, *Le Corbusier*, 280.
27. Nicholas Weber, *Le Corbusier*, 282.
28. Nicholas Weber, *Le Corbusier*, 281, 284.
29. Bernard and Dubief, *Decline of the Third Republic*, 131.
30. Duménil, *Parfum d'empire*, 164.
31. Toledano and Coty, *François Coty*, 150, 151.
32. Bazin, *Jean Renoir*, 155.
33. Bertin, *Jean Renoir*, 78.
34. Picardie, *Coco Chanel*, 184.

14 The Bubble Bursts (1929)

Selected sources for this chapter: Charters, *This Must Be the Place*; Fitch, *Sylvia Beach and the Lost Generation*; Kiki, *Kiki's Memoirs*; Lottman, *Man Ray's Montparnasse*; Crespelle, *La Vie quotidienne à Montparnasse*; Wambly Bald, *On the Left Bank, 1929–1933* (Athens: Ohio University Press, 1987); Bougault, *Paris, Montparnasse*; Baldwin, *Man Ray*; Man Ray, *Self Portrait*; Buñuel, *My Last Sigh*; Abel, *French Cinema*; Browder, *André Breton*; Steegmuller, *Cocteau*; Bertin, *Jean Renoir*; Jean Renoir, *My Life and My Films*; Bazin, *Jean Renoir*; Watson, *Georges Clemenceau*; Clemenceau, *Georges Clemenceau à son ami Claude Monet*; Madsen, *Chanel*; Serge Lifar, *Serge Diaghilev, His Life, His Work, His Legend: An Intimate Biography* (New York: Da Capo, 1976); Scheijen, *Diaghilev*; Walsh, *Stravinsky: A Creative Spring*; Gold and Fizdale, *Misia*; Misia Sert, *Misia and the Muses*; Kessler, *Diaries of a Cosmopolitan*; McBrien, *Cole Porter*; Mme Duffet-Bourdelle, "Bourdelle, Sa Vie, Son Oeuvre," *Dossier de L'Art 10* (Janvier–Février 1993): 17–23; Nicholas Weber, *Le Corbusier*; Benton, *Villas of Le Corbusier*; Blake, *Master Builders*; Gans, *Le Corbusier Guide*; Jean-Claude Baker and Chris Chase, *Josephine*; Perriand, *A Life of Creation*; Vaill, *Everyone Was So Young*; Wullschläger, *Chagall*; Richardson, *Life of Picasso: The Triumphant Years*; Coty and Toledano, *François Coty*; Deslandres, *Paul Poiret*; Baudot, *Poiret*; Beach, *Shakespeare and Company*; Ellmann, *James Joyce*; Ravel, *Ravel Reader*; Quinn, *Marie Curie*; Brown, *Embrace of Unreason*; Bernard and Dubief, *Decline of the Third Republic*.

1. "Montparnasse really ended in 1929 with the beginning of the depression in America, but as an artist colony it had been on the wane for some time before that" (Charters, *This Must Be the Place*, 197).
2. Fitch, *Sylvia Beach and the Lost Generation*, 284.

3. Fitch, *Sylvia Beach and the Lost Generation*, 284. On 10 December 1929, Crosby killed himself and his current lover in an apparent suicide pact.

4. Hemingway, intro. to *Kiki's Memoirs*, 47, 49.

5. Foujita, intro. to *Kiki's Memoirs*, 45.

6. Hemingway, intro. to *Kiki's Memoirs*, 50.

7. Klüver and Martin, foreword to *Kiki's Memoirs*, 38.

8. Putnam, intro. to *Kiki's Memoirs*, 61.

9. Bald, *On the Left Bank*, 2 (from his 28 October 1929 "La Vie de Bohème" column).

10. Bald, *On the Left Bank*, 14 (from his 17 February 1930 "La Vie de Bohème" column).

11. Baldwin, *Man Ray*, 149.

12. Baldwin, *Man Ray*, 155, 156.

13. Man Ray, *Self Portrait*, 227.

14. Man Ray, *Self Portrait*, 229.

15. Man Ray, *Self Portrait*, 235.

16. Buñuel, *My Last Sigh*, 104.

17. According to Buñuel, *tout* Paris attended, including Picasso, Le Corbusier, Cocteau, and the composer Georges Auric, and he was so worried that he had "put some stones in my pocket to throw at the audience in case of disaster." This did not prove necessary (Buñuel, *My Last Sigh*, 105, 106).

18. Steegmuller, *Cocteau*, 325.

19. Steegmuller, *Cocteau*, 396.

20. Jean Renoir, *My Life and My Films*, 103.

21. Bazin, *Jean Renoir*, 155.

22. Jean Renoir, *My Life and My Films*, 101.

23. Jean Renoir, *My Life and My Films*, 101.

24. Clemenceau à Monet, 17 avril 1922, in *Georges Clemenceau à son ami Claude Monet*, 101.

25. Watson, *Georges Clemenceau*, 394.

26. Lifar, *Serge Diaghilev*, 333. Diaghilev told Lifar that this was only the second time he had kissed a dancer's leg. The first was Nijinsky's, after his performance in *Le Spectre de la rose* (333).

27. Misia Sert joined Diaghilev at the end of the Ballets Russes London season, after he asked her to join him "as soon as possible." She "found him completely exhausted. . . . His face was drawn with suffering. A septic ulcer in the lower stomach refused to respond to treatment, and the doctors insisted that he should take a rest and undergo a cure. But at that moment Markevitch was his only pre-occupation" (Misia Sert, *Misia and the Muses*, 156).

28. Gold and Fizdale, *Misia*, 260. Misia recalled that she had returned from London to Paris, where she received his telegram. She does not include the cruise with Chanel and Bendor in her memoirs [which Gold and Fizdale conclude are "generally accurate,"

although "much is omitted, episodes are romanticized, outlines are blurred," 5], and says she went directly from Paris to Venice (Misia Sert, *Misia and the Muses*, 156).

29. Misia Sert, *Misia and the Muses*, 159.

30. Gold and Fizdale, *Misia*, 262. Misia had a different recollection of events. After giving the only money she had with her to the Baroness d'Erlanger, "who happened to be in Venice," Misia asked the baroness to make the necessary arrangements for the Mass and funeral. Without money, Misia was en route to a jewelers to pawn a diamond necklace, when she "met a dearly loved friend [Chanel] who, following a presentiment, had hurried to Venice." Chanel had been in Venice earlier but had "left town the day before on the yacht of the Duke of Westminster. . . . The boat had hardly reached the open sea when she began to fear the worst and begged the Duke to turn back." Misia credited this "dearly loved friend" with moral support, but gave the Baroness d'Erlanger credit for organizing the funeral. Presumably Chanel provided financial support as well (*Misia and the Muses*, 159).

31. Gold and Fizdale, *Misia*, 263.

32. Kessler, 10 April 1930, in *Diaries of a Cosmopolitan*, 381–82.

33. Beach told Lawrence that she was too busy, but privately did not care for the book, which she called a "kind of sermon-on-the-mount—of Venus" (Fitch, *Sylvia Beach and the Lost Generation*, 280).

34. Bourdelle's quote, as remembered by his daughter, is in Duffet-Bourdelle, "Bourdelle, Sa Vie, Son Oeuvre," 23.

35. The new Institut Giacometti, at 46 Rue Hippolyte Maindron, with Giacometti's tiny atelier at its heart, is scheduled to open to the public in late 2016.

36. The Cité de Refuge is located at 12 Rue Cantagrel (13th), and the Asile Flottant, a humble barge of reinforced concrete named the *Louise-Catherine*, is moored on the Seine just below the Gare d'Austerlitz (13th). Both the Cité de Refuge and the *Louise-Catherine* are at this writing under renovation, but despite ongoing construction, the *Louise-Catherine* is currently open to visitors Wed.–Sun., 2:00–8:00 p.m.

37. Nicholas Weber, *Le Corbusier*, 300.

38. Neither the house nor the village would be built, although Baker would in time adopt and house a tribe of international orphans at her château in the Dordogne.

39. Nicholas Weber, *Le Corbusier*, 302.

40. Nicholas Weber, *Le Corbusier*, 307.

41. Nicholas Weber includes these in *Le Corbusier*, plates 23–25.

42. Nicholas Weber, *Le Corbusier*, 312.

43. Nicholas Weber interview with Jean-Claude Baker, in *Le Corbusier*, 312.

44. Perriand, *A Life of Creation*, 35.

45. Perriand, *A Life of Creation*, 35.

46. Fitch, *Sylvia Beach and the Lost Generation*, 264.

47. Dunoyer, in *Ravel Reader*, appendix F, 527–28.

48. Quinn, *Marie Curie*, 419.

49. Charters and Cody, *This Must Be the Place*, xv.

50. Kiki, *Kiki's Memoirs*, 184, 188, 191.

Bibliography

Abel, Richard. *French Cinema: The First Wave, 1915–1929*. Princeton, N.J.: Princeton University Press, 1984.

Adam, Helen Pearl. *Paris Sees It Through: A Diary, 1914–1919*. New York: Hodder & Stoughton, 1919.

Albaret, Céleste. *Monsieur Proust: A Memoir*. Recorded by Georges Belmont. Translated by Barbara Bray. New York: McGraw-Hill, 1976.

Anderson, Sherwood. *Sherwood Anderson/Gertrude Stein: Correspondence and Personal Essays*. Edited by Ray Lewis White. Chapel Hill: University of North Carolina Press, 1972.

———. *Sherwood Anderson's Memoirs: A Critical Edition*. Edited by Ray Lewis White. Chapel Hill: University of North Carolina Press, 1969.

Assouline, Pierre. *Simenon: A Biography*. Translated by Jon Rothschild. New York: Knopf, 1997.

Baker, Jean-Claude, and Chris Chase. *Josephine: The Hungry Heart*. New York: Cooper Square Press, 2001. First published 1993.

Baker, Josephine, and Jo Bouillon. *Josephine*. Translated by Mariana Fitzpatrick. New York: Harper & Row, 1977.

Bald, Wambly. *On the Left Bank, 1929–1933*. Edited by Benjamin Franklin V. Athens: Ohio University Press, 1987.

Baldwin, Neil. *Man Ray, American Artist*. New York: Da Capo, 2001. First published 1988.

Barr, Alfred H., Jr. *Picasso: Fifty Years of His Art*. New York: for the Trustees of the Museum of Modern Art by Plantin Press, 1951.

Baudot, François. *Poiret*. Translated by Caroline Beamish. New York: Assouline, 2006.

Bazin, André. *Jean Renoir*. Translated by W. W. Halsey II and William H. Simon. Edited and with introduction by François Truffaut. New York: De Capo, 1992.

Beach, Sylvia. *Shakespeare and Company*. Lincoln: University of Nebraska Press, 1980.

Benstock, Shari. *Women of the Left Bank, Paris, 1900–1940*. Austin: University of Texas Press, 1986.

Benton, Tim. *The Villas of Le Corbusier, 1920–1930*. With photographs in the Lucien Hervé collection. New Haven, Conn.: Yale University Press, 1987.

Bernard, Philippe, and Henri Dubief. *The Decline of the Third Republic, 1914–1938*. Translated by Anthony Forster. New York: Cambridge University Press, 1988. First published in English, 1985.

Bernhardt, Lysiane Sarah, and Marion Dix. *Sarah Bernhardt, My Grandmother*. N.p., 1949.

Bertaut, Jules. *Paris, 1870–1935*. Translated by R. Millar. Edited by John Bell. London: Eyre & Spottiswoode, 1936.

Bertin, Célia. *Jean Renoir: A Life in Pictures*. Translated by Mireille Muellner and Leonard Muellner. Baltimore, Md.: Johns Hopkins University Press, 1991.

Birmingham, Kevin. *The Most Dangerous Book: The Battle for James Joyce's* Ulysses. New York: Penguin, 2014.

Blake, Peter. *The Master Builders*. New York: Knopf, 1960.

Blanche, Jacques-Emile. *More Portraits of a Lifetime: 1918–1938*. Translated and edited by Walter Clement. London: J. M. Dent, 1939.

Bougault, Valérie. *Paris, Montparnasse: The Heyday of Modern Art, 1910–1940*. Paris: Editions Pierre Terrail, 1997.

Brandon, Ruth. *Ugly Beauty: Helena Rubinstein, L'Oréal, and the Blemished History of Looking Good*. New York: Harper, 2011.

Bréon, Emmanuel, and Philippe Rivoirard, eds. *1925, quand l'art deco séduit le monde*. Paris: Cité de l'Architecture et du Patrimoine, 2013.

Breton, André. *Manifestoes of Surrealism*. Translated by Richard Seaver and Helen R. Lane. Ann Arbor: University of Michigan Press, 1969.

Brinnin, John Malcolm. *The Third Rose: Gertrude Stein and Her World*. Reading, Mass.: Addison-Wesley, 1987. First published 1959.

Broca, Henri. *T'en fais pas, viens à Montparnasse! Enquête sur le Montparnasse actuel*. Paris: 71 Rue de Rennes, 1928.

Brooks, H. Allen. *Le Corbusier's Formative Years: Charles-Edouard Jeanneret at La Chaux-de-Fonds*. Chicago: University of Chicago Press, 1997.

Browder, Clifford. *André Breton, Arbiter of Surrealism*. Geneva, Switzerland: Droz, 1967.

Brown, Frederick. *The Embrace of Unreason: France, 1914–1940*. New York: Knopf, 2014.

Buñuel, Luis. *My Last Sigh*. Translated by Abigail Israel. New York: Vintage, 1984.

Carter, William C. *Marcel Proust: A Life*. New Haven, Conn.: Yale University Press, 2000.

Casadesus, Gaby. *Mes noces musicales: Gaby Casadesus, Conversation avec Jacqueline Muller*. Paris: Buchet-Chastel, 1989.

Cendrars, Blaise. *J'ai tué*. Paris: G. Crès, 1919.

Ceroni, Ambrogio. *Amedeo Modigliani, peintre: suivi des 'souvenirs' de Lunia Czechowska*. Milan: Edizioni del Milione, 1958.

Charters, Jimmie, as told to Morrill Cody. *This Must Be the Place: Memoirs of Montparnasse*. Edited and with a preface by Hugh Ford. Introduction by Ernest Hemingway. New York: Collier Macmillan, 1989. First published 1934.

Church, Roy. "Family Firms and Managerial Capitalism: The Case of the International Motor Industry." In *Business in the Age of Depression and War*, edited by R. P. T. Davenport-Hines. Savage, Md.: Frank Cass, 1990.

Clemenceau, Georges. *Claude Monet: The Water Lilies*. Translated by George Boas. Garden City, N.Y.: Doubleday, Doran, 1930.

———. *Georges Clemenceau à son ami Claude Monet: Correspondance*. Paris: Editions de la Réunion des Musées Nationaux, 1993.

Clement, Russell T. *Les Fauves: A Sourcebook*. Westport, Conn.: Greenwood, 1994.

Cocteau, Jean. *The Journals of Jean Cocteau*. Edited and translated with an introduction by Wallace Fowlie. New York: Criterion Books, 1956.

———. *Lettre à Jacques Maritain*. Paris: Stock, 1983.

———. *Lettres à sa mère*. Vol. 1 (1989–1918). Edited and annotated by Pierre Caizergues. Paris: Gallimard, 1989.

———. *Lettres à sa mère*. Vol. 2 (1919–1938). Edited and annotated by Pierre Caizergues. Paris: Gallimard, 1989.

Cossart, Michael de. *The Food of Love: Princesse Edmond de Polignac (1865–1943) and Her Salon*. London: Hamish Hamilton, 1978.

Crespelle, Jean-Paul. *La Vie quotidienne à Montparnasse à la Grande Epoque, 1905–1930*. Paris: Hachette, 1976.

Curie, Eve. *Madame Curie: A Biography*. Translated by Vincent Sheean. New York: Da Capo, 2001. Reprint of 1937 original.

Danchev, Alex. *Georges Braque: A Life*. New York: Arcade, 2012.

De Francia, Peter. *Fernand Léger*. New Haven, Conn.: Yale University Press, 1983.

DeKoven, Marianne. *A Different Language: Gertrude Stein's Experimental Writing*. Madison: University of Wisconsin Press, 1983.

Deslandres, Yvonne, assisted by Dorothée Lalanne. *Poiret: Paul Poiret, 1879–1944*. Paris: Editions du Regard, 1986.

Desti, Mary. *The Untold Story: The Life of Isadora Duncan*. New York: Da Capo, 1981. First published 1929.

Diliberto, Gioia. *Paris without End: The True Story of Hemingway's First Wife*. New York: Harper Perennial, 2011. First published 1992 as *Hadley*.

Duffet-Bourdelle, Mme. "Bourdelle, Sa Vie, Son Oeuvre." *Dossier de L'Art* 10 (Janvier–Février 1993): 17–23.

Duménil, Alain. *Parfum d'empire: la vie extraordinaire de François Coty*. Paris, France: Plon, 2009.

Duncan, Irma. *Duncan Dancer*. New York: Books for Libraries, 1980. First published 1963.

Duncan, Isadora. *My Life*. New York: Liveright, 2013. First published 1927.

Easton, Laird McLeod. *The Red Count: The Life and Times of Harry Kessler*. Berkeley: University of California Press, 2002.

Eliel, Carol S. *L'Esprit nouveau: Purism in Paris, 1918–1925*. With essays by Françoise Ducros and Tag Gronberg and an English translation of *After Cubism* by Amédée Ozenfant and Charles-Edouard Jeanneret. Los Angeles, Calif.: Los Angeles County Museum of Art in association with Harry N. Abrams, 2001.

Ellmann, Richard. *James Joyce*. New York: Oxford University Press, 1982.

Evenson, Norma. *Paris: A Century of Change, 1878–1978*. New Haven, Conn.: Yale University Press, 1979.

Fitch, Noel Riley. *Sylvia Beach and the Lost Generation: A History of Literary Paris in the Twenties and Thirties*. New York: Norton, 1983.

Fitzgerald, F. Scott. *A Life in Letters: F. Scott Fitzgerald*. Edited by Matthew J. Bruccoli. New York: Scribner, 1995.

———. *The Great Gatsby*. New York: Scribner, 2004. First published 1925.

Flanner, Janet. *Paris Was Yesterday, 1925–1939*. New York: Viking, 1972.

Ford, Hugh D. *Four Lives in Paris*. San Francisco, Calif.: North Point Press, 1987.

Franck, Dan. *Bohemian Paris: Picasso, Modigliani, Matisse, and the Birth of Modern Art*. Translated by Cynthia Hope Liebow. New York: Grove Press, 2001.

Frèrejean, Alain. *André Citroën, Louis Renault: un duel sans merci*. Paris: A. Michel, 1998.

Fuss-Amore, Gustave, and Maurice des Ombiaux. *Montparnasse*. Paris: Albin Michel, 1925.

Gans, Deborah. *The Le Corbusier Guide*. New York: Princeton Architectural Press, 2006. First published 1987.

Gillmor, Alan M. *Erik Satie*. Boston: Twayne, 1988.

Gold, Arthur, and Robert Fizdale. *The Divine Sarah: A Life of Sarah Bernhardt*. New York: Vintage, 1992.

———. *Misia: The Life of Misia Sert*. New York: Morrow, 1981.

Green, Christopher. *Léger and the Avant-Garde*. New Haven, Conn.: Yale University Press, 1976.

Greenfeld, Howard. *The Devil and Dr. Barnes: Portrait of an American Art Collector*. Philadelphia, Pa.: Camino Books, 2006.

Hamnett, Nina. *Laughing Torso: Reminiscences*. New York: Ray Long & R. R. Smith, 1932.

Hansen, Arlen J. *Expatriate Paris: A Cultural and Literary Guide to Paris of the 1920s*. New York: Arcade, 1990.

Harvie, David I. *Eiffel: The Genius Who Reinvented Himself*. Stroud, UK: Sutton, 2004.

Hays, Peter L. *Fifty Years of Hemingway Criticism*. Lanham, Md.: Scarecrow Press, 2014.

Hemingway, Ernest. *A Moveable Feast*. New York: Touchstone, 1996. First published 1964.

———. *Selected Letters, 1917–1961*. New York: Scribner, 1981.

———. *The Sun Also Rises*. New York: Scribner, 1968. First published 1926.

Hillier, Bevis. *Art Deco Style*. London: Phaidon, 1997.

Hotchner, A. E. *Papa Hemingway: A Personal Memoir*. New York: Random House, 1966.

Huddleston, Sisley. *Back to Montparnasse: Glimpses of Broadway in Bohemia*. Philadelphia: J. B. Lippincott, 1931.

———. *Bohemian Literary and Social Life in Paris: Salons, Cafés, Studios*. London: G. G. Harrap, 1928.

———. *In and About Paris*. London: Methuen, 1927.

Hugo, Jean. *Avant d'oublier: 1918–1931*. Paris: Fayard, 1976.

Ingpen, Roger. *The Fighting Retreat to Paris*. New York: Hodder & Stoughton, 1914.

Jablonski, Edward. *Gershwin*. Garden City, N.Y.: Doubleday, 1987.

Jacob, Max, and Jean Cocteau. *Correspondance, 1917–1944*. Edited and introduction by Anne Kimball. Paris: Paris–Méditerranée, 2000.

Jencks, Charles. *Le Corbusier and the Continual Revolution in Architecture*. New York: Monacelli Press, 2000.

Jones, Colin. *Paris: Biography of a City*. New York: Viking, 2005.

Jordan, Robert Furneaux. *Le Corbusier*. New York: Lawrence Hill, 1972.

Joyce, James. *Ulysses*. New York: Vintage, 1993. First published 1922, Paris, by Shakespeare and Company; first American edition, 1934, Random House.

Kelly, Barbara L. *Music and Ultra-Modernism in France: A Fragile Consensus, 1913–1939*. Woodbridge, Suffolk, UK: Boydell Press, 2013.

Kessler, Harry. *The Diaries of a Cosmopolitan: Count Harry Kessler, 1918–1937*. Translated and edited by Charles Kessler. London: Weidenfeld & Nicolson, 1971.

Kessner, Thomas. *The Flight of the Century: Charles Lindbergh and the Rise of American Aviation*. New York: Oxford University Press, 2010.

Kiki. *Kiki's Memoirs*. Introductions by Ernest Hemingway and Tsuguharu Foujita. Photography by Man Ray. Edited and foreword by Billy Klüver and Julie Martin. Translated by Samuel Putnam. Hopewell, N.J.: Ecco Press, 1996.

Kimball, Robert, and Alfred Simon. *The Gershwins*. New York: Atheneum, 1973.

Klüver, Billy, and Julie Martin. *Kiki's Paris: Artists and Lovers, 1900–1930*. New York: Abrams, 1989.

Kurth, Peter. *Isadora: A Sensational Life*. Boston: Little, Brown, 2001.

Lacouture, Jean. *De Gaulle: The Rebel, 1890–1944*. Translated by Patrick O'Brian. New York: Norton, 1993.

Le Corbusier. *The City of To-morrow and Its Planning*. Translated by Frederick Etchells. London: J. Rodker, 1929.

Leymarie, Jean. *Chanel*. Translated by Antony Shugaar. New York: Abrams, 2010. First published 1987.

Lifar, Serge. *Serge Diaghilev, His Life, His Work, His Legend: An Intimate Biography.* New York: Da Capo, 1976. First published 1940.

Loeb, Harold. *The Way It Was.* New York: Criterion Books, 1959.

Long, Marguerite. *Au piano avec Maurice Ravel.* Paris: Juillard, 1971.

Lottman, Herbert R. *Man Ray's Montparnasse.* New York: Harry N. Abrams, 2001.

———. *The Michelin Men: Driving an Empire.* New York: I. B. Tauris, 2003.

Ludington, Townsend. *John Dos Passos: A Twentieth Century Odyssey.* New York: Dutton, 1980.

MacMillan, Margaret. *Paris 1919: Six Months That Changed the World.* New York: Random House, 2002.

Madsen, Axel. *Chanel: A Woman of Her Own.* New York: Henry Holt, 1990.

Maltby, Richard, and Melvyn Stokes, eds. *Hollywood Abroad: Audiences and Cultural Exchange.* London: BFI, 2004.

Man Ray. *Self Portrait.* Boston: Little, Brown, 1988. First published 1963.

Mare, André. *André Mare, cubisme et camouflage, 1914–1918.* Bernay, France: Musée de Bernay, 1998.

———. *Carnets de guerre, 1914–1918.* Edited by Laurence Graffin. Paris: Herscher, 1996.

Matisse, Henri. *Matisse on Art.* Rev. ed. Edited by Jack Flam. Berkeley: University of California Press, 1995.

Mawer, Deborah. *Darius Milhaud: Modality and Structure in Music of the 1920s.* Brookfield, Vt.: Ashgate, 1997.

Maxwell, Elsa. *R.S.V.P.: Elsa Maxwell's Own Story.* Boston: Little, Brown, 1954.

McAlmon, Robert. *Being Geniuses Together, 1920–1930.* San Francisco, Calif.: North Point Press, 1984.

McAuliffe, Mary. *Dawn of the Belle Epoque: The Paris of Monet, Zola, Bernhardt, Eiffel, Debussy, Clemenceau, and Their Friends.* Lanham, Md.: Rowman & Littlefield, 2011.

———. *Twilight of the Belle Epoque: The Paris of Picasso, Stravinsky, Proust, Renault, Marie Curie, Gertrude Stein, and Their Friends through the Great War.* Lanham, Md.: Rowman & Littlefield, 2014.

McBrien, William. *Cole Porter: A Biography.* New York: Vintage, 1998.

Meyers, Jeffrey. *Scott Fitzgerald: A Biography.* New York: HarperCollins, 1994.

Milhaud, Darius. *Notes without Music: An Autobiography.* Edited by Rollo H. Myers and Herbert Weinstock. Translated by Donald Evans and Arthur Ogden. New York: Knopf, 1953.

Monet, Claude. *Monet by Himself: Paintings, Drawings, Pastels, Letters.* Edited by Richard R. Kendall. Translated by Bridget Strevens Romer. London: Macdonald, 1989.

Morand, Paul. *The Allure of Chanel.* Translated by Euan Cameron. London: Pushkin Press, 2008. First published 1976.

Mugnier, Abbé (Arthur). *Journal de l'Abbé Mugnier: 1879–1939.* Paris: Mercure de France, 1985.

Musée des Arts Décoratifs (Paris, France). *Fernand Léger, 1881–1955: [Exposition] juin–octobre 1956.* Paris: F. Hazan, 1956.

Mussolini, Benito. *My Autobiography*. Foreword by Richard Washburn Child. Westport, Conn.: Greenwood, 1970.

Myers, Rollo H. *Erik Satie*. Rev. ed. New York: Dover, 1968. First published 1948.

Nichols, Roger. *Ravel*. New Haven, Conn.: Yale University Press, 2011.

Nicholson, Harold George. *Peacemaking, 1919*. New York: Grosset & Dunlap, 1965.

O'Mahony, Mike. *Olympic Visions: Images of the Games through History*. London: Reaktion Books, 2012.

Orenstein, Arbie. *Ravel: Man and Musician*. New York: Dover Publications, 1991. First published 1975.

Orledge, Robert, ed. *Satie Remembered*. Translated by Roger Nichols. Portland, Ore.: Amadeus Press, 1995.

Paul, Elliot. *The Last Time I Saw Paris*. New York: Random House, 1942.

Penrose, Roland. *Man Ray*. New York: Thames & Hudson, 1989.

Perriand, Charlotte. *A Life of Creation: An Autobiography*. Translated by Odile Jacob. New York: Monacelli Press, 2003.

Petit, Jean. *Le Corbusier lui-même*. Geneva, Switzerland: Editions Rousseau, 1970.

Picardie, Justine. *Coco Chanel: The Legend and the Life*. New York: itbooks, 2010.

Poiret, Paul. *Art et Phynance*. Paris: Editions Lutetia, 1934.

———. *King of Fashion: The Autobiography of Paul Poiret*. Translated by Stephen Haden Guest. London: V & A Publishing, 2009. First published 1931.

Pollack, Howard. *George Gershwin: His Life and Work*. Berkeley: University of California Press, 2006.

Potter, Caroline. *Nadia and Lili Boulanger*. Burlington, Vt.: Ashgate, 2006.

Poulenc, Francis. *Moi et mes amis*. Confidences recueillies par Stéphane Audel. Paris: La Palatine, 1963.

Proust, Marcel. *La Correspondance de Marcel Proust*. Edited and annotated by Philip Kolb. Vols. 17–21 (1918–1922). Paris: Plon, 1989–1993.

———. *In Search of Lost Time: The Captive; The Fugitive*. Translated by C. K. Scott Moncrieff and Terence Kilmartin; revised by D. J. Enright. New York: Modern Library, 1993.

———. *In Search of Lost Time: The Guermantes Way*. Translated by C. K. Scott Moncrieff and Terence Kilmartin; revised by D. J. Enright. New York: Modern Library, 2003.

———. *In Search of Lost Time: Sodom and Gomorrah*. Translated by C. K. Scott Moncrieff and Terence Kilmartin; revised by D. J. Enright. New York: Modern Library, 1993.

———. *In Search of Lost Time: Time Regained*. Translated by Andreas Mayor and Terence Kilmartin; revised by D. J. Enright. New York: Modern Library, 1999.

———. *In Search of Lost Time: Within a Budding Grove*. Translated by C. K. Scott Moncrieff and Terence Kilmartin; revised by D. J. Enright. New York: Modern Library, 1998.

———. *Selected Letters*. Vol. 4 (1918–1922). Edited by Philip Kolb. Translated with introduction by Joanna Kilmartin. Foreword by Alain de Botton. London: HarperCollins, 2000.

Putnam, Samuel. *Paris Was Our Mistress: Memoirs of a Lost and Found Generation*. New York: Viking, 1947.

Quinn, Susan. *Marie Curie: A Life*. New York: Simon & Schuster, 1995.

Radiguet, Raymond. *Count d'Orgel*. Translated by Violet Schiff. London: Pushkin Press, 2001. First published 1924.

———. *The Devil in the Flesh*. Translated by A. M. Sheridan Smith. New York: Marion Boyars, 2005. First published 1923.

Ravel, Maurice. *A Ravel Reader: Correspondence, Articles, Interviews*. Compiled and edited by Arbie Orenstein. Mineola, N.Y.: Dover, 2003. First published 1990.

Renoir, Jean. *My Life and My Films*. Translated by Norman Denny. New York: Atheneum, 1974.

———. *Renoir on Renoir: Interviews, Essays, and Remarks*. Translated by Carol Volk. New York: Cambridge University Press, 1989.

Reynolds, John. *André Citroën: The Man and the Motor Cars*. Thrupp, Stroud, UK: Sutton, 1996.

Reynolds, Michael. *Hemingway: The American Homecoming*. Cambridge, Mass: Blackwell, 1992.

———. *Hemingway: The Final Years*. New York: Norton, 1999.

———. *Hemingway: The Paris Years*. New York: Norton, 1999. First published 1989.

———. *The Young Hemingway*. New York: Norton, 1998. First published 1986.

Rhodes, Anthony. *Louis Renault: A Biography*. New York: Harcourt, Brace & World, 1970.

Richardson, John. *A Life of Picasso: The Triumphant Years, 1917–1932*. New York: Knopf, 2007.

Rideout, Walter B. *Sherwood Anderson: A Writer in America*. Vol. 1. Introduction by Charles E. Modlin. Madison: University of Wisconsin Press, 2006.

Roy, Jean. *L'Intemporel: Robert Casadesus, Pianiste et compositeur*. Paris: Buchet-Chastel, 1999.

Sachs, Maurice. *Day of Wrath: Confessions of a Turbulent Youth*. Translated by Robin King. London: A. Barker, 1953.

———. *The Decade of Illusion: Paris, 1918–1928*. Translated by Gwladys Matthew Sachs. New York: Knopf, 1933.

Salmon, André. *Montparnasse*. Paris: A. Bonne, 1950.

Sassoon, Siegfried. *Sherston's Progress*. London: Faber & Faber, 1936.

Satie, Erik. *Satie Seen through His Letters*. Edited by Ornella Volta. Translated by Michael Bullock. New York: Marion Boyars, 1989.

Schack, William. *Art and Argyrol: The Life and Career of Dr. Albert C. Barnes*. New York: T. Yoseloff, 1960.

Scheijen, Sjeng. *Diaghilev: A Life*. Translated by Jane Hedley-Prôle and S. J. Leinbach. New York: Oxford University Press, 2009.

Schmidt, Carl B. *Entrancing Muse: A Documented Biography of Francis Poulenc*. Hillsdale, N.Y.: Pendragon Press, 2001.

Secrest, Meryle. *Modigliani: A Life*. New York: Knopf, 2011.

Sert, Misia. *Misia and the Muses: The Memoirs of Misia Sert*. Translated by Moura Budberg. New York: John Day, 1953.

Sicard-Picchiottino, Ghislaine. *François Coty: un industriel corse sous la IIIe République*. Ajaccio, France: Albiana, 2006.

Silver, Kenneth E. *Esprit de Corps: The Art of the Parisian Avant-Garde and the First World War, 1914–1925*. Princeton, N.J.: Princeton University Press, 1989.

Spurling, Hilary. *Matisse the Master: A Life of Henri Matisse, the Conquest of Colour, 1909–1954*. New York: Knopf, 2005.

Staggs, Sam. *Inventing Elsa Maxwell: How an Irrepressible Nobody Conquered High Society, Hollywood, the Press, and the World*. New York: St. Martin's, 2012.

Steegmuller, Francis. *Cocteau: A Biography*. Boston: Little, Brown, 1970.

Stein, Gertrude. *The Autobiography of Alice B. Toklas*. New York: Vintage, 1990. First published 1933.

———. *Everybody's Autobiography*. New York: Random House, 1937.

Stokes, Melvyn. *D. W. Griffith's* The Birth of a Nation: *A History of "The Most Controversial Motion Picture of All Time."* New York: Oxford University Press, 2007.

———. "Race, Politics, and Censorship: D. W. Griffith's *The Birth of a Nation* in France, 1916–1923." *Cinema Journal* 50, no. 1 (Fall 2010): 19–38.

Stovall, Tyler Edward. *The Rise of the Paris Red Belt*. Berkeley: University of California Press, 1990.

Strauss, Walter A. "Jean Cocteau: The Difficulty of Being Orpheus." In *Reviewing Orpheus: Essays on the Cinema and Art of Jean Cocteau*, edited by Cornelia A. Tsakiridou. Lewisburg, Pa.: Bucknell University Press, 1997.

Stravinsky, Igor. *An Autobiography*. New York: Norton, 1998. First published 1936.

Stravinsky, Igor, and Robert Craft. *Memories and Commentaries*. New York: Faber & Faber, 2002.

Sutcliffe, Anthony. *The Autumn of Central Paris: The Defeat of Town Planning, 1950–1970*. London: Edward Arnold, 1970.

Thurman, Judith. *Secrets of the Flesh: A Life of Colette*. New York: Ballantine, 1999.

Toledano, Roulhac B., and Elizabeth Z. Coty. *François Coty: Fragrance, Power, Money*. Gretna, La.: Pelican, 2009.

Tours, Hugh. *Parry Thomas, Designer-Driver*. London: B. T. Batsford, 1959.

U.S. Department of State. *The Flight of Captain Charles A. Lindbergh from New York to Paris, May 20–21, 1927. As compiled from the official records of the Department of State*. Facsimile of presentation copy. Washington, D.C.: Government Printing Office, 1927.

Vaill, Amanda. *Everybody Was So Young: Gerald and Sara Murphy, a Lost Generation Love Story*. New York: Broadway Books, 1999.

Walsh, Stephen. *Stravinsky: A Creative Spring; Russia and France, 1882–1934*. Berkeley: University of California Press, 2002. First published 1999.

Watson, David Robin. *Georges Clemenceau: A Political Biography*. New York: David McKay, 1974.

Weber, Eugen Joseph. *Action Française: Royalism and Reaction in Twentieth Century France*. Stanford, Calif.: Stanford University Press, 1962.

Weber, Nicholas Fox. *Le Corbusier: A Life*. New York: Knopf, 2008.

Wells, H. G. *The War That Will End War*. New York: Duffield, 1914.

Wiéner, Jean. *Allegro appassionato*. Paris: Pierre Belfond, 1978.

Wildenstein, Daniel. *Monet, or the Triumph of Impressionism*. Vol. 1. Translated by Chris Miller and Peter Snowdon. Cologne, Germany, and Paris, France: Taschen/ Wildenstein Institute, 1999.

Williams, Charles. *The Last Great Frenchman: A Life of General de Gaulle*. New York: Wiley, 1993.

Wullschläger, Jackie. *Chagall: A Biography*. New York: Knopf, 2008.

Zapata-Aubé, Nicole, ed. *André Mare, Cubisme et camouflage, 1914–1918*. Bernay, France: Musée de Bernay, 1998.

Index

Geffroy, Gustave, 7, 59
Gershwin, George, 140; *An American
  in Paris*, 238–39, 241; background
  of, 241; Concerto in F, 239; lessons,
  requests for, 240–41, 301nn14–15;
  and Milhaud, 241, 301n15; and Cole
  Porter, 239
Giacometti, Alberto, 264–65,
  304nn34–35
Gide, André, 58, 232; and Cocteau,
  34–35, 260; and Proust, 104
Godebski, Cipa, 32
Goncharova, Natalya, 137
Gris, Juan, 120, 233
Groupe des Six, 32–33, 44, 75, 92, 148,
  241, 277nn26–27, 282n15, 285n6
Guggenheim, Peggy, 140
Guillaume, Paul, 136

Hamnett, Nina, 125–26, 153
Hastings, Beatrice, 93
Hemingway, Ernest, 22, *54, 108*,
  144, 155, 253, 271; and Sherwood
  Anderson, 98, 110, 115, 206,
  208–10, 296nn34–35; background
  of, 109–10; and Josephine Baker,
  217–18, 299n5; and Sylvia Beach,
  111, 113, 270; and bullfights, 149,
  156–57; and cafés, 157, 142, 187,
  290n20; and Jimmie Charters, 210;
  and Cocteau, 157–58, 161; and Dos
  Passos, 163–64, 292n26, 296n34;
  fabrications of, 217–18, 299n5,
  299n8; *A Farewell to Arms*, 242,
  270; and financial woes, 157, 164,
  291n6; and Fitzgerald, 187, 206,
  207, 296n35, 296n37; and Ford
  Madox Ford, 157–58, 209, 292n7,
  292n10; and Hadley Hemingway,
  98, 107, *108*, 110–11, 115, 117,
  118, 119, 149, 150, 155, 164, 188,
  206, 207–8, 243; and John (Bumby,
  or Jack) Hemingway (son), 119,

149–50, 164, 288n26; and Pauline
  Pfeiffer Hemingway, 187, 188,
  206, 207–8, 218, 242; and Patrick
  Hemingway (son), 242; and James
  Joyce, 190, 270; and Kiki, 253, 264;
  loss of manuscripts, 119; and the
  Lost Generation, 109, 115, 188; Ada
  and Archibald MacLeish, 218, 243;
  and Man Ray, 120; and Miró, 98;
  and Montparnasse, 253–54, 290n20;
  and Sara and Gerald Murphy, 134,
  290n7; Paris, arrives in, 98, 107,
  109, 110–11; Paris publications
  of, 149; Paris, returns to, 150; and
  Pascin, 142; and Max Perkins, 187,
  206, 207, 208–9; and Ezra Pound,
  117, 118, 149, 157, 164, 292n10;
  rejection by publishers, 118, 157,
  164; and sports, 118, 149; and
  Gertrude Stein, 110, 114, 115, 117,
  119, 157, 188, 209–10, 287n16,
  287n20, 292n7; *The Sun Also Rises*,
  118, 149, 188, 206–7, 208, 287n20,
  296n37, 297n39, 297n41; *Torrents
  of Spring*, 206–7, 208–9; travels of,
  118, 149; and Lady Duff Twysden,
  187–88
Hemingway, Hadley, 98, 107, *108*,
  110–11, 115, 117, 118, 119, 149–50,
  155, 164, 188, 291n6; break-up of
  marriage to Ernest, 188, 206, 207–8,
  243; marries Paul Mowrer, 243; as
  single mother in Paris, 242–43
Hemingway, Pauline Pfeiffer, 187, 188,
  206, 207–8, 218, 242
Hessling, Catherine. *See* Renoir, Dédée
Hitler, Adolf, 132, 144–45, 249; and
  Nazi party, 234, 245, 249
Honegger, Arthur, 32, 33, 126
Hugo, Jean, 44, *74*, 75, 78, 93, 119,
  125, 160, 185, 186, 187, 259
Hugo, Valentine, *74*, 78, 93, 143, 152,
  160, 184, 185, 186, 187, 259

~

About the Author

Mary McAuliffe holds a PhD in history from the University of Maryland, has taught at several universities, and lectured at the Smithsonian Institution. She has traveled extensively in France, and for many years she was a regular contributor to *Paris Notes*. Her books include *Paris Discovered*, *Dawn of the Belle Epoque*, *Twilight of the Belle Epoque*, and *Clash of Crowns*. She lives in New York City with her husband and shares her insights and photos of Paris with her readers on her Paris Facebook photo blog (www.ParisMSM.com).